VIZ Media Edition

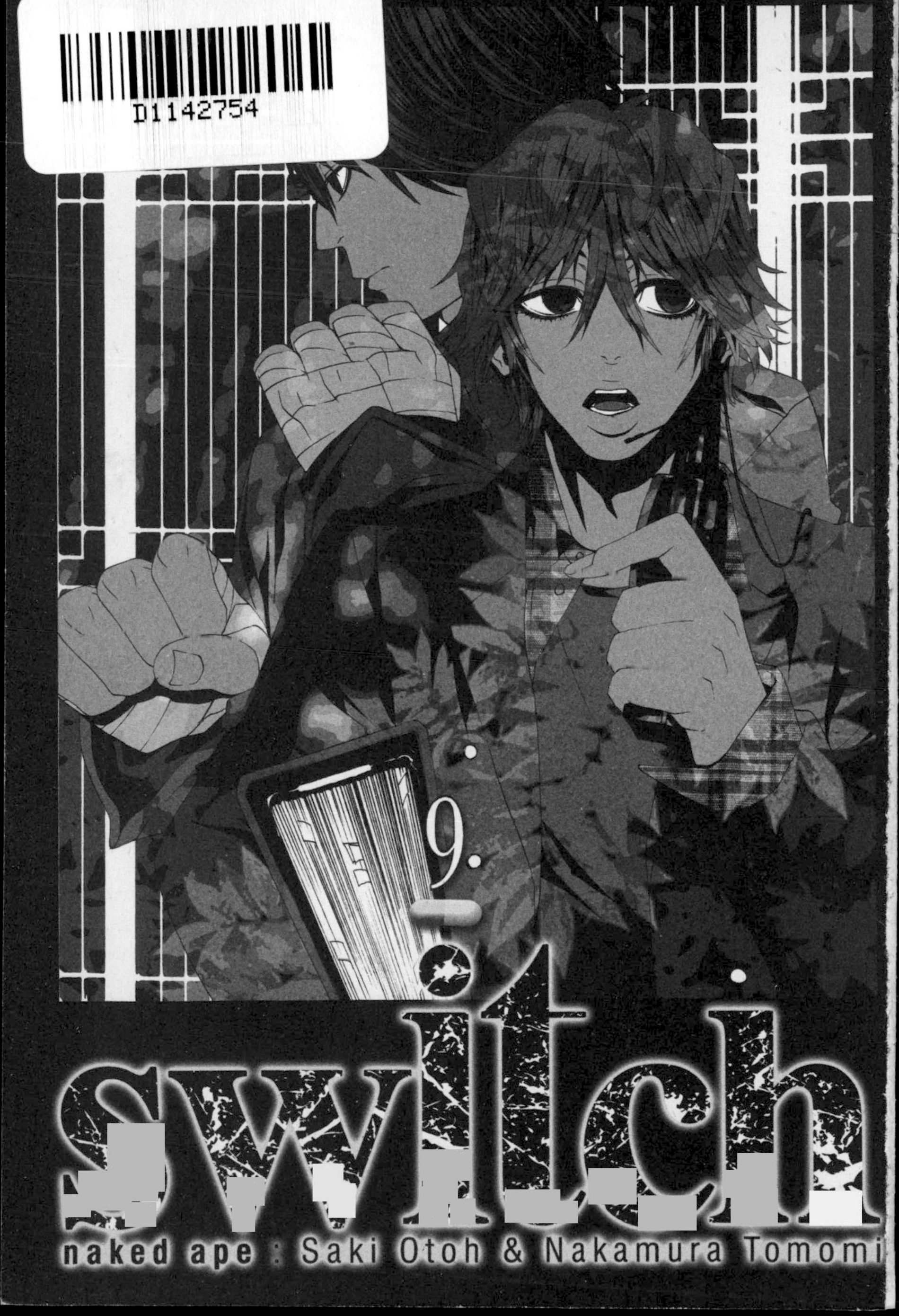

9

switch

naked ape : Saki Otoh & Nakamura Tomomi

switch

9

CONTENTS

Act.39

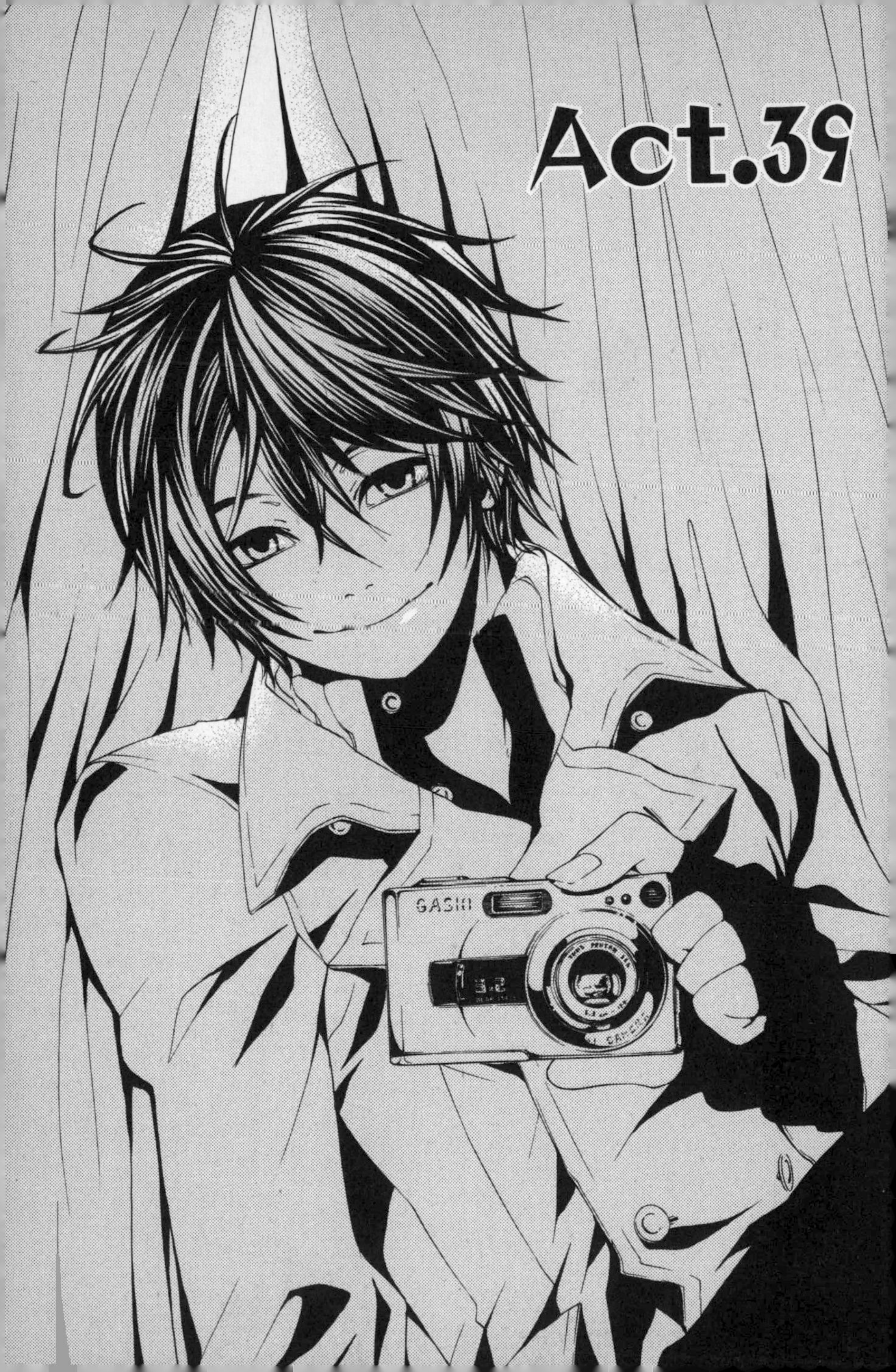

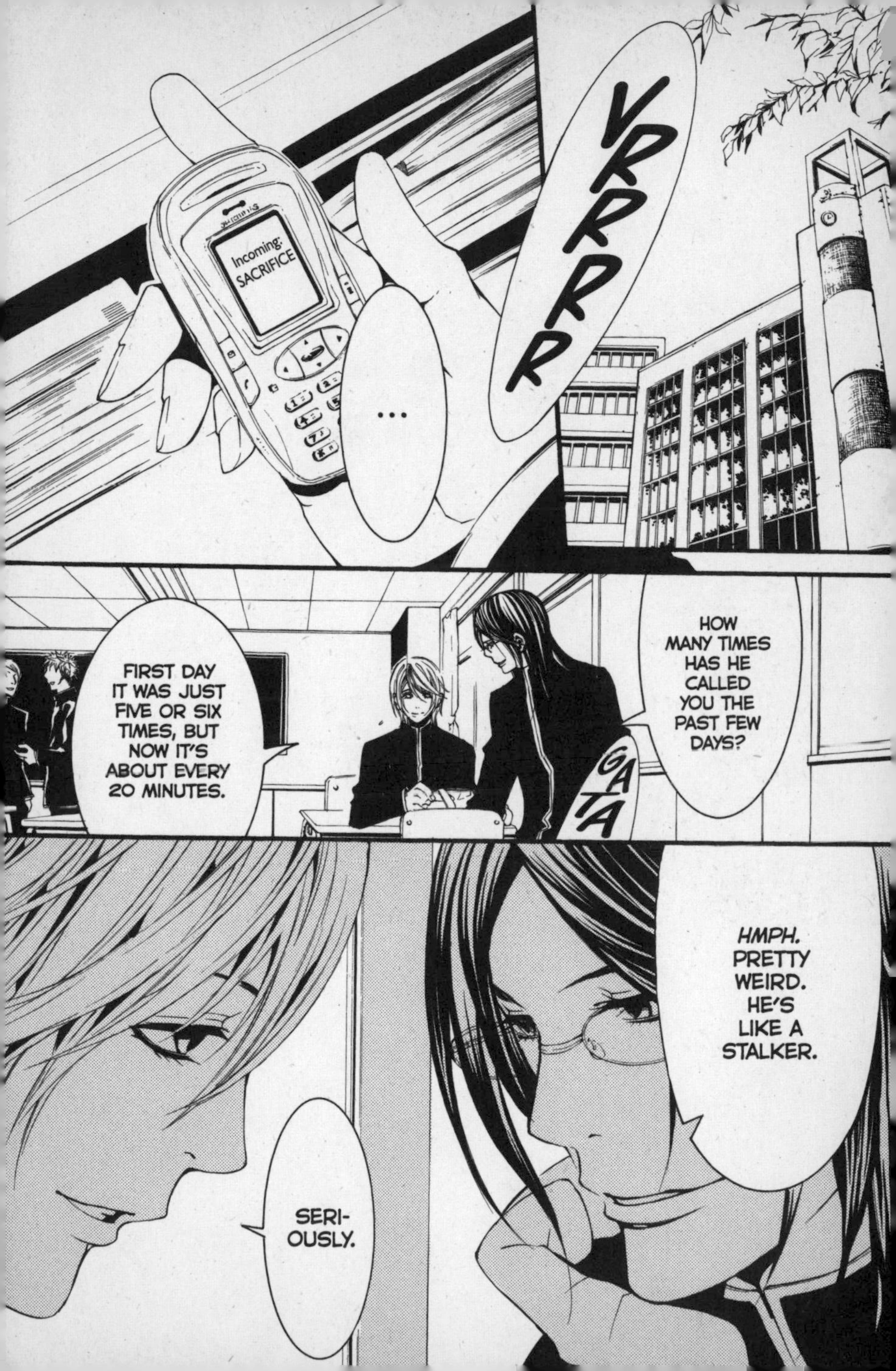
VRRRR
Incoming: SACRIFICE
...
HOW MANY TIMES HAS HE CALLED YOU THE PAST FEW DAYS?
GATA
FIRST DAY IT WAS JUST FIVE OR SIX TIMES, BUT NOW IT'S ABOUT EVERY 20 MINUTES.
HMPH. PRETTY WEIRD. HE'S LIKE A STALKER.
SERI-OUSLY.

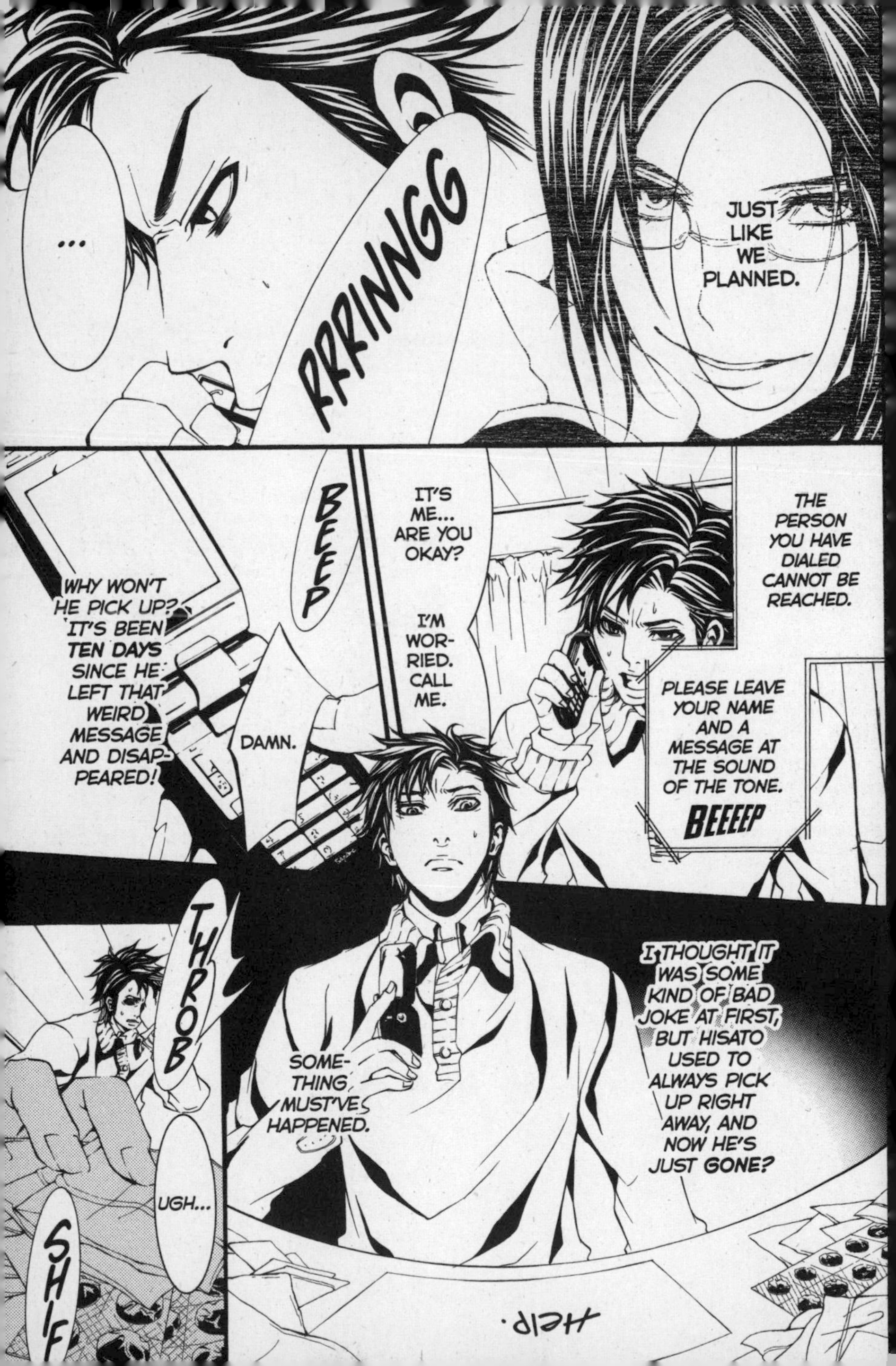
JUST LIKE WE PLANNED.
RRRINNGG
...
THE PERSON YOU HAVE DIALED CANNOT BE REACHED.
PLEASE LEAVE YOUR NAME AND A MESSAGE AT THE SOUND OF THE TONE.
BEEEEP
IT'S ME... ARE YOU OKAY?
I'M WOR-RIED. CALL ME.
BEEP
DAMN.
WHY WON'T HE PICK UP? IT'S BEEN TEN DAYS SINCE HE LEFT THAT WEIRD MESSAGE AND DISAP-PEARED!
I THOUGHT IT WAS SOME KIND OF BAD JOKE AT FIRST, BUT HISATO USED TO ALWAYS PICK UP RIGHT AWAY, AND NOW HE'S JUST GONE?
SOME-THING MUST'VE HAPPENED.
THROB
UGH...
SHIF
HELP.

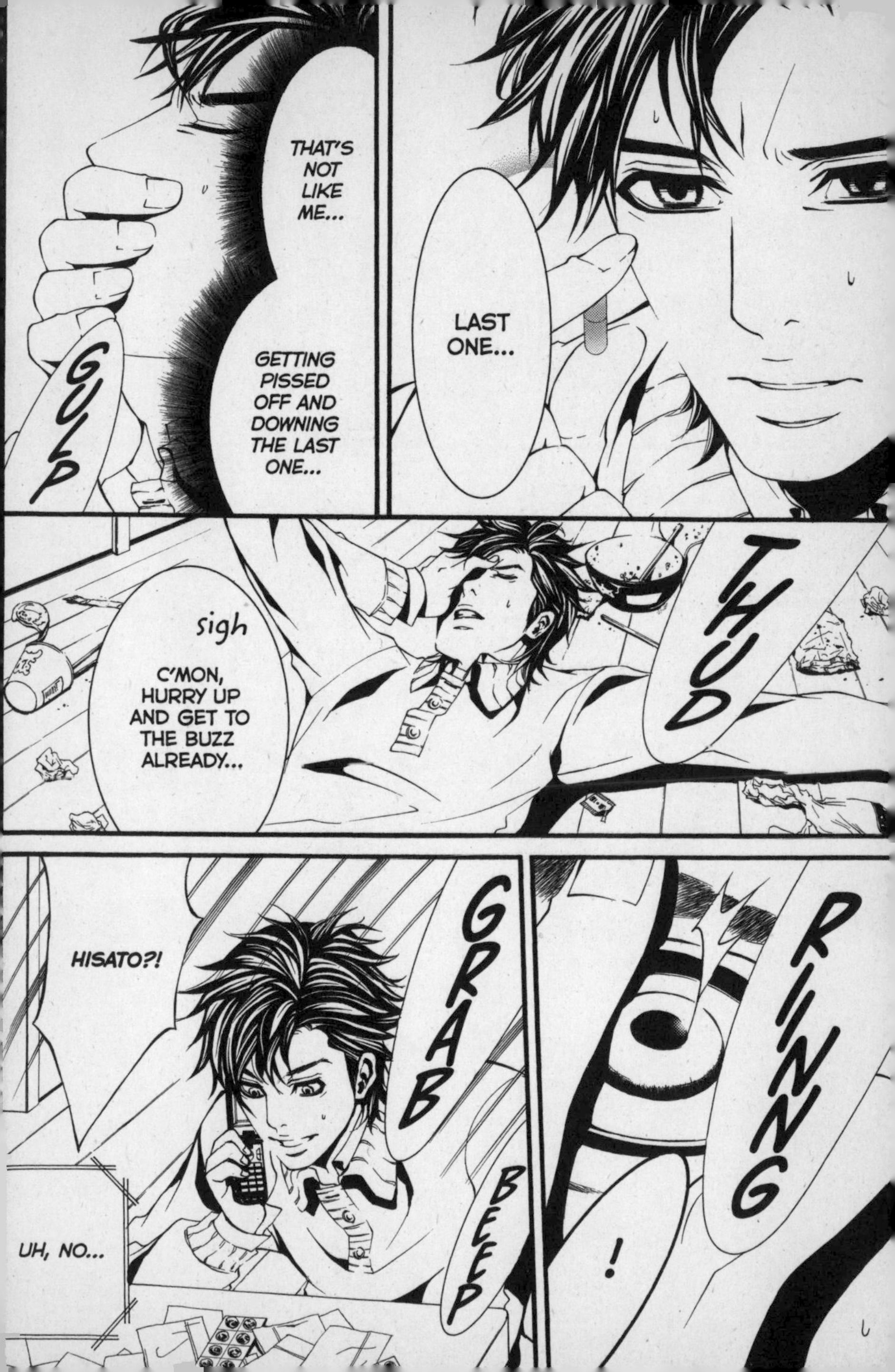
LAST ONE...
THAT'S NOT LIKE ME...
GETTING PISSED OFF AND DOWNING THE LAST ONE...
GULP
THUD
sigh
C'MON, HURRY UP AND GET TO THE BUZZ ALREADY...
RIINNG
!
GRAB
BEEP
HISATO?!
UH, NO...

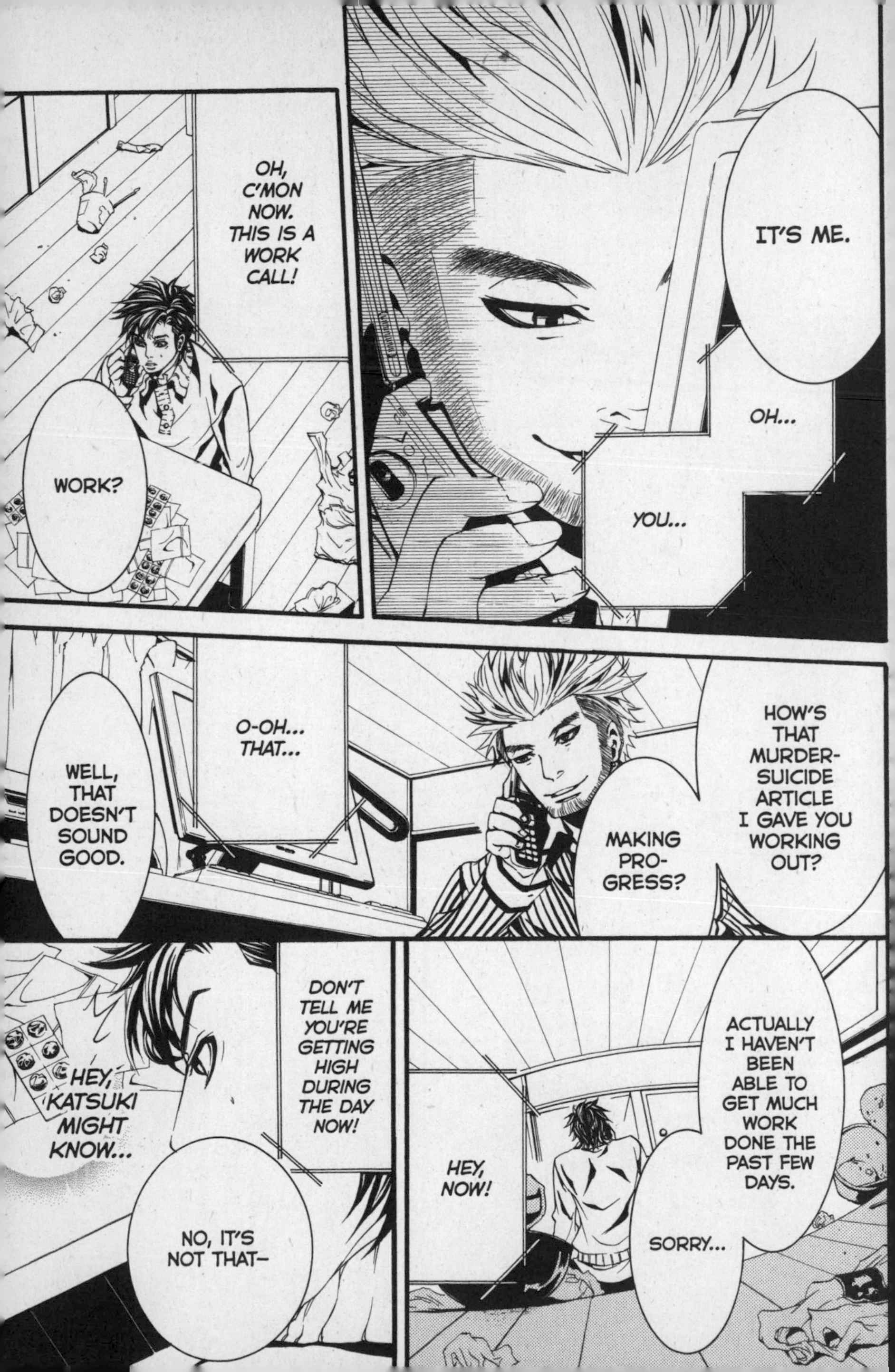
IT'S ME.
OH...
YOU...
OH, C'MON NOW. THIS IS A WORK CALL!
WORK?
HOW'S THAT MURDER-SUICIDE ARTICLE I GAVE YOU WORKING OUT?
MAKING PRO-GRESS?
O-OH... THAT...
WELL, THAT DOESN'T SOUND GOOD.
ACTUALLY I HAVEN'T BEEN ABLE TO GET MUCH WORK DONE THE PAST FEW DAYS.
SORRY...
HEY, NOW!
DON'T TELL ME YOU'RE GETTING HIGH DURING THE DAY NOW!
HEY, KATSUKI MIGHT KNOW...
NO, IT'S NOT THAT–

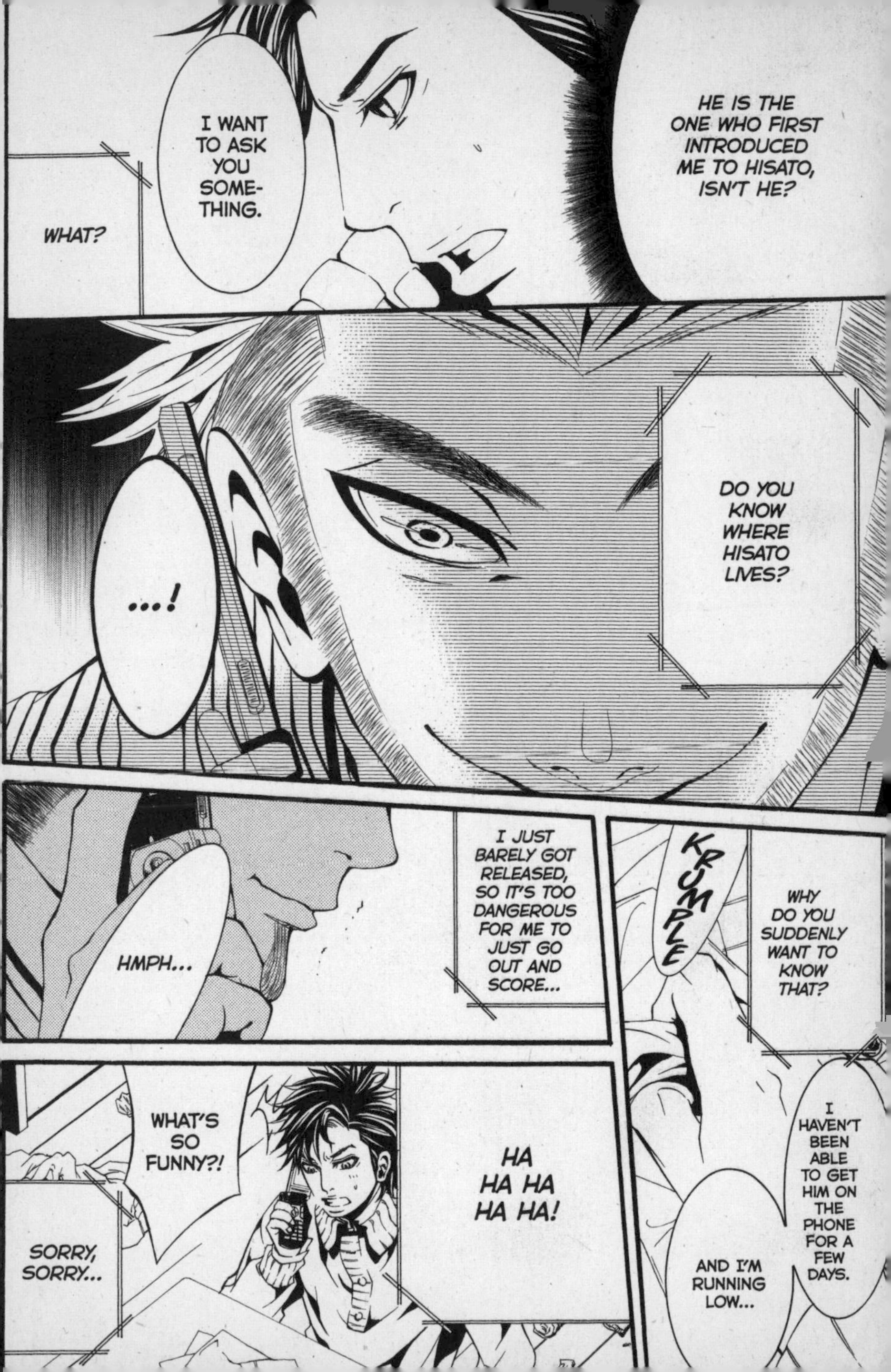
HE IS THE ONE WHO FIRST INTRODUCED ME TO HISATO, ISN'T HE?
I WANT TO ASK YOU SOME-THING.
WHAT?
DO YOU KNOW WHERE HISATO LIVES?
...!
KRUMPLE
WHY DO YOU SUDDENLY WANT TO KNOW THAT?
I HAVEN'T BEEN ABLE TO GET HIM ON THE PHONE FOR A FEW DAYS.
AND I'M RUNNING LOW...
I JUST BARELY GOT RELEASED, SO IT'S TOO DANGEROUS FOR ME TO JUST GO OUT AND SCORE...
HMPH...
HA HA HA HA HA!
WHAT'S SO FUNNY?!
SORRY, SORRY...

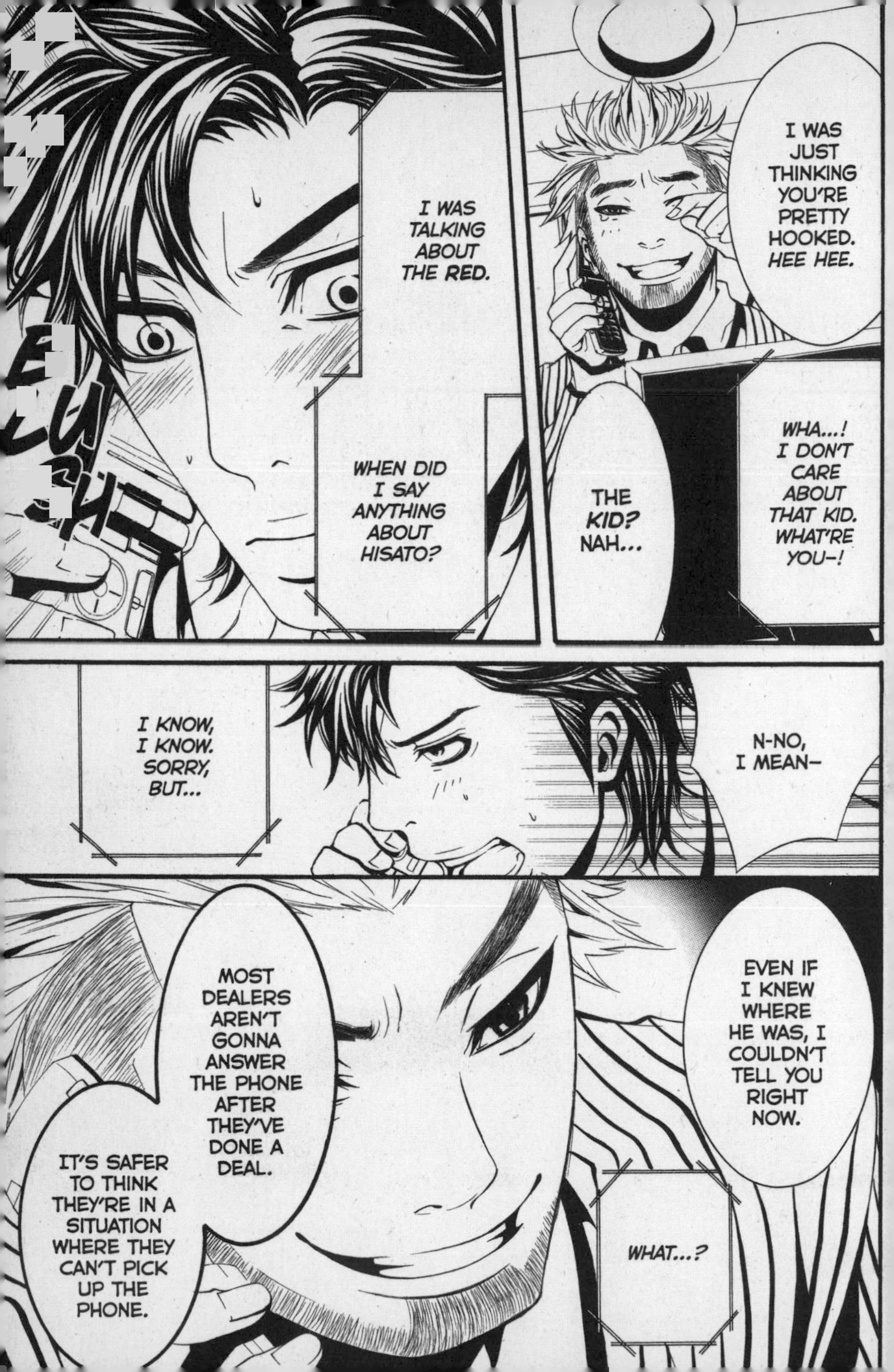
I WAS JUST THINKING YOU'RE PRETTY HOOKED. HEE HEE.
WHA...! I DON'T CARE ABOUT THAT KID. WHAT'RE YOU–!
THE KID? NAH...
I WAS TALKING ABOUT THE RED.
WHEN DID I SAY ANYTHING ABOUT HISATO?
N-NO, I MEAN–
I KNOW, I KNOW. SORRY, BUT...
EVEN IF I KNEW WHERE HE WAS, I COULDN'T TELL YOU RIGHT NOW.
WHAT...?
MOST DEALERS AREN'T GONNA ANSWER THE PHONE AFTER THEY'VE DONE A DEAL.
IT'S SAFER TO THINK THEY'RE IN A SITUATION WHERE THEY CAN'T PICK UP THE PHONE.

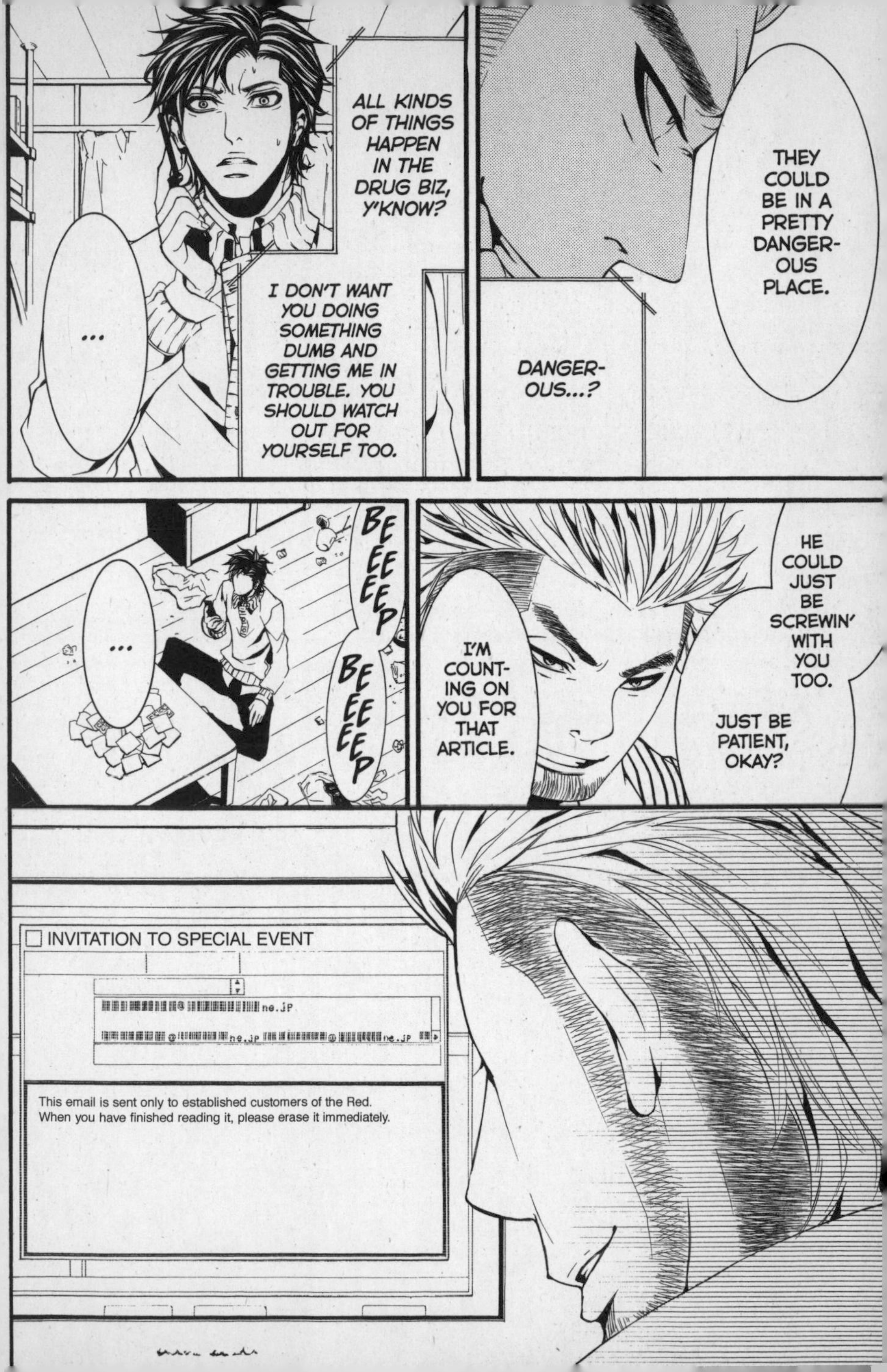
THEY COULD BE IN A PRETTY DANGER-OUS PLACE.
DANGER-OUS...?
ALL KINDS OF THINGS HAPPEN IN THE DRUG BIZ, Y'KNOW?
I DON'T WANT YOU DOING SOMETHING DUMB AND GETTING ME IN TROUBLE. YOU SHOULD WATCH OUT FOR YOURSELF TOO.
...
HE COULD JUST BE SCREWIN' WITH YOU TOO.
JUST BE PATIENT, OKAY?
I'M COUNT-ING ON YOU FOR THAT ARTICLE.
BEEEEP
BEEEEEP
...
INVITATION TO SPECIAL EVENT
This email is sent only to established customers of the Red.
When you have finished reading it, please erase it immediately.

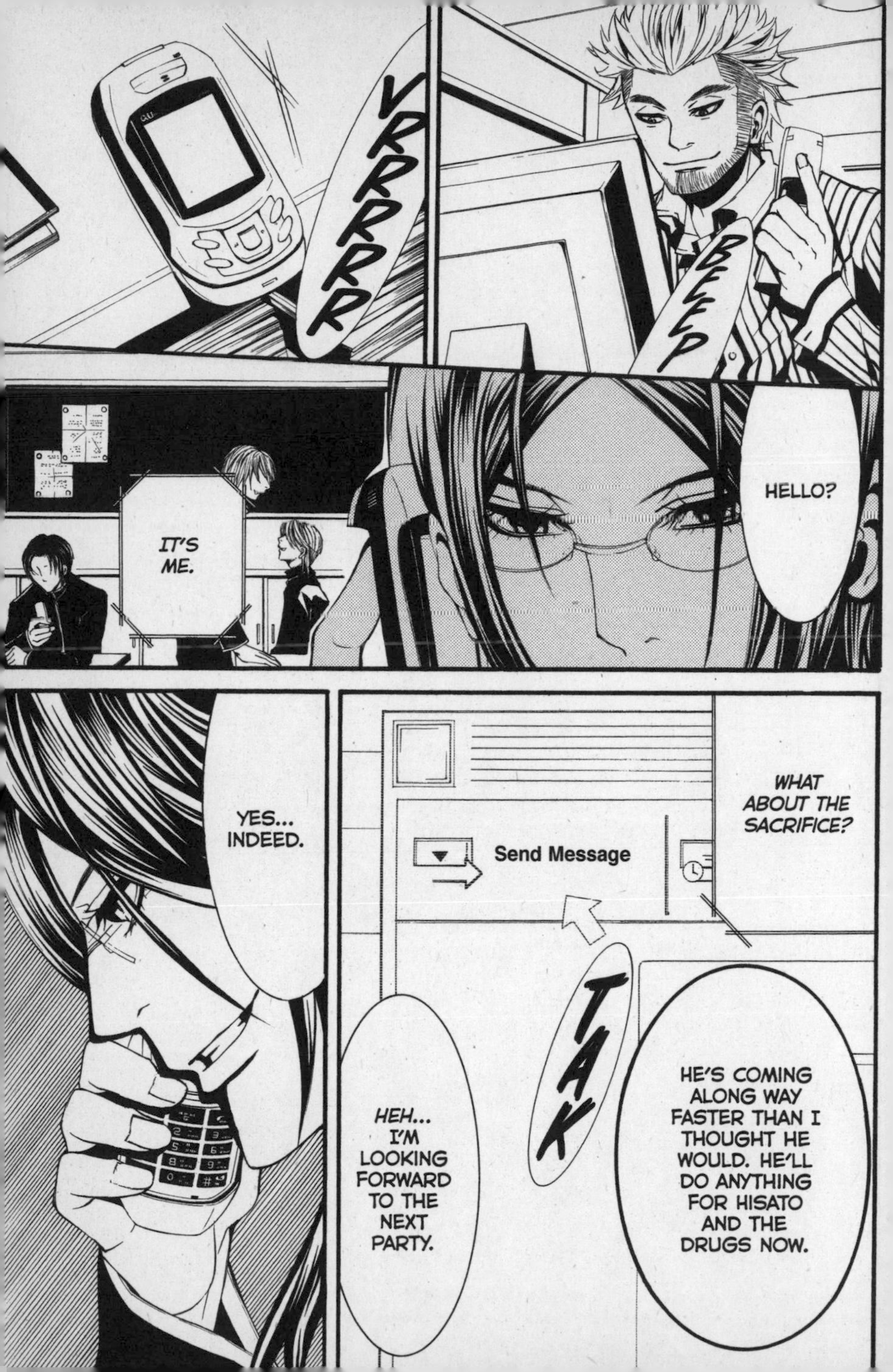
BEEP
VRRRRR
HELLO?
IT'S ME.
WHAT ABOUT THE SACRIFICE?
Send Message
TAK
HE'S COMING ALONG WAY FASTER THAN I THOUGHT HE WOULD. HE'LL DO ANYTHING FOR HISATO AND THE DRUGS NOW.
HEH... I'M LOOKING FORWARD TO THE NEXT PARTY.
YES... INDEED.

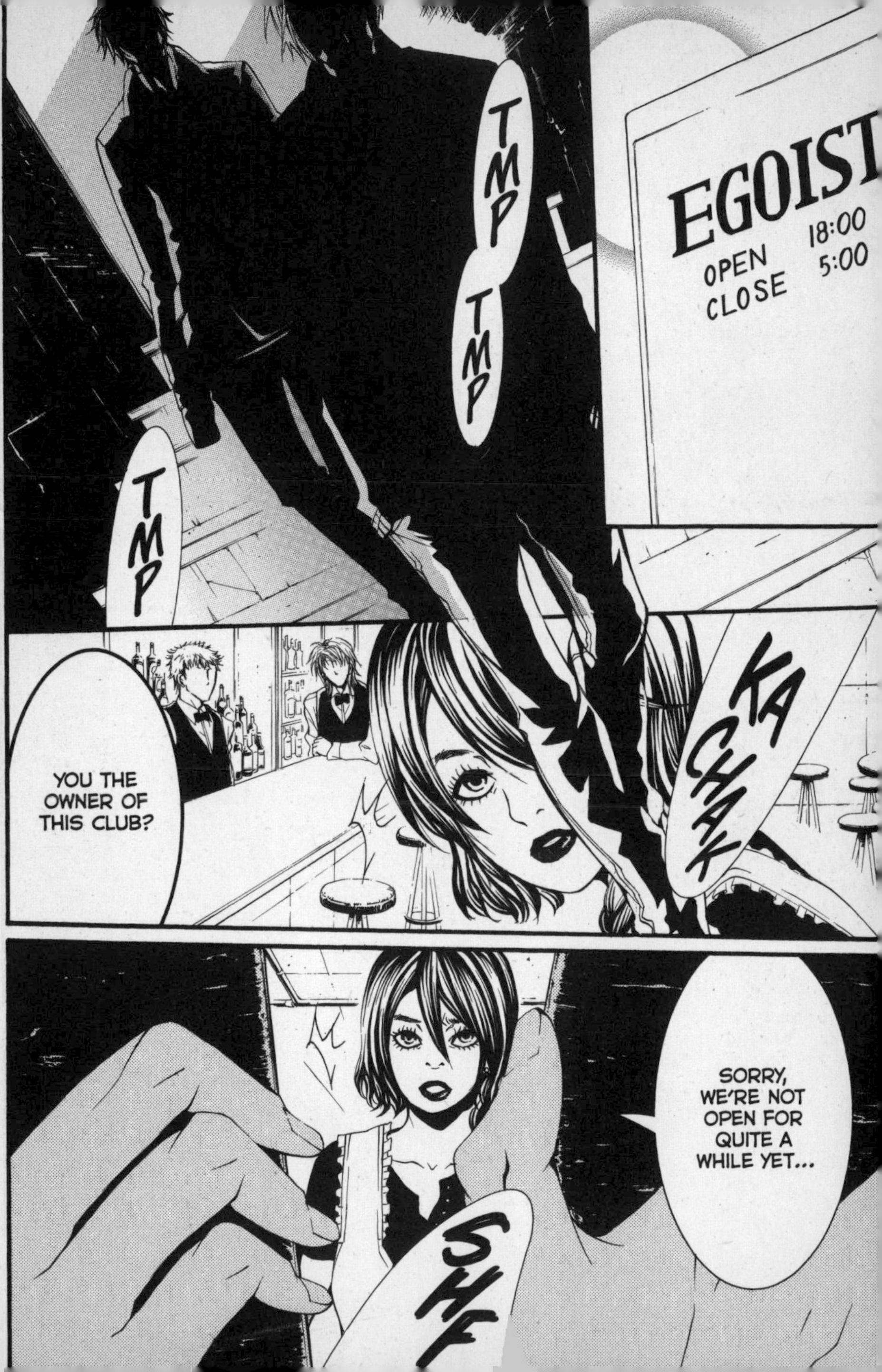
EGOIST
OPEN 18:00
CLOSE 5:00
TMP
TMP
TMP
KA CHAK
YOU THE OWNER OF THIS CLUB?
SORRY, WE'RE NOT OPEN FOR QUITE A WHILE YET...
SHF

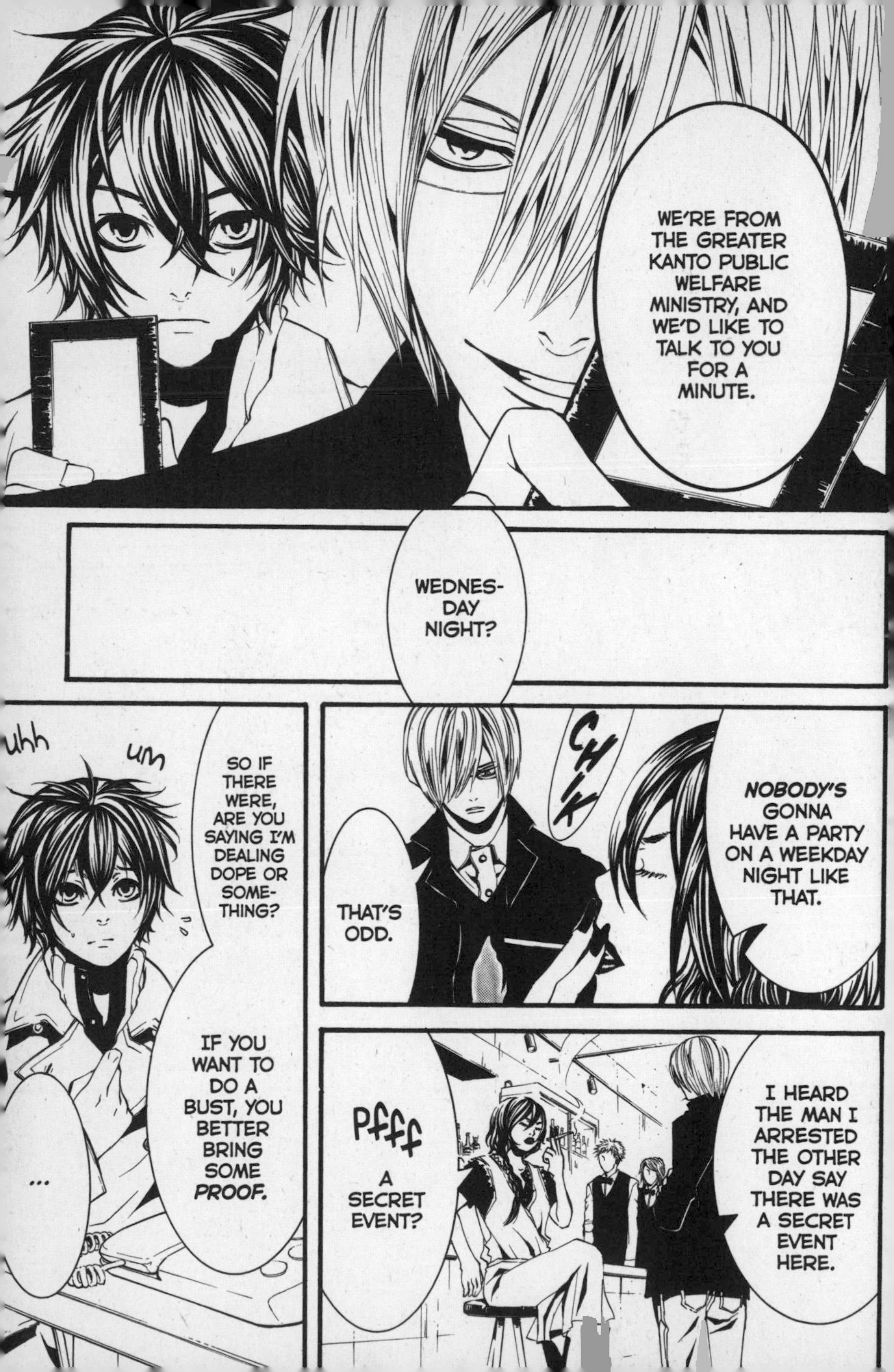
WE'RE FROM THE GREATER KANTO PUBLIC WELFARE MINISTRY, AND WE'D LIKE TO TALK TO YOU FOR A MINUTE.
WEDNES-DAY NIGHT?
NOBODY'S GONNA HAVE A PARTY ON A WEEKDAY NIGHT LIKE THAT.
CHIK
THAT'S ODD.
I HEARD THE MAN I ARRESTED THE OTHER DAY SAY THERE WAS A SECRET EVENT HERE.
Pfff
A SECRET EVENT?
uhh
um
SO IF THERE WERE, ARE YOU SAYING I'M DEALING DOPE OR SOME-THING?
IF YOU WANT TO DO A BUST, YOU BETTER BRING SOME *PROOF.*
...

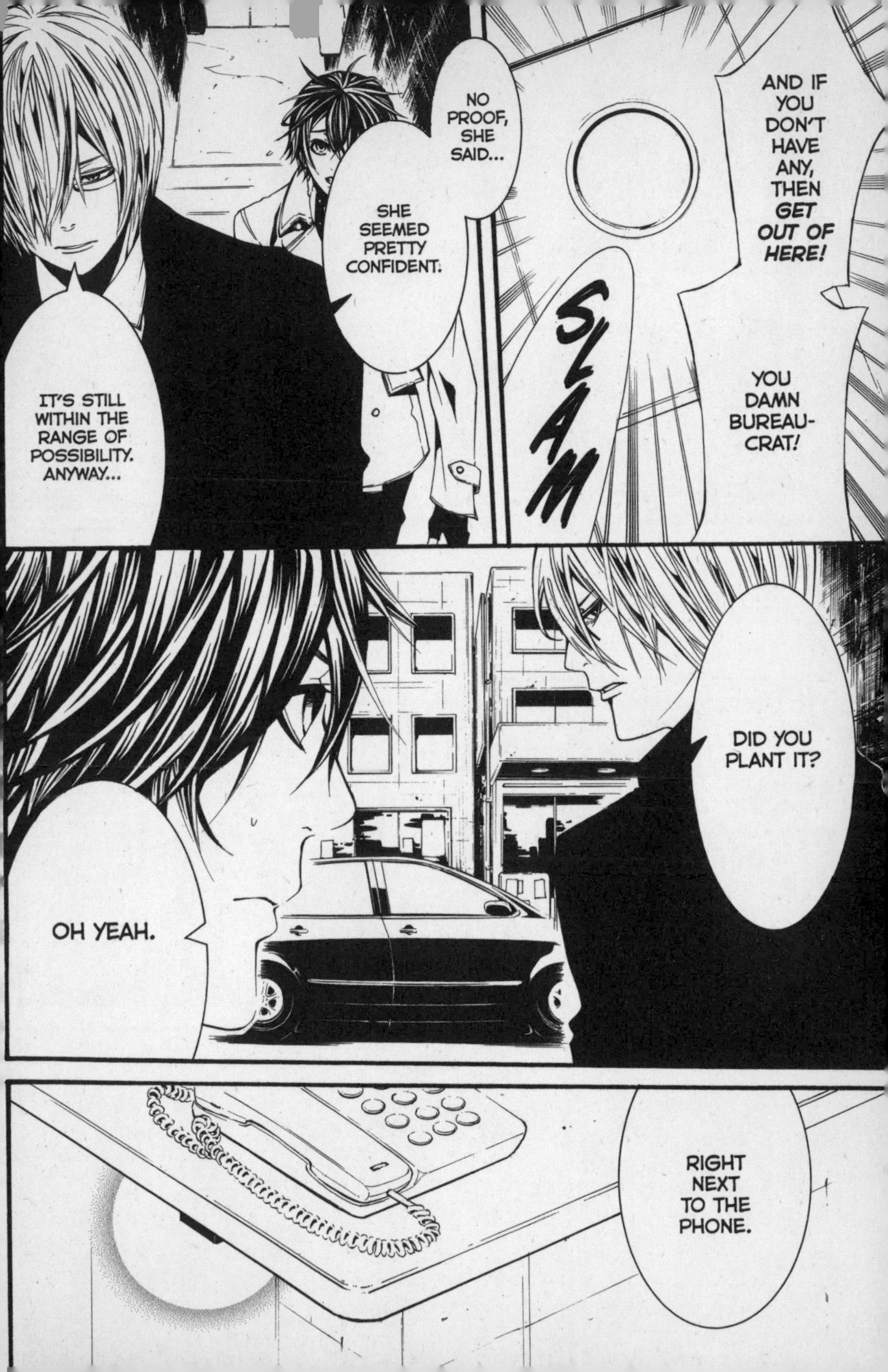
AND IF YOU DON'T HAVE ANY, THEN *GET OUT OF HERE!*
YOU DAMN BUREAU-CRAT!
SLAM
NO PROOF, SHE SAID...
SHE SEEMED PRETTY CONFIDENT.
IT'S STILL WITHIN THE RANGE OF POSSIBILITY. ANYWAY...
DID YOU PLANT IT?
OH YEAH.
RIGHT NEXT TO THE PHONE.

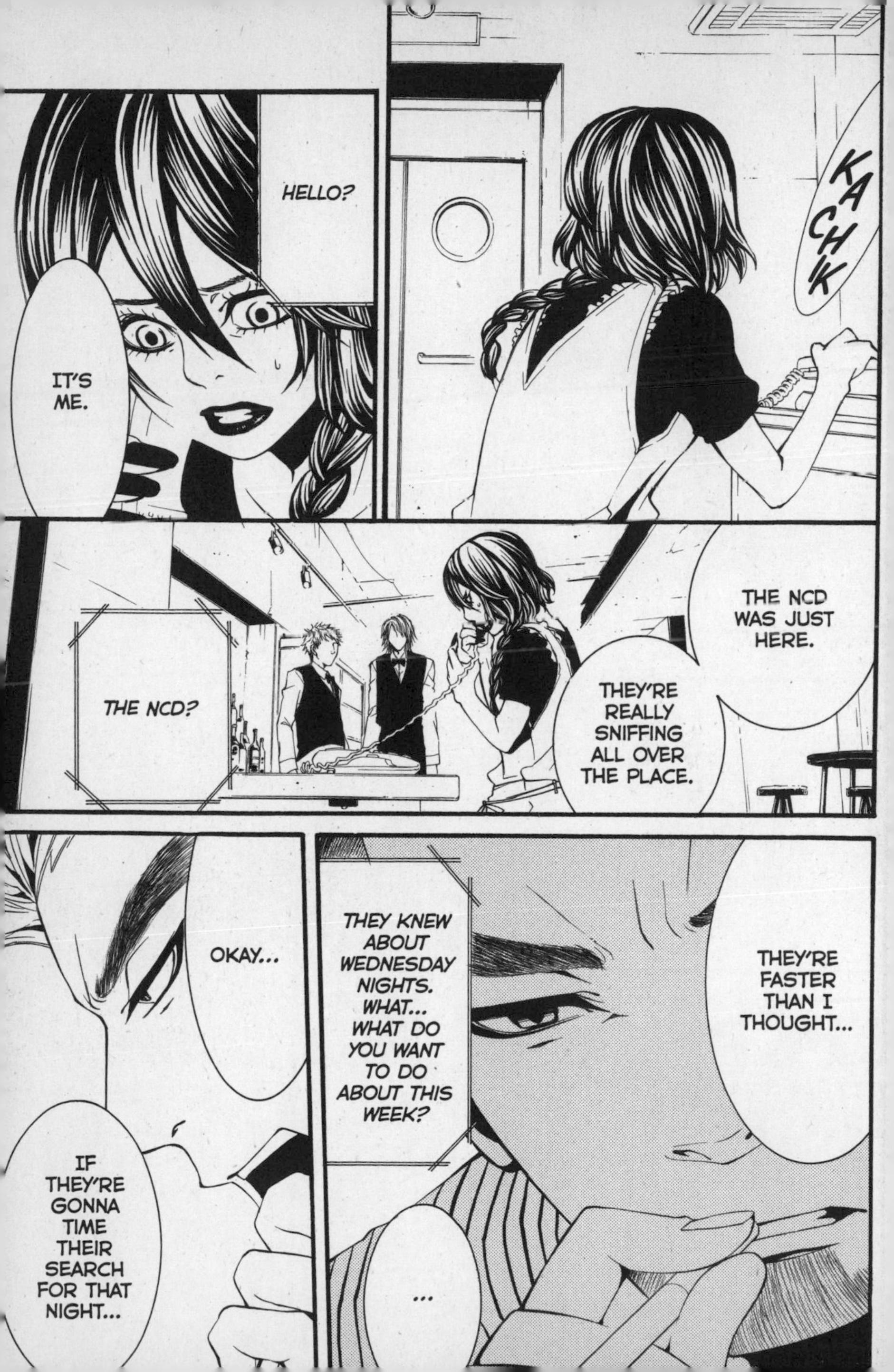
KACHK
HELLO?
IT'S ME.
THE NCD WAS JUST HERE.
THEY'RE REALLY SNIFFING ALL OVER THE PLACE.
THE NCD?
THEY'RE FASTER THAN I THOUGHT...
THEY KNEW ABOUT WEDNESDAY NIGHTS. WHAT... WHAT DO YOU WANT TO DO ABOUT THIS WEEK?
...
OKAY...
IF THEY'RE GONNA TIME THEIR SEARCH FOR THAT NIGHT...

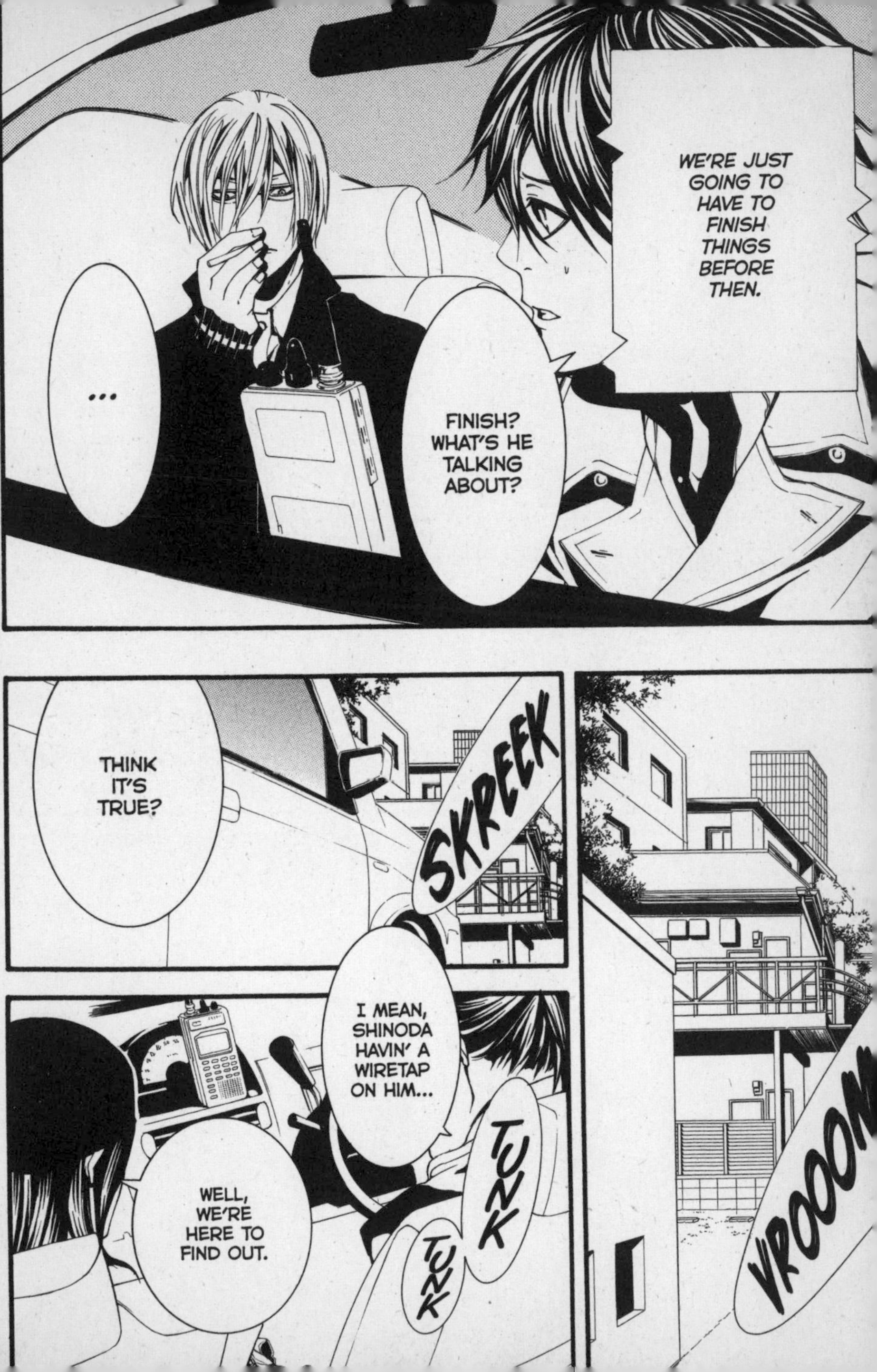
WE'RE JUST GOING TO HAVE TO FINISH THINGS BEFORE THEN.
FINISH? WHAT'S HE TALKING ABOUT?
...
VROOOM
SKREEK
THINK IT'S TRUE?
I MEAN, SHINODA HAVIN' A WIRETAP ON HIM...
TUNK
WELL, WE'RE HERE TO FIND OUT.
TUNK

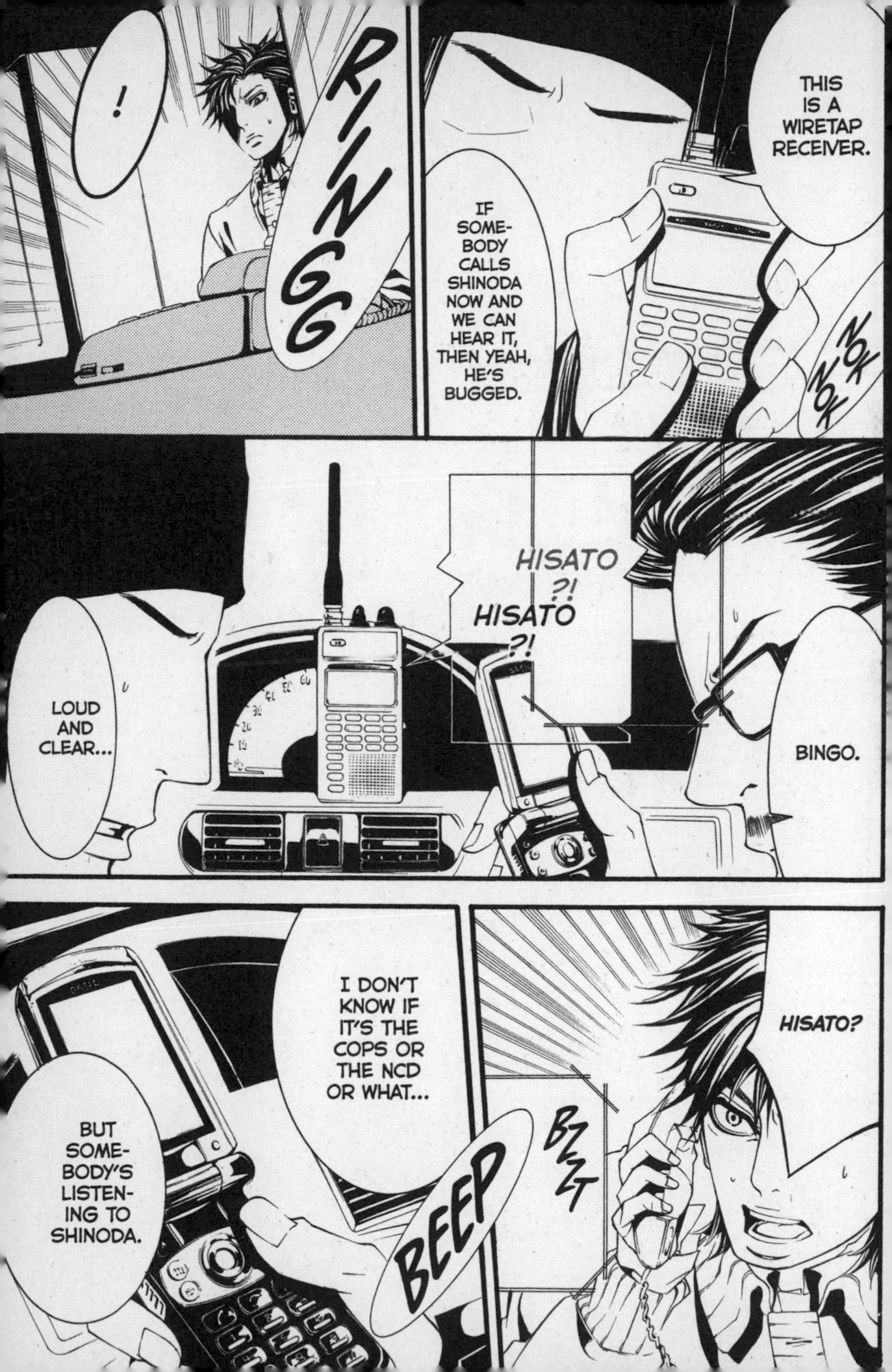
THIS IS A WIRETAP RECEIVER.
IF SOMEBODY CALLS SHINODA NOW AND WE CAN HEAR IT, THEN YEAH, HE'S BUGGED.
NOK NOK
RIINGG
!
BINGO.
HISATO ?!
HISATO ?!
LOUD AND CLEAR...
HISATO?
BZZT
BEEP
I DON'T KNOW IF IT'S THE COPS OR THE NCD OR WHAT...
BUT SOMEBODY'S LISTENING TO SHINODA.

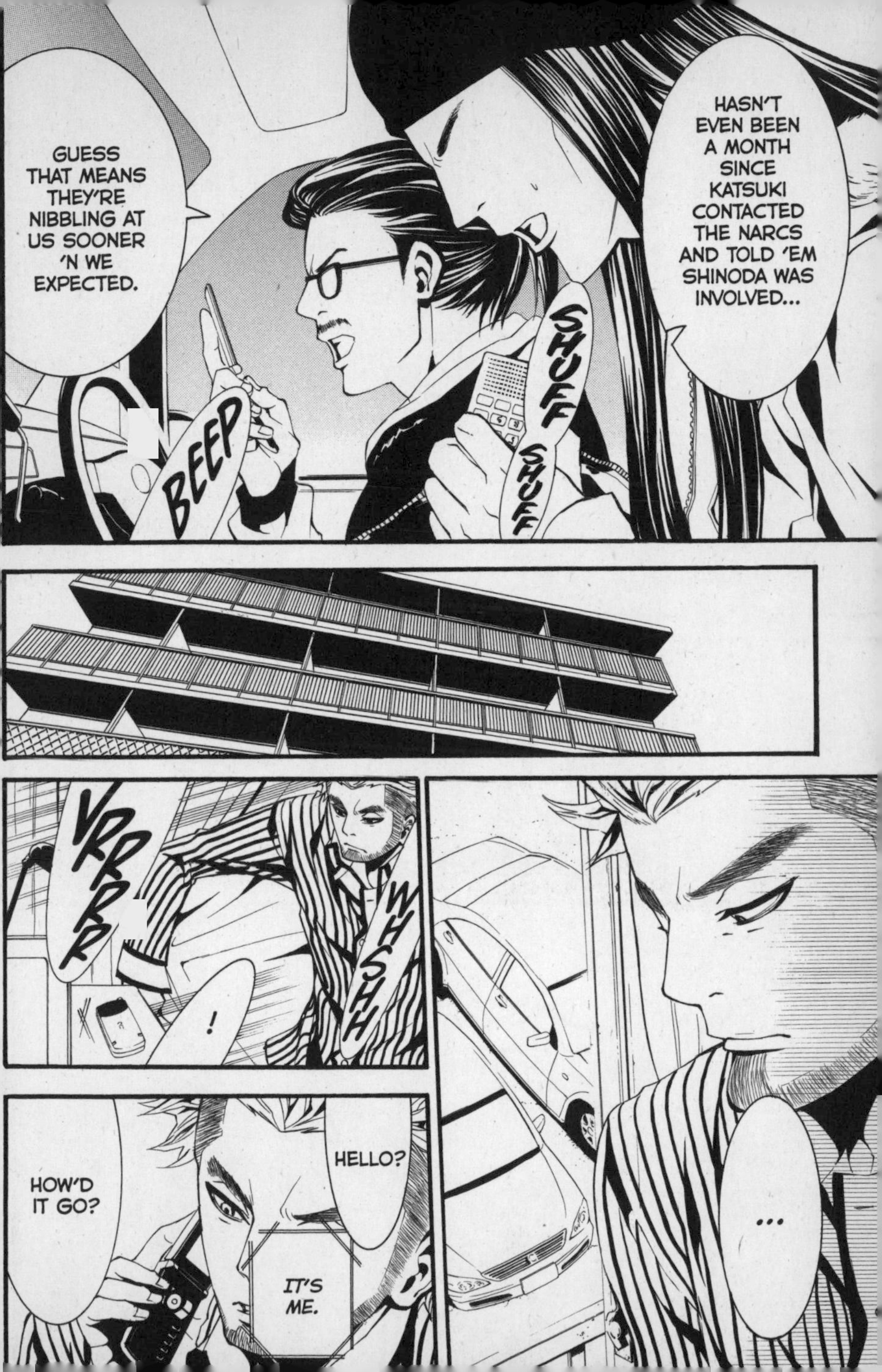
HASN'T EVEN BEEN A MONTH SINCE KATSUKI CONTACTED THE NARCS AND TOLD 'EM SHINODA WAS INVOLVED...
SHUFF SHUFF
BEEP
GUESS THAT MEANS THEY'RE NIBBLING AT US SOONER 'N WE EXPECTED.
...
VRRRR
WHSHH
!
HELLO?
IT'S ME.
HOW'D IT GO?

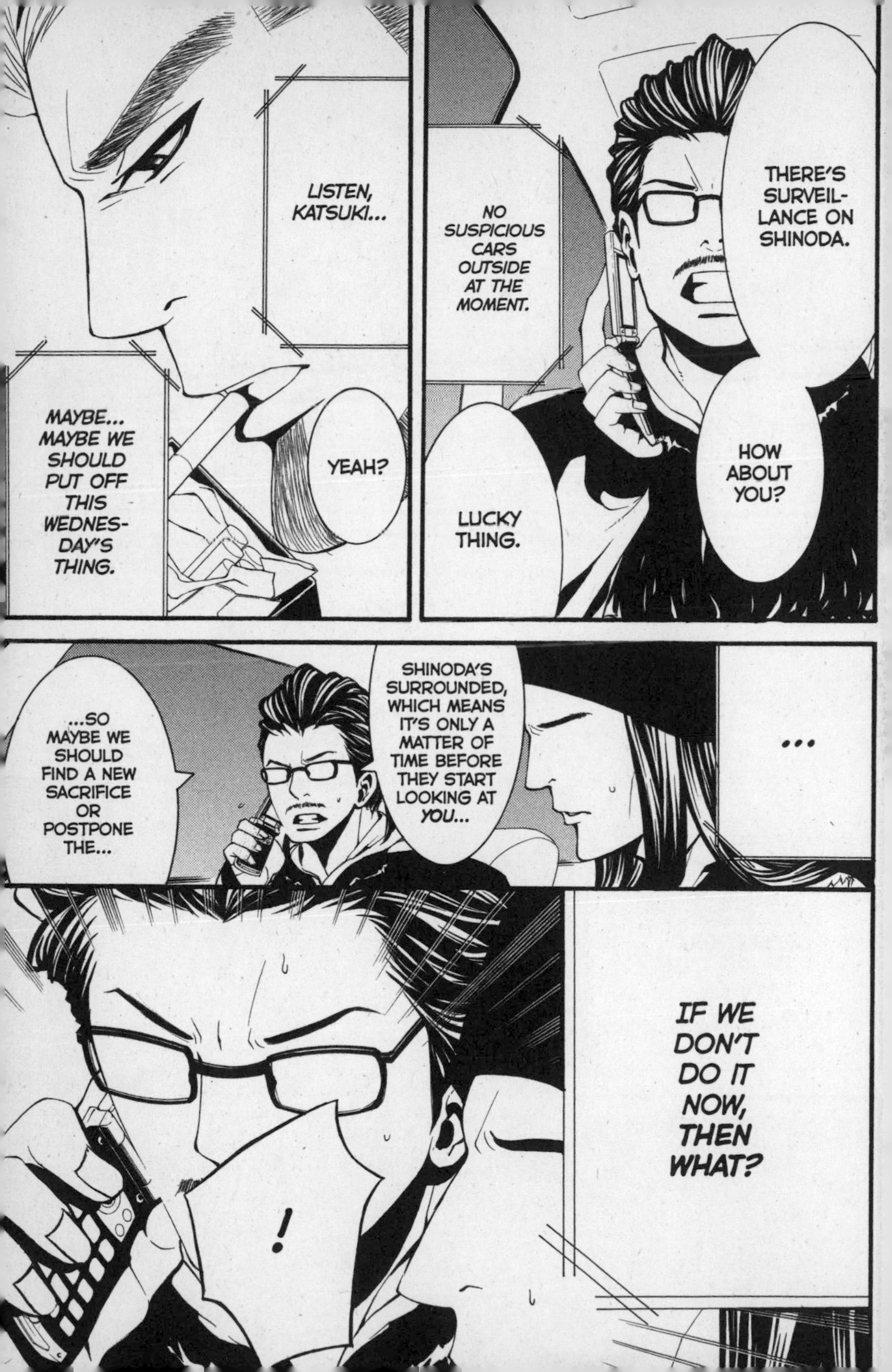
THERE'S SURVEIL-LANCE ON SHINODA.
NO SUSPICIOUS CARS OUTSIDE AT THE MOMENT.
HOW ABOUT YOU?
LUCKY THING.
LISTEN, KATSUKI...
YEAH?
MAYBE... MAYBE WE SHOULD PUT OFF THIS WEDNES-DAY'S THING.
...
SHINODA'S SURROUNDED, WHICH MEANS IT'S ONLY A MATTER OF TIME BEFORE THEY START LOOKING AT YOU...
...SO MAYBE WE SHOULD FIND A NEW SACRIFICE OR POSTPONE THE...
IF WE DON'T DO IT NOW, THEN WHAT?
!

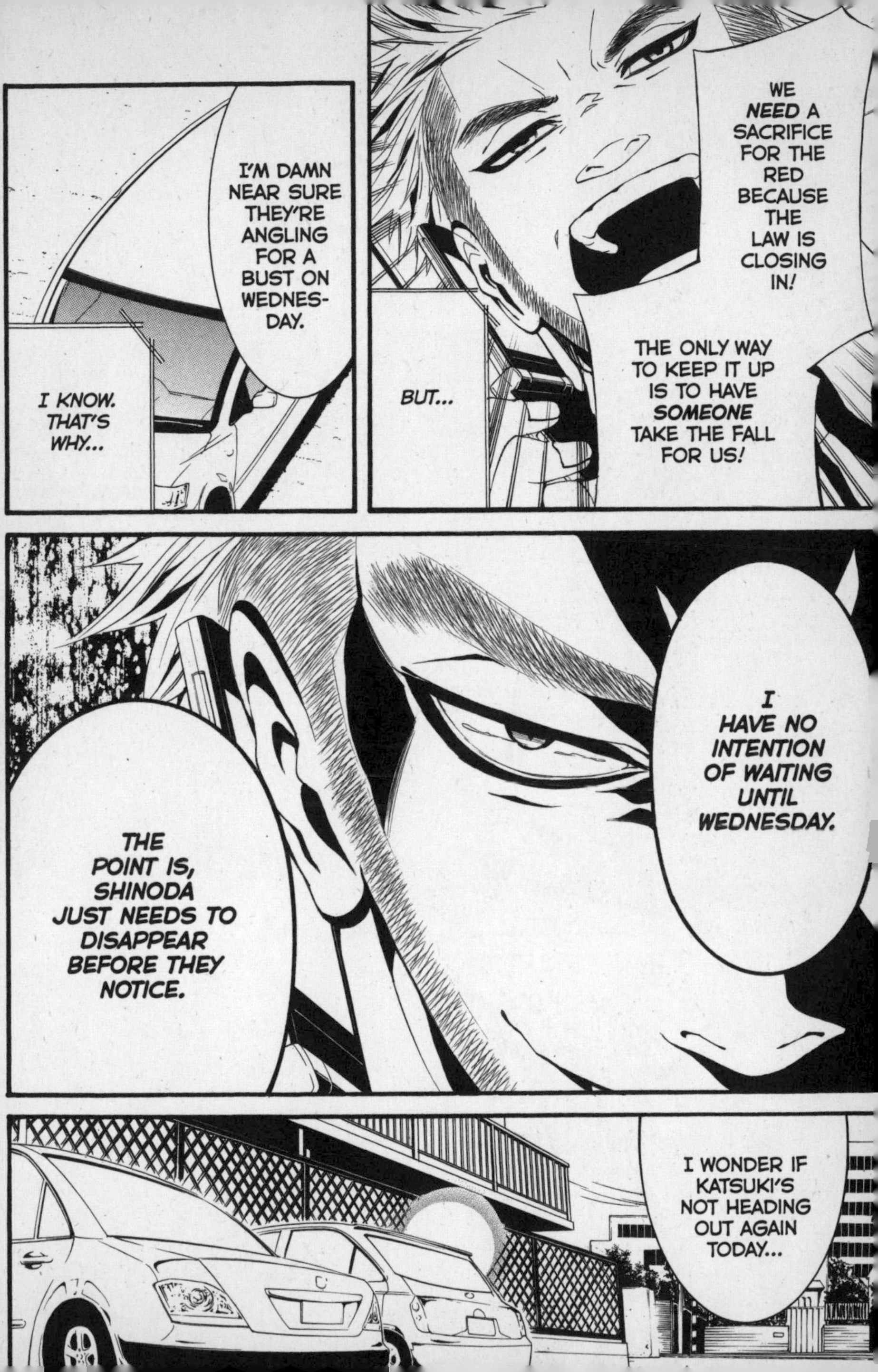
WE NEED A SACRIFICE FOR THE RED BECAUSE THE LAW IS CLOSING IN!
THE ONLY WAY TO KEEP IT UP IS TO HAVE SOMEONE TAKE THE FALL FOR US!
BUT...
I'M DAMN NEAR SURE THEY'RE ANGLING FOR A BUST ON WEDNES-DAY.
I KNOW. THAT'S WHY...
I HAVE NO INTENTION OF WAITING UNTIL WEDNESDAY.
THE POINT IS, SHINODA JUST NEEDS TO DISAPPEAR BEFORE THEY NOTICE.
I WONDER IF KATSUKI'S NOT HEADING OUT AGAIN TODAY...

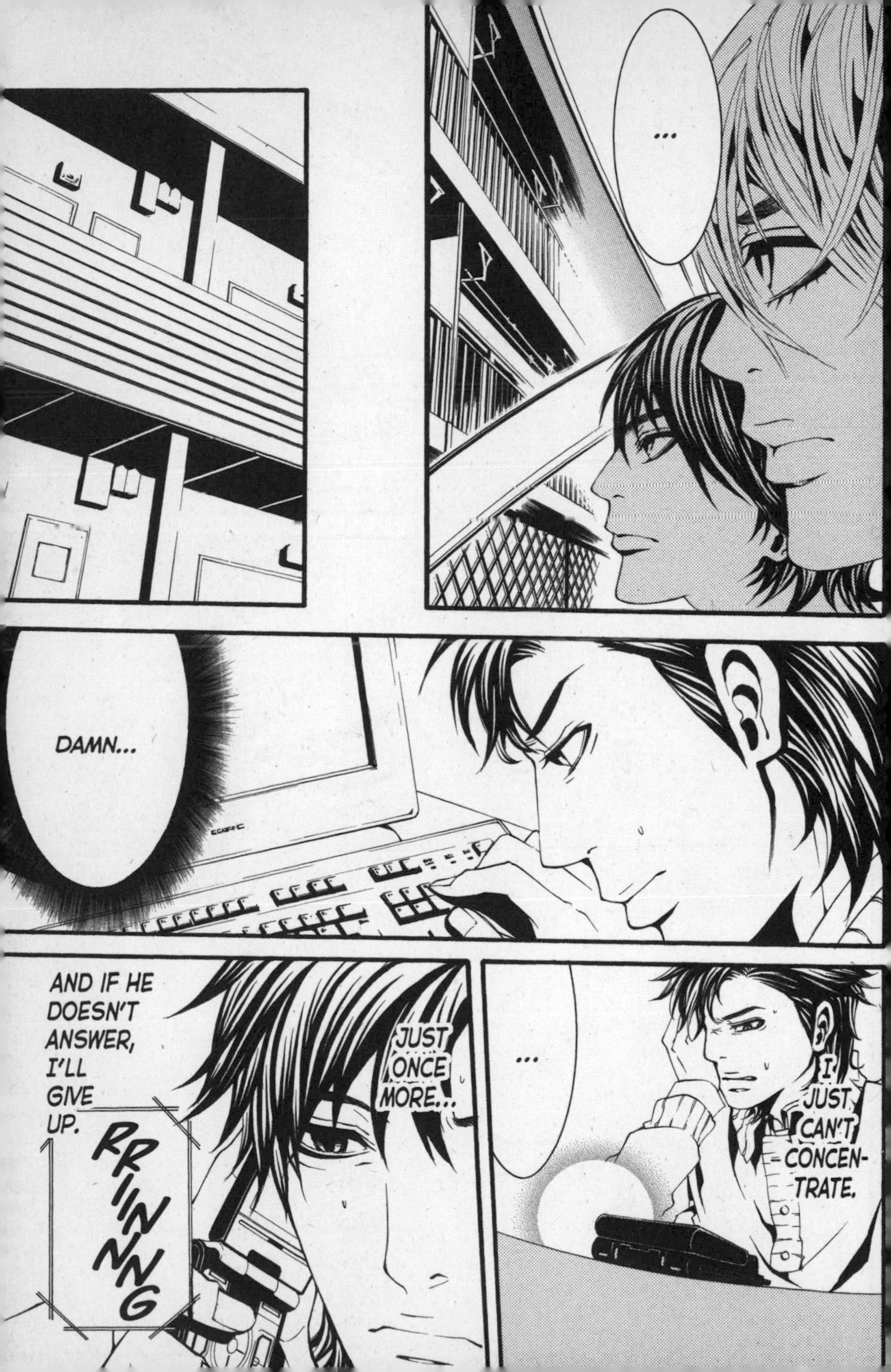
...
DAMN...
I JUST CAN'T CONCENTRATE.
...
JUST ONCE MORE...
AND IF HE DOESN'T ANSWER, I'LL GIVE UP.
RRIINNNG

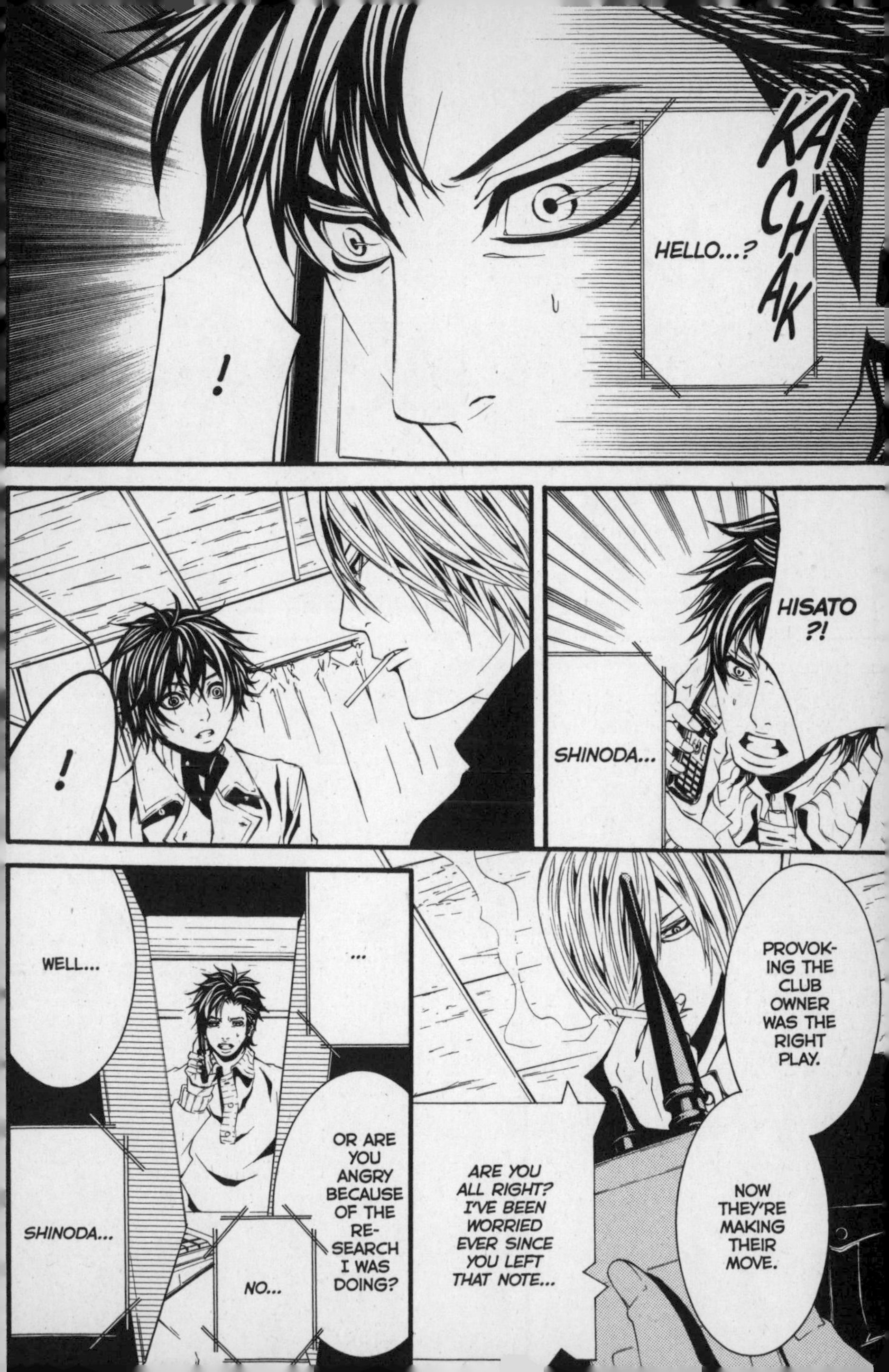
KACHAK
HELLO...?
!
HISATO ?!
SHINODA...
!
PROVOKING THE CLUB OWNER WAS THE RIGHT PLAY.
NOW THEY'RE MAKING THEIR MOVE.
ARE YOU ALL RIGHT? I'VE BEEN WORRIED EVER SINCE YOU LEFT THAT NOTE...
...
WELL...
OR ARE YOU ANGRY BECAUSE OF THE RESEARCH I WAS DOING?
NO...
SHINODA...

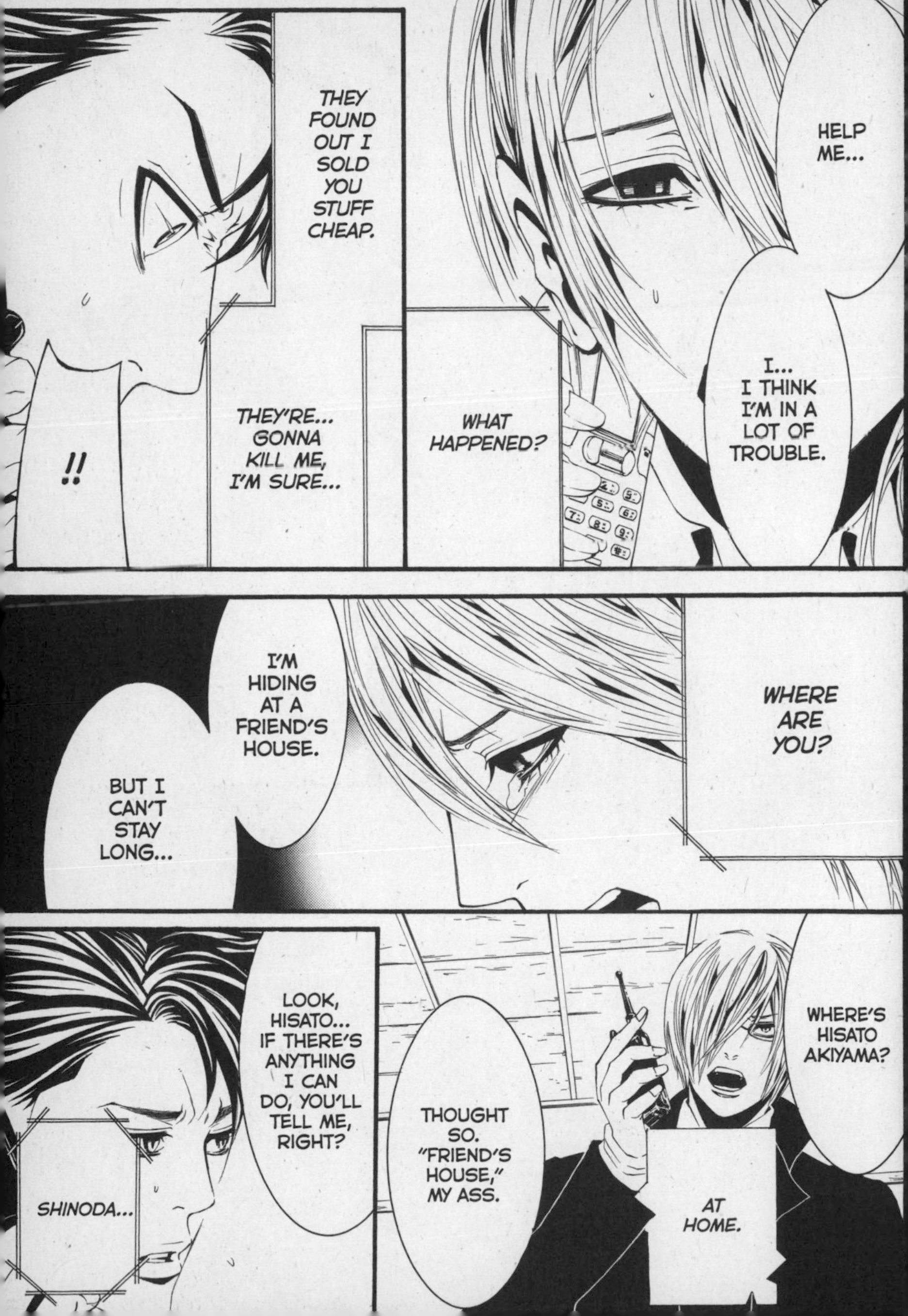
HELP ME...
I... I THINK I'M IN A LOT OF TROUBLE.
WHAT HAPPENED?
THEY FOUND OUT I SOLD YOU STUFF CHEAP.
THEY'RE... GONNA KILL ME, I'M SURE...
!!
WHERE ARE YOU?
I'M HIDING AT A FRIEND'S HOUSE.
BUT I CAN'T STAY LONG...
WHERE'S HISATO AKIYAMA?
AT HOME.
THOUGHT SO. "FRIEND'S HOUSE," MY ASS.
LOOK, HISATO... IF THERE'S ANYTHING I CAN DO, YOU'LL TELL ME, RIGHT?
SHINODA...

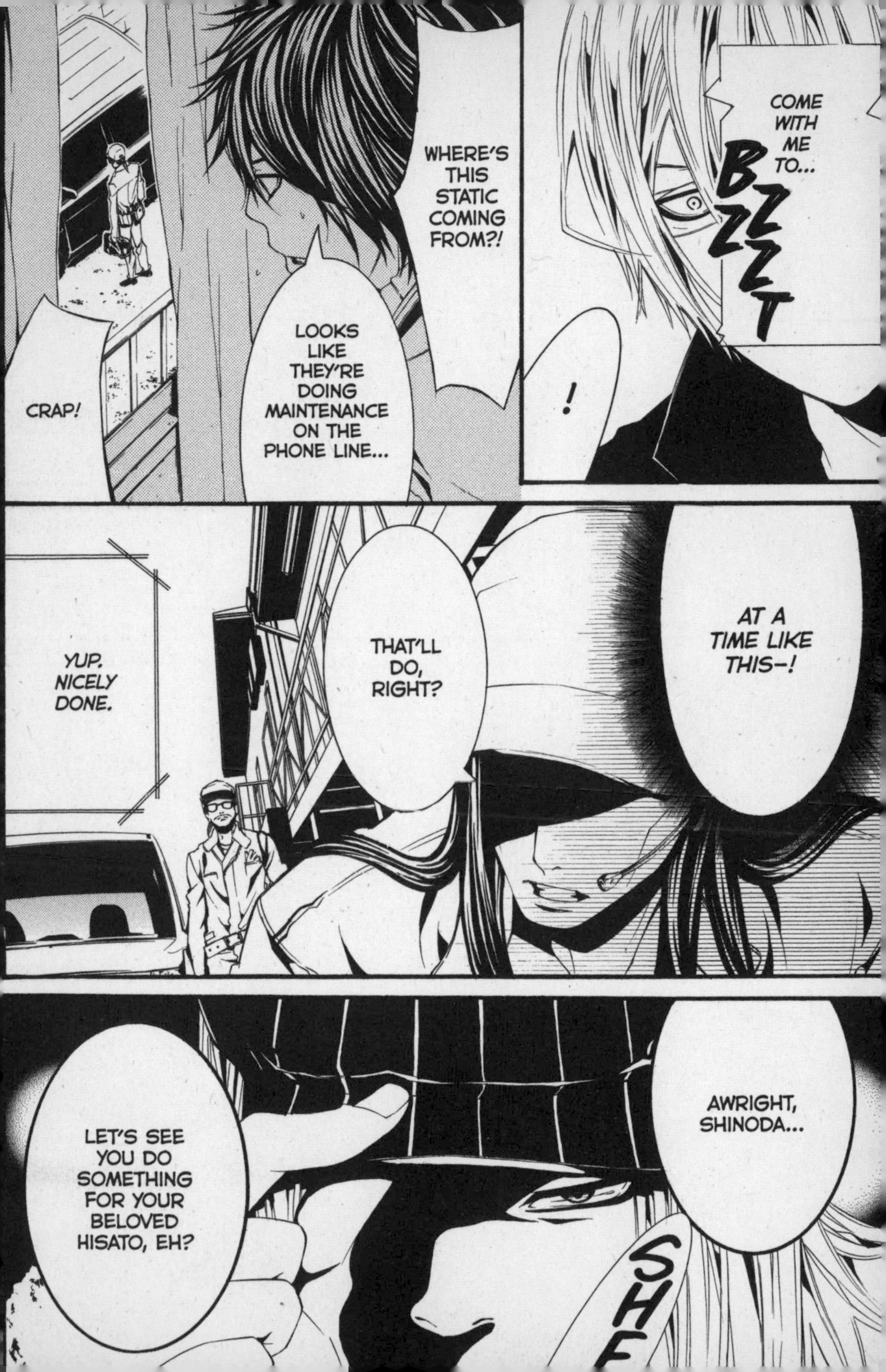
COME WITH ME TO...
BZZZT
!
WHERE'S THIS STATIC COMING FROM?!
LOOKS LIKE THEY'RE DOING MAINTENANCE ON THE PHONE LINE...
CRAP!
AT A TIME LIKE THIS–!
THAT'LL DO, RIGHT?
YUP. NICELY DONE.
AWRIGHT, SHINODA...
LET'S SEE YOU DO SOMETHING FOR YOUR BELOVED HISATO, EH?
SHF

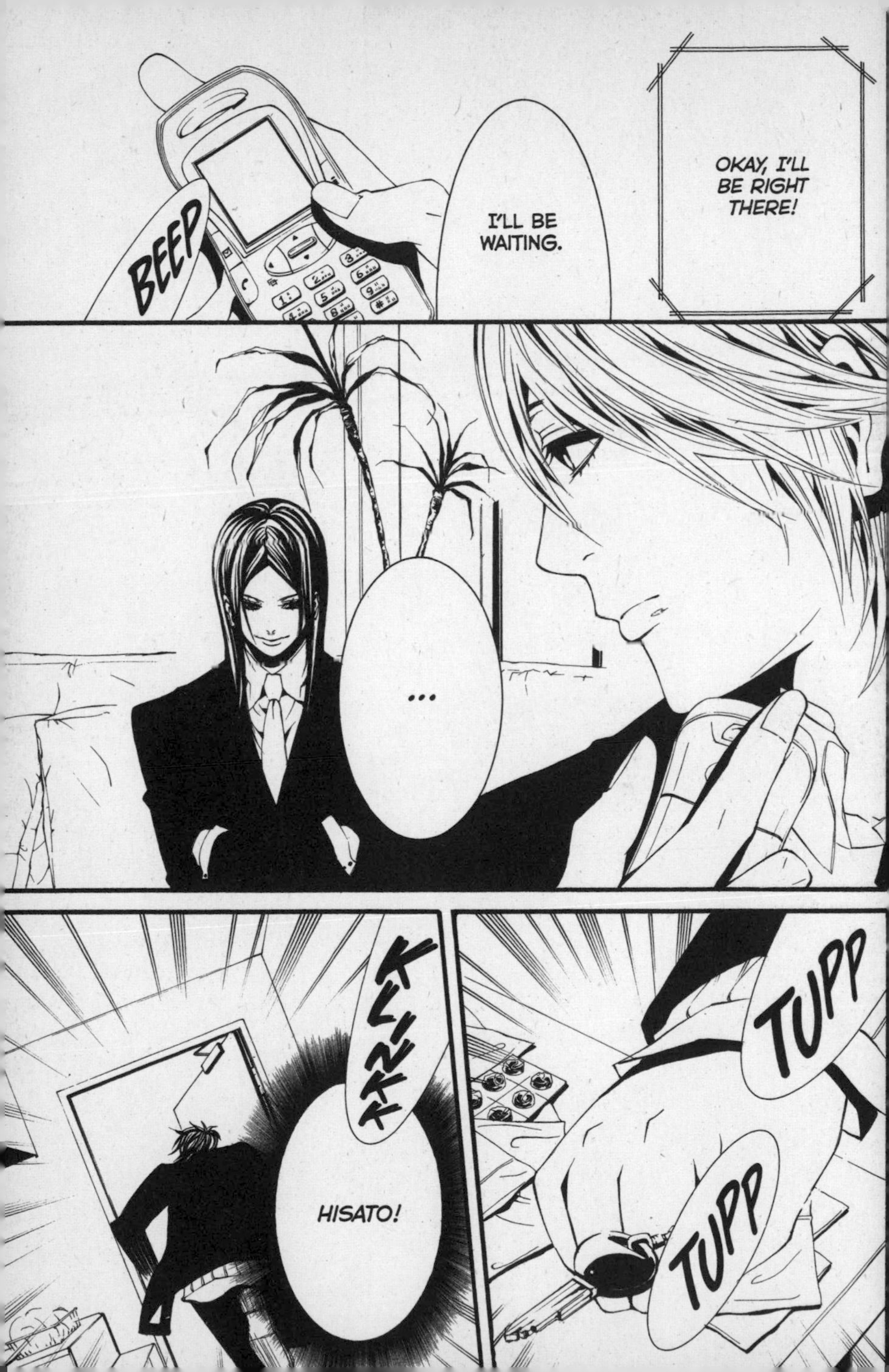
OKAY, I'LL BE RIGHT THERE!
I'LL BE WAITING.
BEEP
...
TUPP
TUPP
KLINK
HISATO!

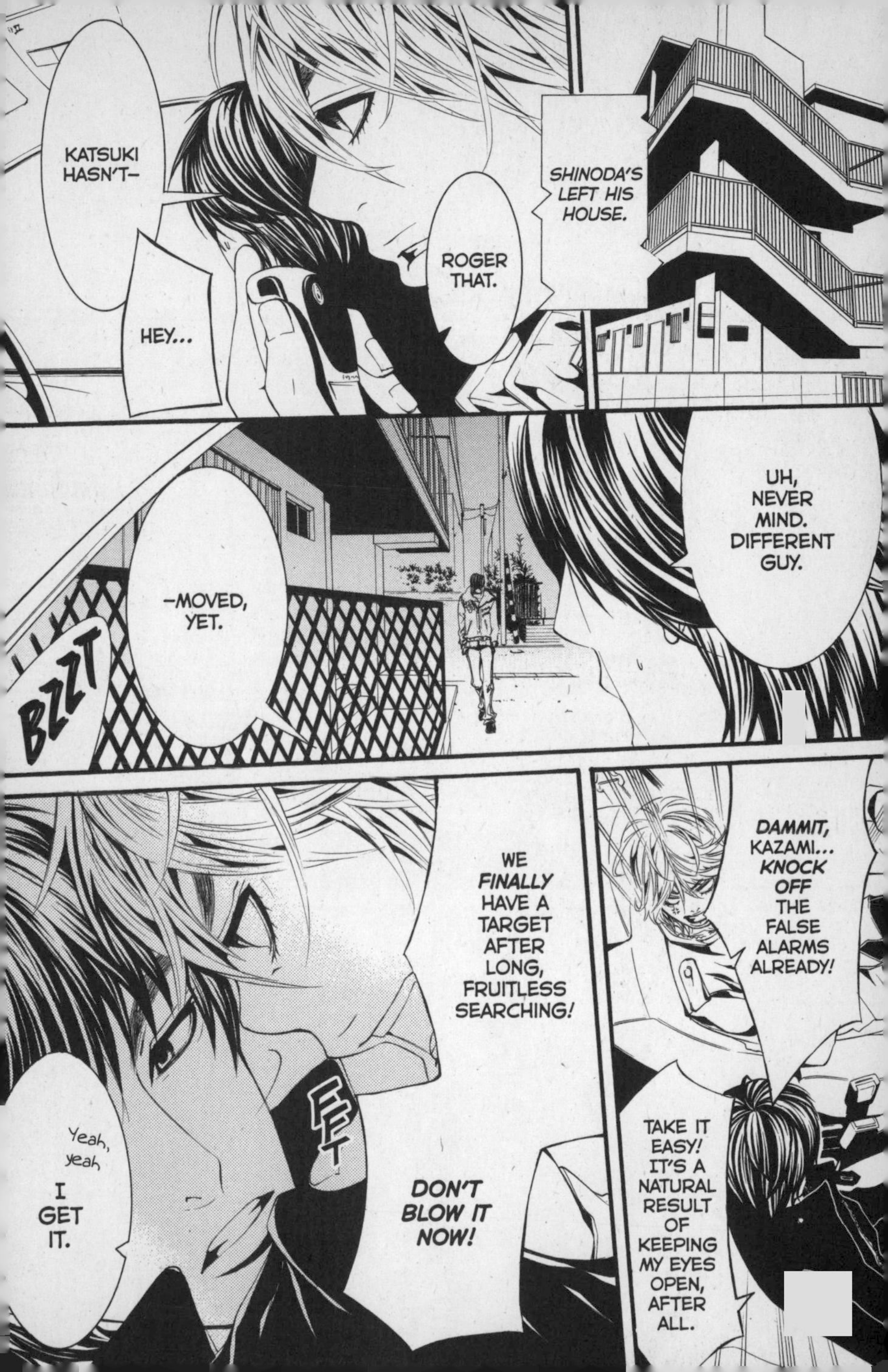
SHINODA'S LEFT HIS HOUSE.
ROGER THAT.
KATSUKI HASN'T—
HEY...
UH, NEVER MIND. DIFFERENT GUY.
—MOVED, YET.
BZZT
DAMMIT, KAZAMI... *KNOCK OFF* THE FALSE ALARMS ALREADY!
TAKE IT EASY! IT'S A NATURAL RESULT OF KEEPING MY EYES OPEN, AFTER ALL.
WE *FINALLY* HAVE A TARGET AFTER LONG, FRUITLESS SEARCHING!
FFT
DON'T BLOW IT NOW!
Yeah, yeah
I GET IT.

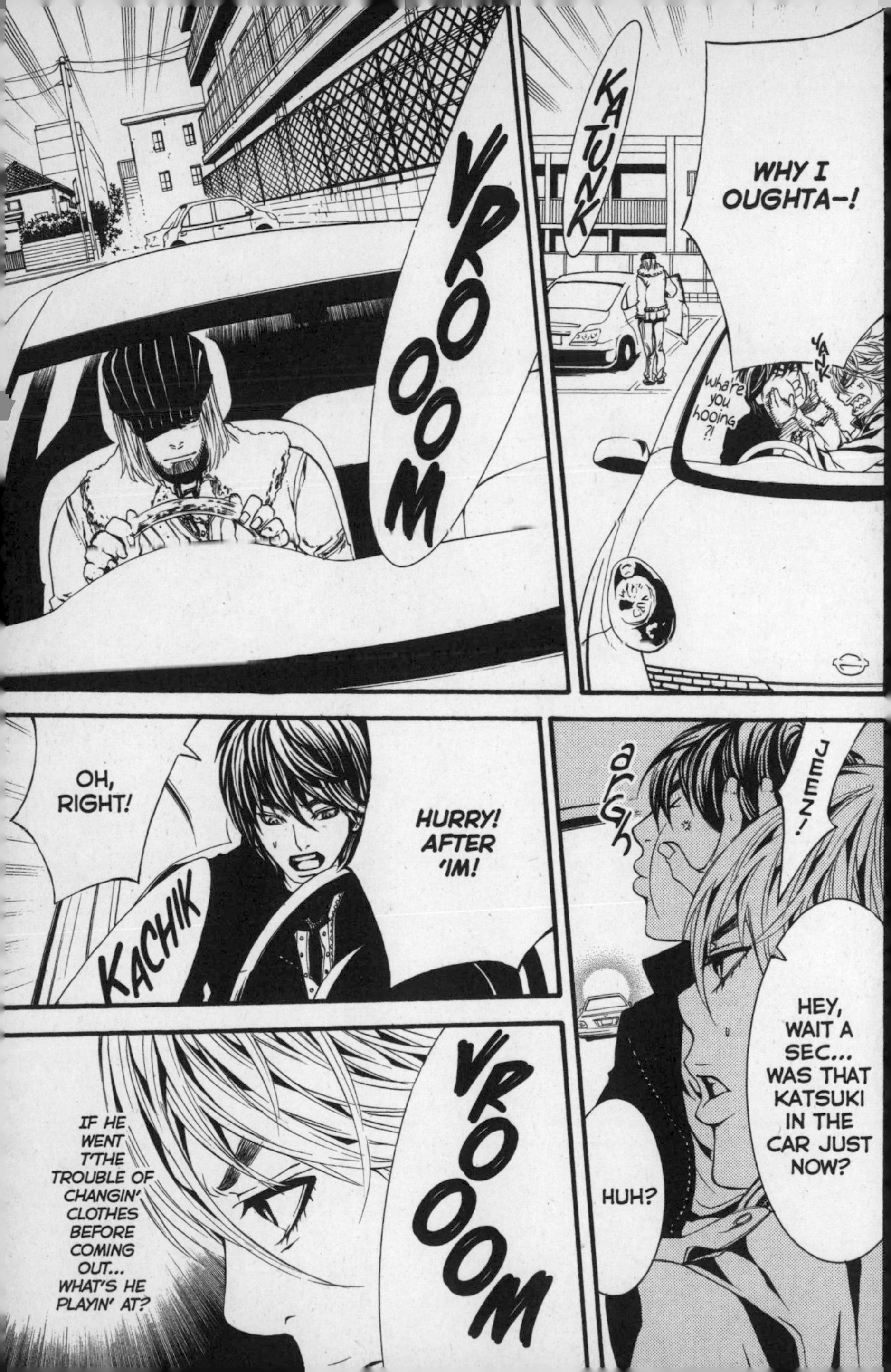
KATUNK
WHY I OUGHTA-!
YANK
Wha're you hooing ?!
VROOOOM
JEEZ!
argh
HEY, WAIT A SEC... WAS THAT KATSUKI IN THE CAR JUST NOW?
HUH?
HURRY! AFTER 'IM!
OH, RIGHT!
KACHIK
VROOOOM
IF HE WENT T'THE TROUBLE OF CHANGIN' CLOTHES BEFORE COMING OUT... WHAT'S HE PLAYIN' AT?

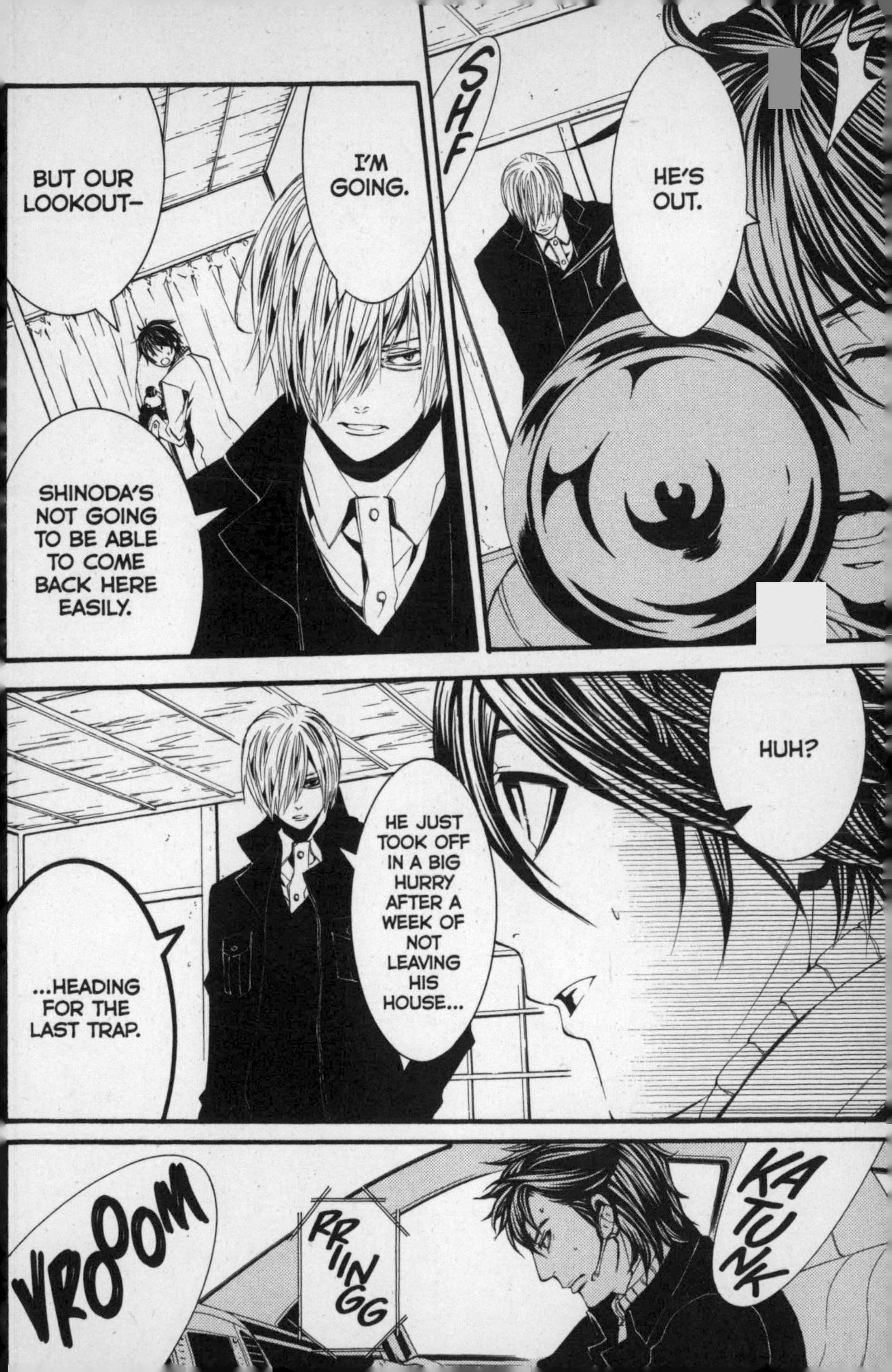
HE'S OUT.
SHF
I'M GOING.
BUT OUR LOOKOUT—
SHINODA'S NOT GOING TO BE ABLE TO COME BACK HERE EASILY.
HUH?
HE JUST TOOK OFF IN A BIG HURRY AFTER A WEEK OF NOT LEAVING HIS HOUSE...
...HEADING FOR THE LAST TRAP.
KATUNK
RRIINGG
VROOOM

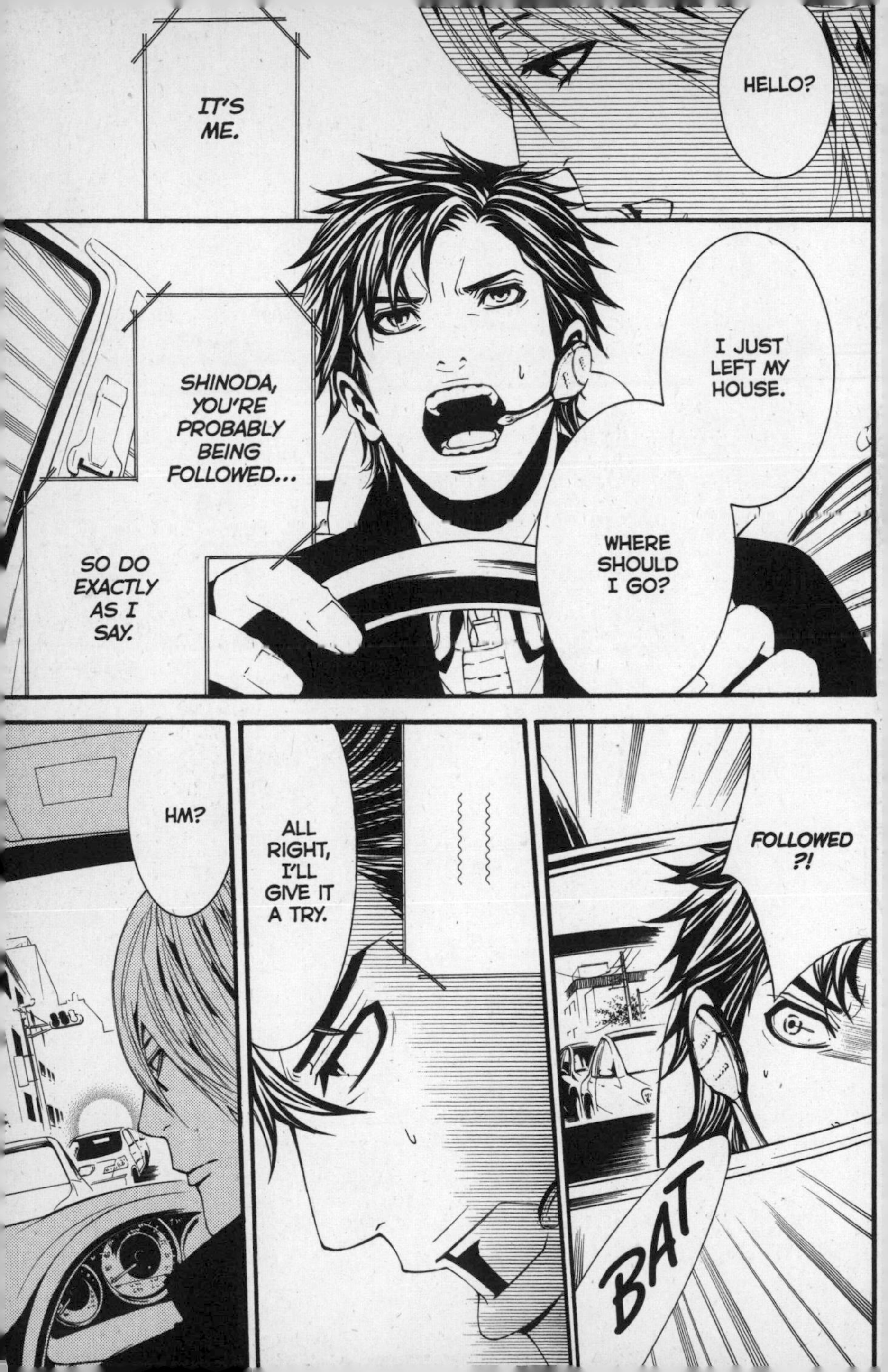
HELLO?
IT'S ME.
I JUST LEFT MY HOUSE.
WHERE SHOULD I GO?
SHINODA, YOU'RE PROBABLY BEING FOLLOWED...
SO DO EXACTLY AS I SAY.
FOLLOWED?!
BAT
ALL RIGHT, I'LL GIVE IT A TRY.
HM?

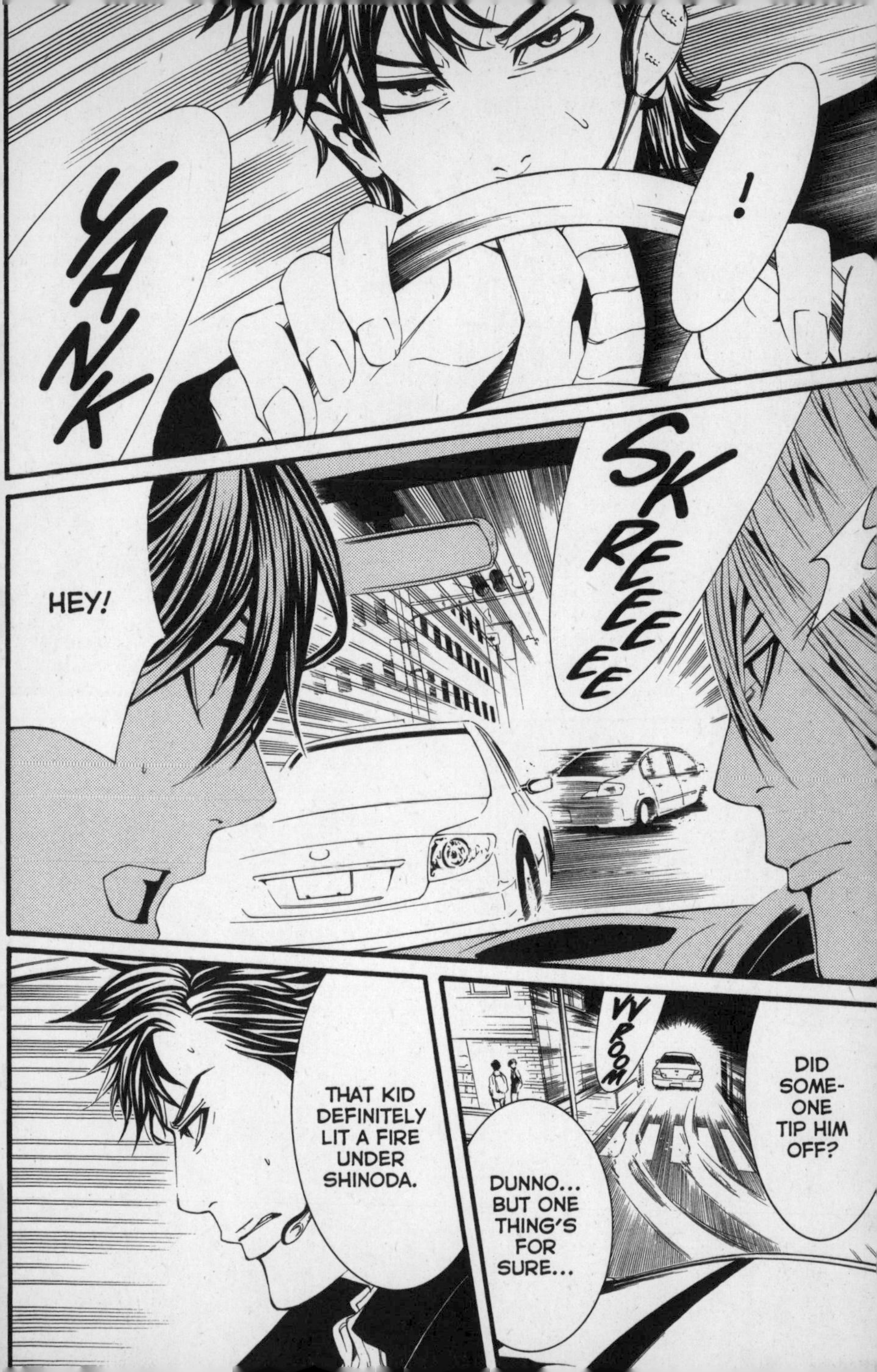
!
YANK
SKREEEEEEE
HEY!
DID SOME-ONE TIP HIM OFF?
VVROOM
DUNNO... BUT ONE THING'S FOR SURE...
THAT KID DEFINITELY LIT A FIRE UNDER SHINODA.

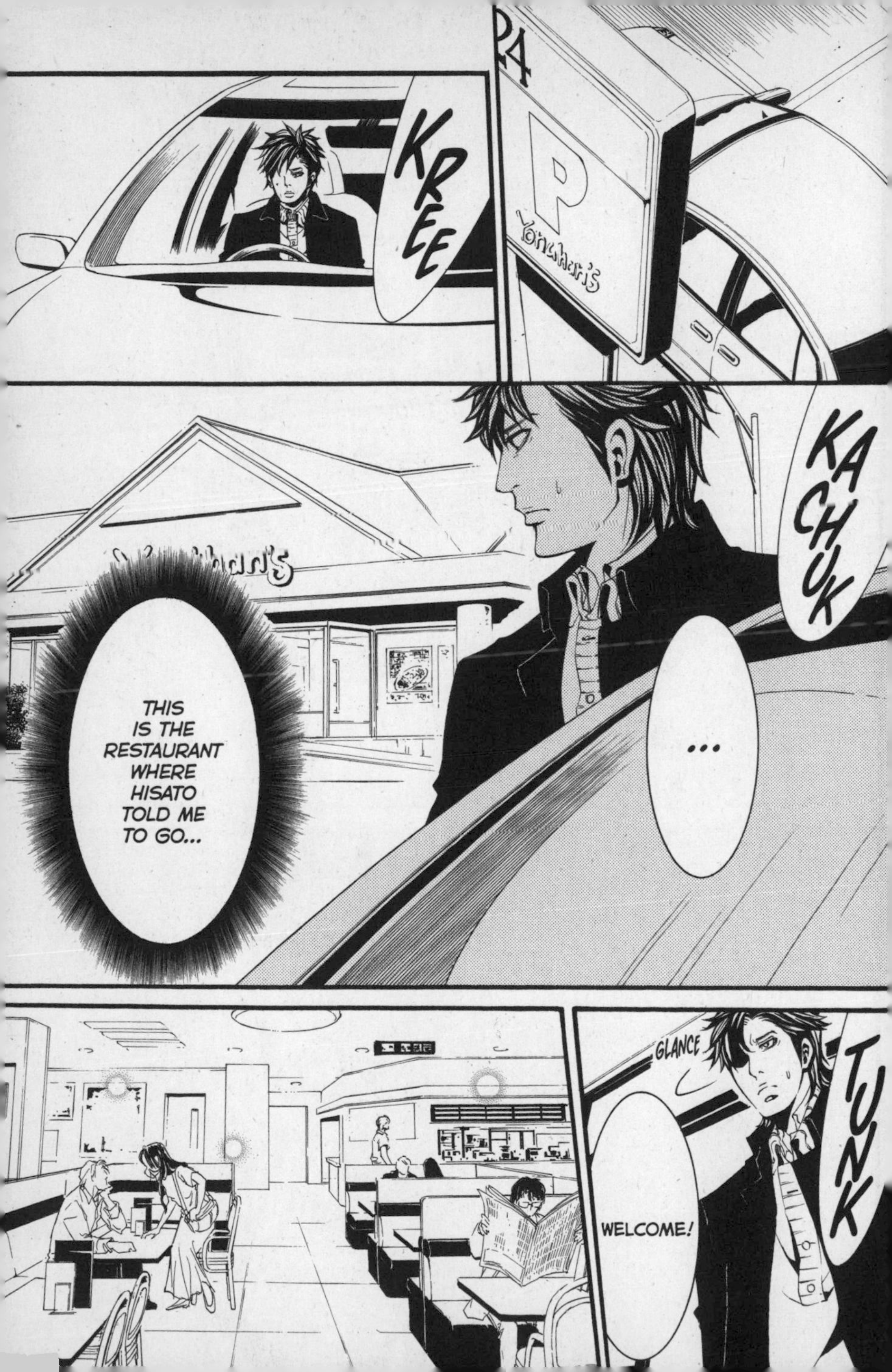
KREE
KACHUK
...
THIS IS THE RESTAURANT WHERE HISATO TOLD ME TO GO...
TUNK
GLANCE
WELCOME!

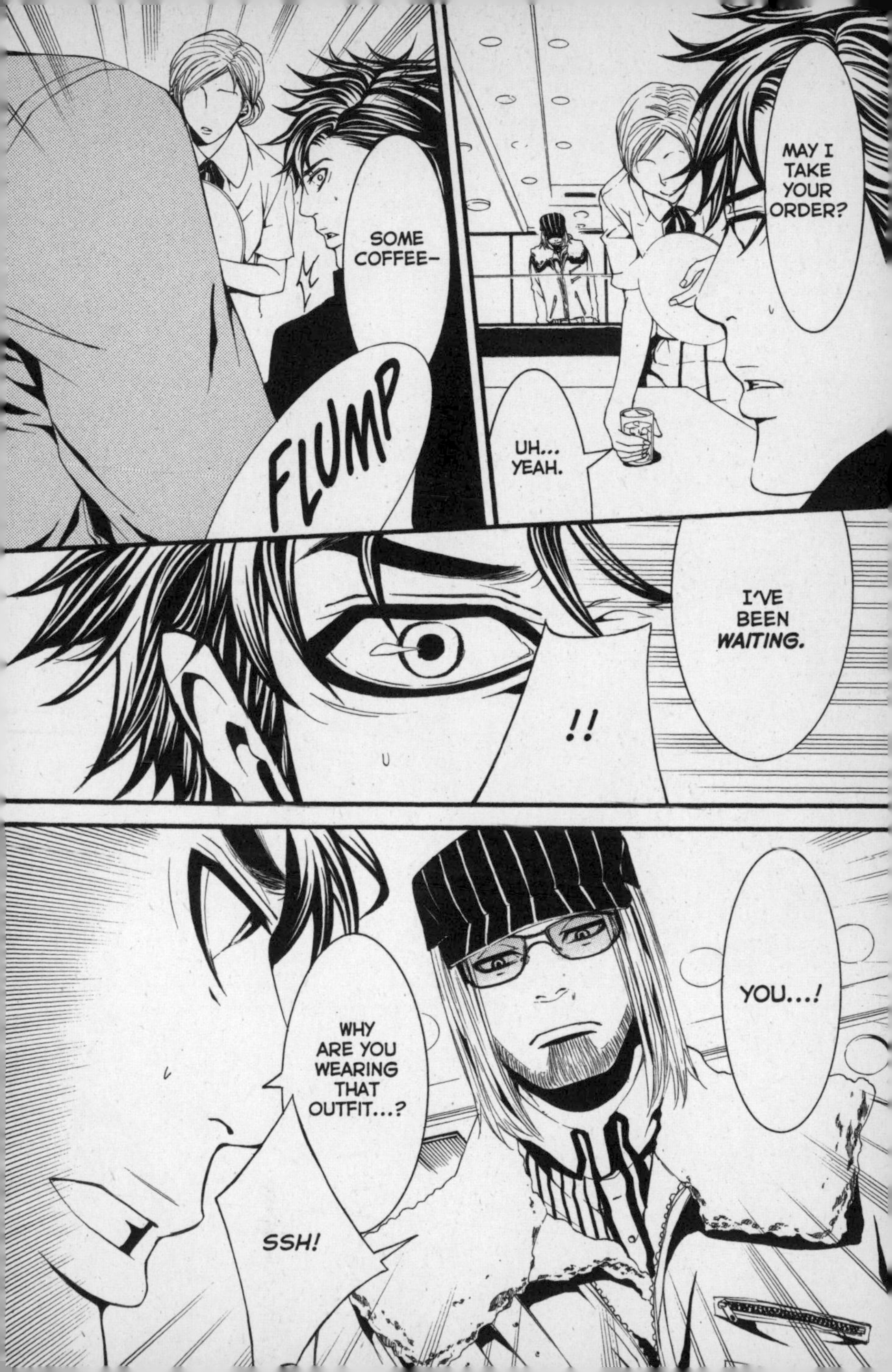
MAY I TAKE YOUR ORDER?
UH... YEAH.
SOME COFFEE–
FLUMP
I'VE BEEN WAITING.
!!
YOU...!
WHY ARE YOU WEARING THAT OUTFIT...?
SSH!

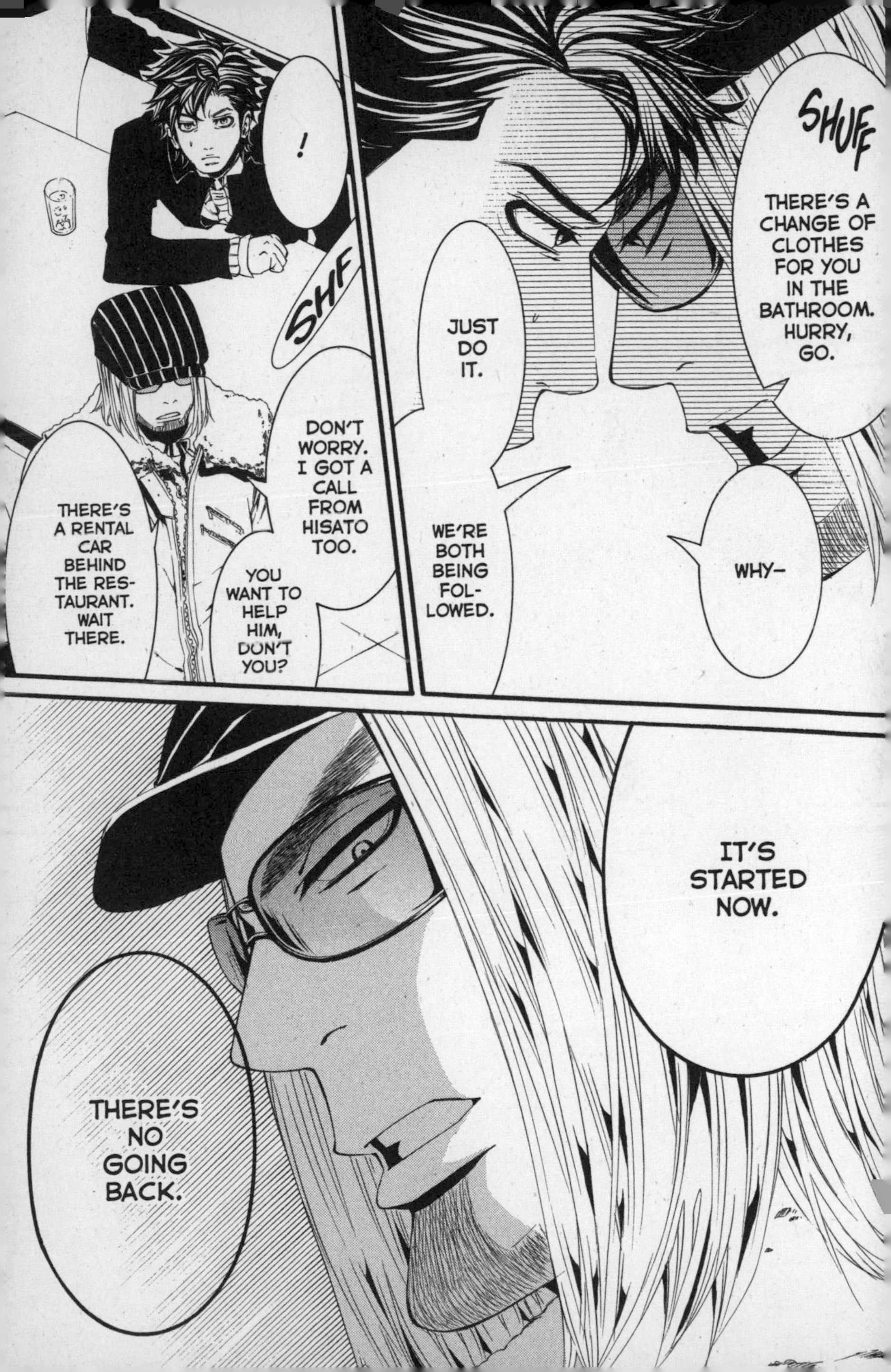
SHUFF
THERE'S A CHANGE OF CLOTHES FOR YOU IN THE BATHROOM. HURRY, GO.
WHY-
JUST DO IT.
WE'RE BOTH BEING FOL-LOWED.
!
SHF
DON'T WORRY. I GOT A CALL FROM HISATO TOO.
YOU WANT TO HELP HIM, DON'T YOU?
THERE'S A RENTAL CAR BEHIND THE RES-TAURANT. WAIT THERE.
IT'S STARTED NOW.
THERE'S NO GOING BACK.

naked ape : Saki Otoh & Nakamura Tomomi

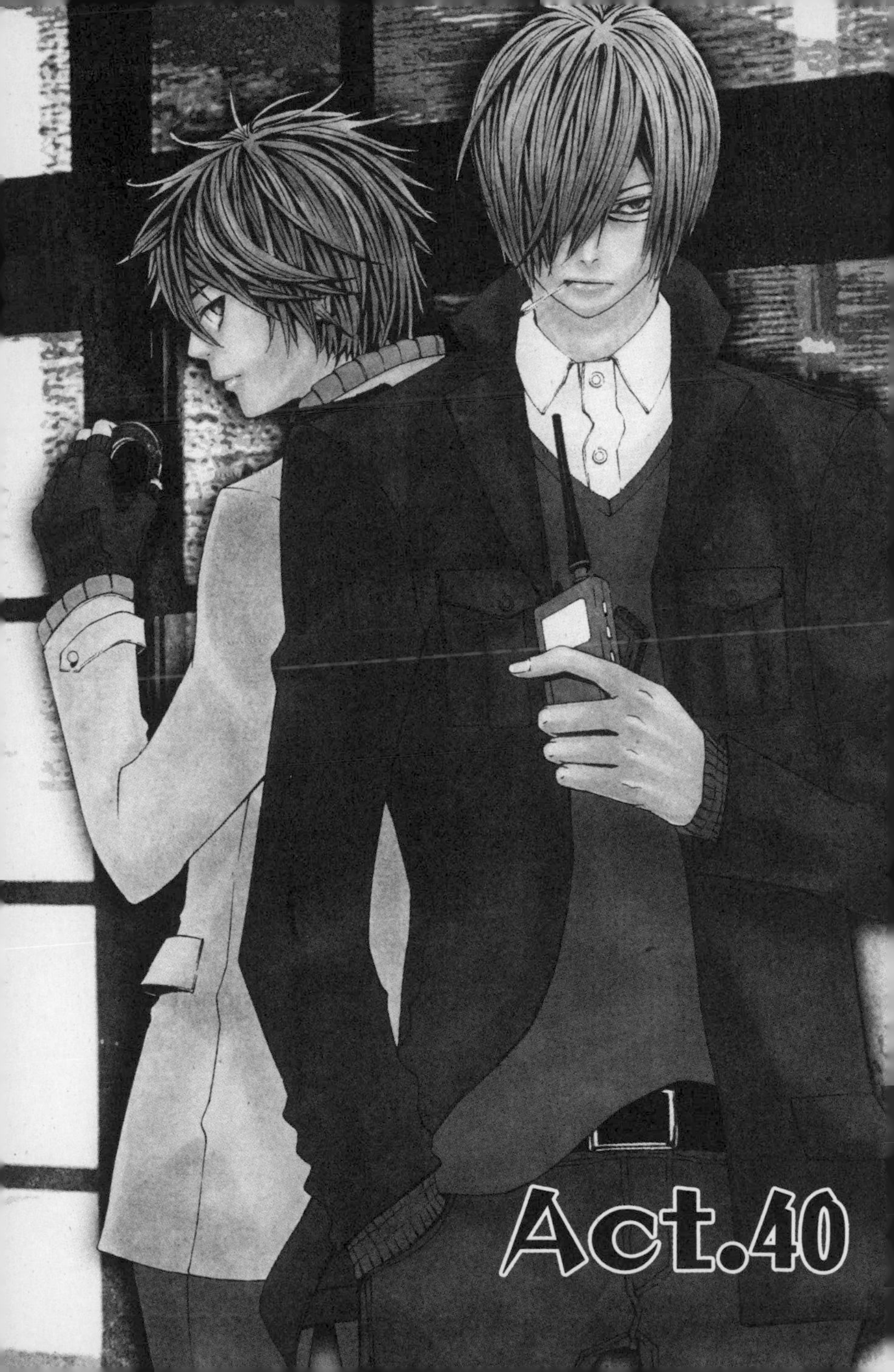
Act.40

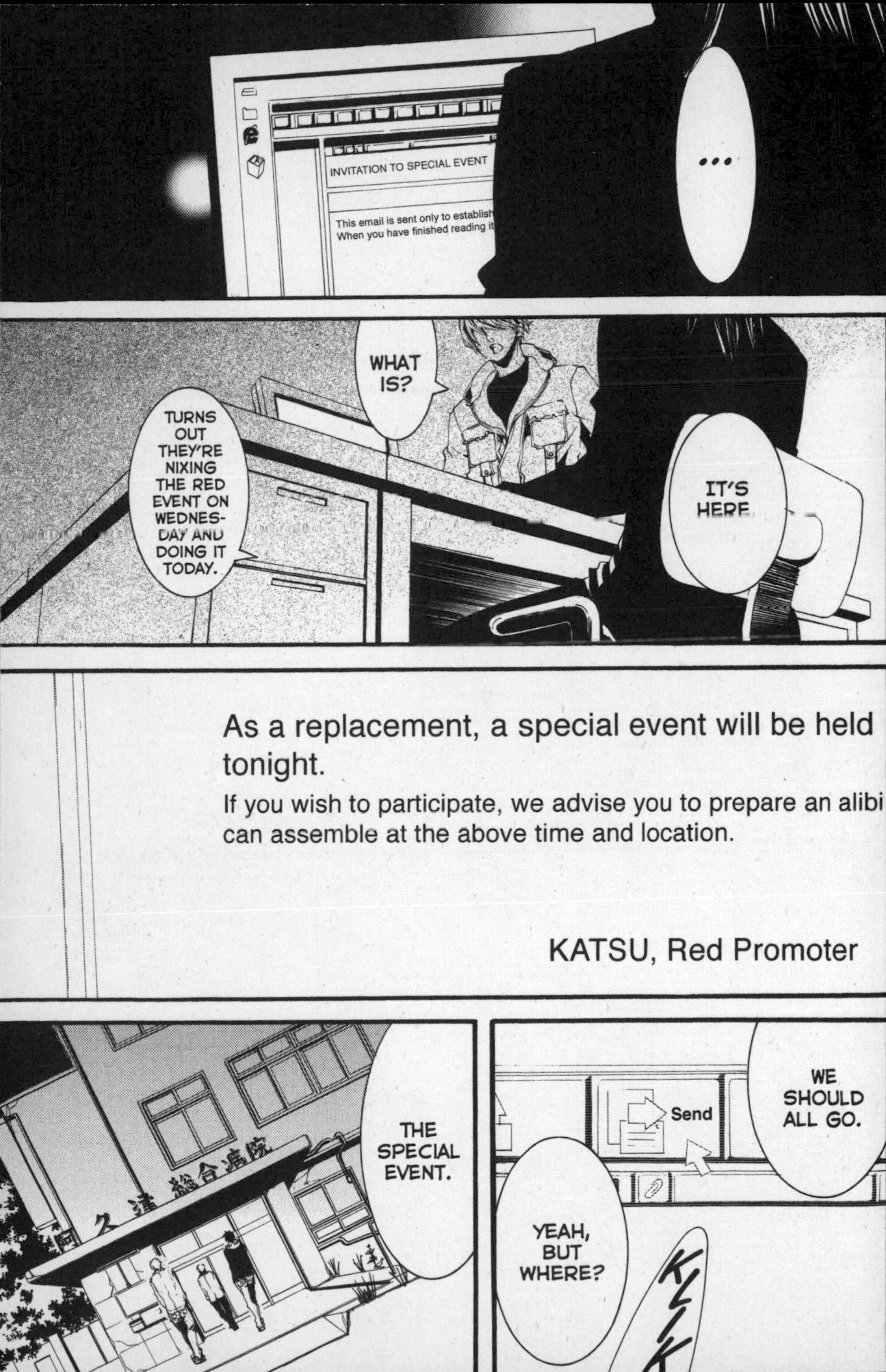
INVITATION TO SPECIAL EVENT
This email is sent only to establish
When you have finished reading it
...
IT'S HERE.
WHAT IS?
TURNS OUT THEY'RE NIXING THE RED EVENT ON WEDNES-DAY AND DOING IT TODAY.
As a replacement, a special event will be held tonight.
If you wish to participate, we advise you to prepare an alibi
can assemble at the above time and location.
KATSU, Red Promoter
WE SHOULD ALL GO.
Send
YEAH, BUT WHERE?
KLIK
THE SPECIAL EVENT.

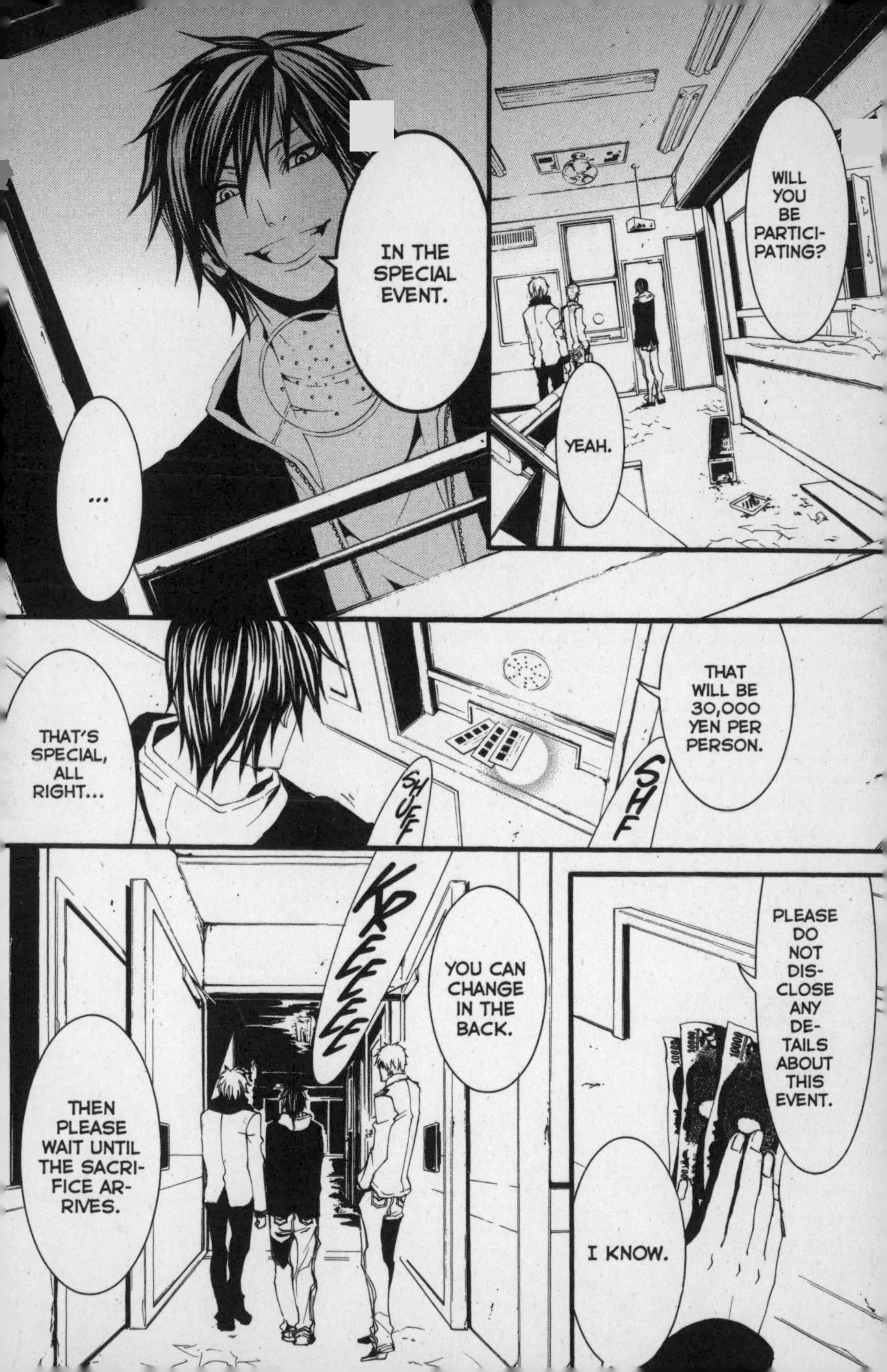
WILL YOU BE PARTICI-PATING?
YEAH.
IN THE SPECIAL EVENT.
...
THAT WILL BE 30,000 YEN PER PERSON.
SHF
SHUFF
THAT'S SPECIAL, ALL RIGHT...
PLEASE DO NOT DIS-CLOSE ANY DE-TAILS ABOUT THIS EVENT.
I KNOW.
KREEEEE
YOU CAN CHANGE IN THE BACK.
THEN PLEASE WAIT UNTIL THE SACRI-FICE AR-RIVES.

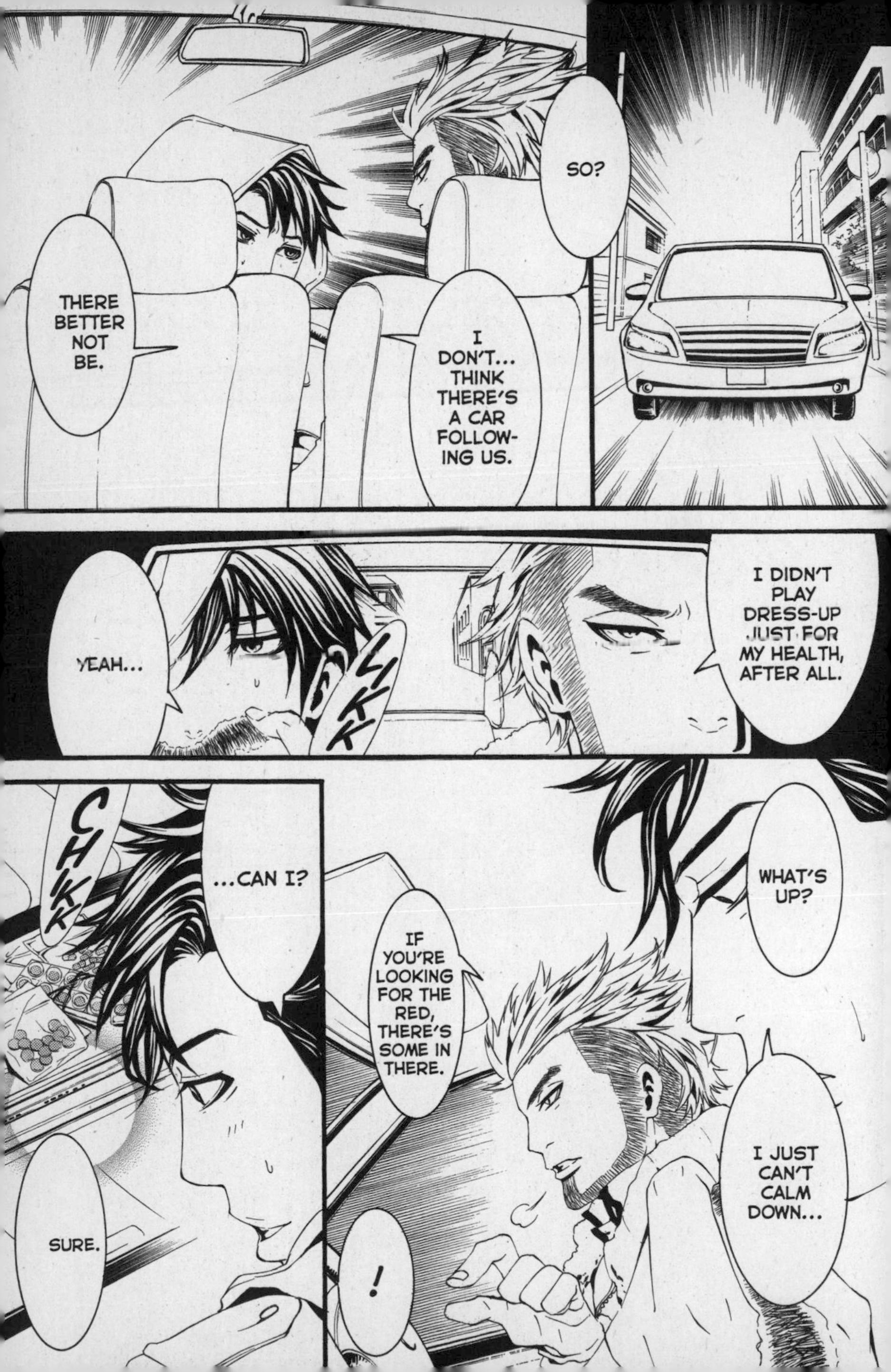
SO?
I DON'T... THINK THERE'S A CAR FOLLOWING US.
THERE BETTER NOT BE.
I DIDN'T PLAY DRESS-UP JUST FOR MY HEALTH, AFTER ALL.
CLIKK
YEAH...
WHAT'S UP?
I JUST CAN'T CALM DOWN...
IF YOU'RE LOOKING FOR THE RED, THERE'S SOME IN THERE.
!
...CAN I?
CHIKK
SURE.

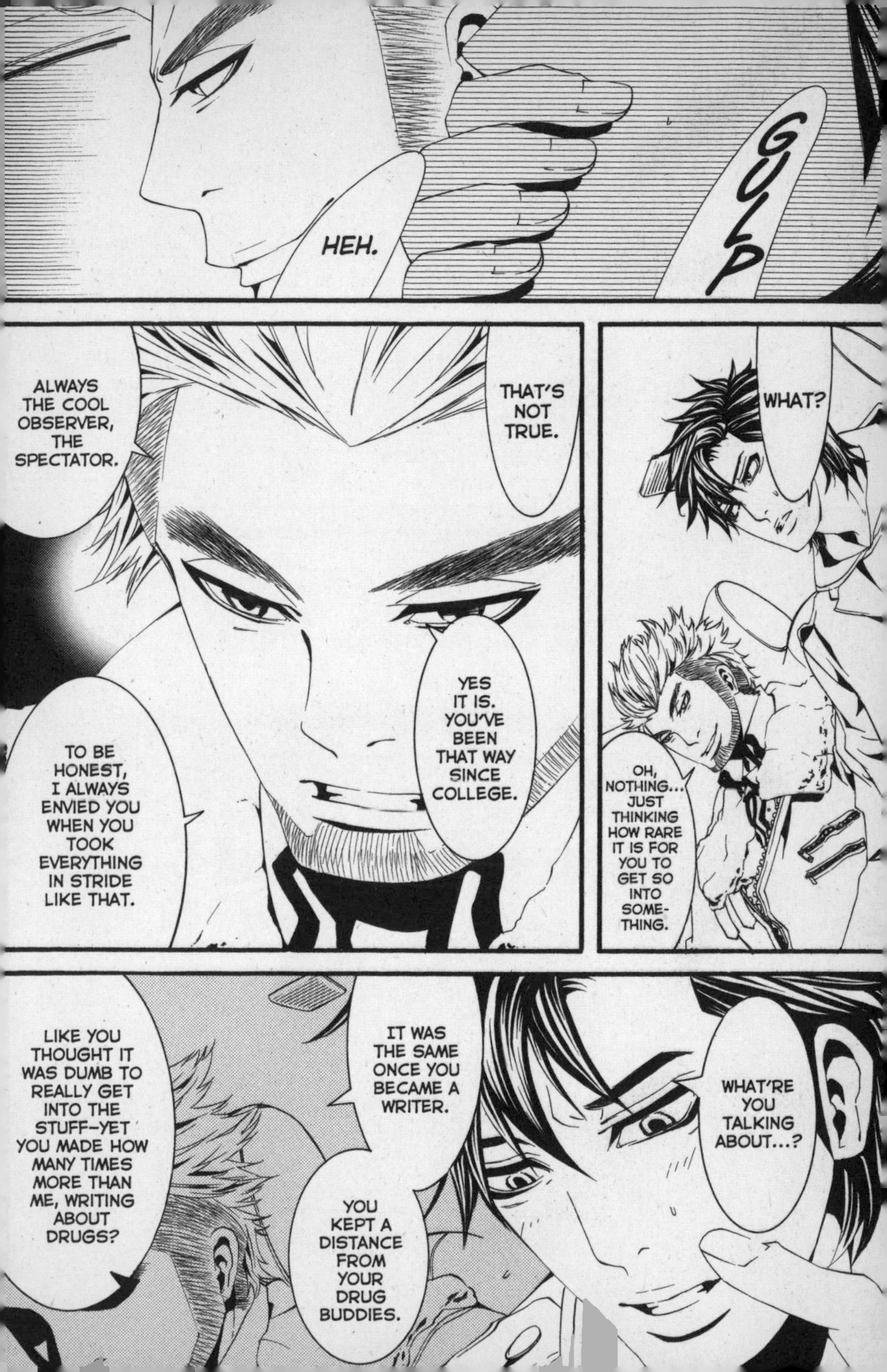
GULP
HEH.
WHAT?
OH, NOTHING... JUST THINKING HOW RARE IT IS FOR YOU TO GET SO INTO SOME-THING.
ALWAYS THE COOL OBSERVER, THE SPECTATOR.
THAT'S NOT TRUE.
YES IT IS. YOU'VE BEEN THAT WAY SINCE COLLEGE.
TO BE HONEST, I ALWAYS ENVIED YOU WHEN YOU TOOK EVERYTHING IN STRIDE LIKE THAT.
WHAT'RE YOU TALKING ABOUT...?
IT WAS THE SAME ONCE YOU BECAME A WRITER.
YOU KEPT A DISTANCE FROM YOUR DRUG BUDDIES.
LIKE YOU THOUGHT IT WAS DUMB TO REALLY GET INTO THE STUFF—YET YOU MADE HOW MANY TIMES MORE THAN ME, WRITING ABOUT DRUGS?

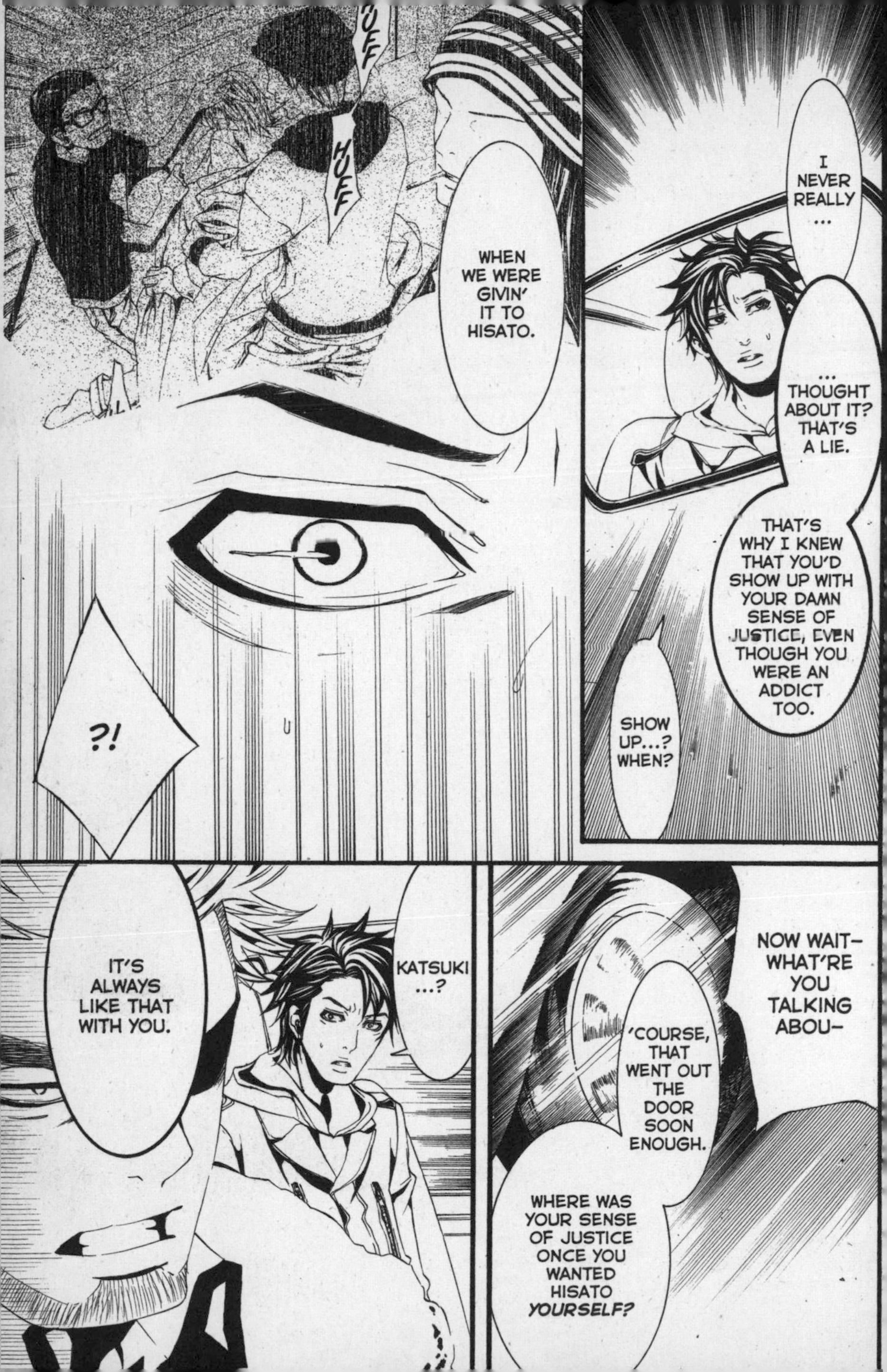
I NEVER REALLY ...
... THOUGHT ABOUT IT? THAT'S A LIE.
THAT'S WHY I KNEW THAT YOU'D SHOW UP WITH YOUR DAMN SENSE OF JUSTICE, EVEN THOUGH YOU WERE AN ADDICT TOO.
SHOW UP...? WHEN?
HUFF
HUFF
WHEN WE WERE GIVIN' IT TO HISATO.
?!
NOW WAIT– WHAT'RE YOU TALKING ABOU–
'COURSE, THAT WENT OUT THE DOOR SOON ENOUGH.
WHERE WAS YOUR SENSE OF JUSTICE ONCE YOU WANTED HISATO *YOURSELF?*
KATSUKI ...?
IT'S ALWAYS LIKE THAT WITH YOU.

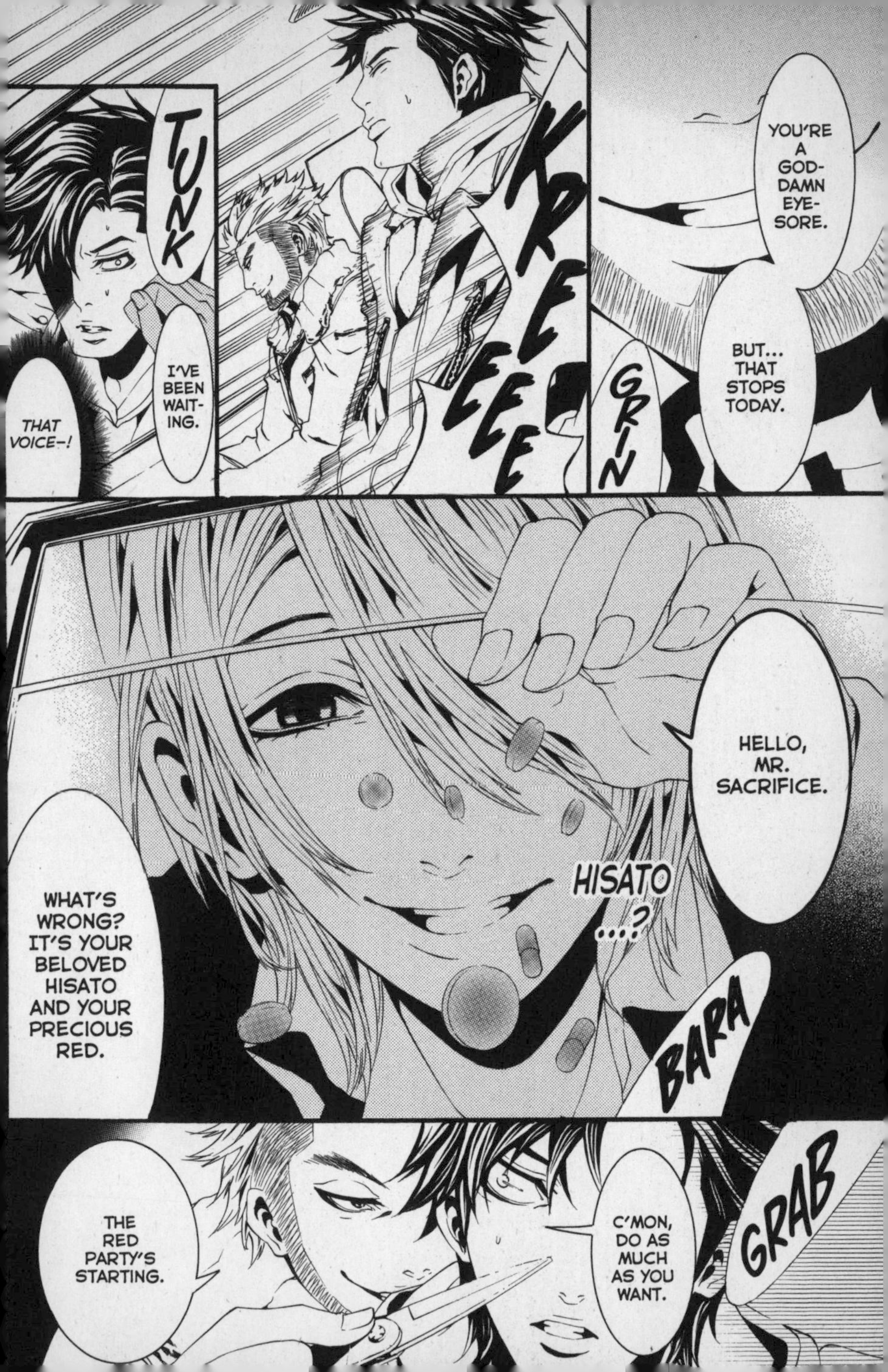
YOU'RE A GOD-DAMN EYE-SORE.
BUT... THAT STOPS TODAY.
GRIN
KREEEEE
I'VE BEEN WAITING.
TUNK
THAT VOICE–!
HELLO, MR. SACRIFICE.
HISATO ...?
BARA
WHAT'S WRONG? IT'S YOUR BELOVED HISATO AND YOUR PRECIOUS RED.
GRAB
C'MON, DO AS MUCH AS YOU WANT.
THE RED PARTY'S STARTING.

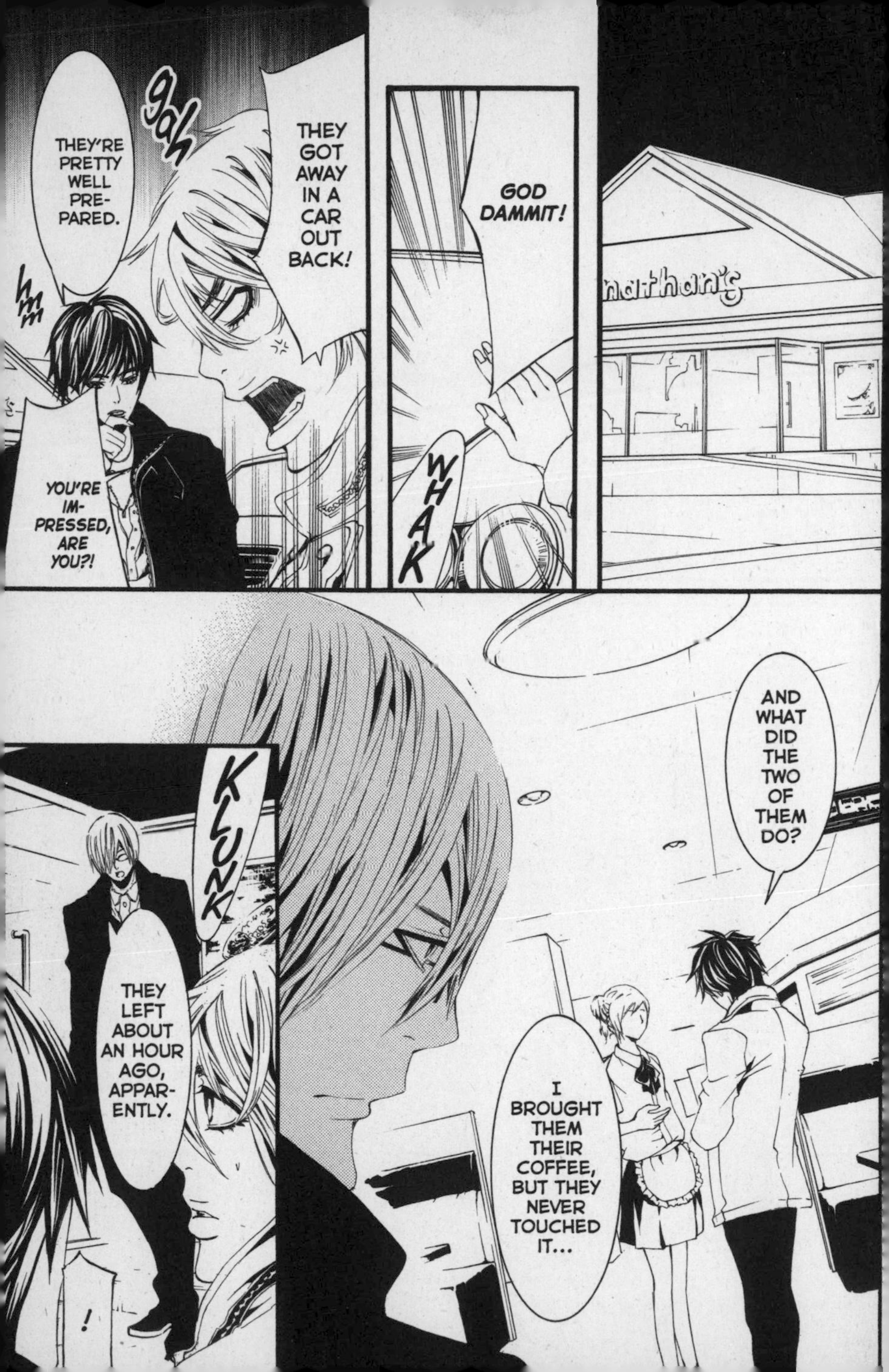
nathan's
GOD DAMMIT!
WHAK
THEY GOT AWAY IN A CAR OUT BACK!
gah
THEY'RE PRETTY WELL PRE-PARED.
hmm
YOU'RE IM-PRESSED, ARE YOU?!
AND WHAT DID THE TWO OF THEM DO?
I BROUGHT THEM THEIR COFFEE, BUT THEY NEVER TOUCHED IT...
KLUNK
THEY LEFT ABOUT AN HOUR AGO, APPAR-ENTLY.
!

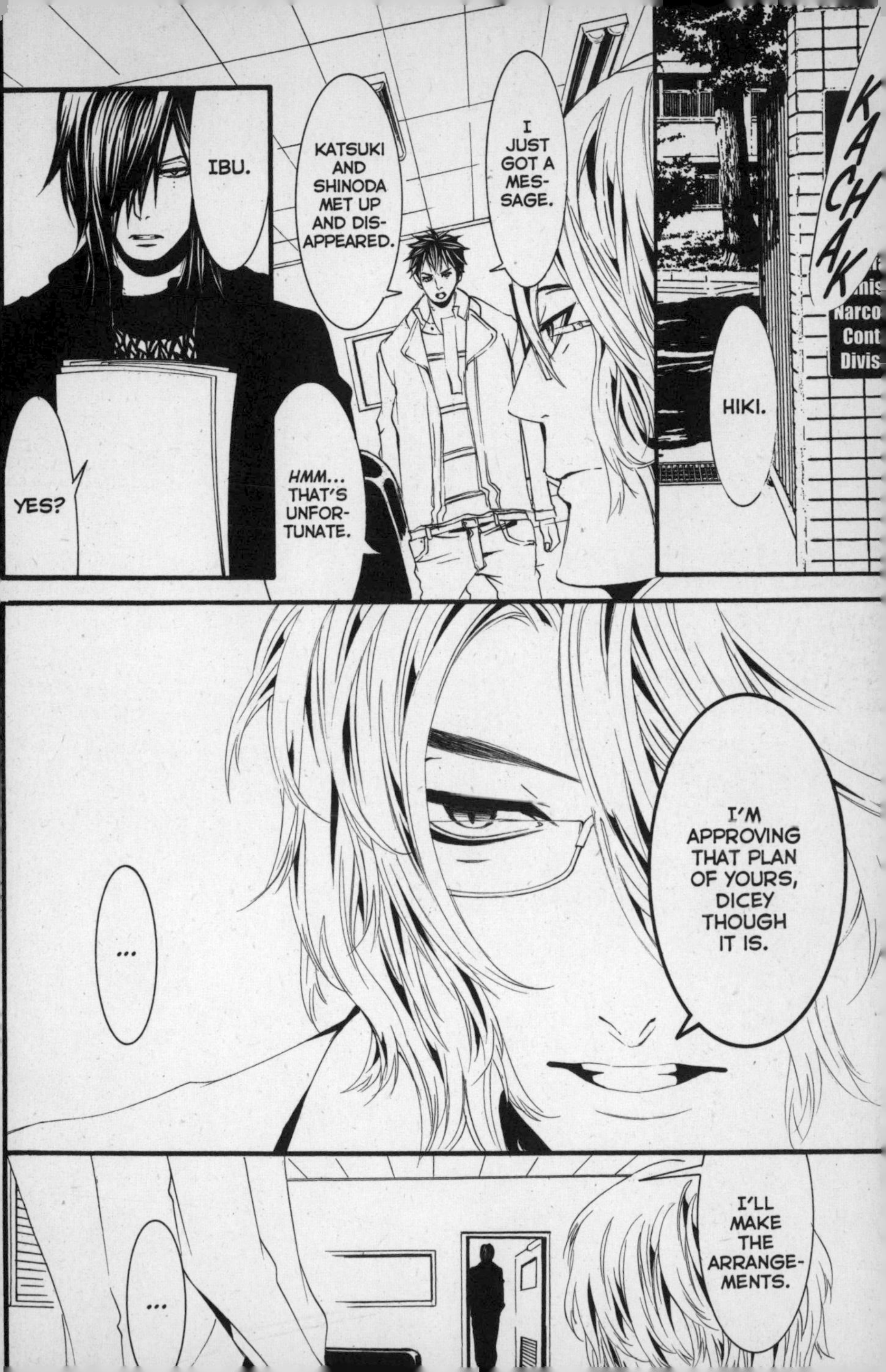
KACHAK
HIKI.
I JUST GOT A MESSAGE.
KATSUKI AND SHINODA MET UP AND DISAPPEARED.
HMM... THAT'S UNFORTUNATE.
IBU.
YES?
I'M APPROVING THAT PLAN OF YOURS, DICEY THOUGH IT IS.
...
I'LL MAKE THE ARRANGEMENTS.
...

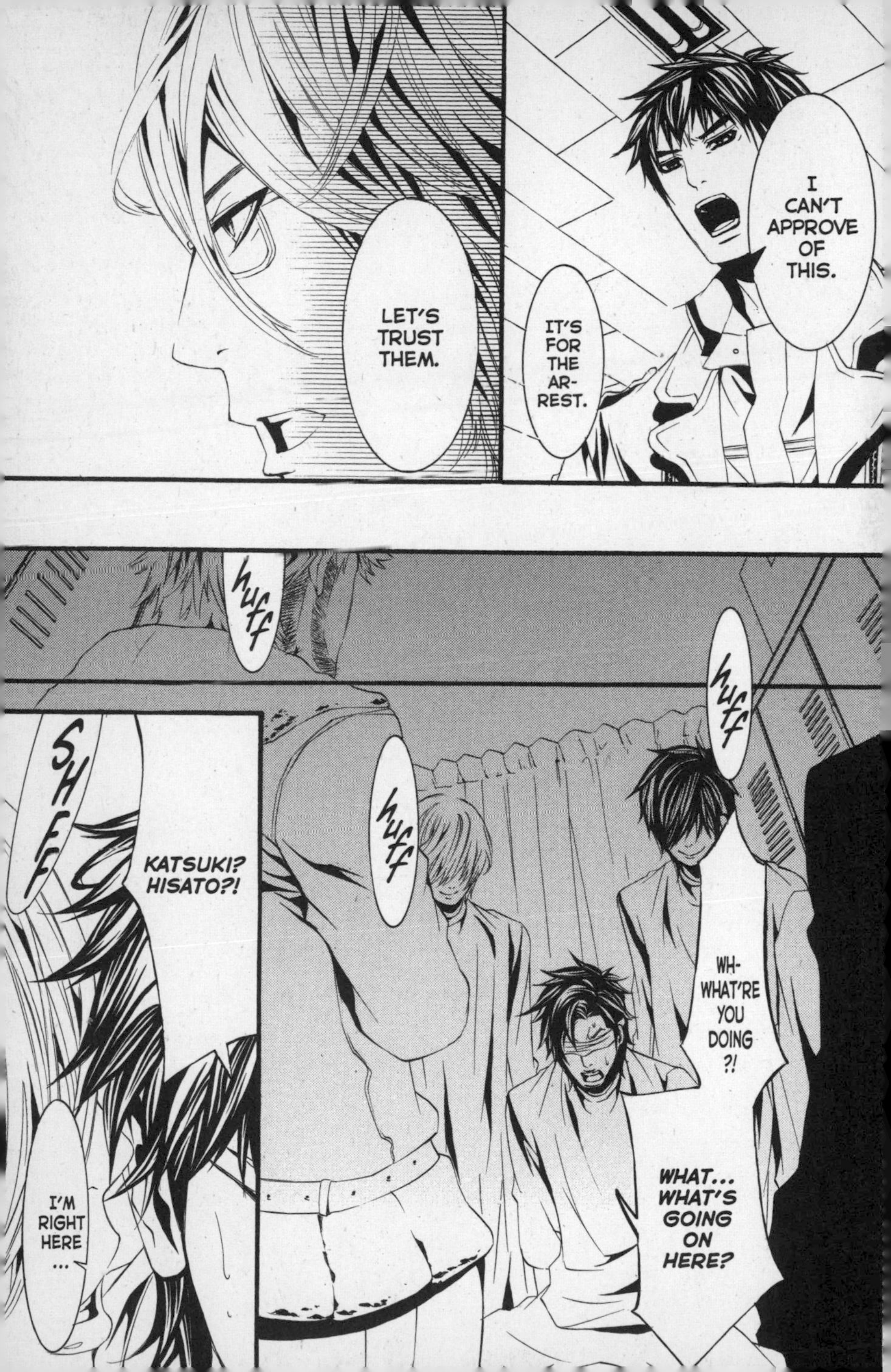
I CAN'T APPROVE OF THIS.
IT'S FOR THE AR-REST.
LET'S TRUST THEM.
huff
huff
huff
WH-WHAT'RE YOU DOING?!
WHAT... WHAT'S GOING ON HERE?
SHFF
KATSUKI? HISATO?!
I'M RIGHT HERE...

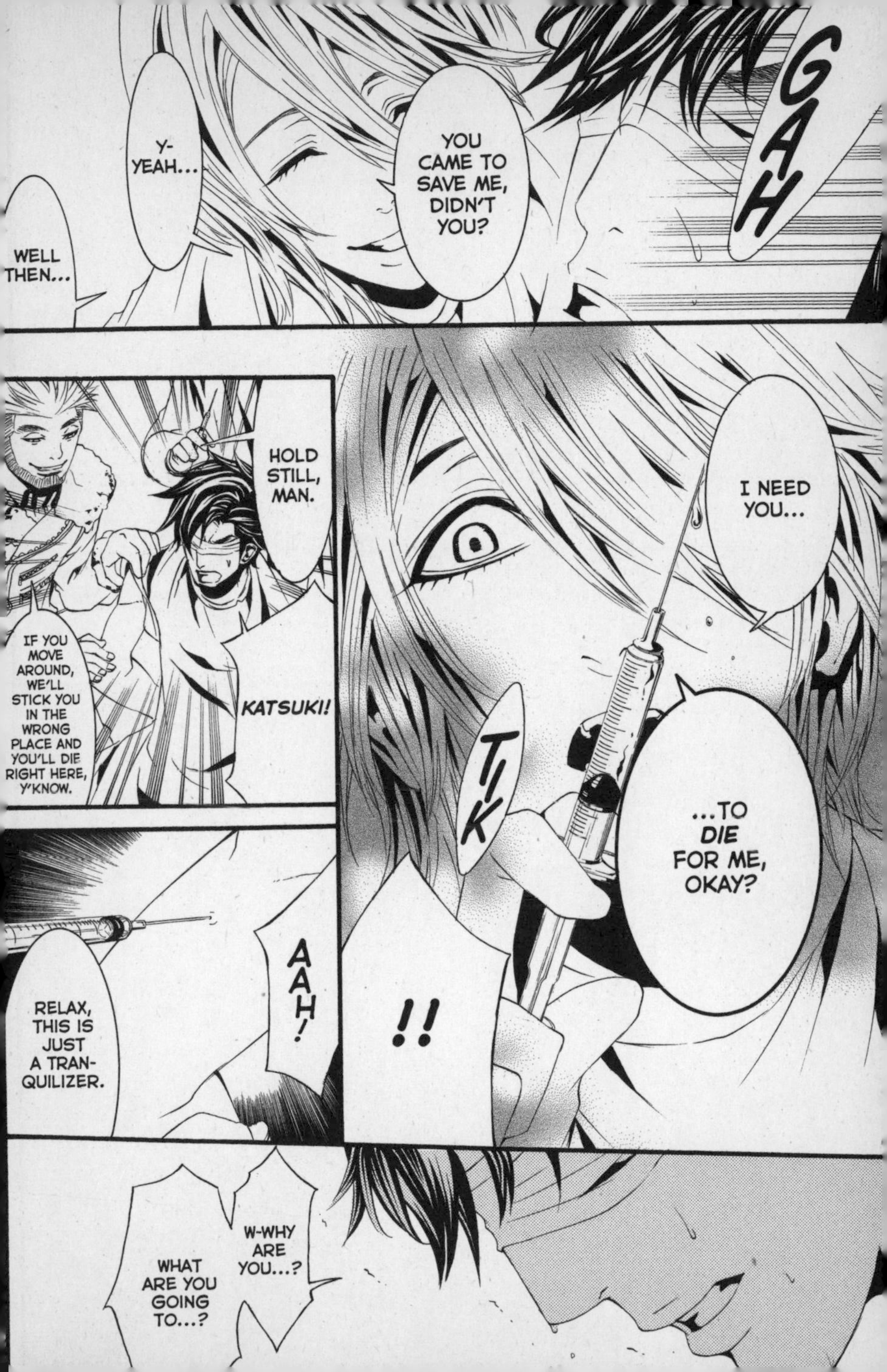
GAH
YOU CAME TO SAVE ME, DIDN'T YOU?
Y-YEAH...
WELL THEN...
I NEED YOU...
TIK
...TO DIE FOR ME, OKAY?
!!
HOLD STILL, MAN.
KATSUKI!
IF YOU MOVE AROUND, WE'LL STICK YOU IN THE WRONG PLACE AND YOU'LL DIE RIGHT HERE, Y'KNOW.
AAH!
RELAX, THIS IS JUST A TRAN-QUILIZER.
W-WHY ARE YOU...?
WHAT ARE YOU GOING TO...?

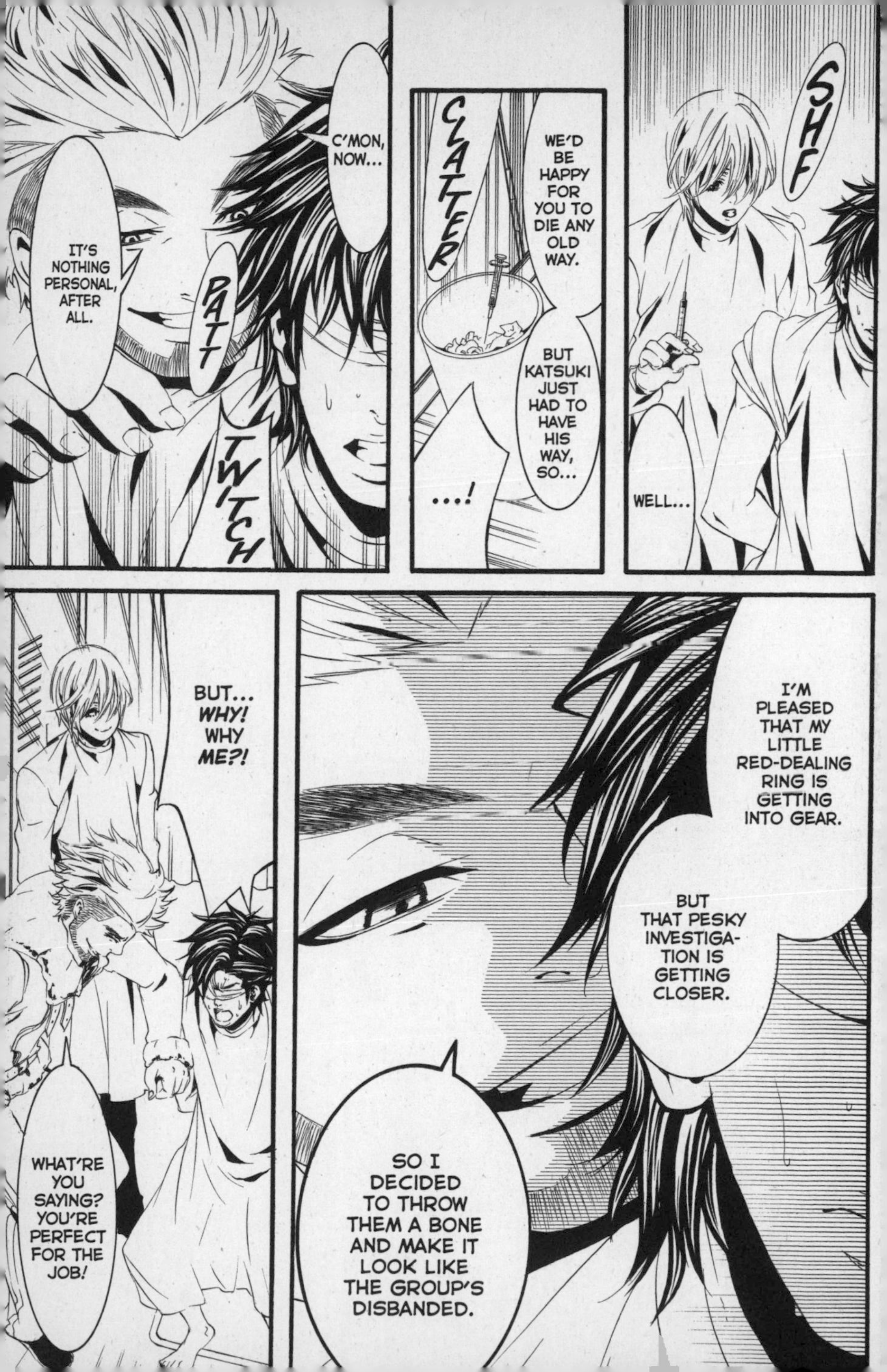
SHF
WELL...
WE'D BE HAPPY FOR YOU TO DIE ANY OLD WAY.
CLATTER
BUT KATSUKI JUST HAD TO HAVE HIS WAY, SO...
...!
C'MON, NOW...
IT'S NOTHING PERSONAL, AFTER ALL.
PATT
TWITCH
I'M PLEASED THAT MY LITTLE RED-DEALING RING IS GETTING INTO GEAR.
BUT THAT PESKY INVESTIGA-TION IS GETTING CLOSER.
SO I DECIDED TO THROW THEM A BONE AND MAKE IT LOOK LIKE THE GROUP'S DISBANDED.
BUT... WHY! WHY ME?!
WHAT'RE YOU SAYING? YOU'RE PERFECT FOR THE JOB!

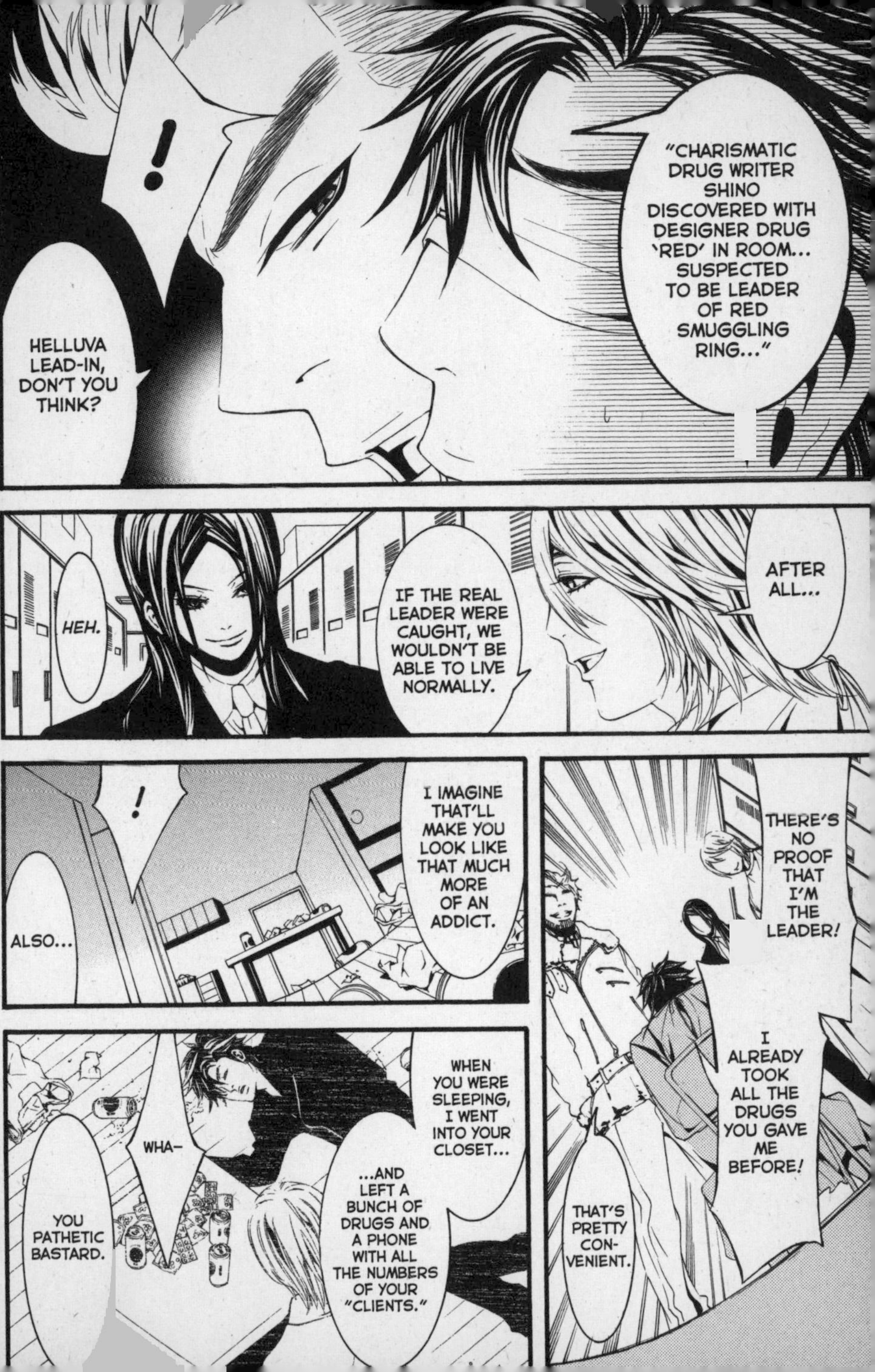
"CHARISMATIC DRUG WRITER SHINO DISCOVERED WITH DESIGNER DRUG 'RED' IN ROOM... SUSPECTED TO BE LEADER OF RED SMUGGLING RING..."
!
HELLUVA LEAD-IN, DON'T YOU THINK?
AFTER ALL...
IF THE REAL LEADER WERE CAUGHT, WE WOULDN'T BE ABLE TO LIVE NORMALLY.
HEH.
THERE'S NO PROOF THAT I'M THE LEADER!
I ALREADY TOOK ALL THE DRUGS YOU GAVE ME BEFORE!
THAT'S PRETTY CON-VENIENT.
I IMAGINE THAT'LL MAKE YOU LOOK LIKE THAT MUCH MORE OF AN ADDICT.
!
ALSO...
WHEN YOU WERE SLEEPING, I WENT INTO YOUR CLOSET...
...AND LEFT A BUNCH OF DRUGS AND A PHONE WITH ALL THE NUMBERS OF YOUR "CLIENTS."
WHA-
YOU PATHETIC BASTARD.

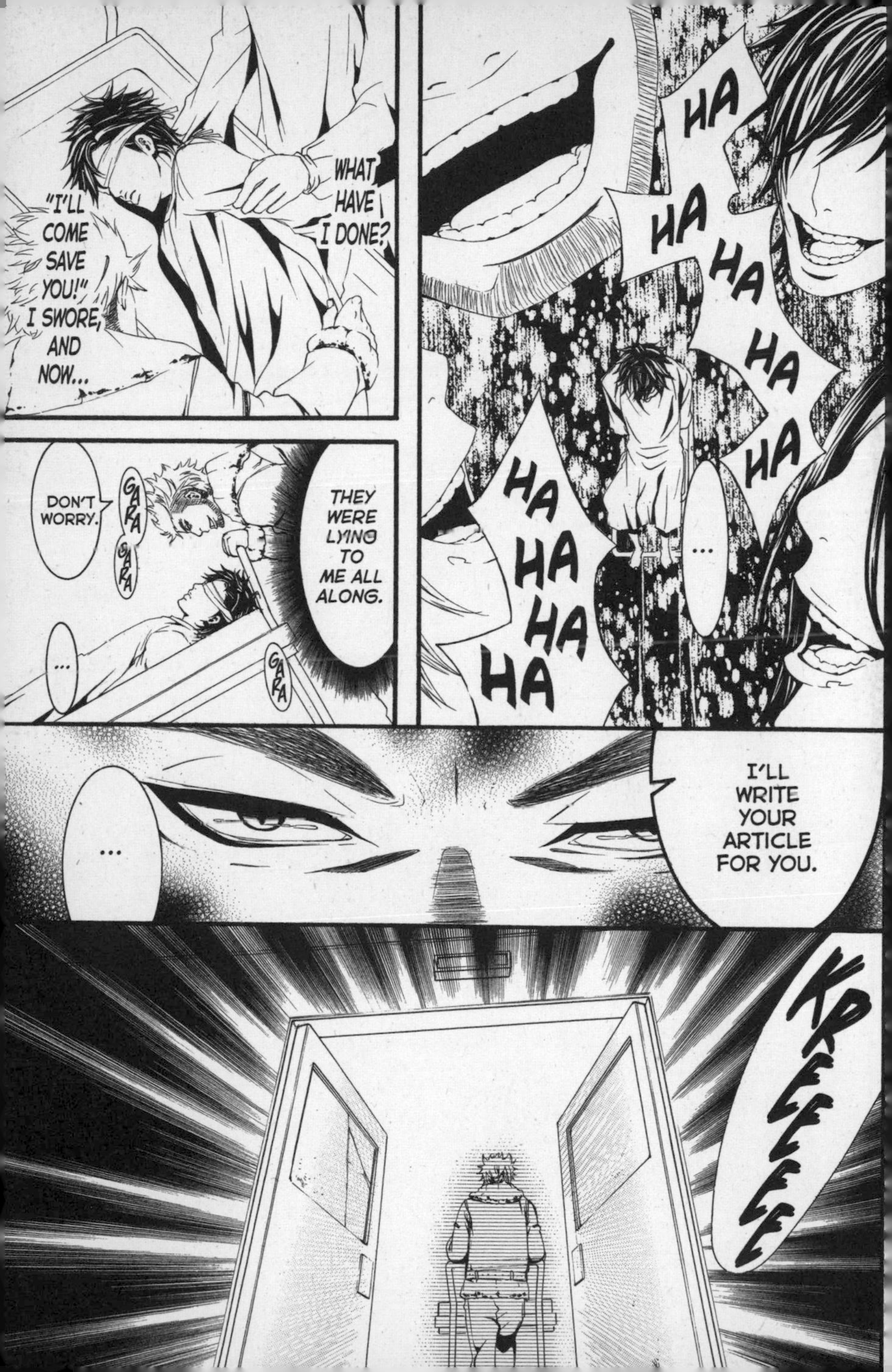
HA
HA
HA
HA
HA
HA
...
HA
HA
HA
HA
HA
WHAT HAVE I DONE?
"I'LL COME SAVE YOU!" I SWORE, AND NOW...
THEY WERE LYING TO ME ALL ALONG.
GARA
GARA
DON'T WORRY.
GARA
...
I'LL WRITE YOUR ARTICLE FOR YOU.
...
KREEEEEE

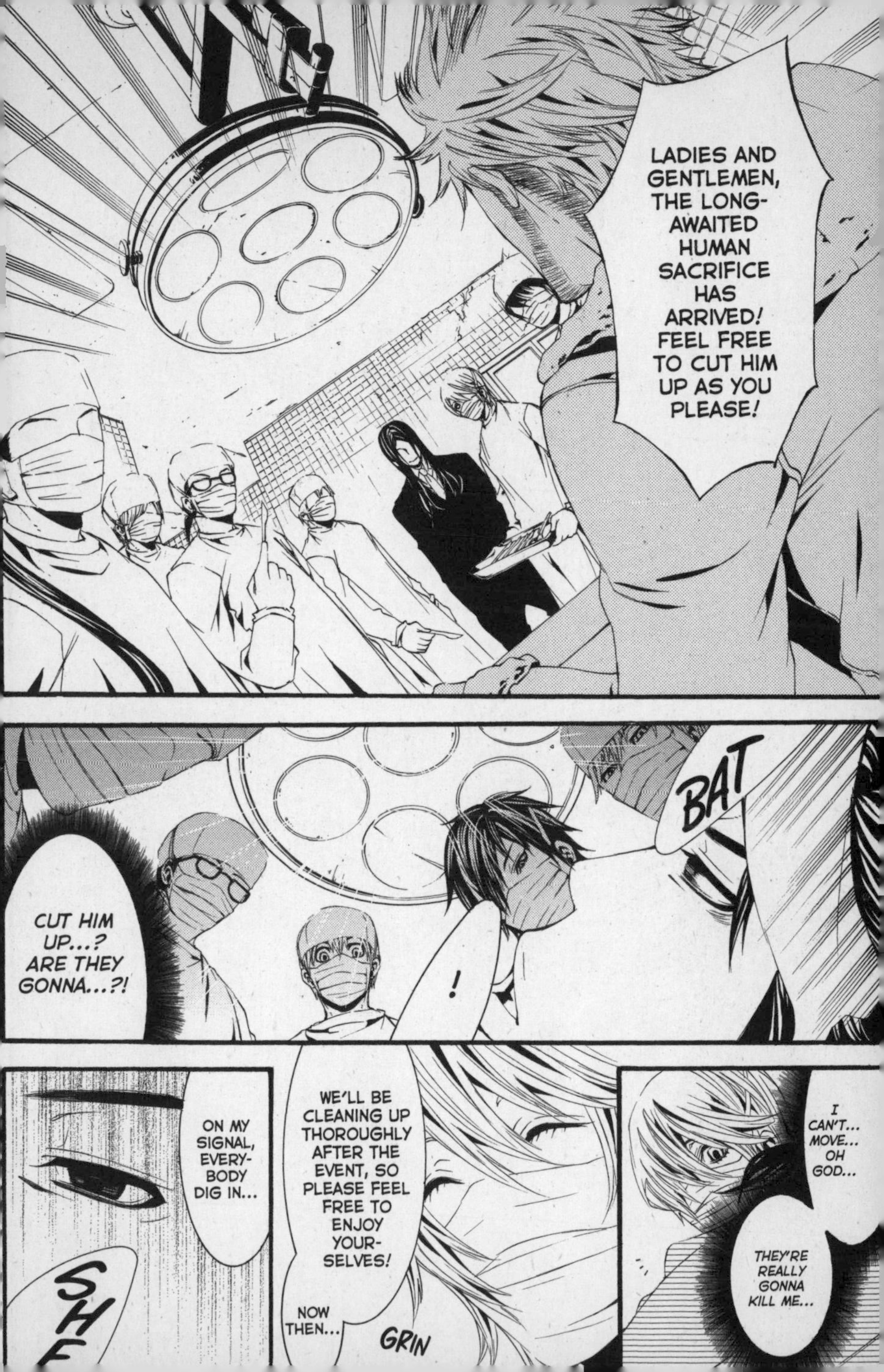
LADIES AND GENTLEMEN, THE LONG-AWAITED HUMAN SACRIFICE HAS ARRIVED! FEEL FREE TO CUT HIM UP AS YOU PLEASE!
BAT
!
CUT HIM UP...? ARE THEY GONNA...?!
I CAN'T... MOVE... OH GOD...
THEY'RE REALLY GONNA KILL ME...
...
WE'LL BE CLEANING UP THOROUGHLY AFTER THE EVENT, SO PLEASE FEEL FREE TO ENJOY YOUR-SELVES!
NOW THEN...
GRIN
ON MY SIGNAL, EVERY-BODY DIG IN...
SHF

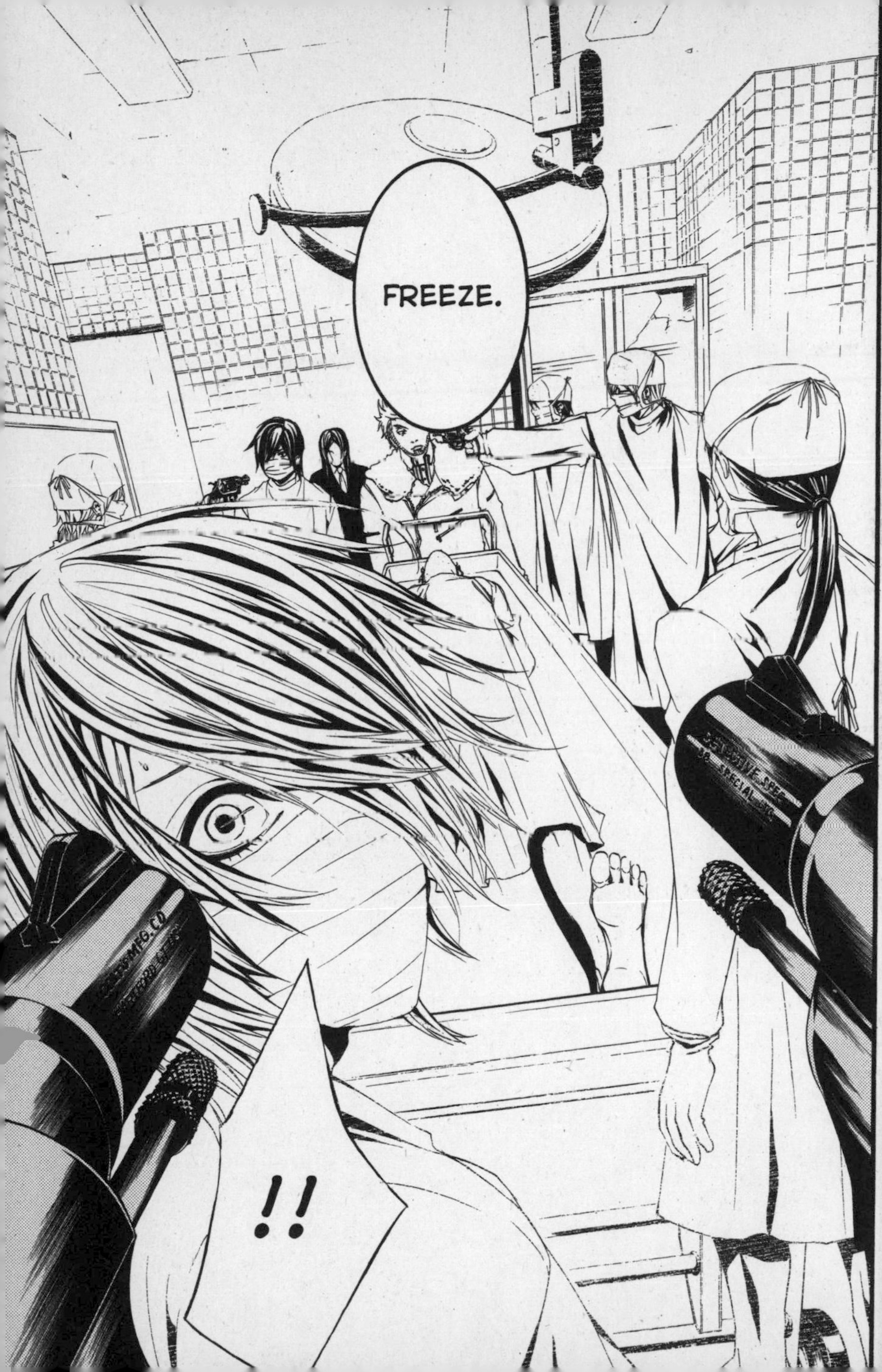
FREEZE.
!!

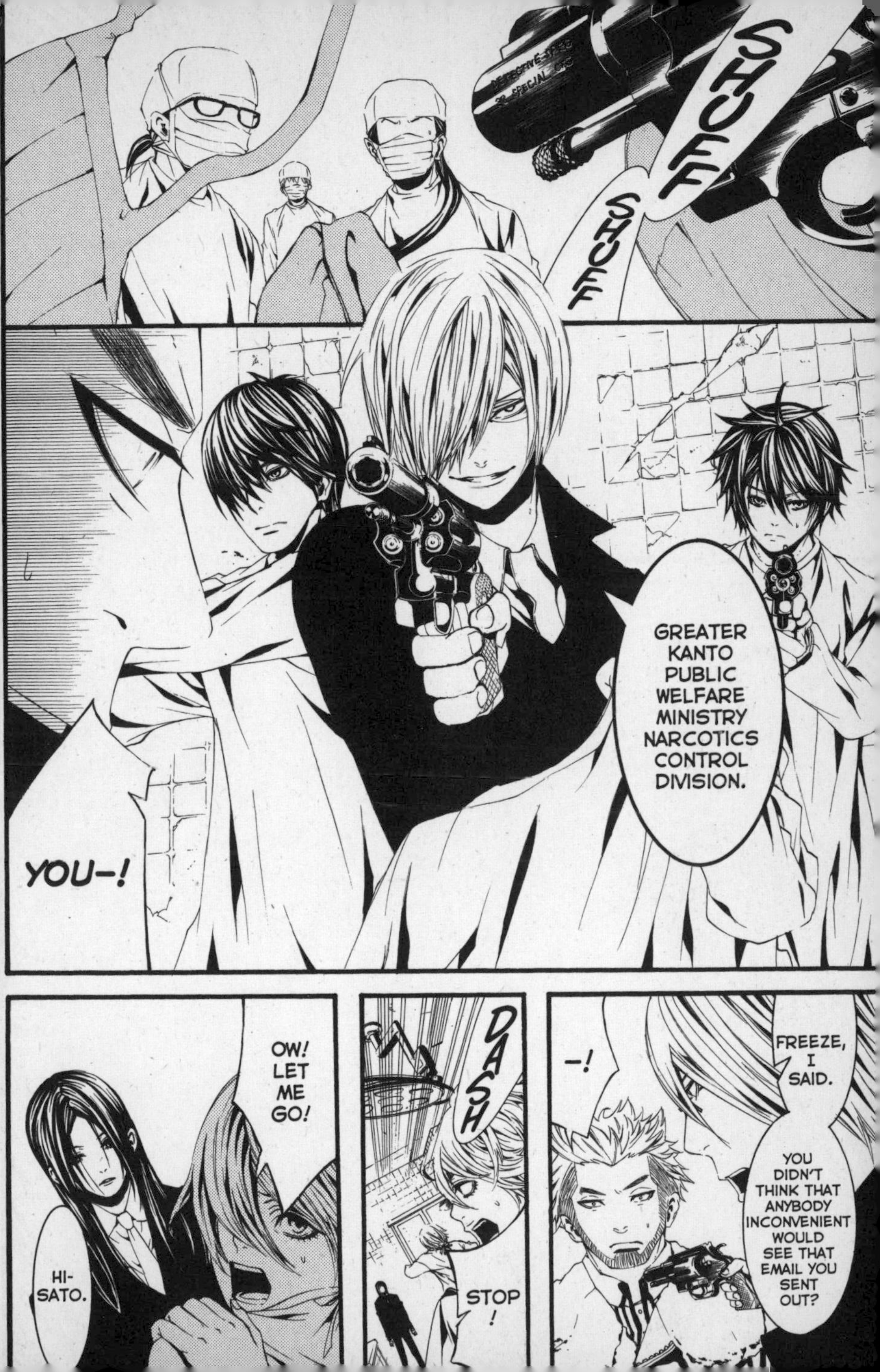
SHUFF
SHUFF
GREATER KANTO PUBLIC WELFARE MINISTRY NARCOTICS CONTROL DIVISION.
YOU-!
FREEZE, I SAID.
YOU DIDN'T THINK THAT ANYBODY INCONVENIENT WOULD SEE THAT EMAIL YOU SENT OUT?
-!
DASH
STOP!
OW! LET ME GO!
HI-SATO.

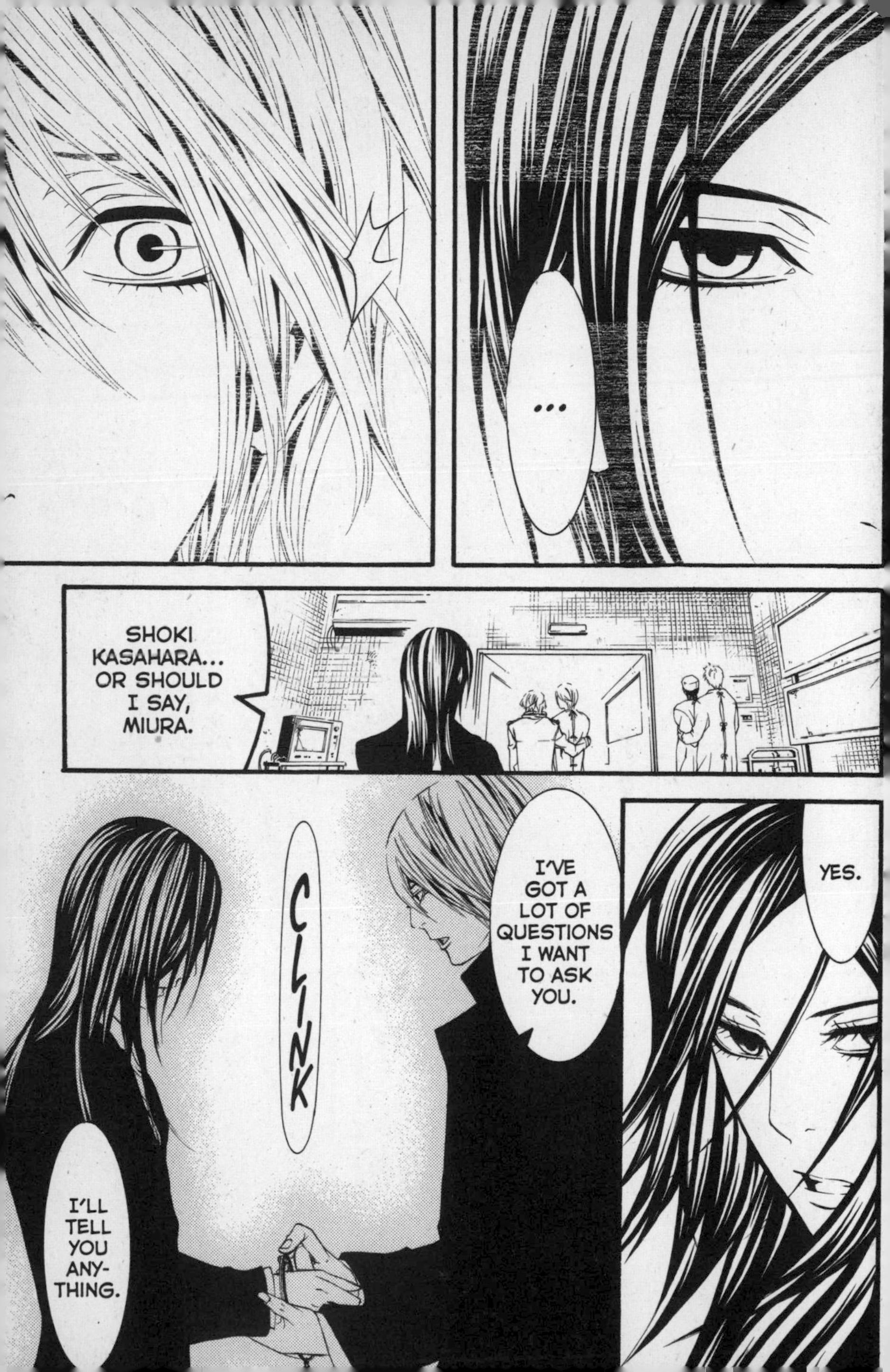
...
SHOKI KASAHARA... OR SHOULD I SAY, MIURA.
YES.
I'VE GOT A LOT OF QUESTIONS I WANT TO ASK YOU.
CLINK
I'LL TELL YOU ANY-THING.

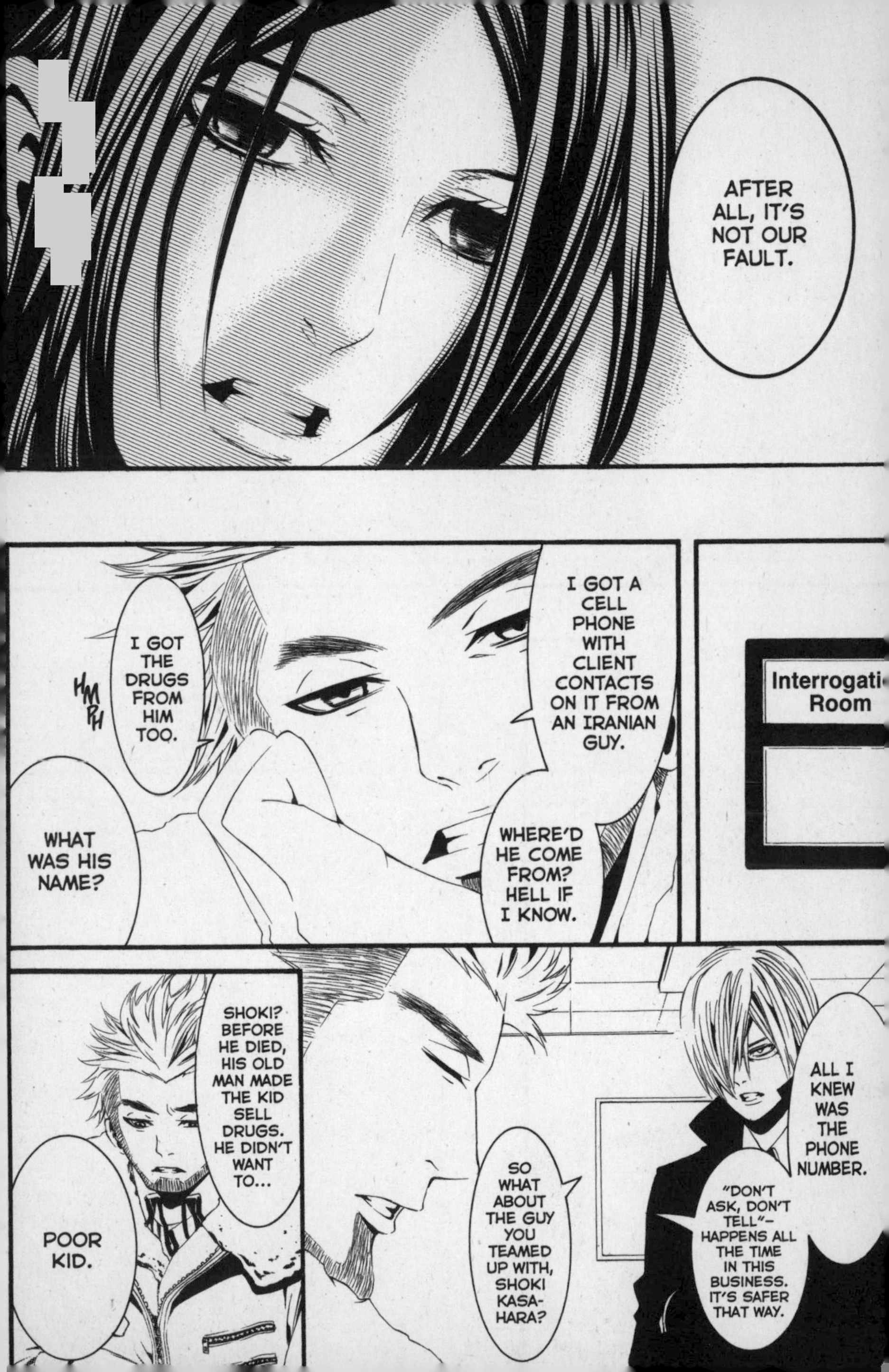
AFTER ALL, IT'S NOT OUR FAULT.
Interrogati
Room
I GOT A CELL PHONE WITH CLIENT CONTACTS ON IT FROM AN IRANIAN GUY.
I GOT THE DRUGS FROM HIM TOO.
HMPH
WHERE'D HE COME FROM? HELL IF I KNOW.
WHAT WAS HIS NAME?
ALL I KNEW WAS THE PHONE NUMBER.
"DON'T ASK, DON'T TELL"—HAPPENS ALL THE TIME IN THIS BUSINESS. IT'S SAFER THAT WAY.
SO WHAT ABOUT THE GUY YOU TEAMED UP WITH, SHOKI KASA-HARA?
SHOKI? BEFORE HE DIED, HIS OLD MAN MADE THE KID SELL DRUGS. HE DIDN'T WANT TO...
POOR KID.

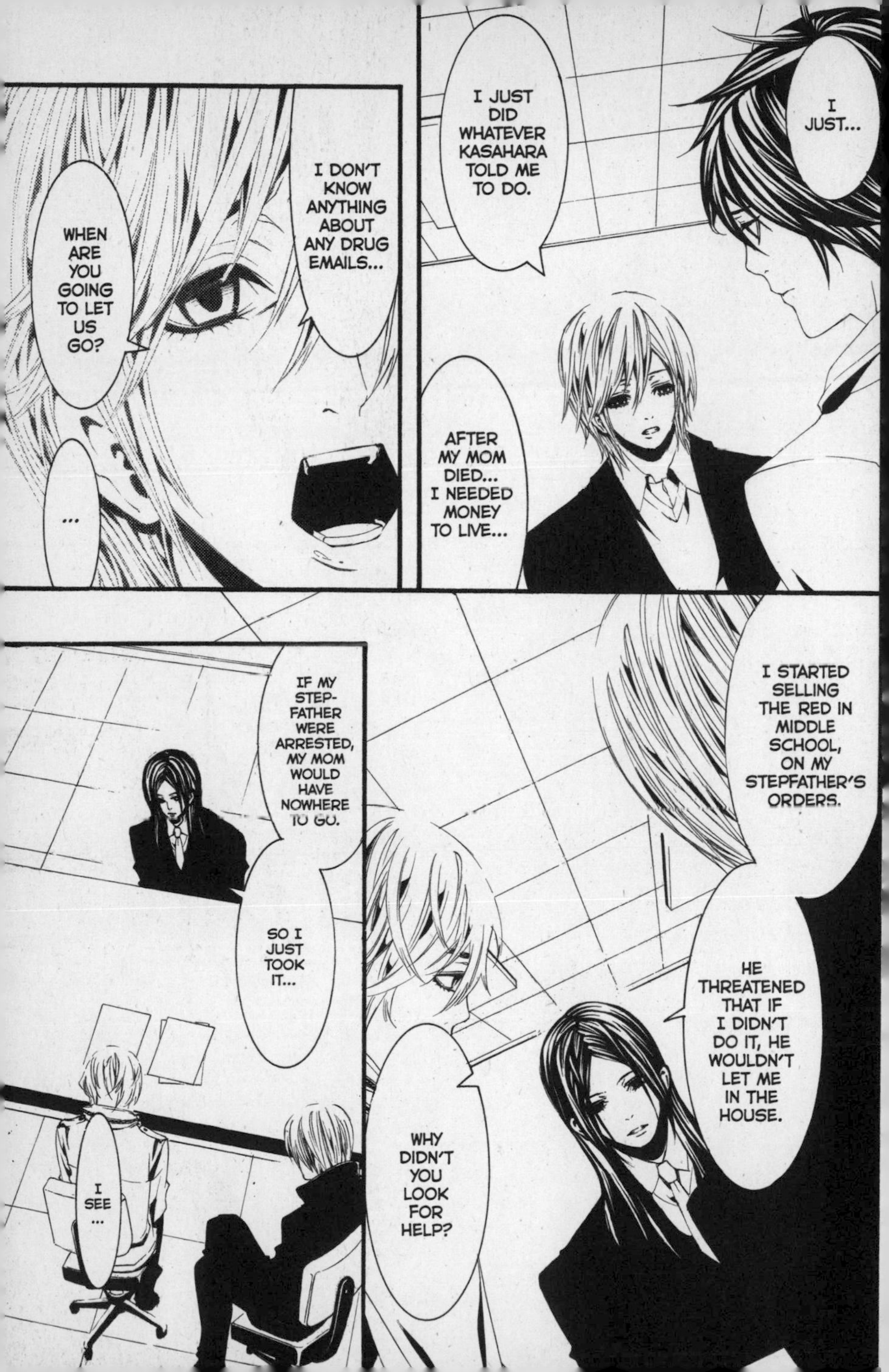
I JUST...
I JUST DID WHATEVER KASAHARA TOLD ME TO DO.
AFTER MY MOM DIED... I NEEDED MONEY TO LIVE...
I DON'T KNOW ANYTHING ABOUT ANY DRUG EMAILS...
WHEN ARE YOU GOING TO LET US GO?
...
I STARTED SELLING THE RED IN MIDDLE SCHOOL, ON MY STEPFATHER'S ORDERS.
HE THREATENED THAT IF I DIDN'T DO IT, HE WOULDN'T LET ME IN THE HOUSE.
WHY DIDN'T YOU LOOK FOR HELP?
IF MY STEP-FATHER WERE ARRESTED, MY MOM WOULD HAVE NOWHERE TO GO.
SO I JUST TOOK IT...
I SEE ...

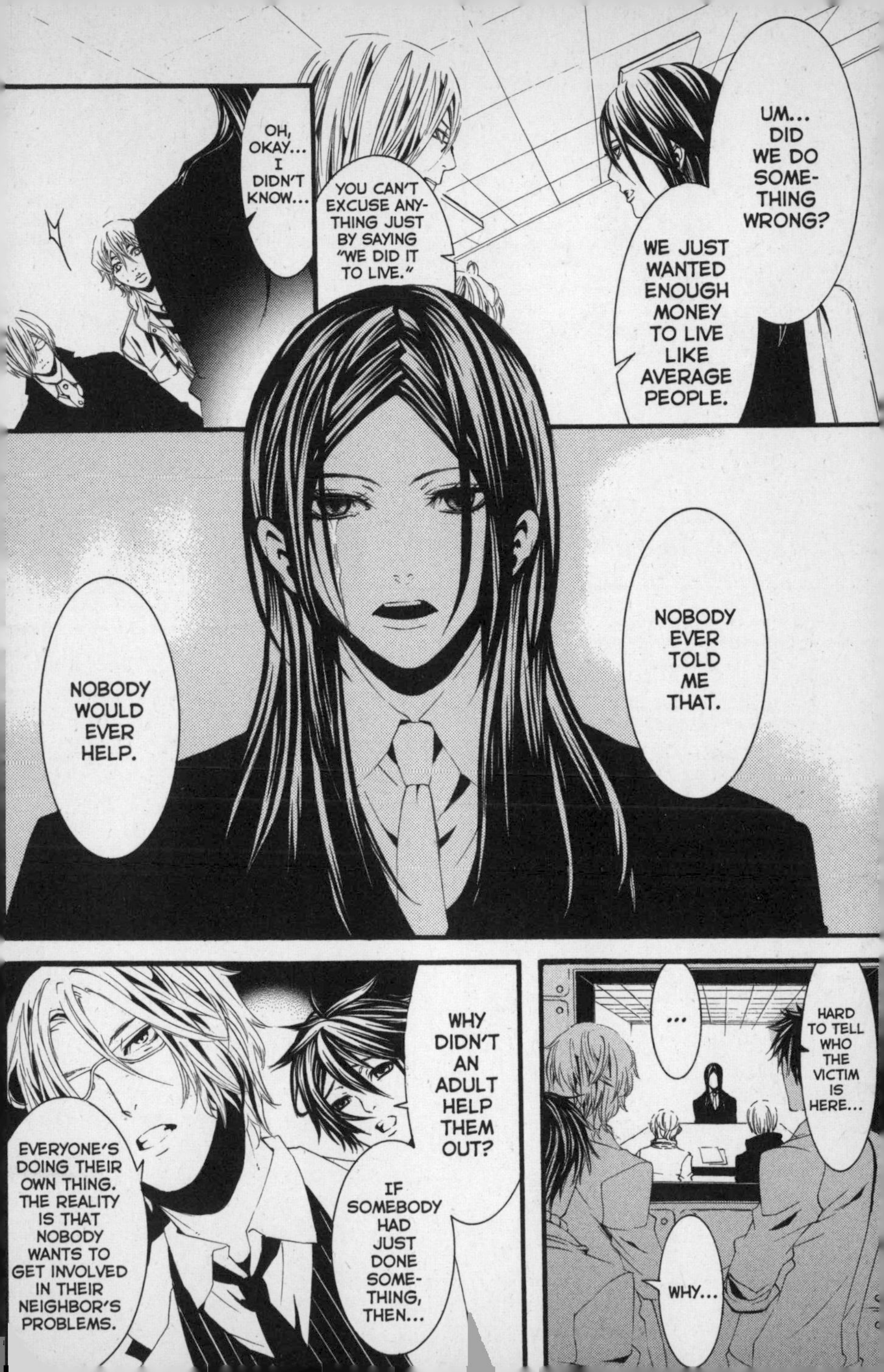
UM... DID WE DO SOMETHING WRONG?
WE JUST WANTED ENOUGH MONEY TO LIVE LIKE AVERAGE PEOPLE.
YOU CAN'T EXCUSE ANYTHING JUST BY SAYING "WE DID IT TO LIVE."
OH, OKAY... I DIDN'T KNOW...
NOBODY EVER TOLD ME THAT.
NOBODY WOULD EVER HELP.
HARD TO TELL WHO THE VICTIM IS HERE...
...
WHY...
WHY DIDN'T AN ADULT HELP THEM OUT?
IF SOMEBODY HAD JUST DONE SOMETHING, THEN...
EVERYONE'S DOING THEIR OWN THING. THE REALITY IS THAT NOBODY WANTS TO GET INVOLVED IN THEIR NEIGHBOR'S PROBLEMS.

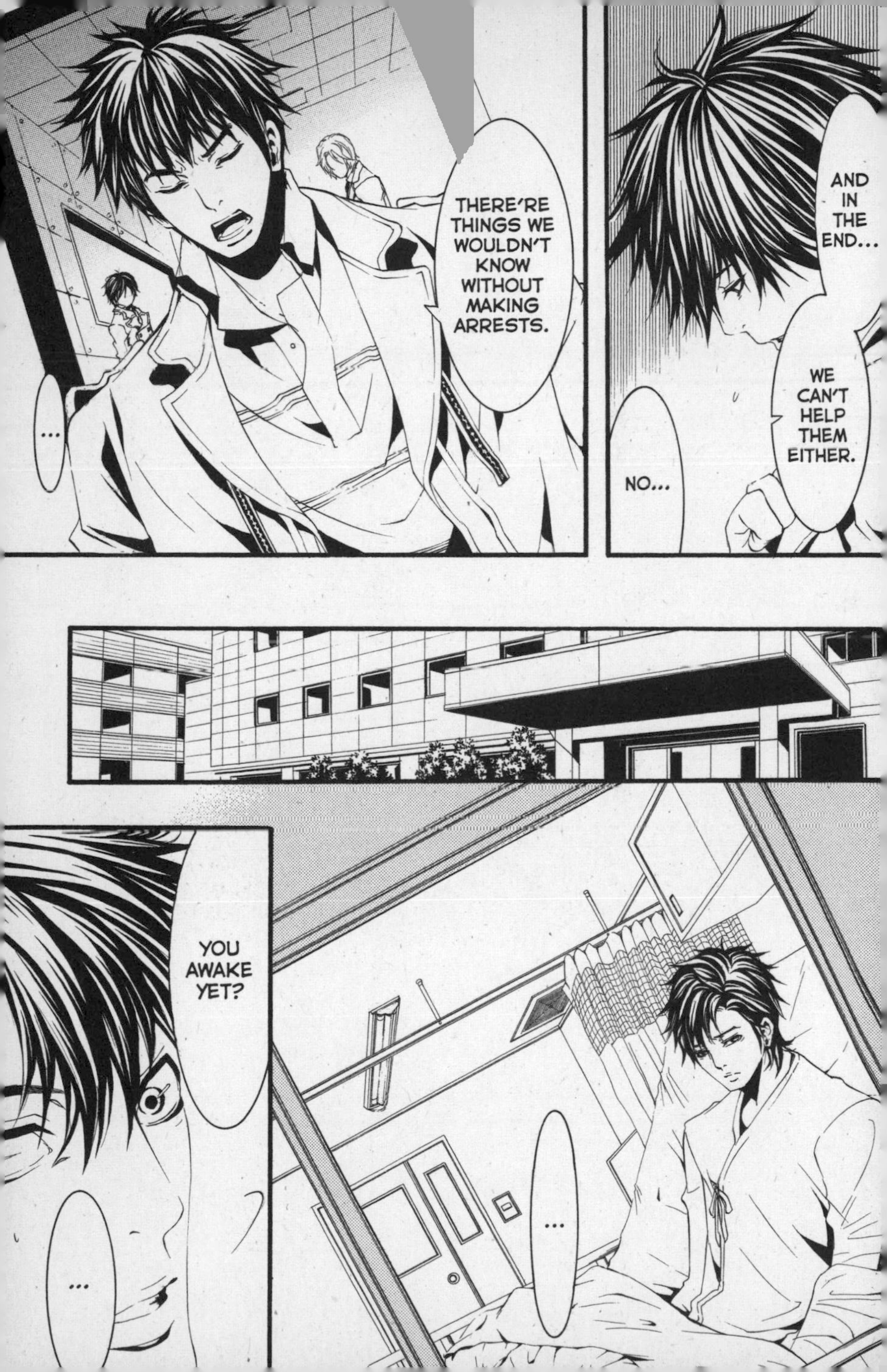
AND IN THE END...
WE CAN'T HELP THEM EITHER.
NO...
THERE'RE THINGS WE WOULDN'T KNOW WITHOUT MAKING ARRESTS.
...
...
YOU AWAKE YET?
...

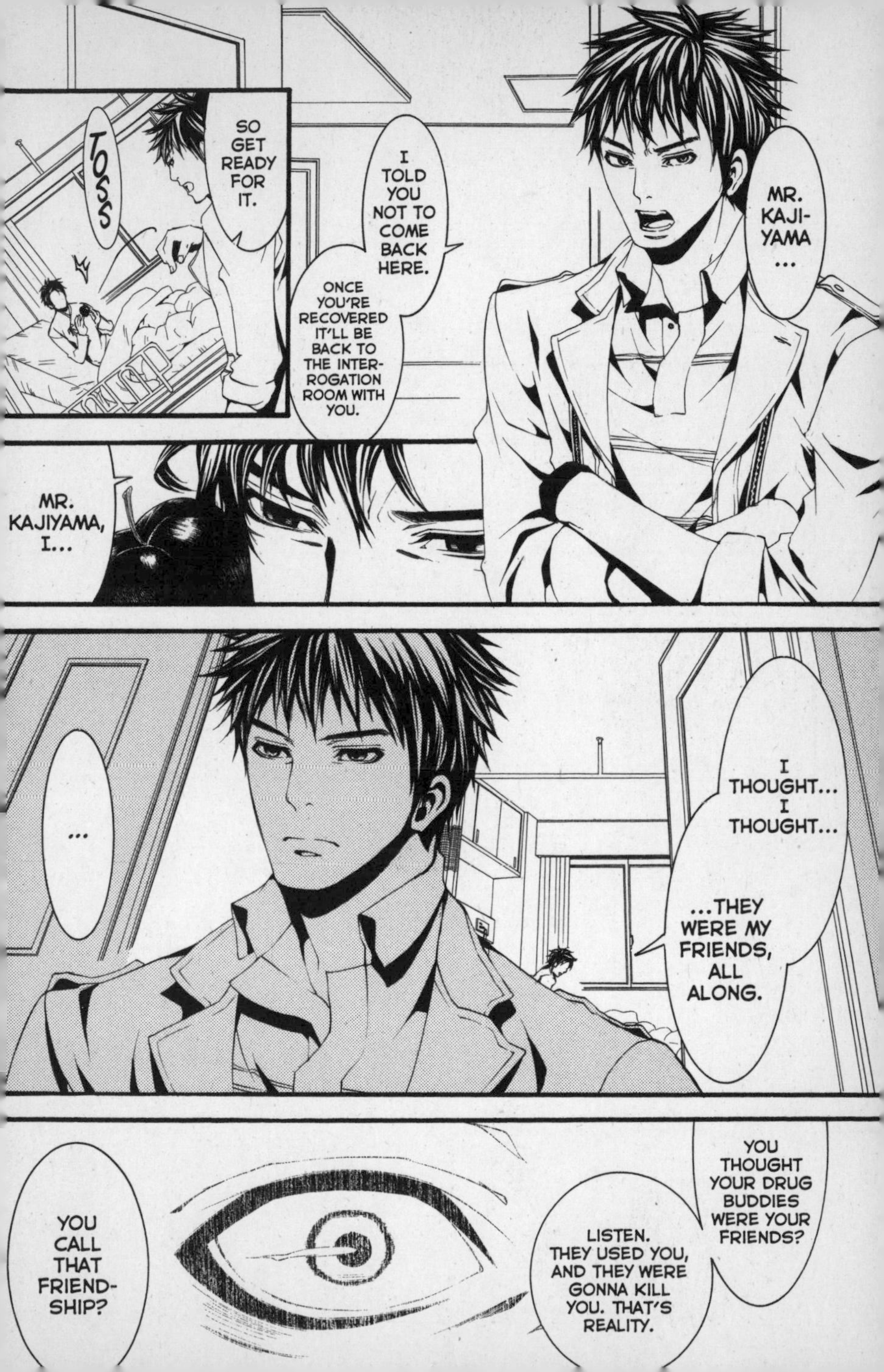
MR. KAJIYAMA...
I TOLD YOU NOT TO COME BACK HERE.
ONCE YOU'RE RECOVERED IT'LL BE BACK TO THE INTERROGATION ROOM WITH YOU.
SO GET READY FOR IT.
TOSS
MR. KAJIYAMA, I...
I THOUGHT... I THOUGHT...
...THEY WERE MY FRIENDS, ALL ALONG.
...
YOU THOUGHT YOUR DRUG BUDDIES WERE YOUR FRIENDS?
LISTEN. THEY USED YOU, AND THEY WERE GONNA KILL YOU. THAT'S REALITY.
YOU CALL THAT FRIENDSHIP?

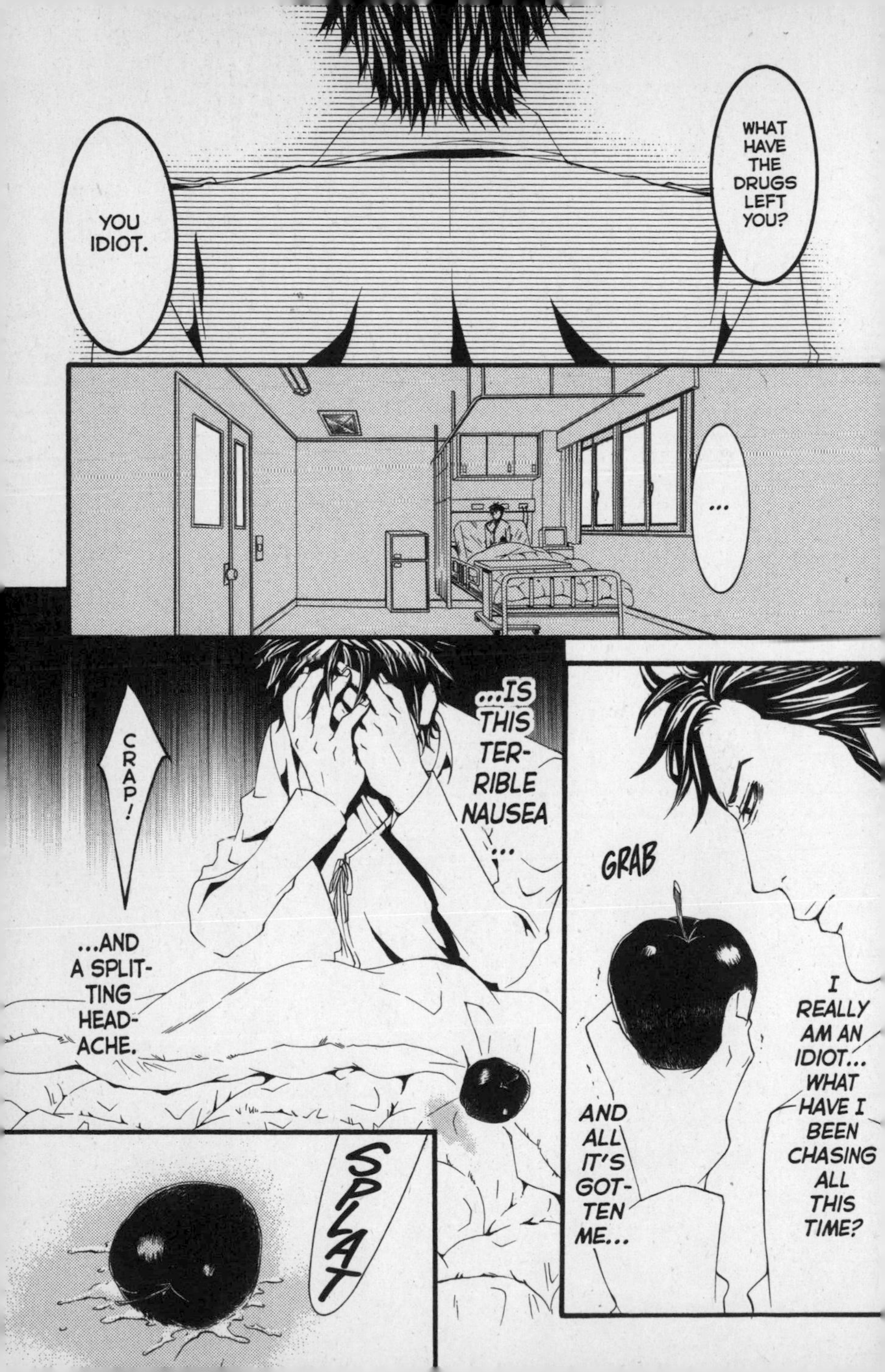
WHAT HAVE THE DRUGS LEFT YOU?
YOU IDIOT.
...
GRAB
I REALLY AM AN IDIOT... WHAT HAVE I BEEN CHASING ALL THIS TIME?
AND ALL IT'S GOTTEN ME...
...IS THIS TERRIBLE NAUSEA...
CRAP!
...AND A SPLITTING HEADACHE.
SPLAT

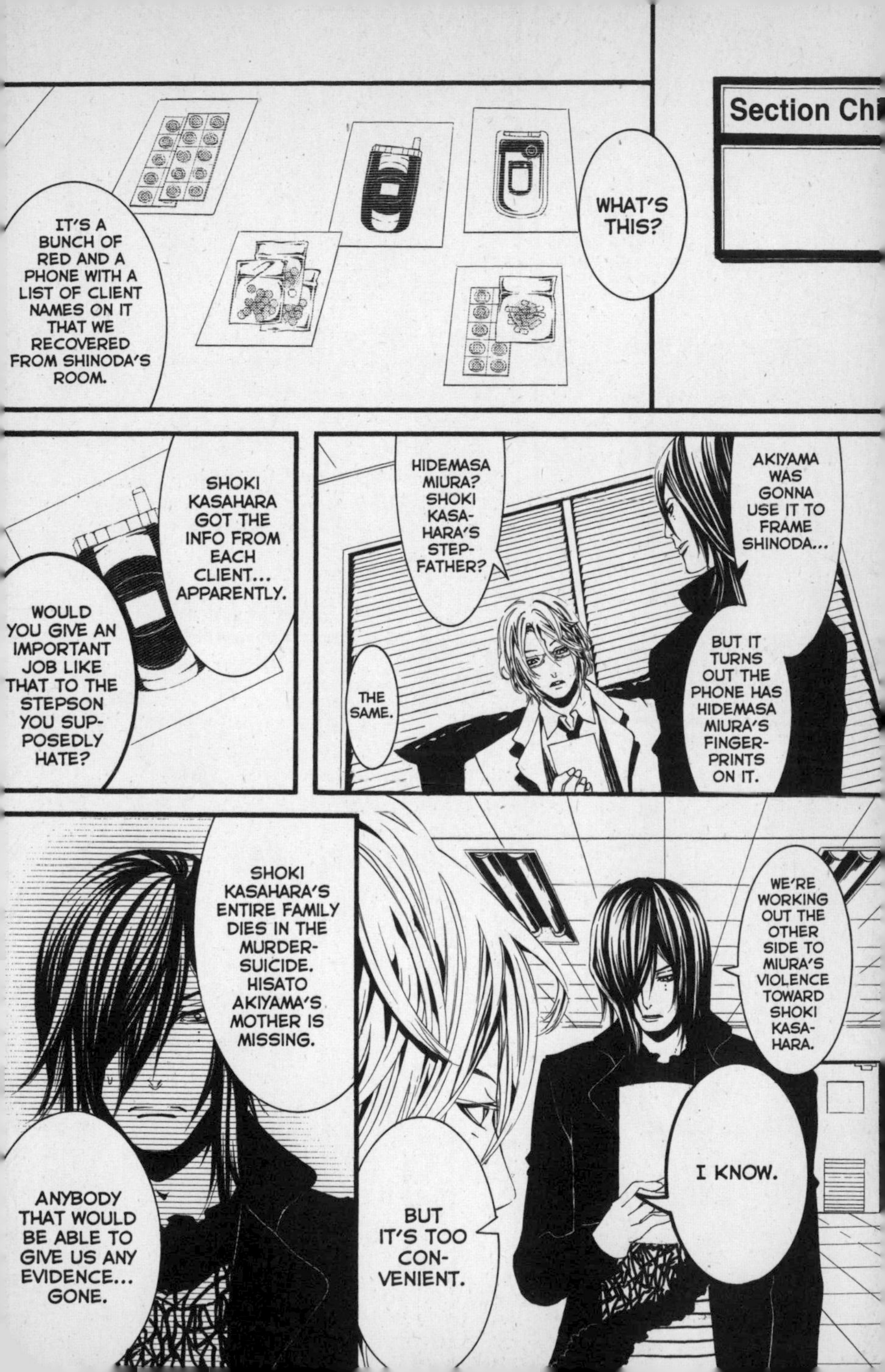
Section Chi
WHAT'S THIS?
IT'S A BUNCH OF RED AND A PHONE WITH A LIST OF CLIENT NAMES ON IT THAT WE RECOVERED FROM SHINODA'S ROOM.
AKIYAMA WAS GONNA USE IT TO FRAME SHINODA...
HIDEMASA MIURA? SHOKI KASA-HARA'S STEP-FATHER?
BUT IT TURNS OUT THE PHONE HAS HIDEMASA MIURA'S FINGER-PRINTS ON IT.
THE SAME.
SHOKI KASAHARA GOT THE INFO FROM EACH CLIENT... APPARENTLY.
WOULD YOU GIVE AN IMPORTANT JOB LIKE THAT TO THE STEPSON YOU SUP-POSEDLY HATE?
WE'RE WORKING OUT THE OTHER SIDE TO MIURA'S VIOLENCE TOWARD SHOKI KASA-HARA.
I KNOW.
BUT IT'S TOO CON-VENIENT.
SHOKI KASAHARA'S ENTIRE FAMILY DIES IN THE MURDER-SUICIDE. HISATO AKIYAMA'S MOTHER IS MISSING.
ANYBODY THAT WOULD BE ABLE TO GIVE US ANY EVIDENCE... GONE.

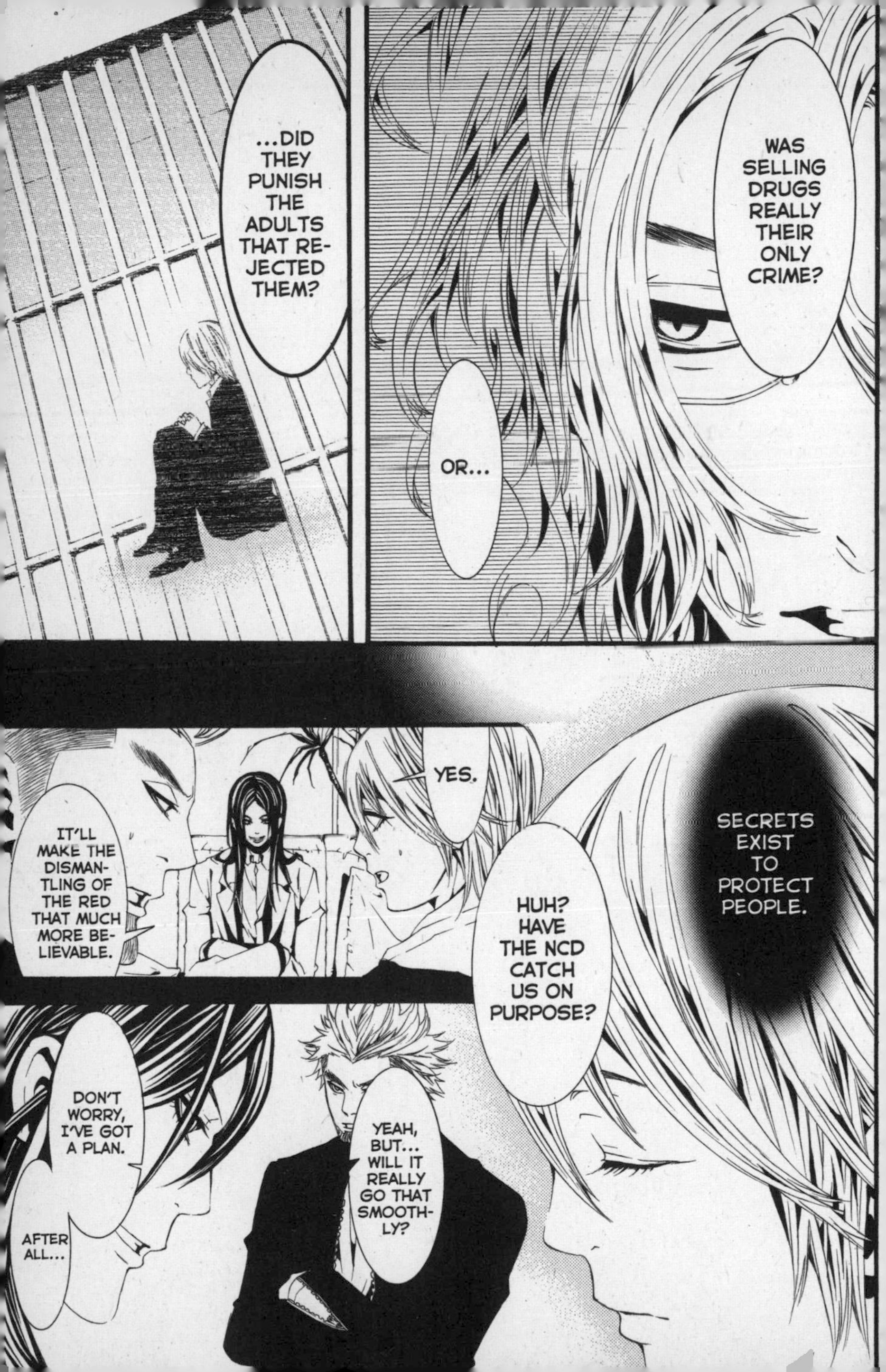
WAS SELLING DRUGS REALLY THEIR ONLY CRIME?
OR...
...DID THEY PUNISH THE ADULTS THAT RE-JECTED THEM?
SECRETS EXIST TO PROTECT PEOPLE.
YES.
HUH? HAVE THE NCD CATCH US ON PURPOSE?
IT'LL MAKE THE DISMAN-TLING OF THE RED THAT MUCH MORE BE-LIEVABLE.
YEAH, BUT... WILL IT REALLY GO THAT SMOOTH-LY?
DON'T WORRY, I'VE GOT A PLAN.
AFTER ALL...

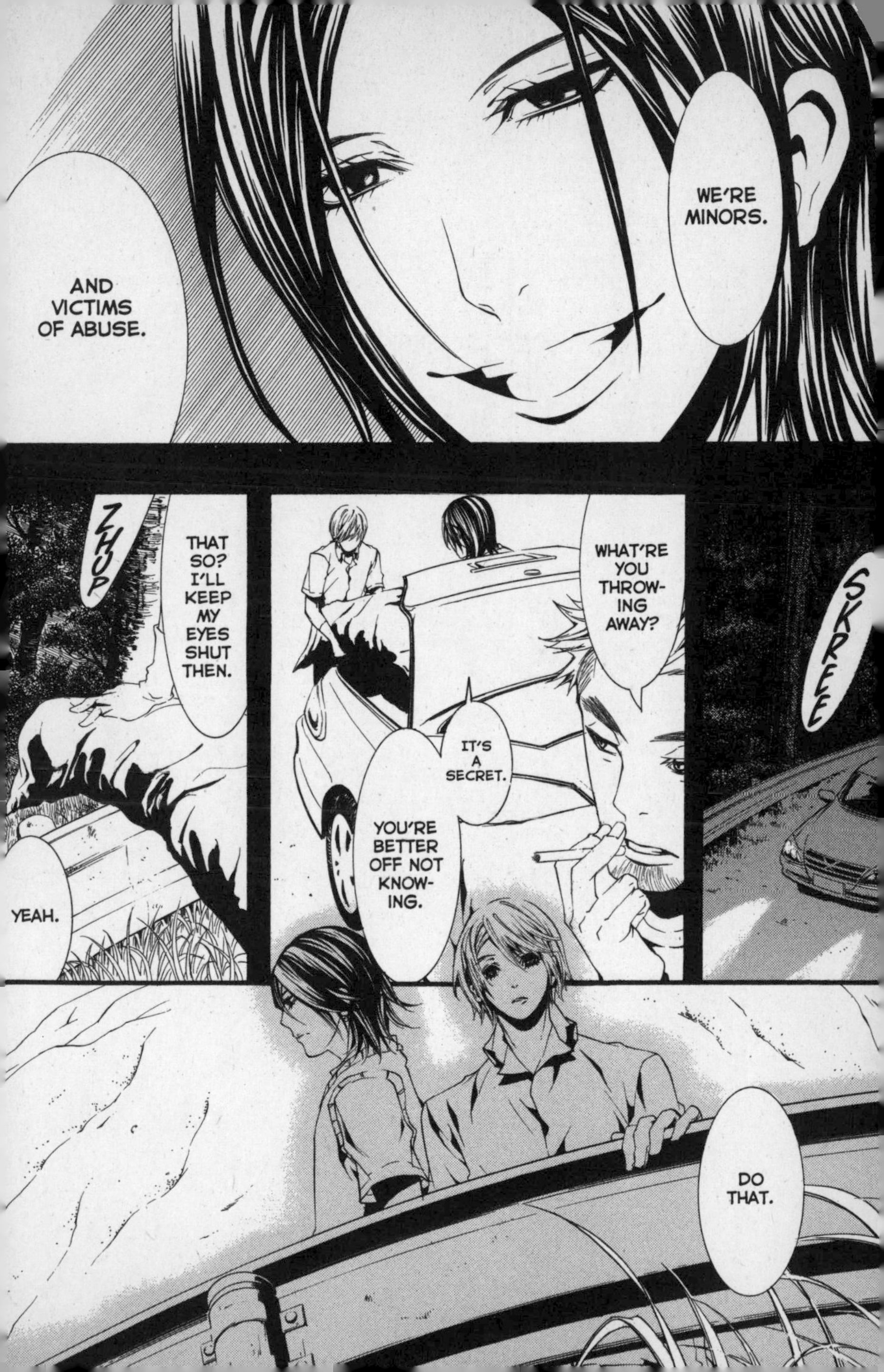
WE'RE MINORS.
AND VICTIMS OF ABUSE.
SKREE
WHAT'RE YOU THROWING-ING AWAY?
IT'S A SECRET.
YOU'RE BETTER OFF NOT KNOW-ING.
ZHUP
THAT SO? I'LL KEEP MY EYES SHUT THEN.
YEAH.
DO THAT.

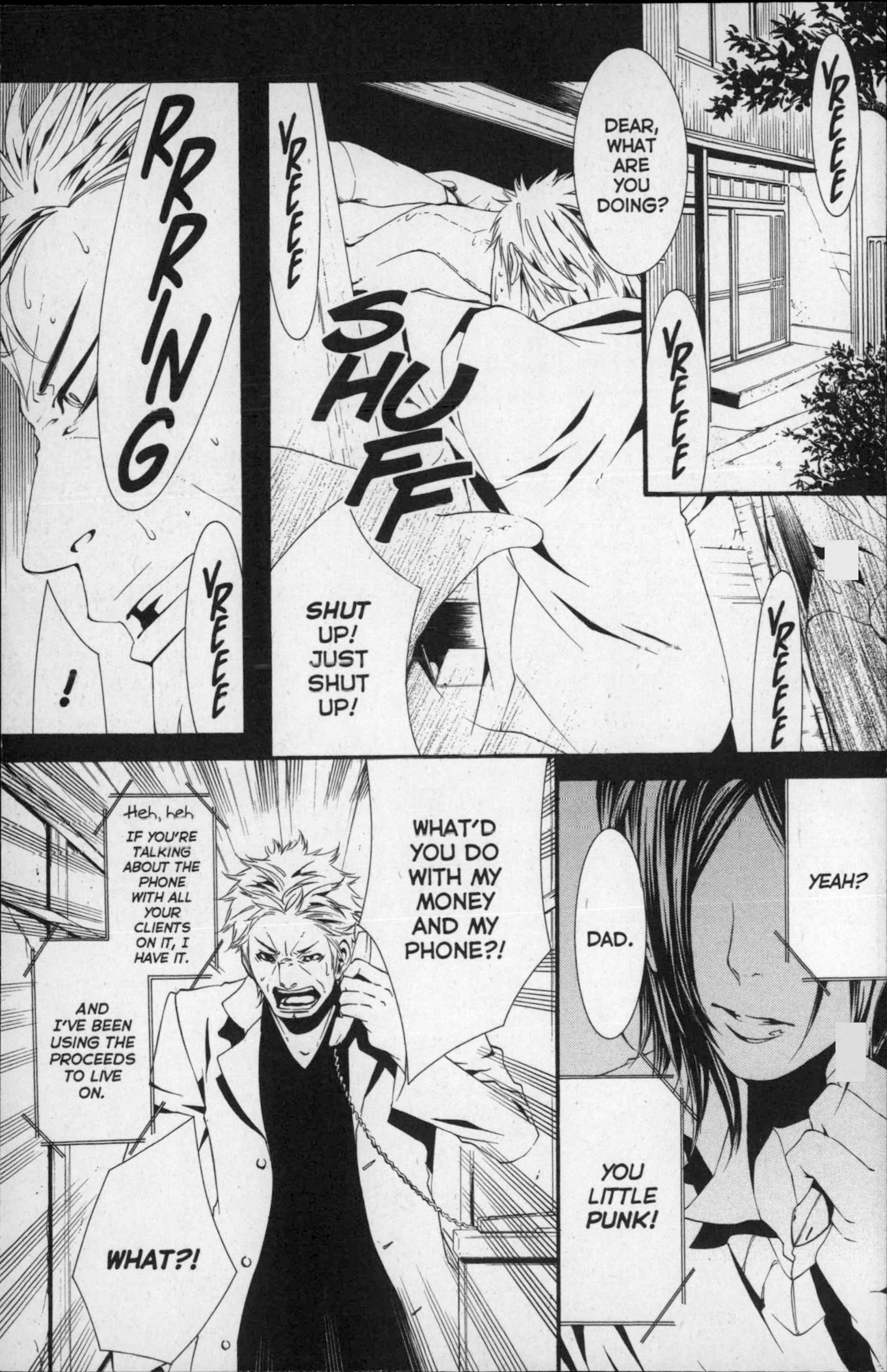
VREEE
DEAR, WHAT ARE YOU DOING?
VREEE
VREEE
SHUFF
VREEE
SHUT UP! JUST SHUT UP!
RRRING
VREEE
!
YEAH?
DAD.
YOU LITTLE PUNK!
WHAT'D YOU DO WITH MY MONEY AND MY PHONE?!
Heh, heh
IF YOU'RE TALKING ABOUT THE PHONE WITH ALL YOUR CLIENTS ON IT, I HAVE IT.
AND I'VE BEEN USING THE PROCEEDS TO LIVE ON.
WHAT?!

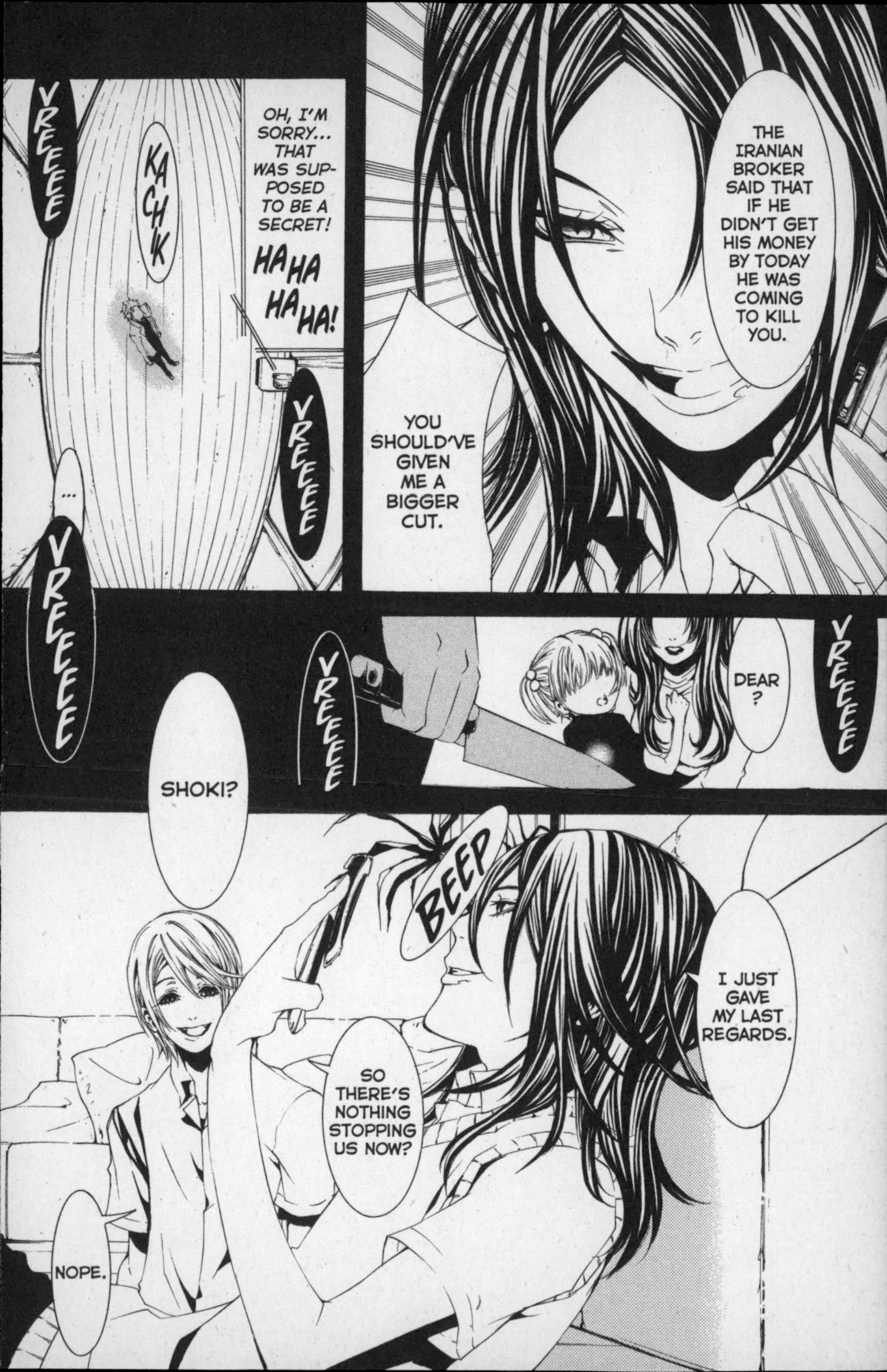
THE IRANIAN BROKER SAID THAT IF HE DIDN'T GET HIS MONEY BY TODAY HE WAS COMING TO KILL YOU.
YOU SHOULD'VE GIVEN ME A BIGGER CUT.
OH, I'M SORRY... THAT WAS SUP-POSED TO BE A SECRET!
HAHA HAHA!
KACHIK
VREEEE
VREEEEE
...
VREEEEE
DEAR?
VREEEEE
VREEEEE
SHOKI?
I JUST GAVE MY LAST REGARDS.
BEEP
SO THERE'S NOTHING STOPPING US NOW?
NOPE.

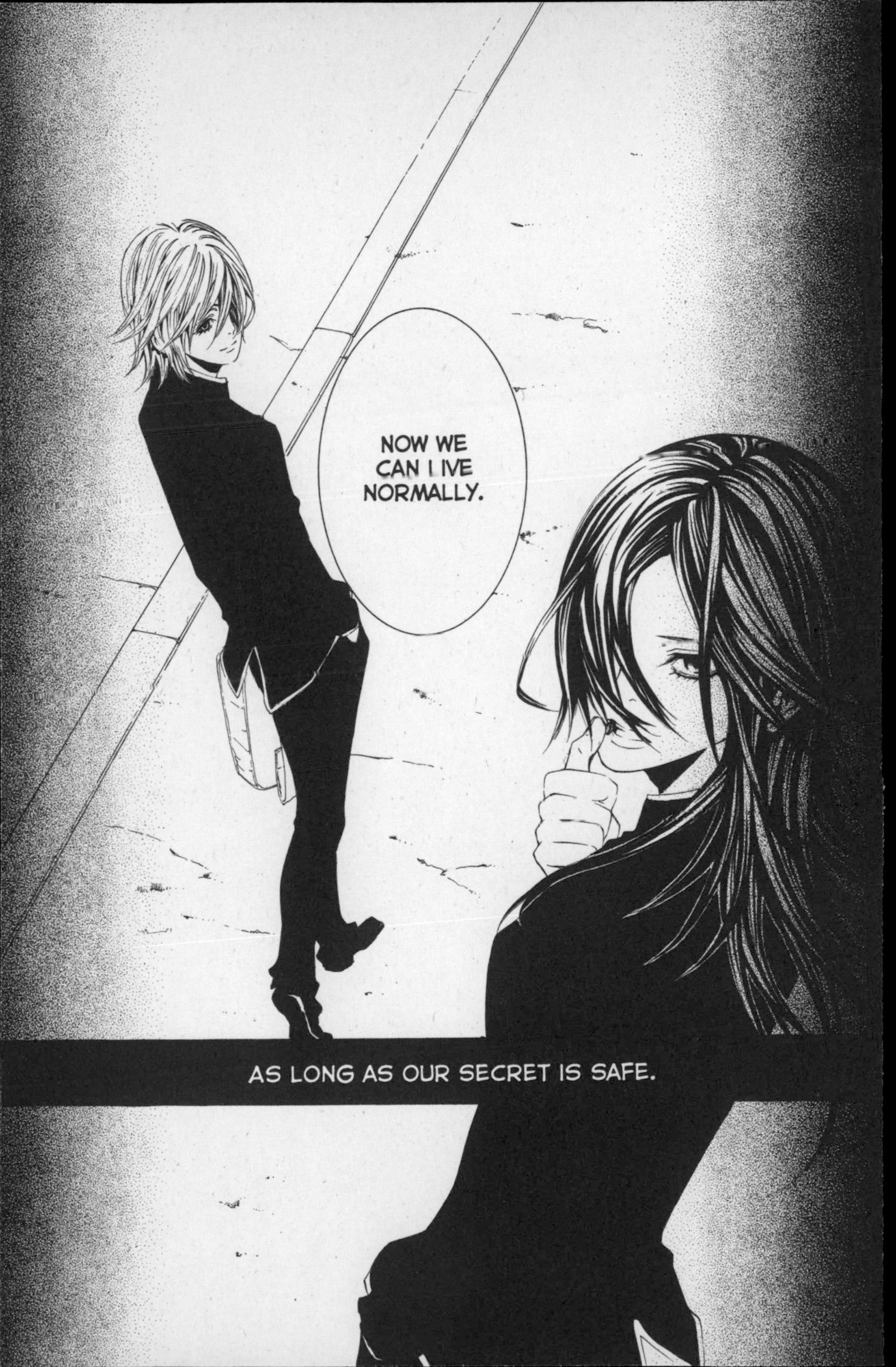
NOW WE CAN LIVE NORMALLY.
AS LONG AS OUR SECRET IS SAFE.

switch

naked ape : Saki Otoh & Nakamura Tomomi

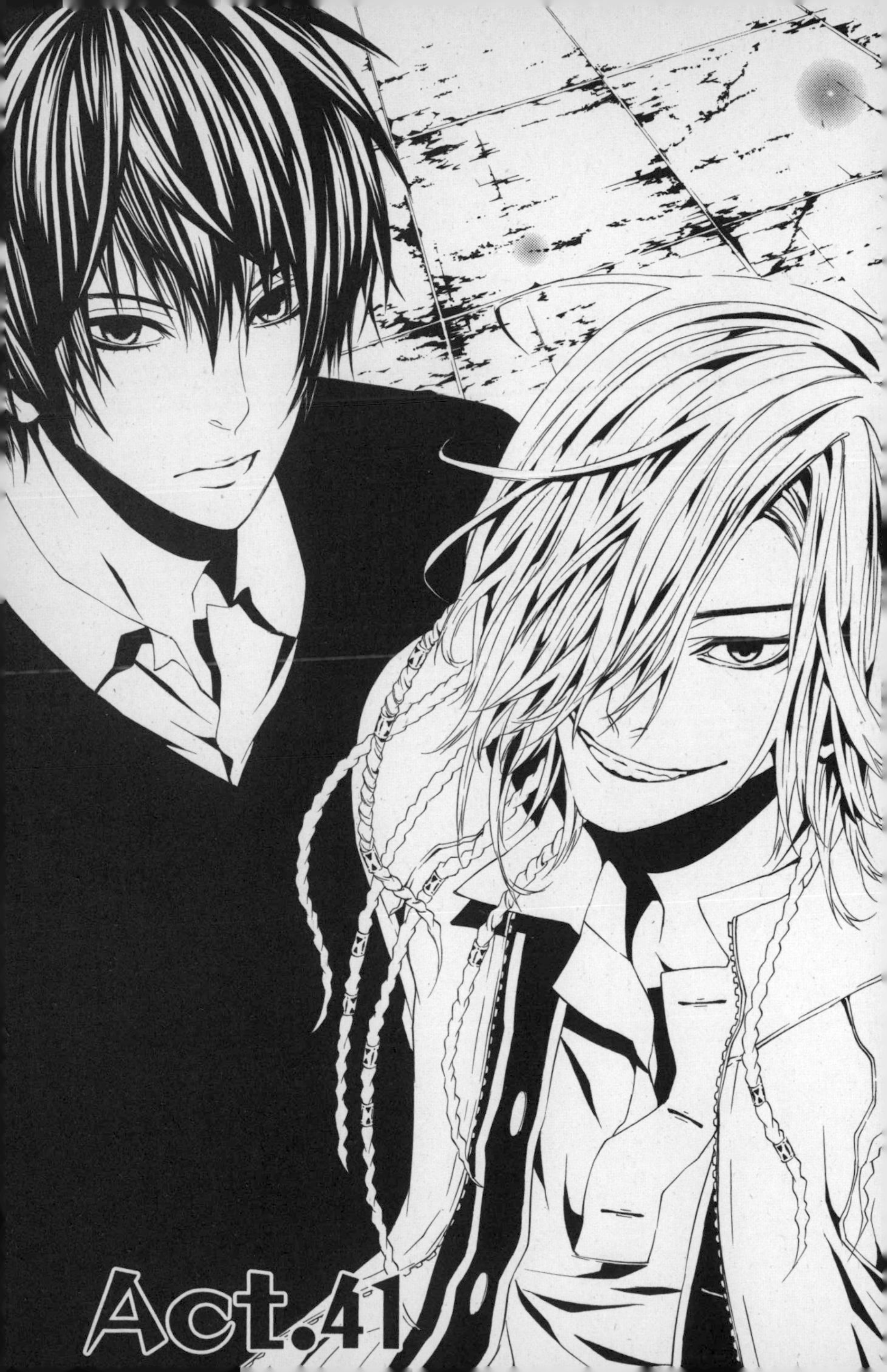
Act.41

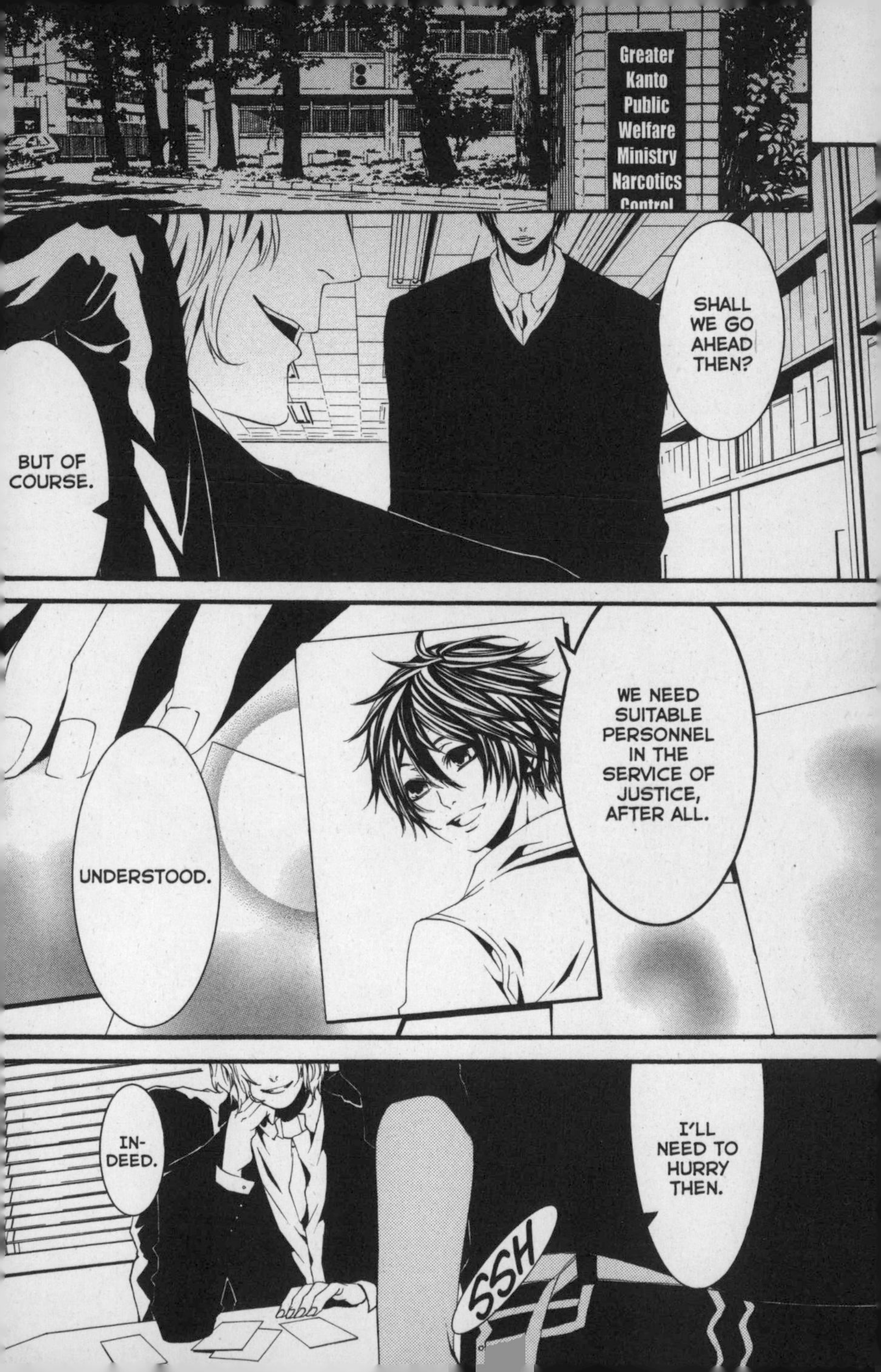
Greater Kanto Public Welfare Ministry Narcotics Control
SHALL WE GO AHEAD THEN?
BUT OF COURSE.
WE NEED SUITABLE PERSONNEL IN THE SERVICE OF JUSTICE, AFTER ALL.
UNDERSTOOD.
I'LL NEED TO HURRY THEN.
SSH
IN-DEED.

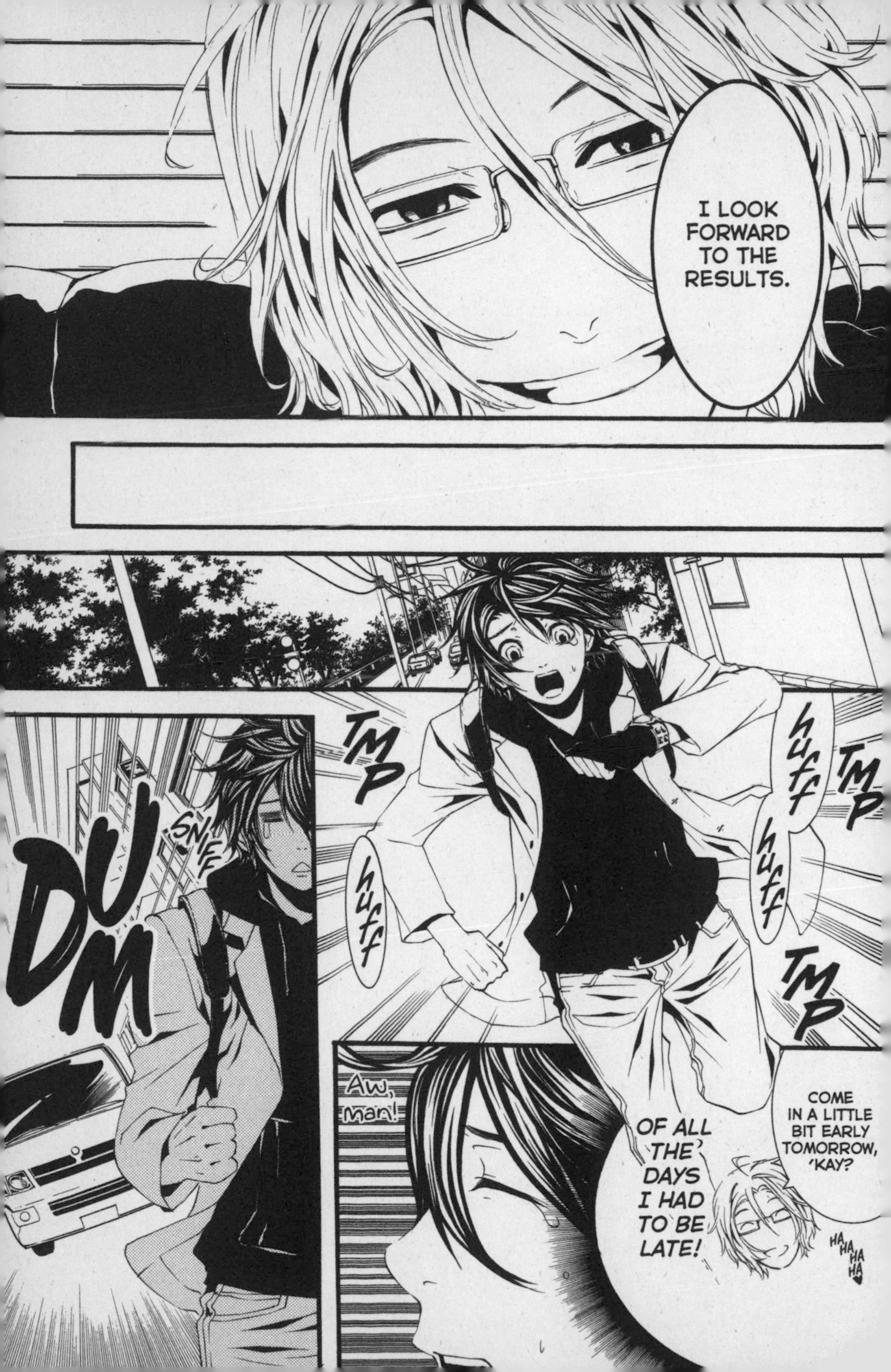

I LOOK FORWARD TO THE RESULTS.
TMP
huff huff
TMP
TMP
huff
COME IN A LITTLE BIT EARLY TOMORROW, 'KAY?
HA HA HA HA
OF ALL THE DAYS I HAD TO BE LATE!
Aw, man!
SNIFF
DUDM

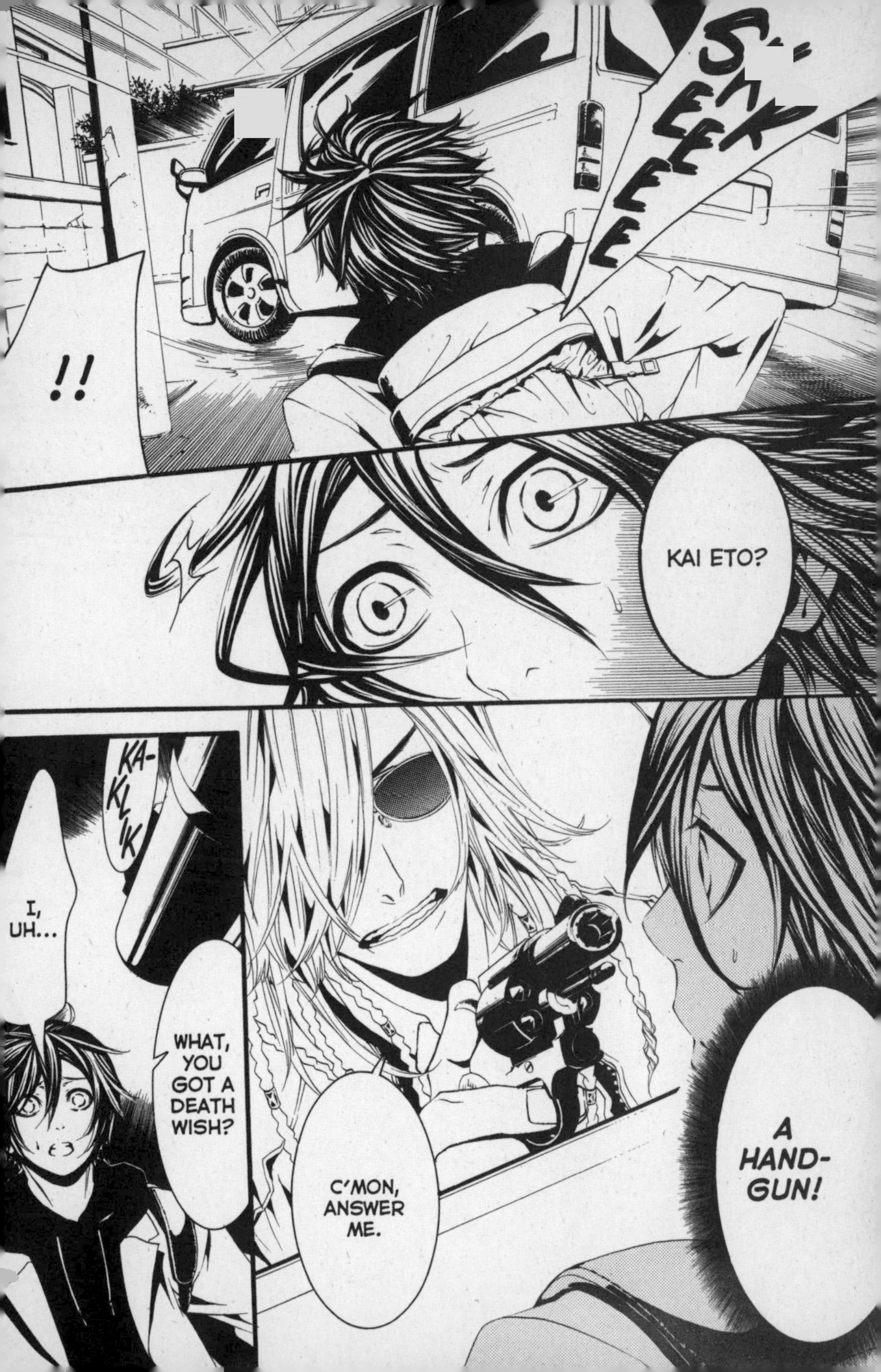
SKREEEE
!!
KAI ETO?
A HAND-GUN!
C'MON, ANSWER ME.
WHAT, YOU GOT A DEATH WISH?
KA-KLIK
I, UH...

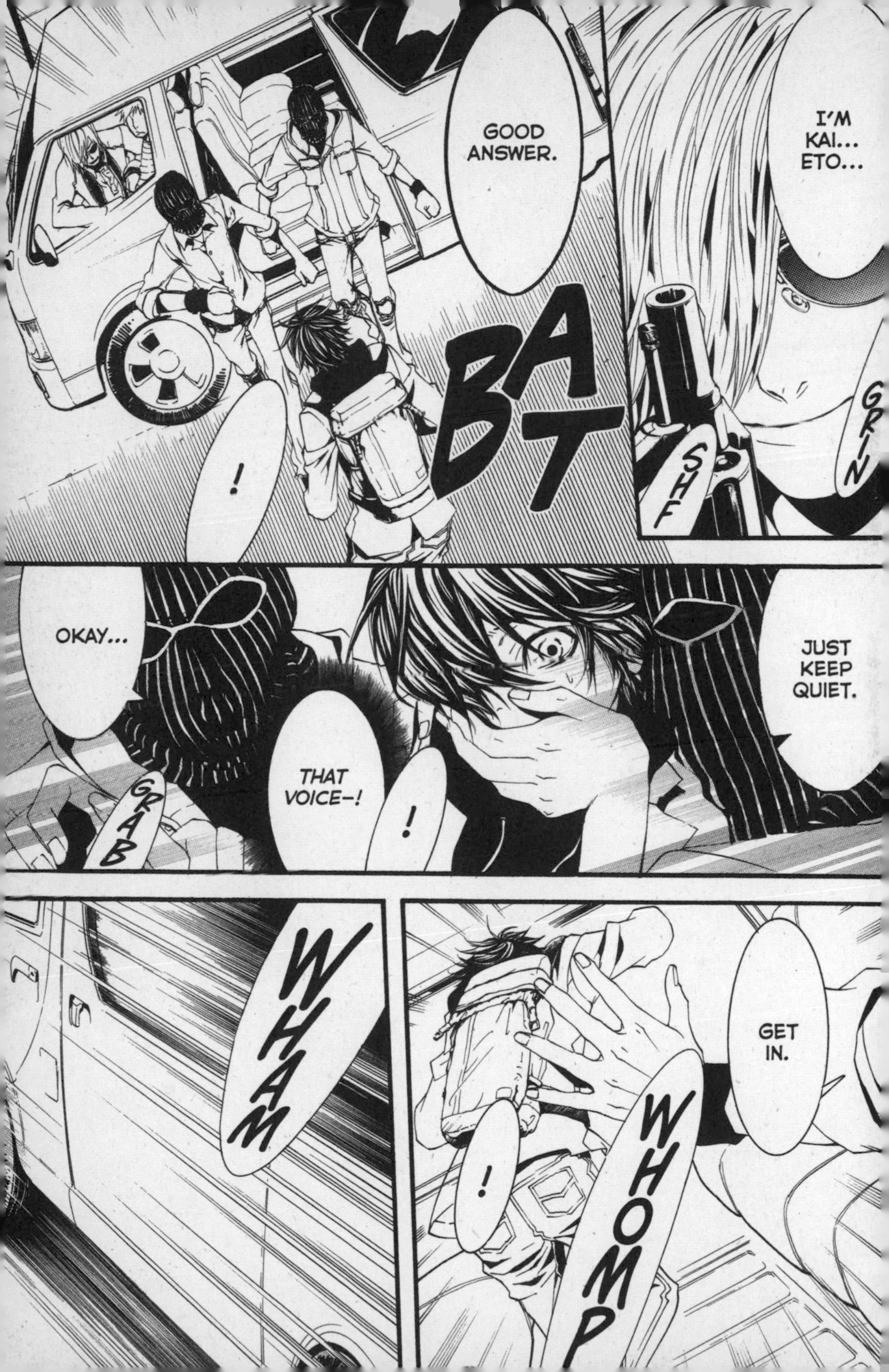
I'M KAI... ETO...
GRIN
SHF
GOOD ANSWER.
BABT
!
JUST KEEP QUIET.
!
THAT VOICE-!
OKAY...
GRAB
GET IN.
WHOMP
!
WHAM

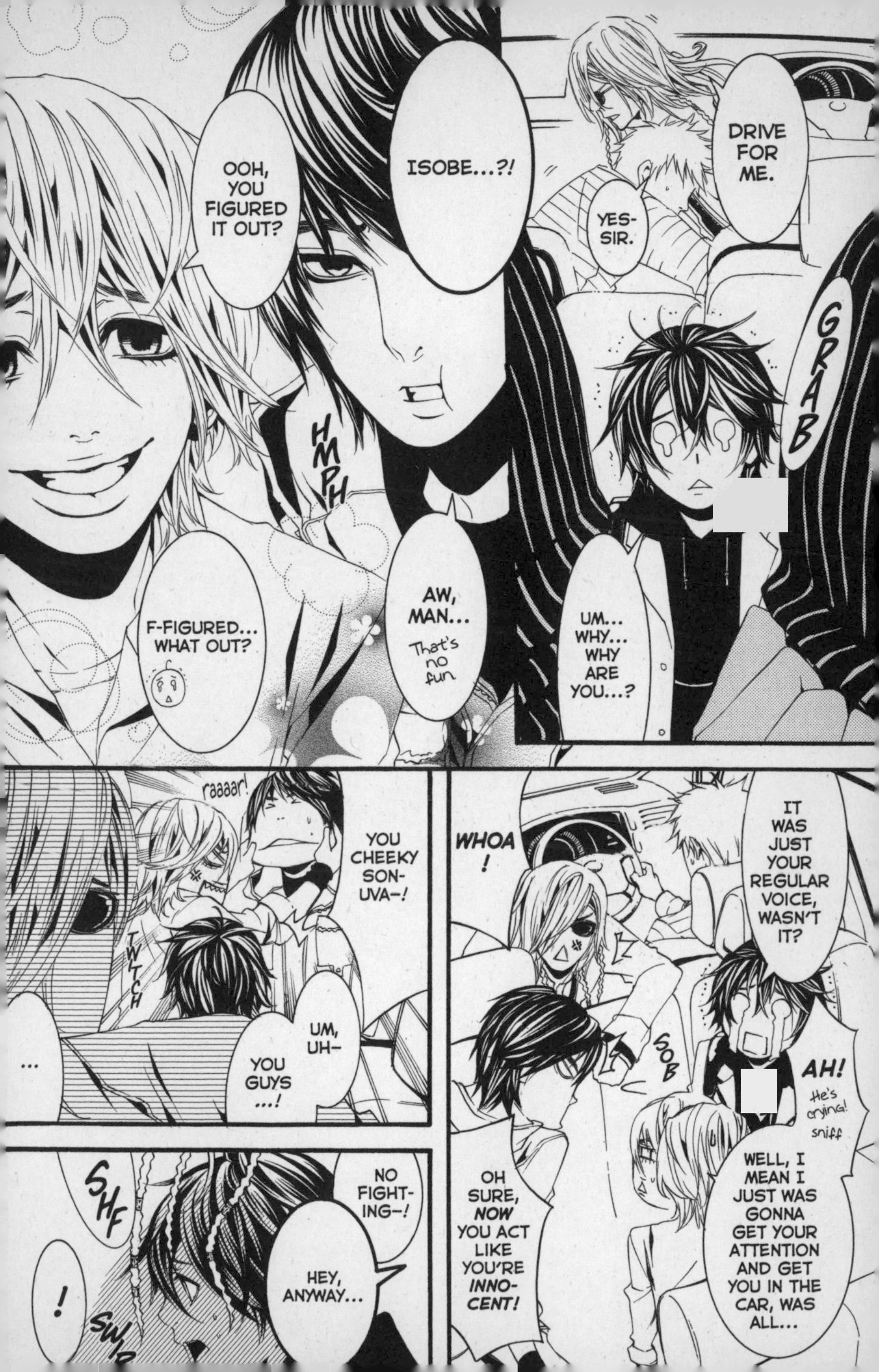

DRIVE FOR ME.
YES-SIR.
GRAB
UM... WHY... WHY ARE YOU...?
ISOBE...?!
OOH, YOU FIGURED IT OUT?
HMPH
AW, MAN...
That's no fun.
F-FIGURED... WHAT OUT?
IT WAS JUST YOUR REGULAR VOICE, WASN'T IT?
WHOA!
SOB
AH!
He's crying!
sniff
WELL, I MEAN I JUST WAS GONNA GET YOUR ATTENTION AND GET YOU IN THE CAR, WAS ALL...
OH SURE, NOW YOU ACT LIKE YOU'RE INNO-CENT!
YOU CHEEKY SON-UVA-!
raaaar!
TWITCH
UM, UH-
YOU GUYS ...!
...
NO FIGHT-ING-!
SHF
HEY, ANYWAY...
!

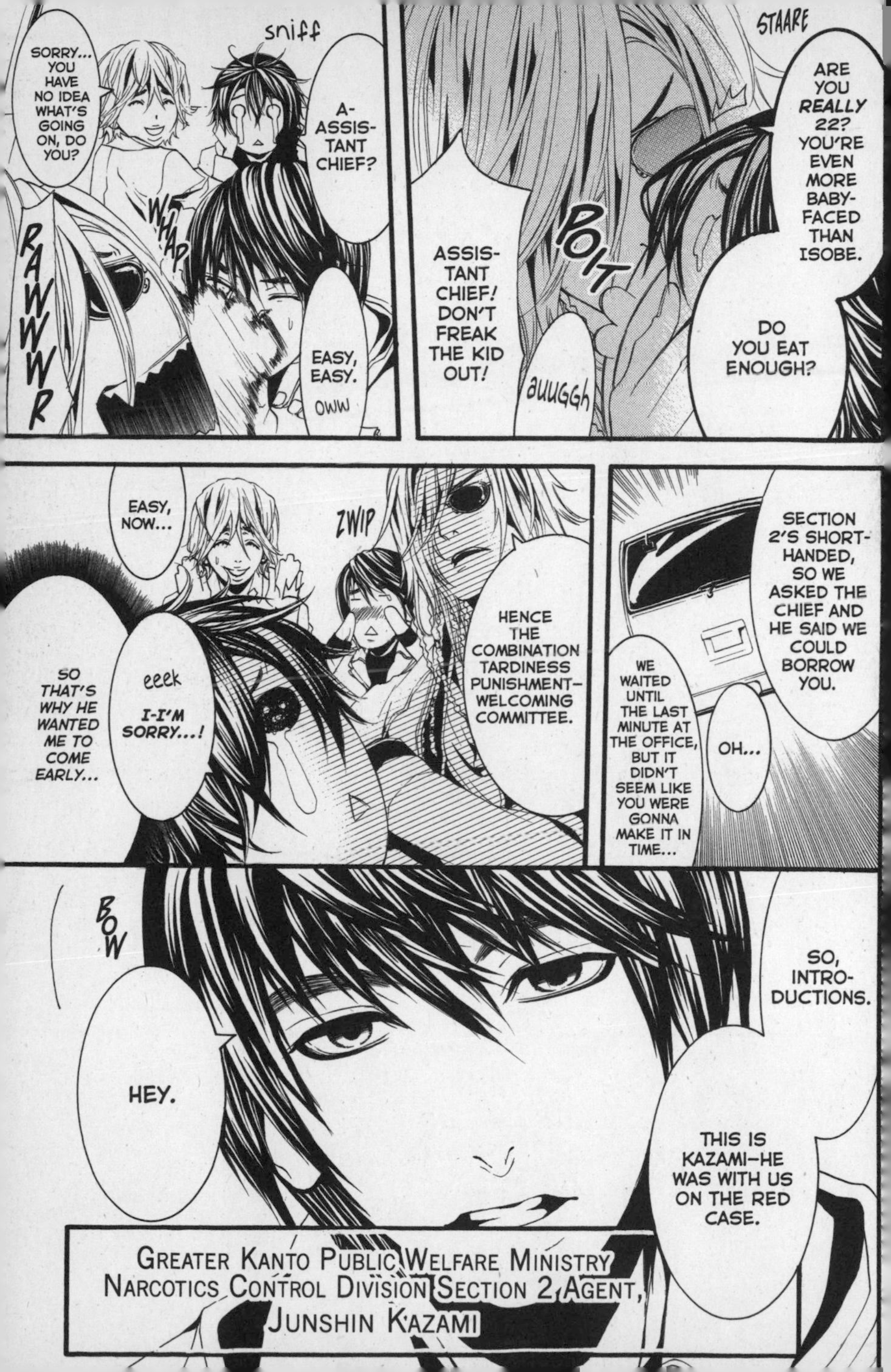
STAARE
ARE YOU REALLY 22? YOU'RE EVEN MORE BABY-FACED THAN ISOBE.
DO YOU EAT ENOUGH?
POIT
auuggh
ASSISTANT CHIEF! DON'T FREAK THE KID OUT!
sniff
A- ASSISTANT CHIEF?
SORRY... YOU HAVE NO IDEA WHAT'S GOING ON, DO YOU?
WHAP
RAWWWR
EASY, EASY.
OWW
SECTION 2'S SHORT-HANDED, SO WE ASKED THE CHIEF AND HE SAID WE COULD BORROW YOU.
OH...
WE WAITED UNTIL THE LAST MINUTE AT THE OFFICE, BUT IT DIDN'T SEEM LIKE YOU WERE GONNA MAKE IT IN TIME...
ZWIP
HENCE THE COMBINATION TARDINESS PUNISHMENT—WELCOMING COMMITTEE.
EASY, NOW...
eeek
I-I'M SORRY...!
SO THAT'S WHY HE WANTED ME TO COME EARLY...
SO, INTRODUCTIONS.
THIS IS KAZAMI—HE WAS WITH US ON THE RED CASE.
BOW
HEY.
GREATER KANTO PUBLIC WELFARE MINISTRY NARCOTICS CONTROL DIVISION SECTION 2 AGENT, JUNSHIN KAZAMI

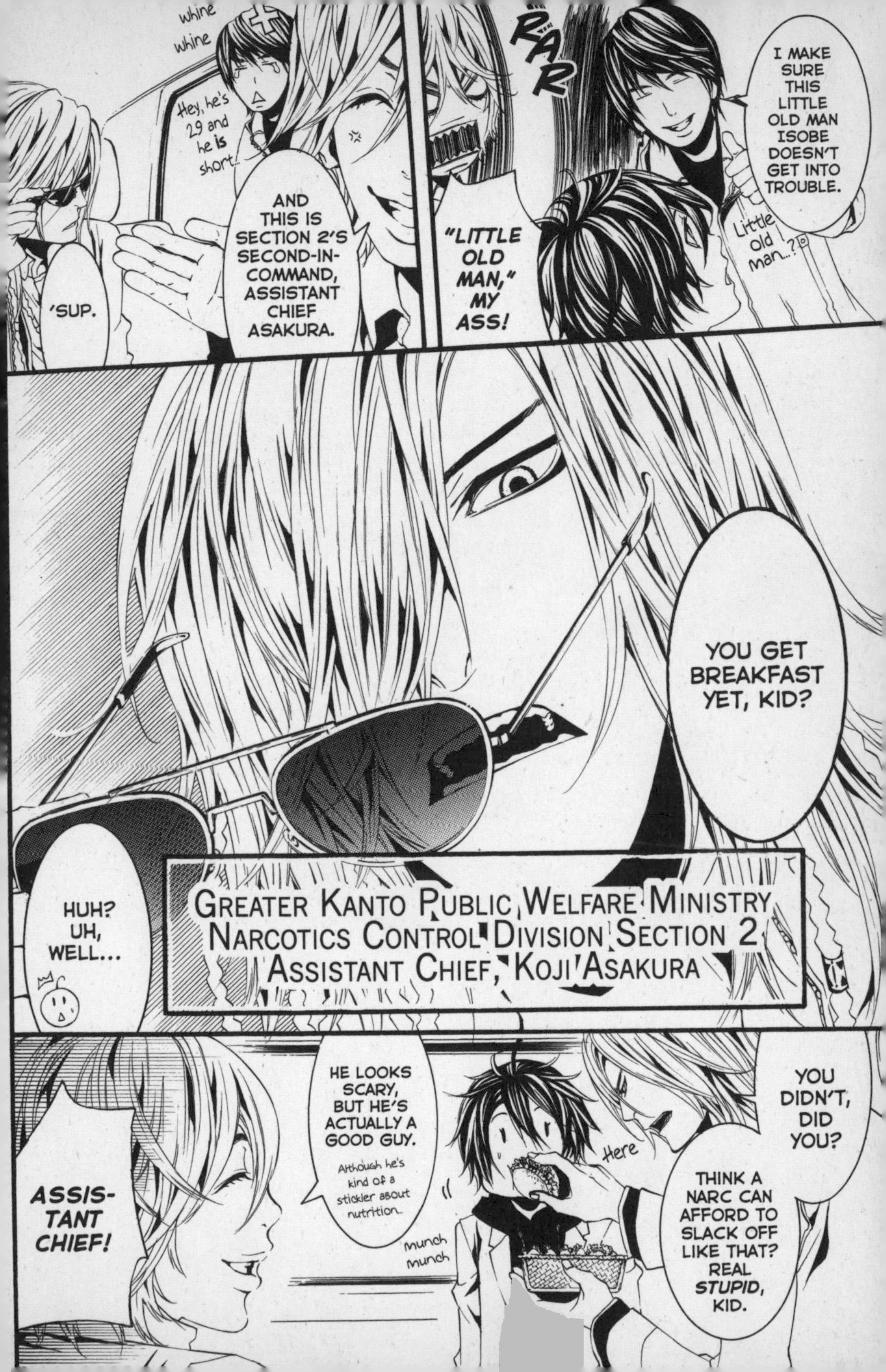
I MAKE SURE THIS LITTLE OLD MAN ISOBE DOESN'T GET INTO TROUBLE.
Little old man...?
RAR
"LITTLE OLD MAN," MY ASS!
whine whine
Hey, he's 29 and he **is** short...
AND THIS IS SECTION 2'S SECOND-IN-COMMAND, ASSISTANT CHIEF ASAKURA.
'SUP.
YOU GET BREAKFAST YET, KID?
GREATER KANTO PUBLIC WELFARE MINISTRY NARCOTICS CONTROL DIVISION SECTION 2 ASSISTANT CHIEF, KOJI ASAKURA
HUH? UH, WELL...
YOU DIDN'T, DID YOU?
THINK A NARC CAN AFFORD TO SLACK OFF LIKE THAT? REAL *STUPID*, KID.
Here
munch munch
HE LOOKS SCARY, BUT HE'S ACTUALLY A GOOD GUY.
Although he's kind of a stickler about nutrition...
ASSISTANT CHIEF!

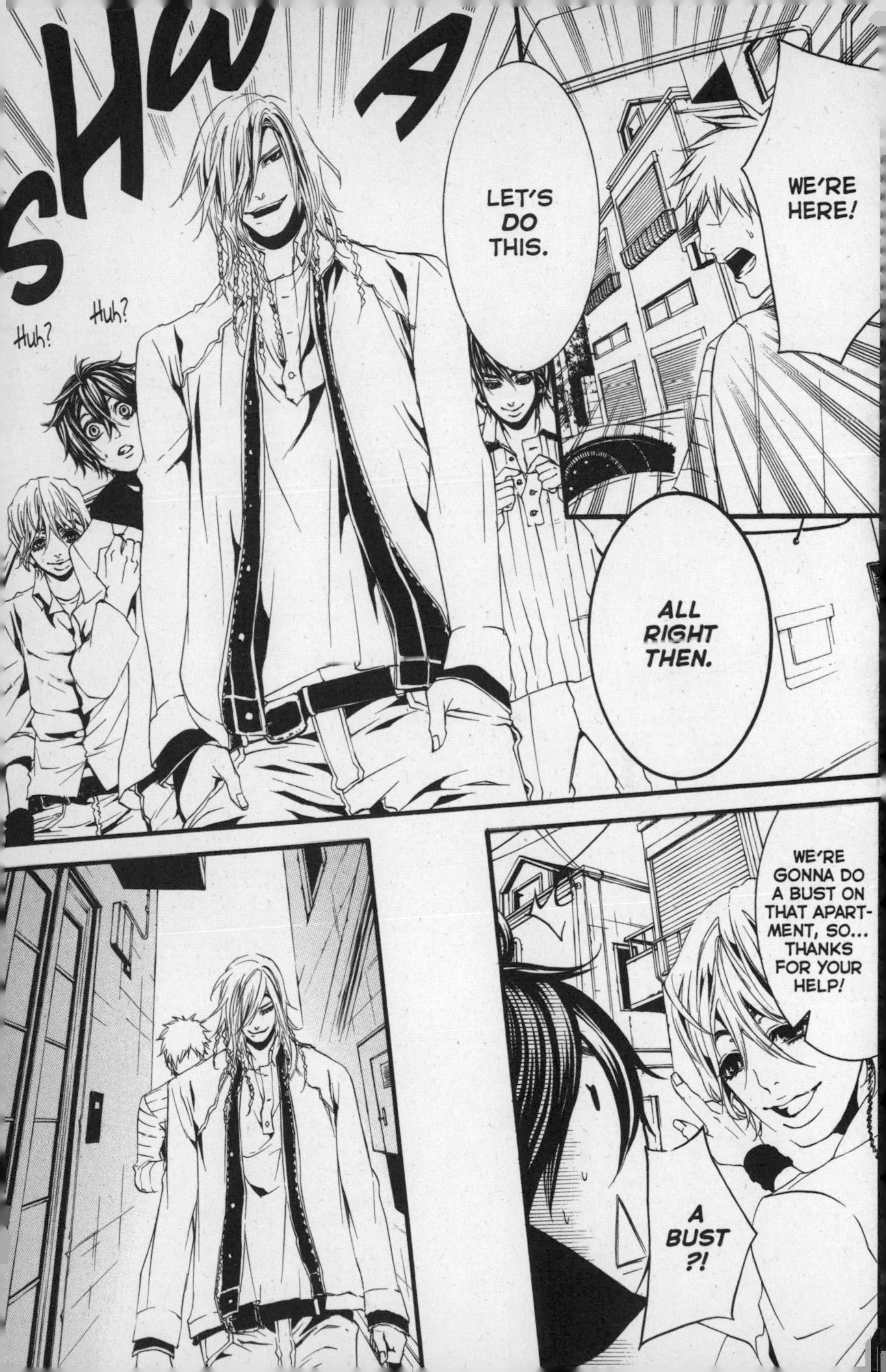
WE'RE HERE!
LET'S DO THIS.
ALL RIGHT THEN.
SHWA
Huh?
Huh?
WE'RE GONNA DO A BUST ON THAT APARTMENT, SO... THANKS FOR YOUR HELP!
A BUST ?!

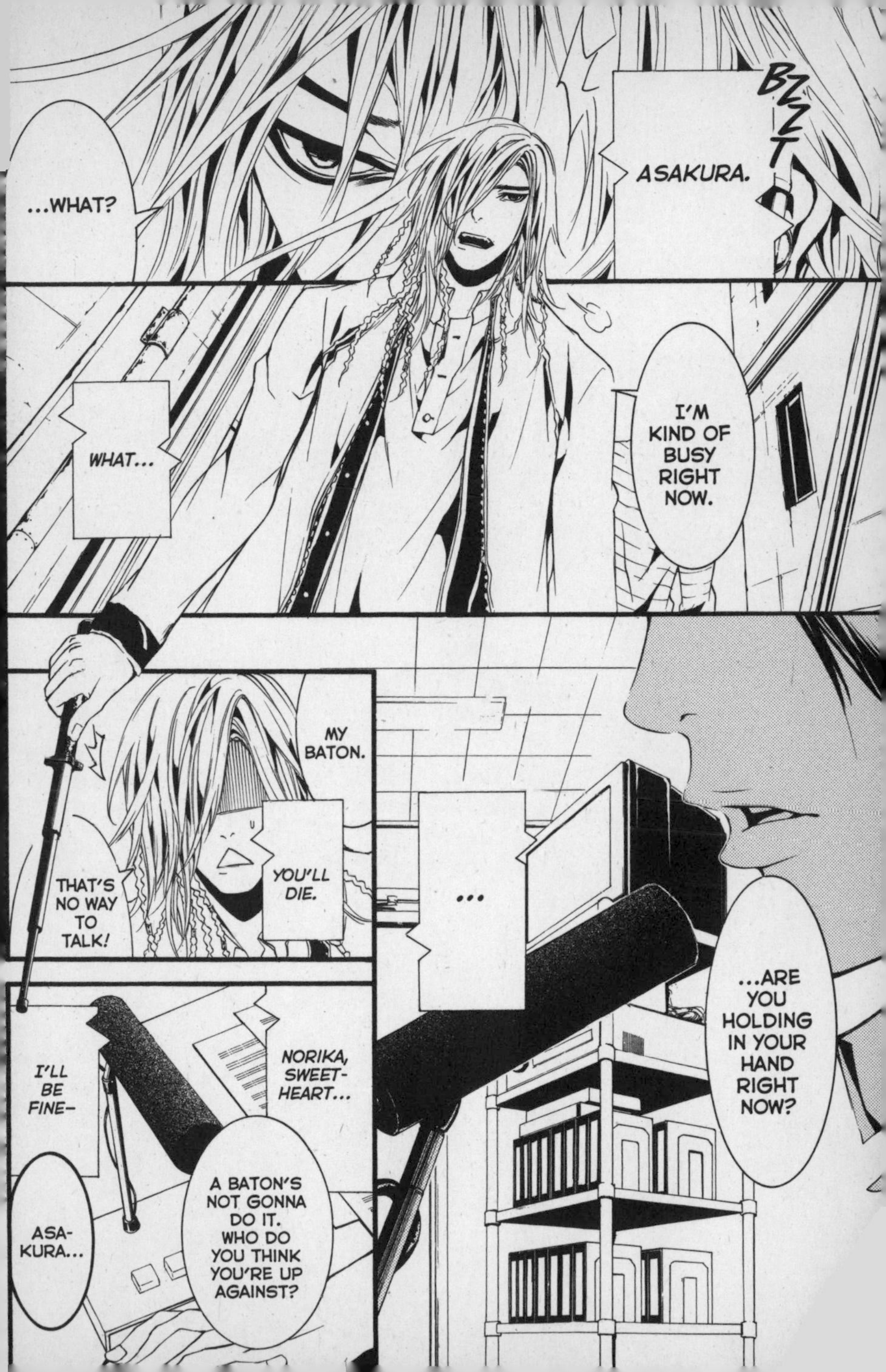
BZZZT
ASAKURA.
...WHAT?
I'M KIND OF BUSY RIGHT NOW.
WHAT...
...ARE YOU HOLDING IN YOUR HAND RIGHT NOW?
MY BATON.
...
YOU'LL DIE.
THAT'S NO WAY TO TALK!
NORIKA, SWEET-HEART...
A BATON'S NOT GONNA DO IT. WHO DO YOU THINK YOU'RE UP AGAINST?
I'LL BE FINE-
ASA-KURA...

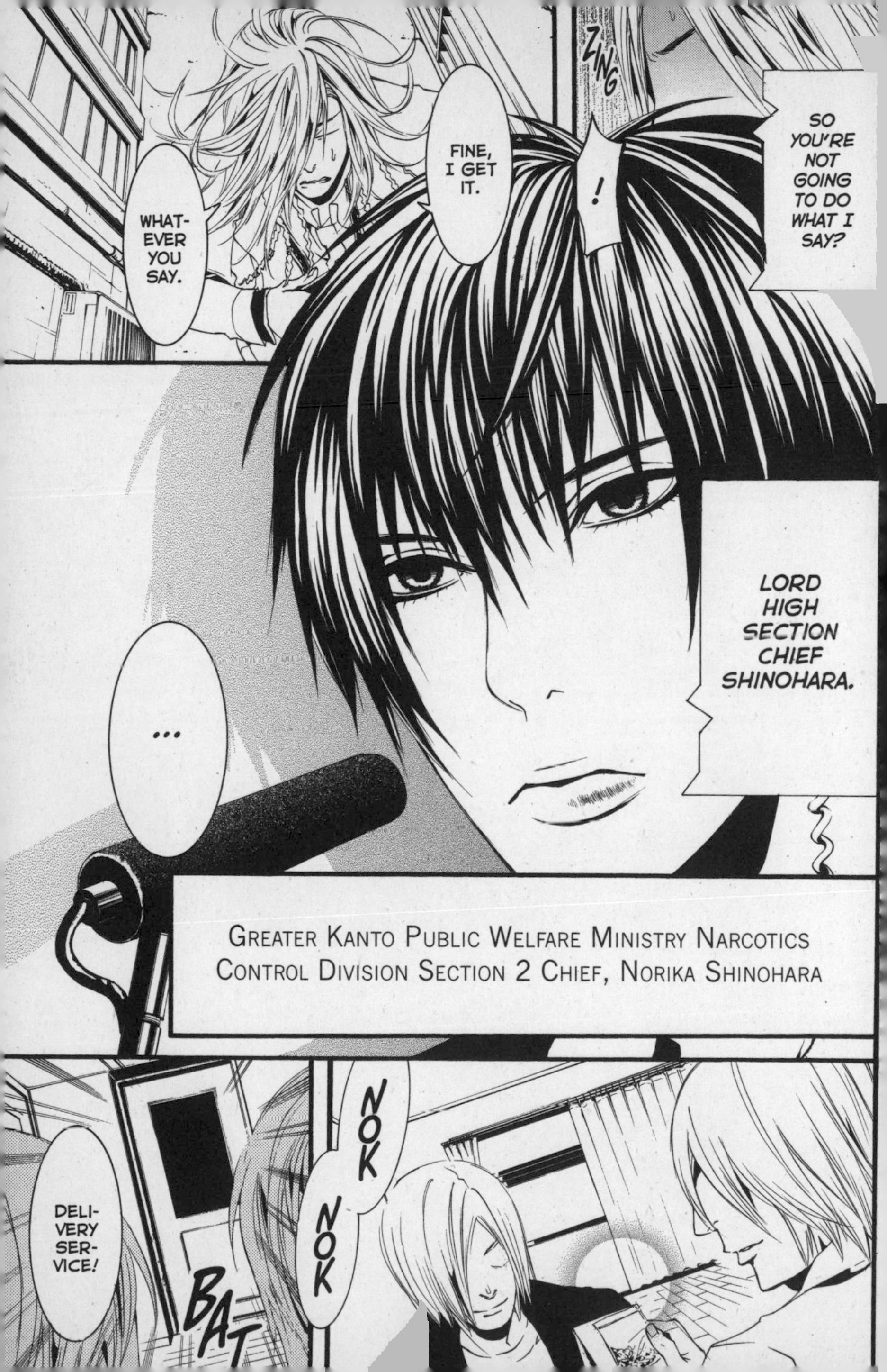
SO YOU'RE NOT GOING TO DO WHAT I SAY?
ZING
!
FINE, I GET IT.
WHAT-EVER YOU SAY.
LORD HIGH SECTION CHIEF SHINOHARA.
...
GREATER KANTO PUBLIC WELFARE MINISTRY NARCOTICS CONTROL DIVISION SECTION 2 CHIEF, NORIKA SHINOHARA
NOK NOK
DELI-VERY SER-VICE!
BAT

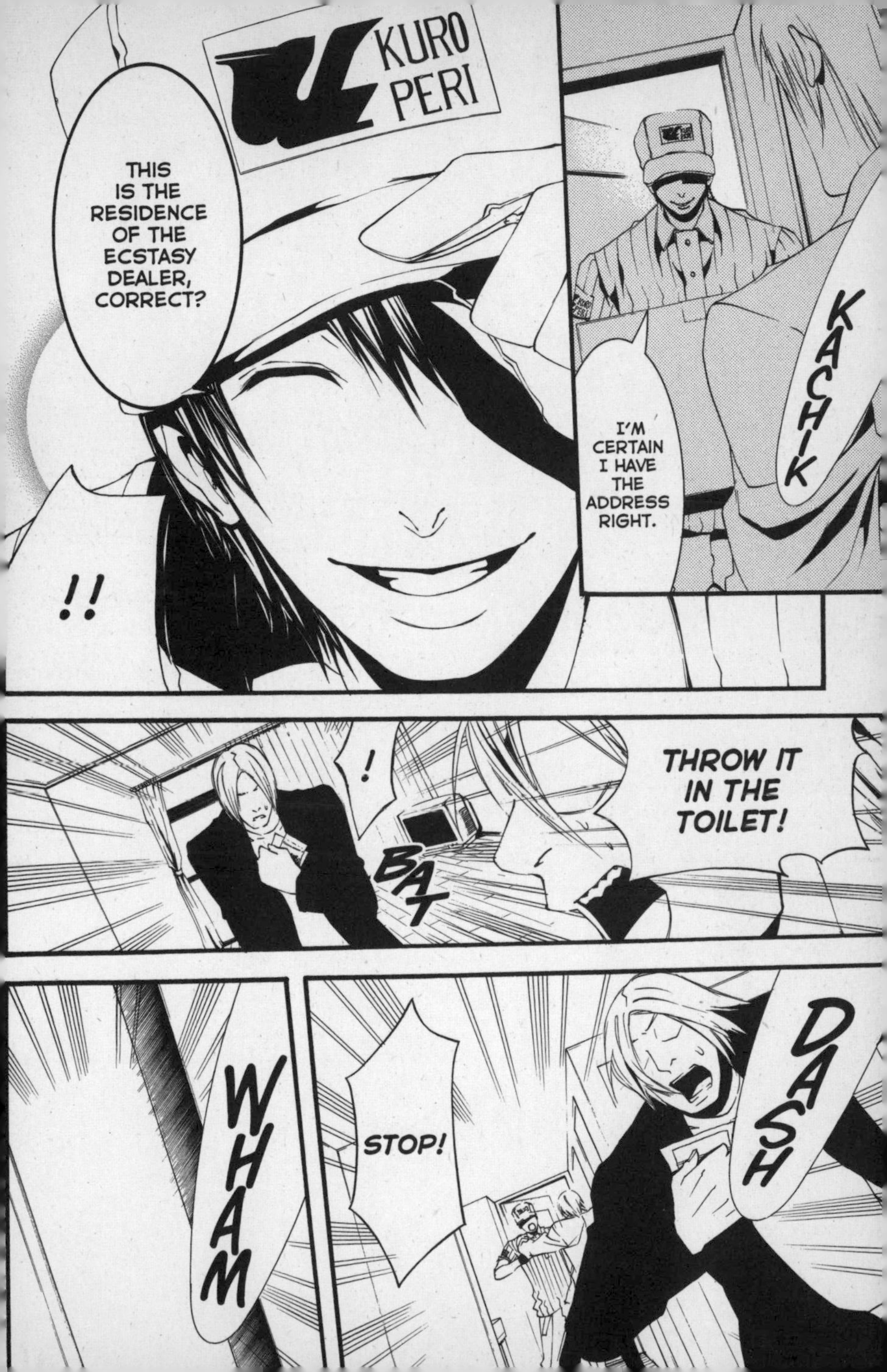
KACHIK
I'M CERTAIN I HAVE THE ADDRESS RIGHT.
KURO PERI
THIS IS THE RESIDENCE OF THE ECSTASY DEALER, CORRECT?
!!
THROW IT IN THE TOILET!
!
BAT
DASH
STOP!
WHAM

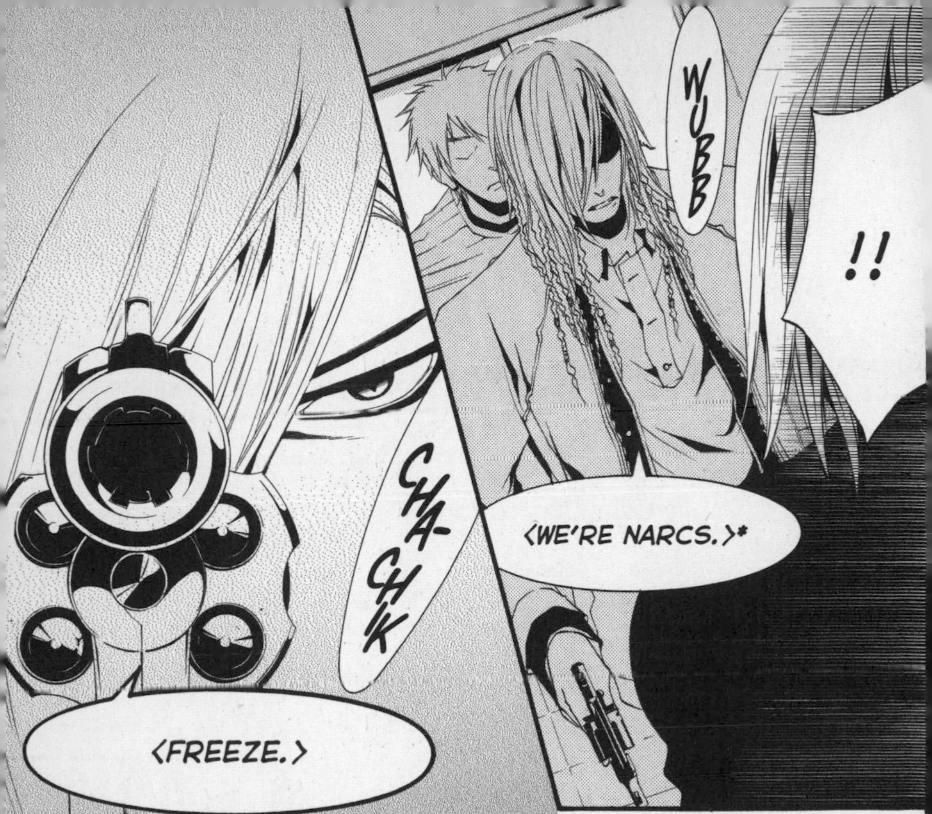
!!
WUBB
‹WE'RE NARCS.›*
CHA-CHIK
‹FREEZE.›

*SPOKEN IN ENGLISH TO THE FOREIGNERS.

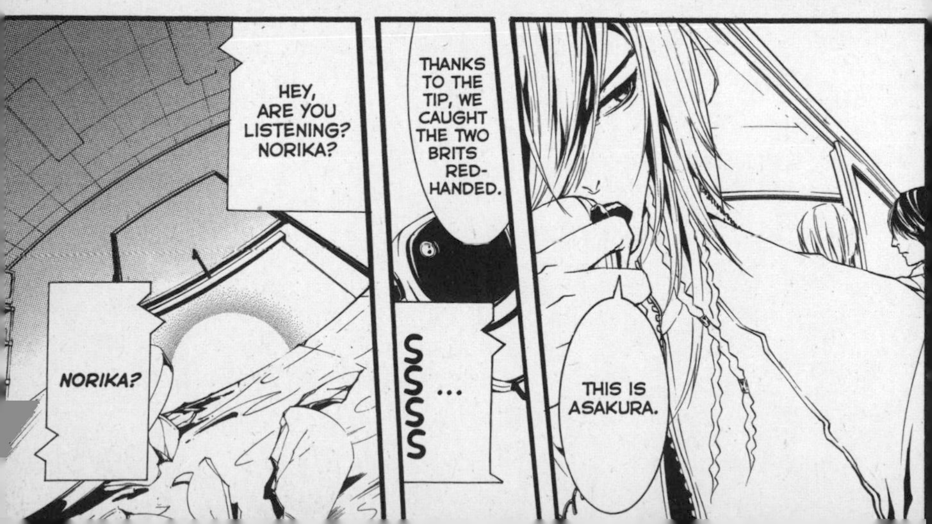
THIS IS ASAKURA.
THANKS TO THE TIP, WE CAUGHT THE TWO BRITS RED-HANDED.
SSSS
...
HEY, ARE YOU LISTENING? NORIKA?
NORIKA?

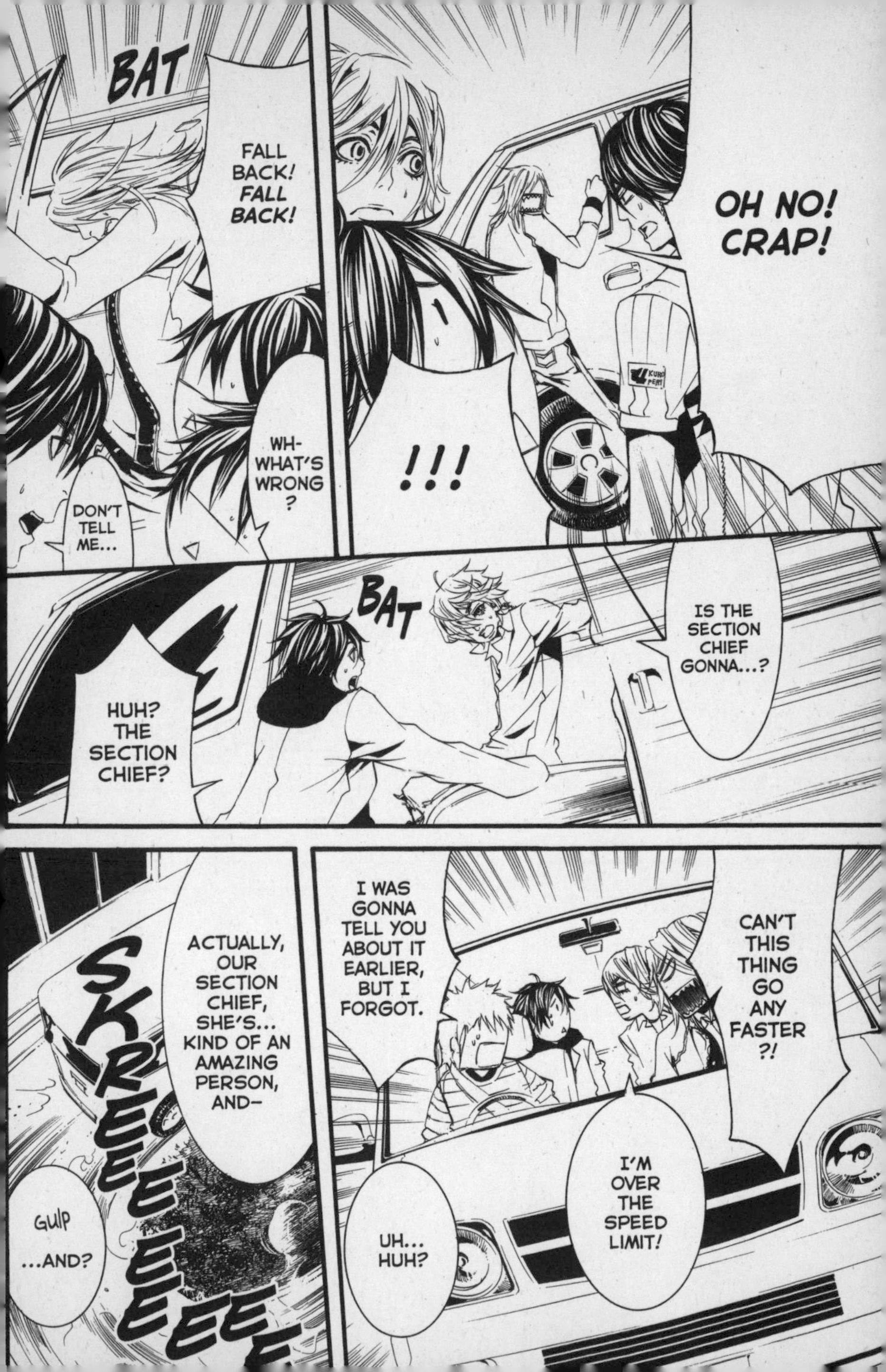
OH NO! CRAP!
!!!
BAT
FALL BACK! FALL BACK!
WH-WHAT'S WRONG?
DON'T TELL ME...
IS THE SECTION CHIEF GONNA...?
BAT
HUH? THE SECTION CHIEF?
CAN'T THIS THING GO ANY FASTER?!
I WAS GONNA TELL YOU ABOUT IT EARLIER, BUT I FORGOT.
I'M OVER THE SPEED LIMIT!
UH... HUH?
ACTUALLY, OUR SECTION CHIEF, SHE'S... KIND OF AN AMAZING PERSON, AND–
SKREEEEEEEE
GULP
...AND?

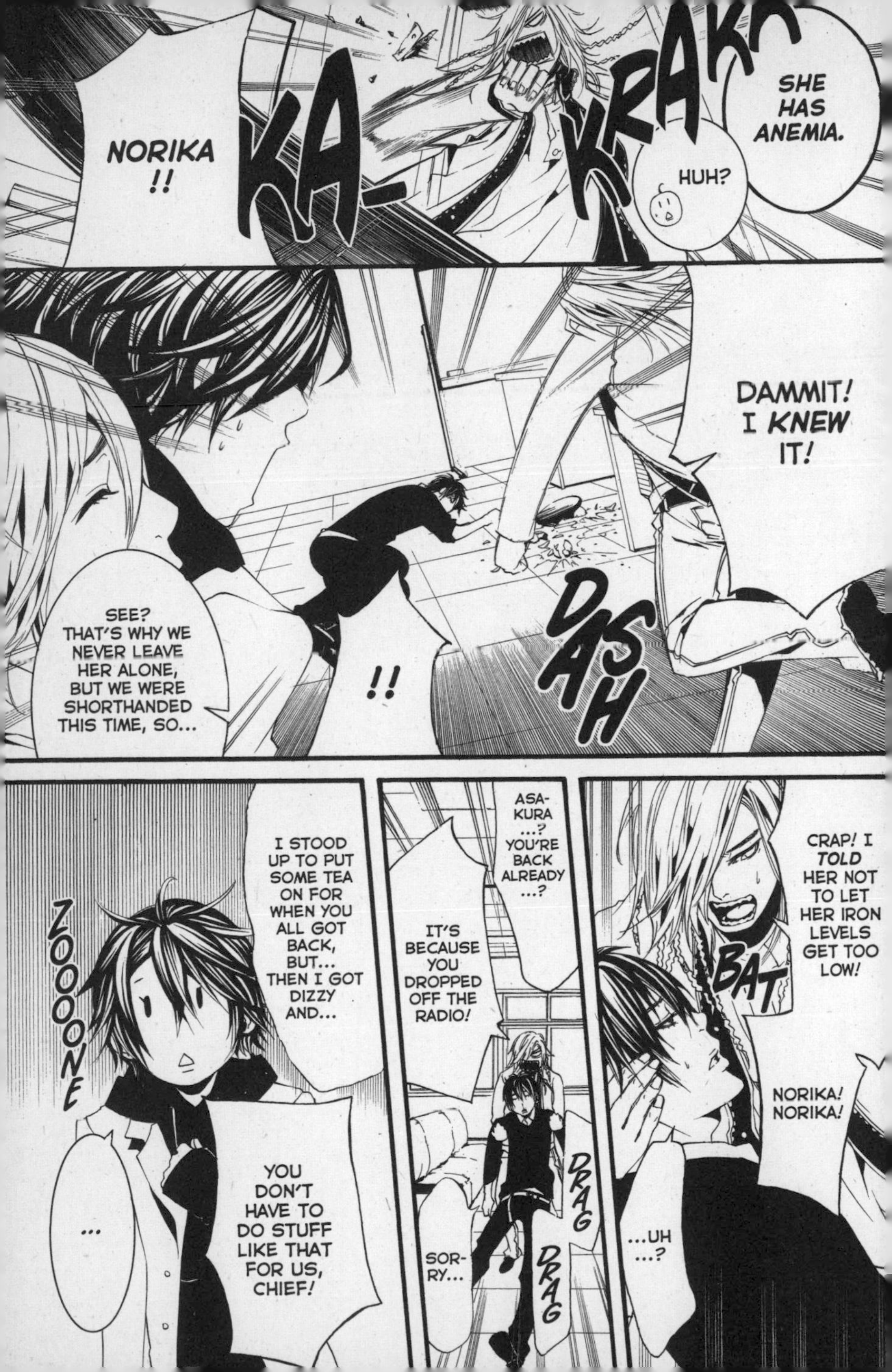
SHE HAS ANEMIA.
HUH?
KA-KRAK
NORIKA !!
DAMMIT! I KNEW IT!
DASH
!!
SEE? THAT'S WHY WE NEVER LEAVE HER ALONE, BUT WE WERE SHORTHANDED THIS TIME, SO...
CRAP! I TOLD HER NOT TO LET HER IRON LEVELS GET TOO LOW!
BAT
NORIKA! NORIKA!
...UH ...?
ASA-KURA ...? YOU'RE BACK ALREADY ...?
IT'S BECAUSE YOU DROPPED OFF THE RADIO!
DRAG
DRAG
SOR-RY...
I STOOD UP TO PUT SOME TEA ON FOR WHEN YOU ALL GOT BACK, BUT... THEN I GOT DIZZY AND...
ZOOOONE
YOU DON'T HAVE TO DO STUFF LIKE THAT FOR US, CHIEF!
...

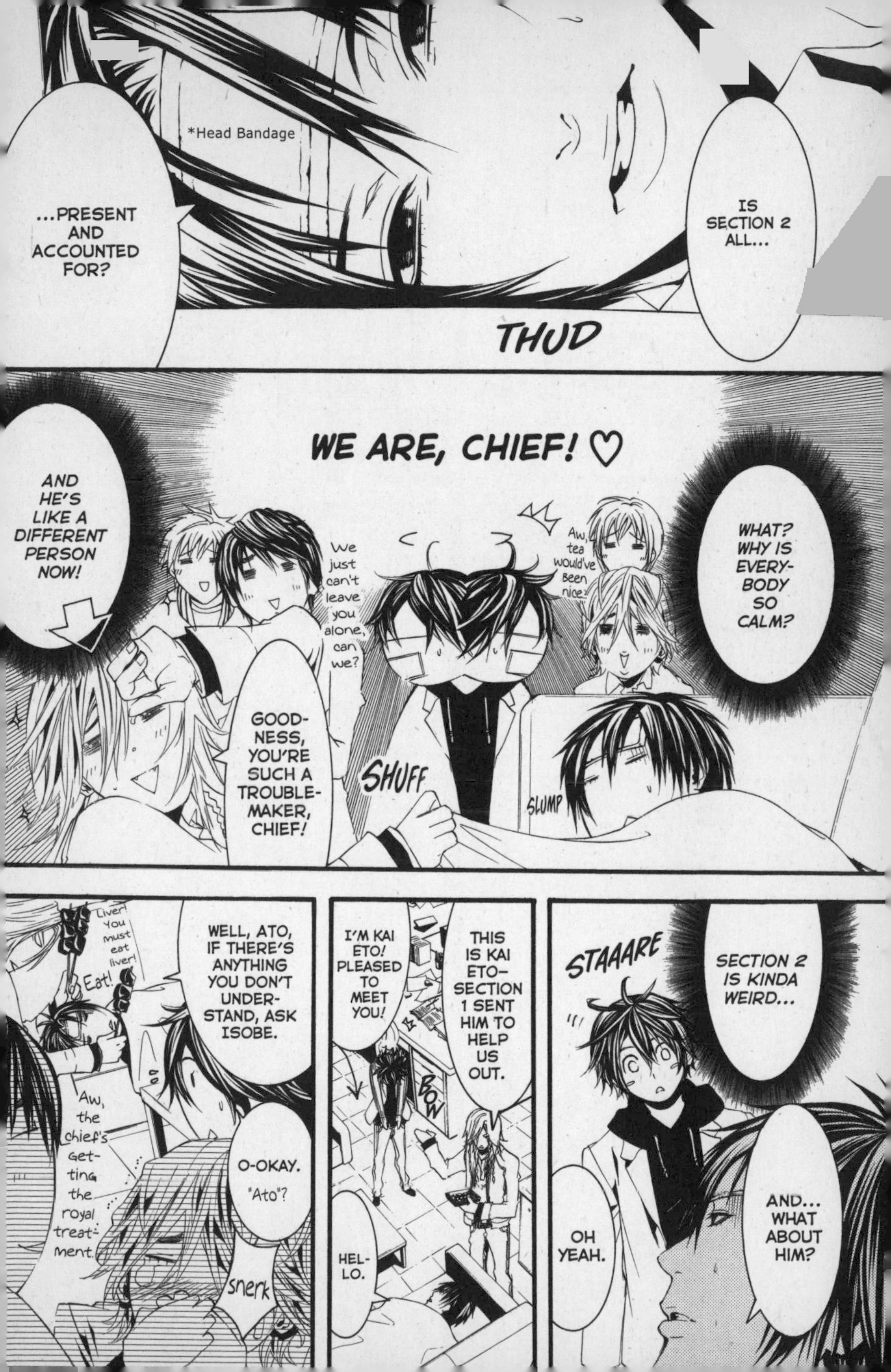
IS SECTION 2 ALL...
*Head Bandage
...PRESENT AND ACCOUNTED FOR?
THUD
WE ARE, CHIEF! ♡
WHAT? WHY IS EVERYBODY SO CALM?
Aw, tea would've Been nice
SLUMP
We just can't leave you alone, can we?
AND HE'S LIKE A DIFFERENT PERSON NOW!
SHUFF
GOODNESS, YOU'RE SUCH A TROUBLE-MAKER, CHIEF!
SECTION 2 IS KINDA WEIRD...
STAAARE
AND... WHAT ABOUT HIM?
OH YEAH.
THIS IS KAI ETO—SECTION 1 SENT HIM TO HELP US OUT.
I'M KAI ETO! PLEASED TO MEET YOU!
BOW
HEL-LO.
WELL, ATO, IF THERE'S ANYTHING YOU DON'T UNDER-STAND, ASK ISOBE.
Liver! You must eat liver!
Eat!
O-OKAY. "Ato"?
Aw, the chief's Get-ting the royal treat-ment.
snerk

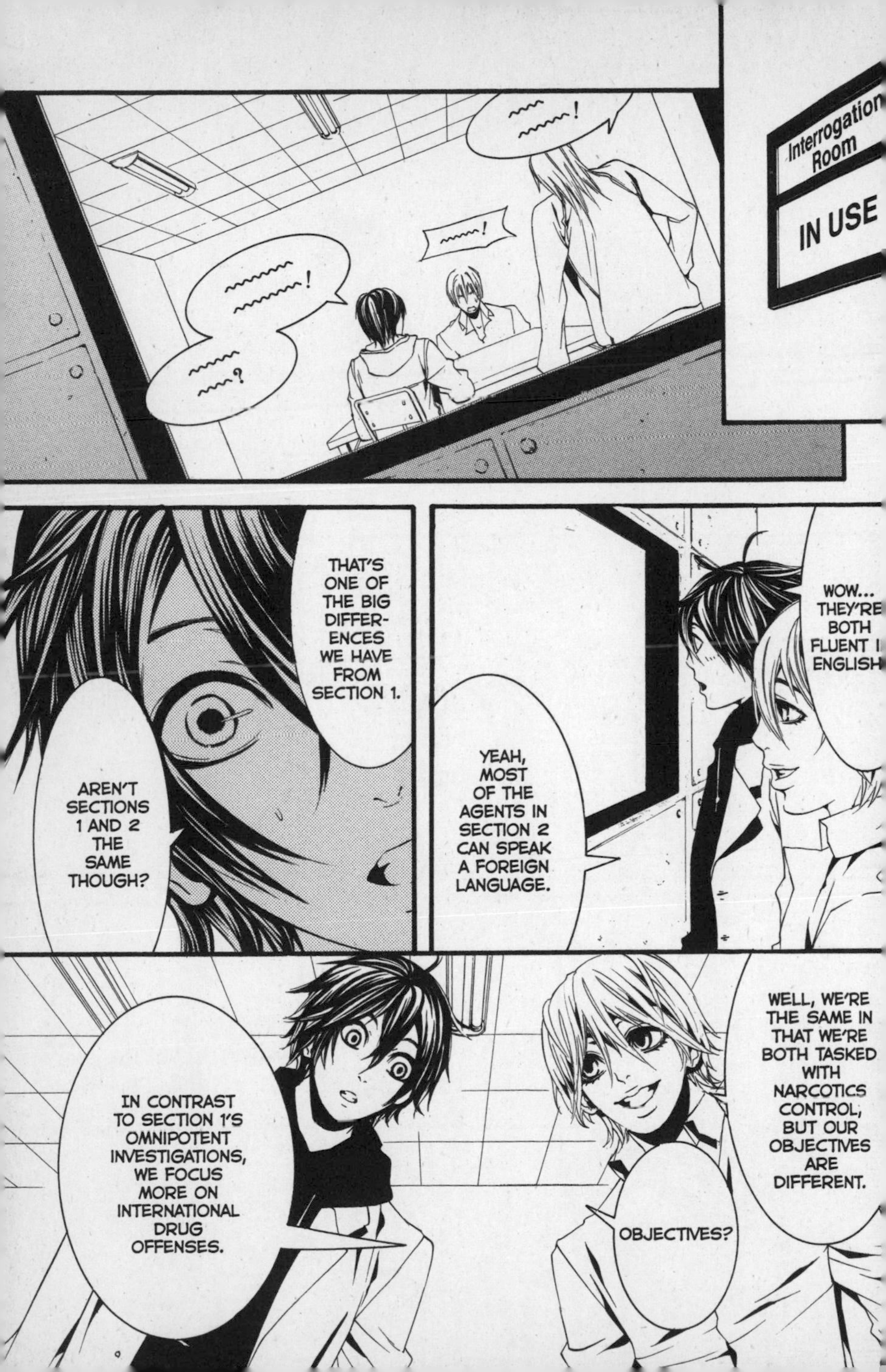
Interrogation Room
IN USE
WOW... THEY'RE BOTH FLUENT I ENGLISH
YEAH, MOST OF THE AGENTS IN SECTION 2 CAN SPEAK A FOREIGN LANGUAGE.
THAT'S ONE OF THE BIG DIFFER-ENCES WE HAVE FROM SECTION 1.
AREN'T SECTIONS 1 AND 2 THE SAME THOUGH?
WELL, WE'RE THE SAME IN THAT WE'RE BOTH TASKED WITH NARCOTICS CONTROL, BUT OUR OBJECTIVES ARE DIFFERENT.
OBJECTIVES?
IN CONTRAST TO SECTION 1'S OMNIPOTENT INVESTIGATIONS, WE FOCUS MORE ON INTERNATIONAL DRUG OFFENSES.

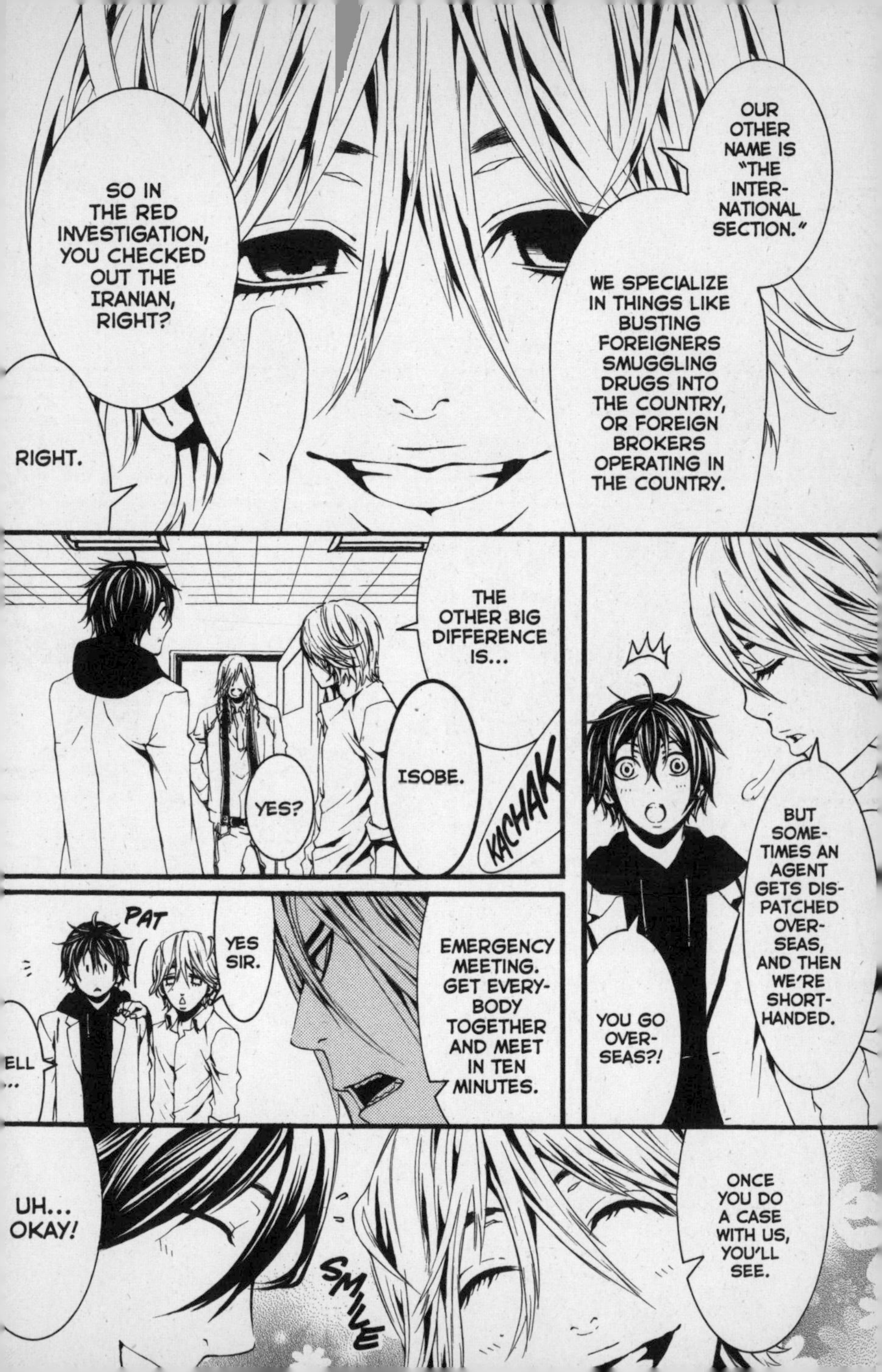
OUR OTHER NAME IS "THE INTERNATIONAL SECTION."
WE SPECIALIZE IN THINGS LIKE BUSTING FOREIGNERS SMUGGLING DRUGS INTO THE COUNTRY, OR FOREIGN BROKERS OPERATING IN THE COUNTRY.
SO IN THE RED INVESTIGATION, YOU CHECKED OUT THE IRANIAN, RIGHT?
RIGHT.
BUT SOMETIMES AN AGENT GETS DISPATCHED OVERSEAS, AND THEN WE'RE SHORTHANDED.
YOU GO OVERSEAS?!
THE OTHER BIG DIFFERENCE IS...
KACHAK
ISOBE.
YES?
EMERGENCY MEETING. GET EVERYBODY TOGETHER AND MEET IN TEN MINUTES.
YES SIR.
PAT
ELL ...
ONCE YOU DO A CASE WITH US, YOU'LL SEE.
SMILE
UH... OKAY!

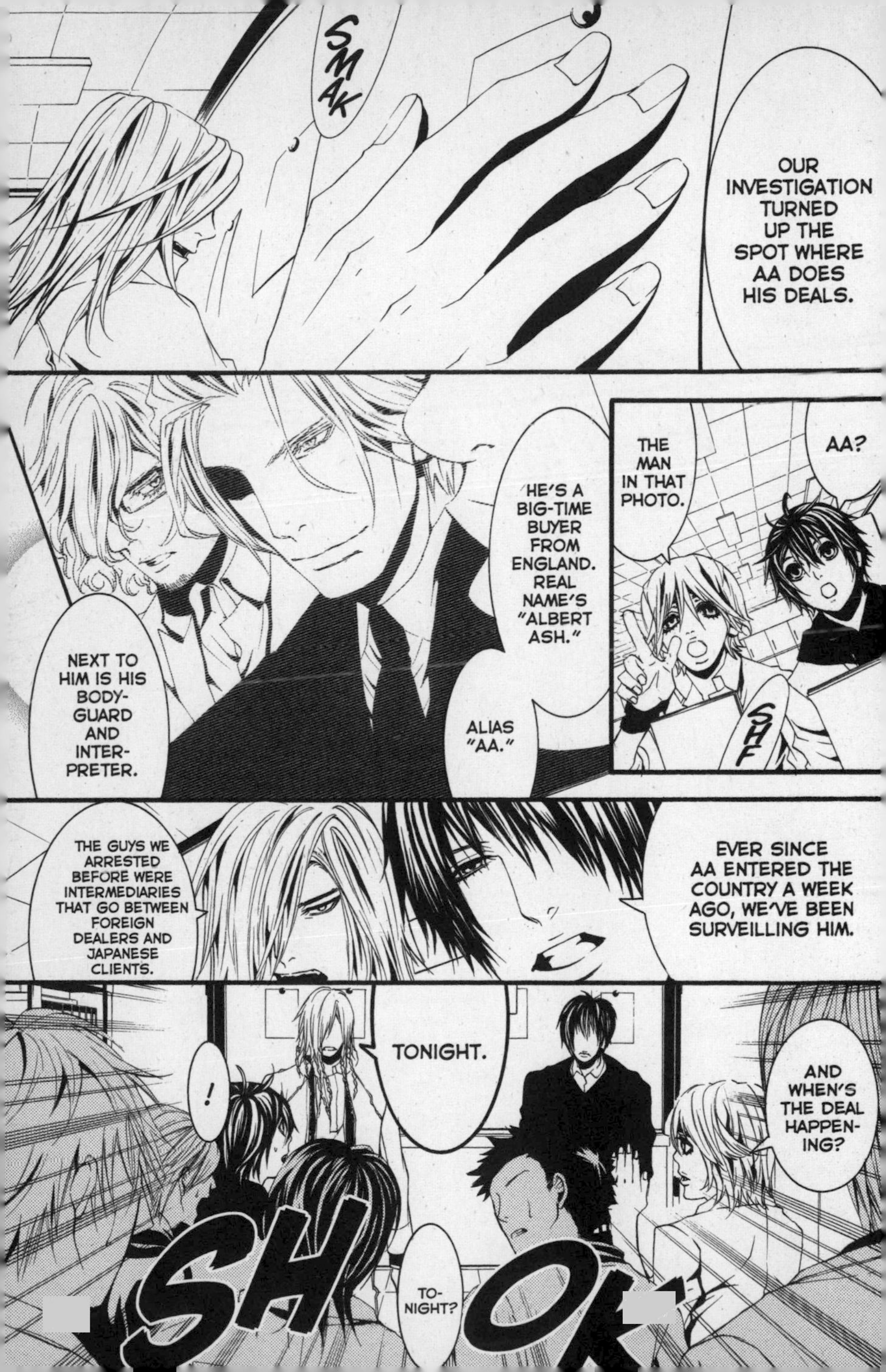
OUR INVESTIGATION TURNED UP THE SPOT WHERE AA DOES HIS DEALS.
SMAK
AA?
THE MAN IN THAT PHOTO.
SHF
HE'S A BIG-TIME BUYER FROM ENGLAND. REAL NAME'S "ALBERT ASH."
ALIAS "AA."
NEXT TO HIM IS HIS BODY-GUARD AND INTER-PRETER.
EVER SINCE AA ENTERED THE COUNTRY A WEEK AGO, WE'VE BEEN SURVEILLING HIM.
THE GUYS WE ARRESTED BEFORE WERE INTERMEDIARIES THAT GO BETWEEN FOREIGN DEALERS AND JAPANESE CLIENTS.
AND WHEN'S THE DEAL HAPPEN-ING?
TONIGHT.
!
TO-NIGHT?
SHOK

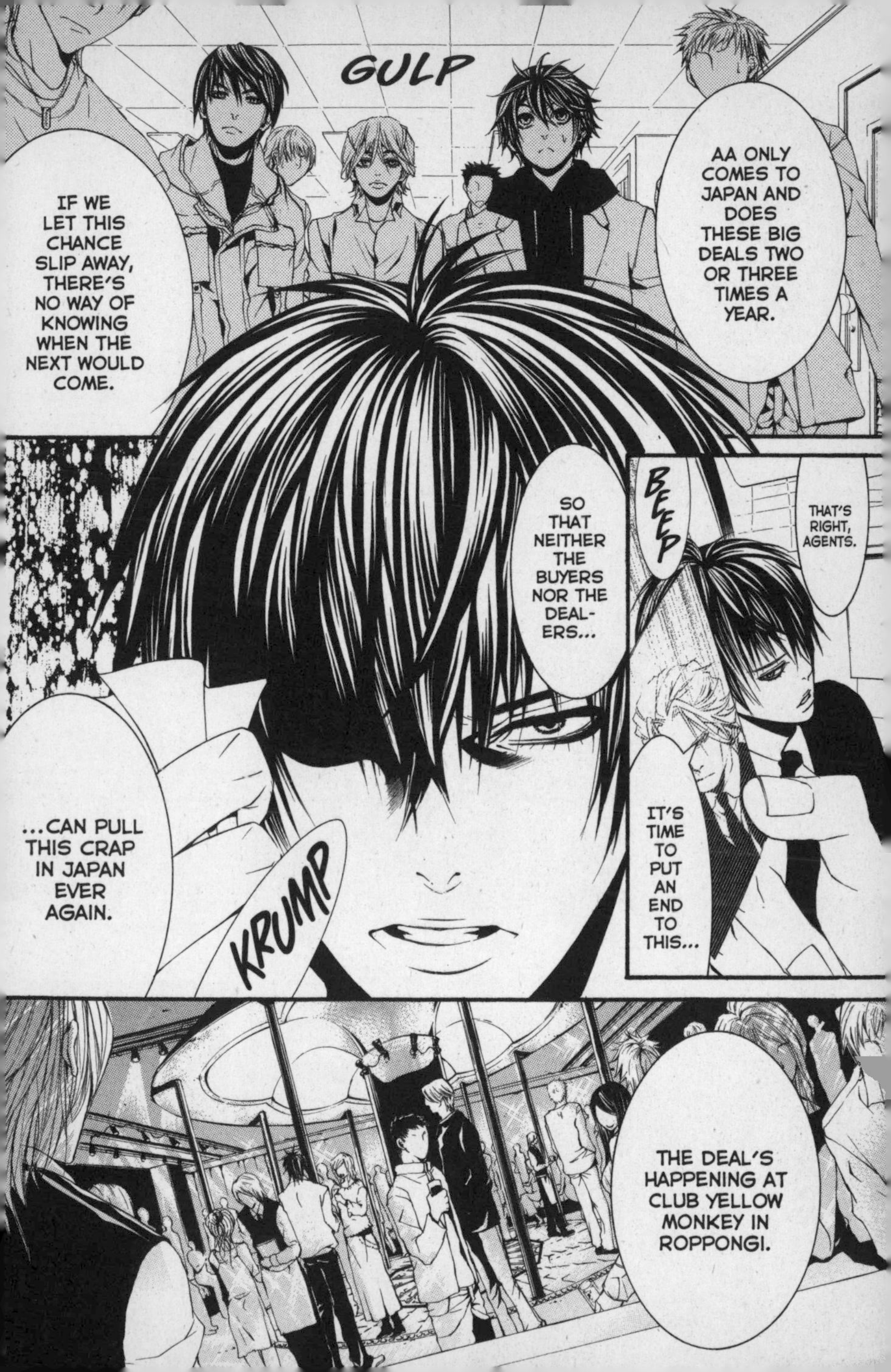
AA ONLY COMES TO JAPAN AND DOES THESE BIG DEALS TWO OR THREE TIMES A YEAR.
GULP
IF WE LET THIS CHANCE SLIP AWAY, THERE'S NO WAY OF KNOWING WHEN THE NEXT WOULD COME.
THAT'S RIGHT, AGENTS.
BEEP
IT'S TIME TO PUT AN END TO THIS...
SO THAT NEITHER THE BUYERS NOR THE DEAL-ERS...
...CAN PULL THIS CRAP IN JAPAN EVER AGAIN.
KRUMP
THE DEAL'S HAPPENING AT CLUB YELLOW MONKEY IN ROPPONGI.

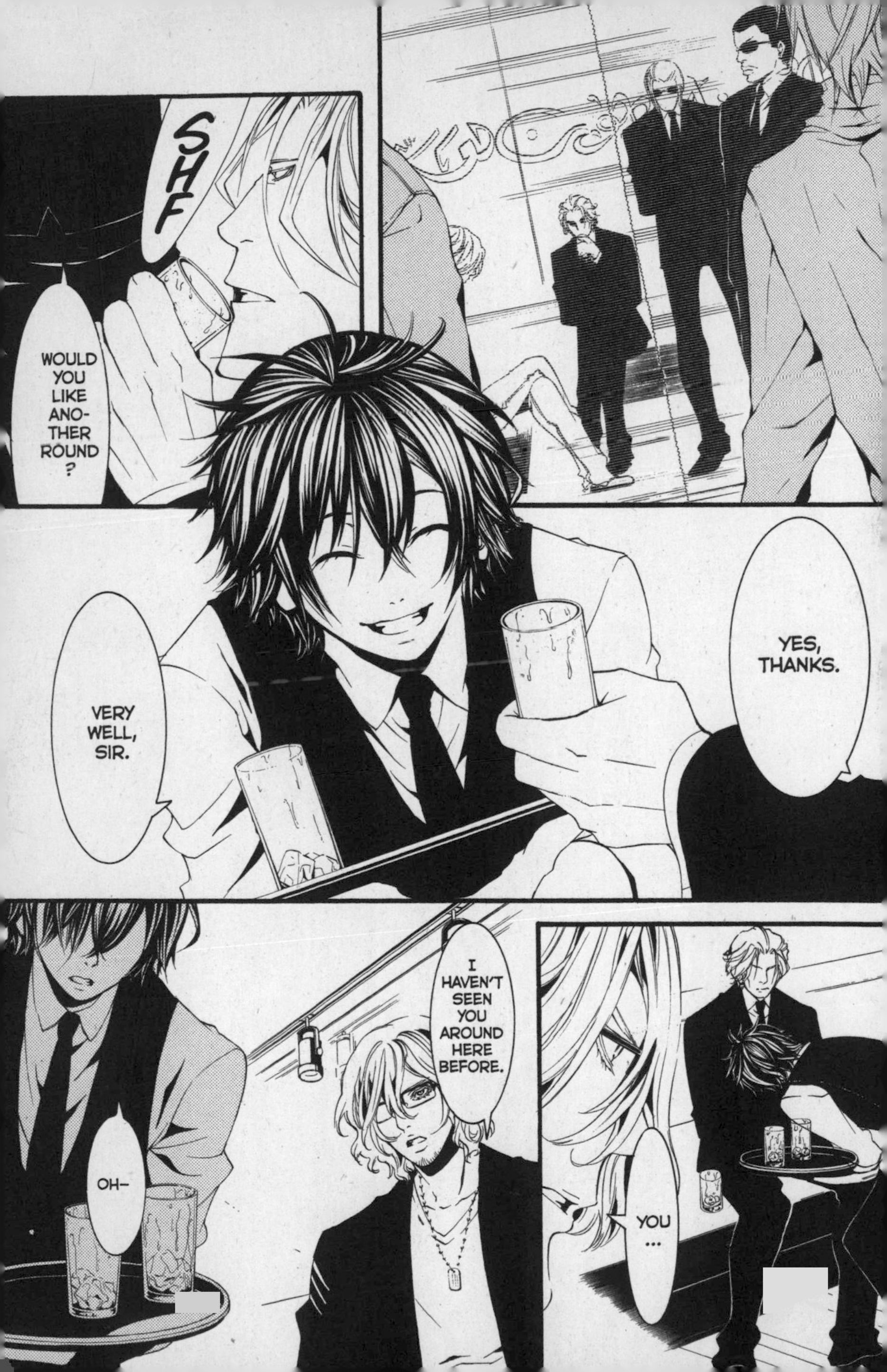
SHF
WOULD YOU LIKE ANO-THER ROUND?
YES, THANKS.
VERY WELL, SIR.
YOU ...
I HAVEN'T SEEN YOU AROUND HERE BEFORE.
OH–

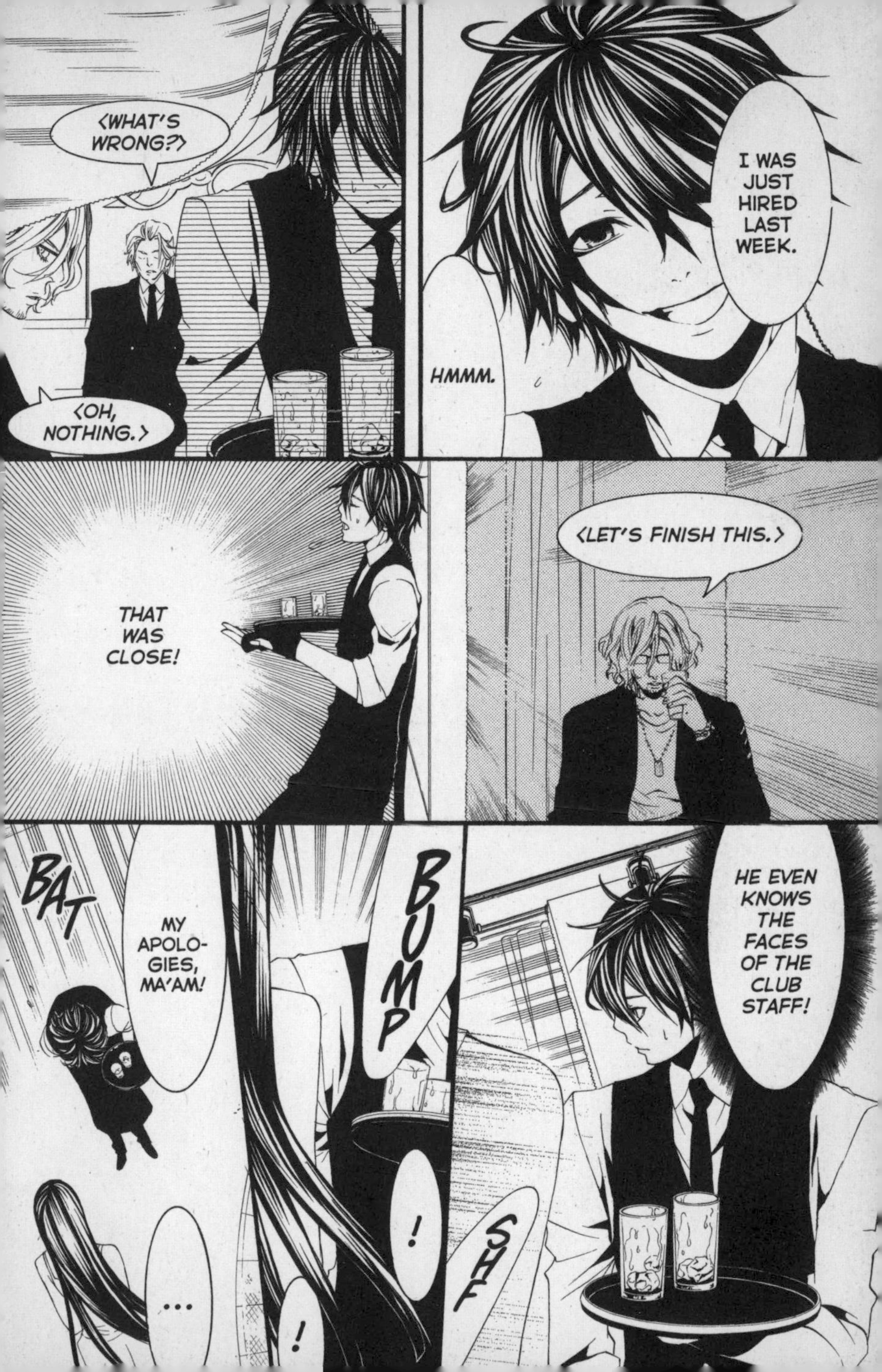
I WAS JUST HIRED LAST WEEK.
HMMM.
<WHAT'S WRONG?>
<OH, NOTHING.>
<LET'S FINISH THIS.>
THAT WAS CLOSE!
HE EVEN KNOWS THE FACES OF THE CLUB STAFF!
BUMP
!
SHF
!
BAT
MY APOLOGIES, MA'AM!
...

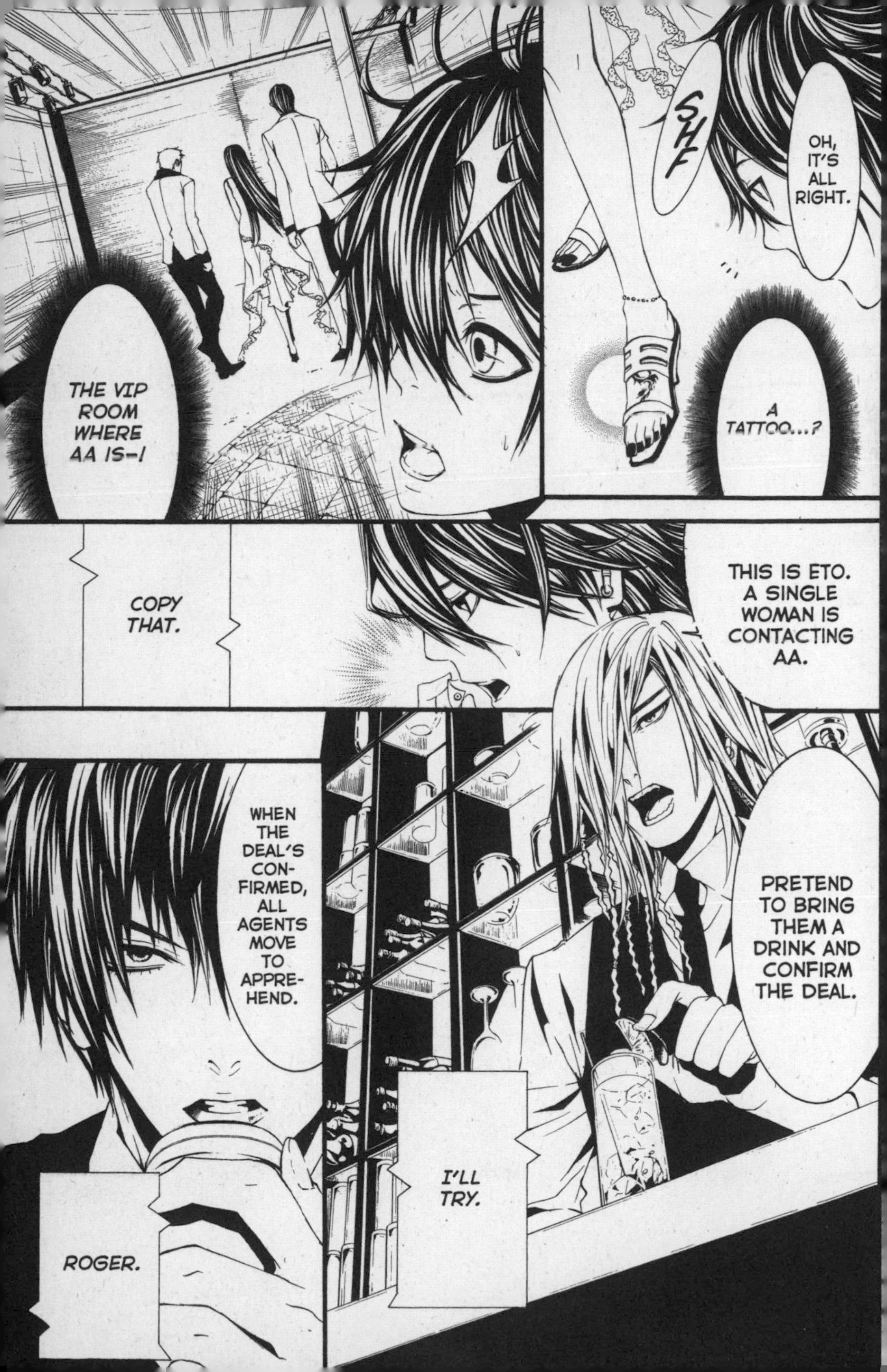
SHF
OH, IT'S ALL RIGHT.
A TATTOO...?
THE VIP ROOM WHERE AA IS—!
THIS IS ETO. A SINGLE WOMAN IS CONTACTING AA.
COPY THAT.
PRETEND TO BRING THEM A DRINK AND CONFIRM THE DEAL.
I'LL TRY.
WHEN THE DEAL'S CONFIRMED, ALL AGENTS MOVE TO APPREHEND.
ROGER.

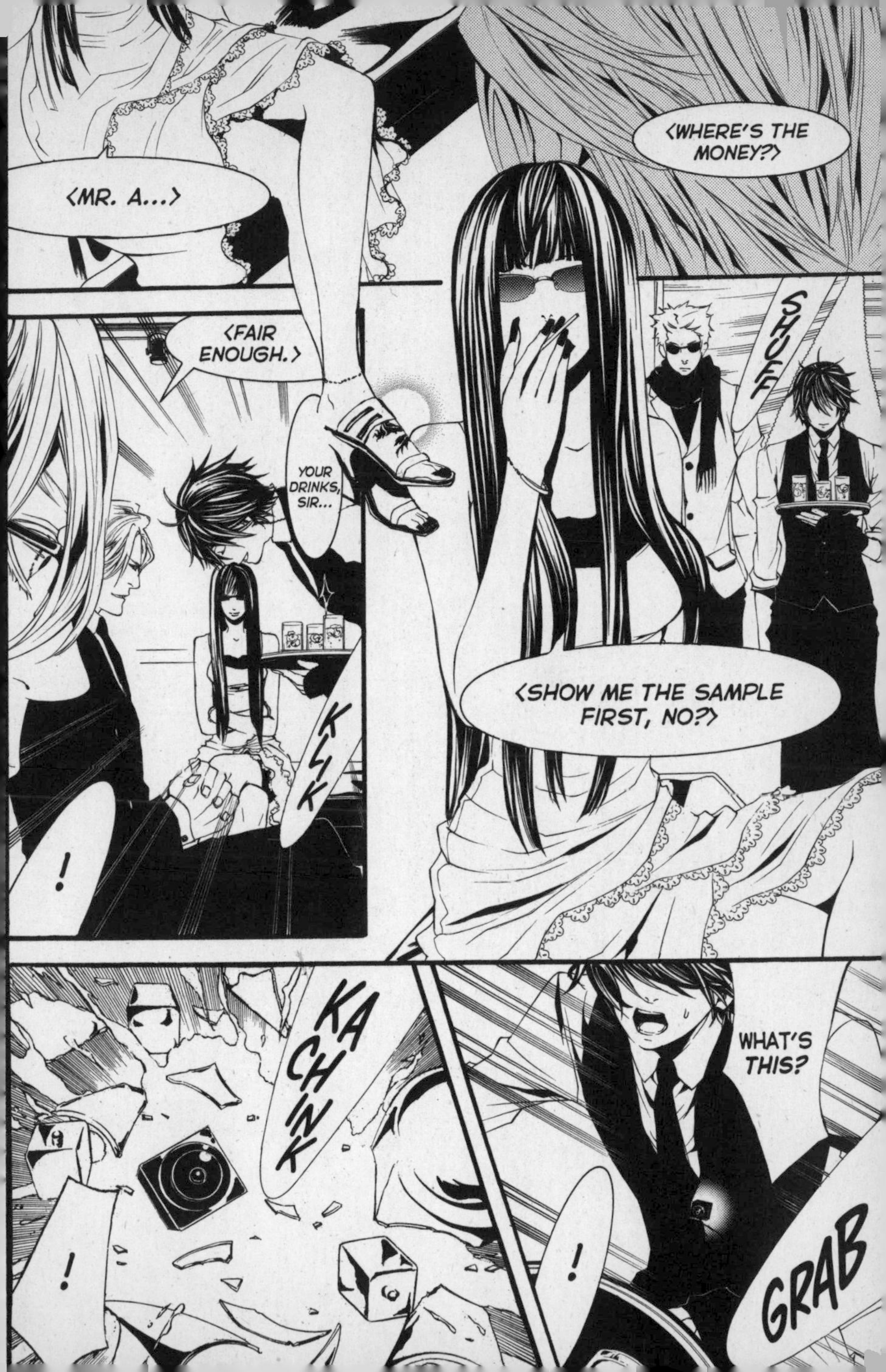

<WHERE'S THE MONEY?>
SHUFF
<SHOW ME THE SAMPLE FIRST, NO?>
<MR. A...>
<FAIR ENOUGH.>
YOUR DRINKS, SIR...
KLIK
!
WHAT'S THIS?
!
GRAB
KACHINK
!

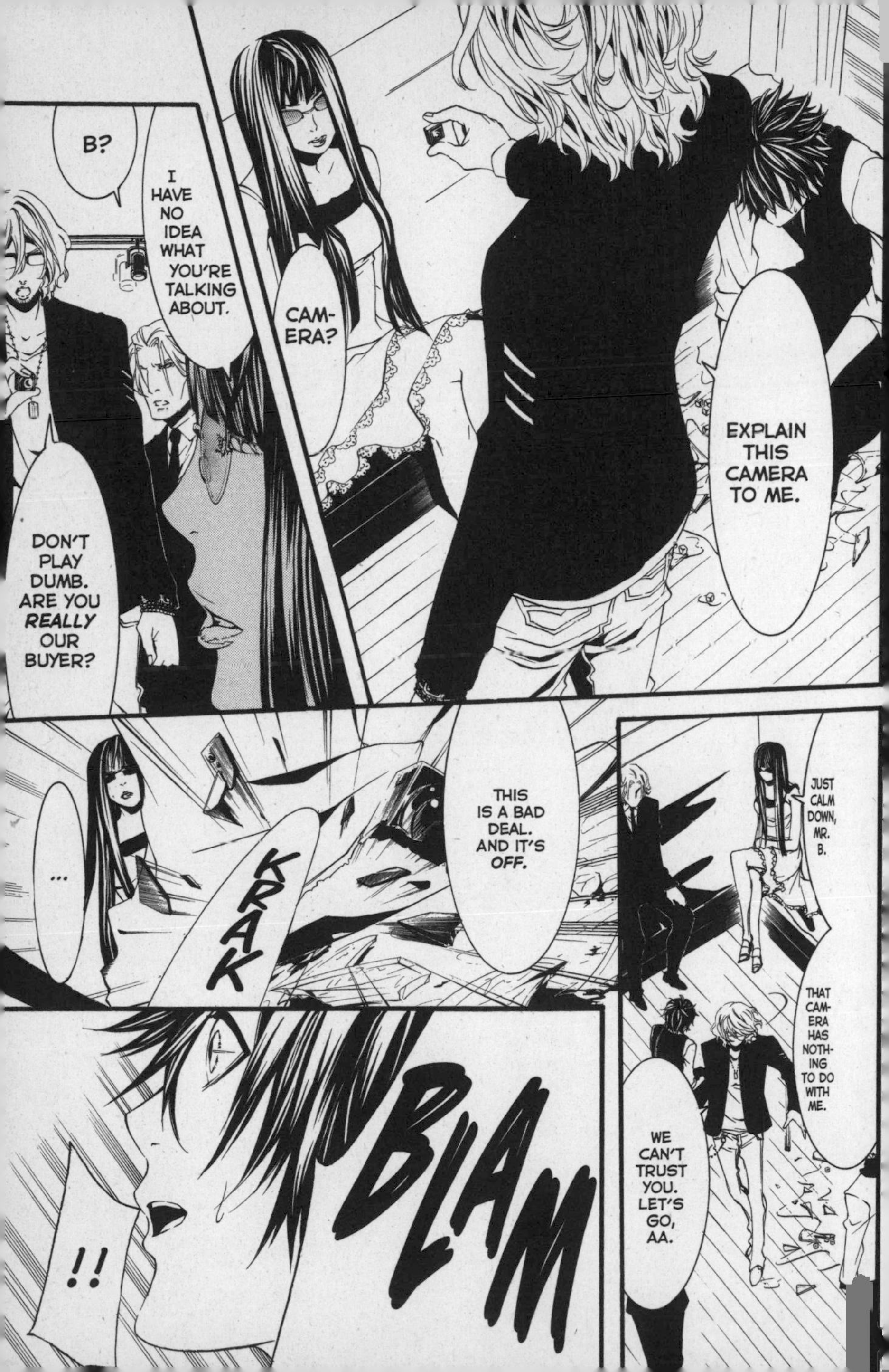
EXPLAIN THIS CAMERA TO ME.
CAM-ERA?
I HAVE NO IDEA WHAT YOU'RE TALKING ABOUT.
B?
DON'T PLAY DUMB. ARE YOU *REALLY* OUR BUYER?
JUST CALM DOWN, MR. B.
THAT CAM-ERA HAS NOTH-ING TO DO WITH ME.
WE CAN'T TRUST YOU. LET'S GO, AA.
THIS IS A BAD DEAL. AND IT'S *OFF.*
KRAK
...
BLAM
!!

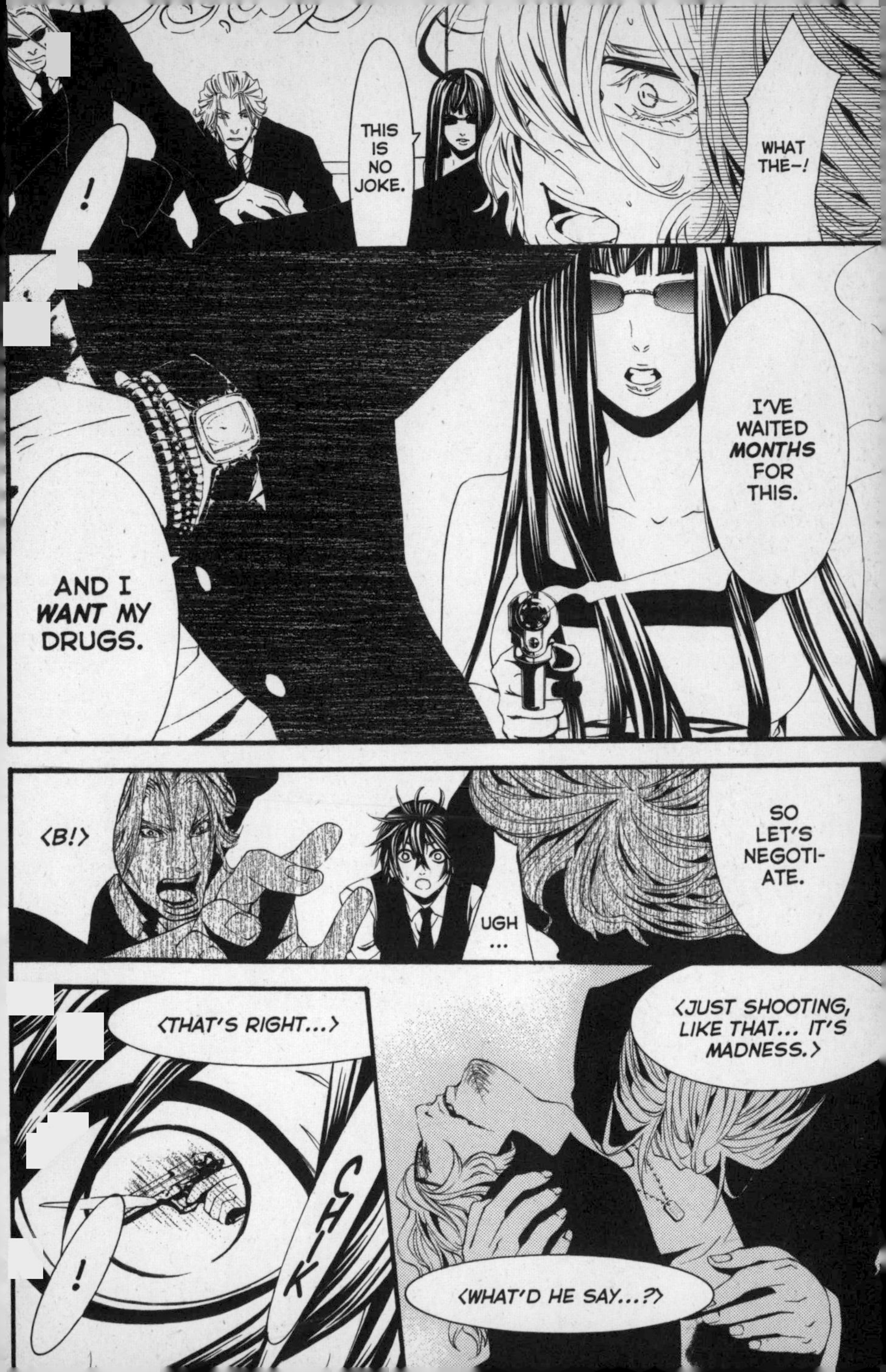
WHAT THE–!
THIS IS NO JOKE.
!
I'VE WAITED *MONTHS* FOR THIS.
AND I *WANT* MY DRUGS.
SO LET'S NEGOTI-ATE.
UGH ...
<B!>
<JUST SHOOTING, LIKE THAT... IT'S MADNESS.>
<WHAT'D HE SAY...?>
<THAT'S RIGHT...>
CHIK
!

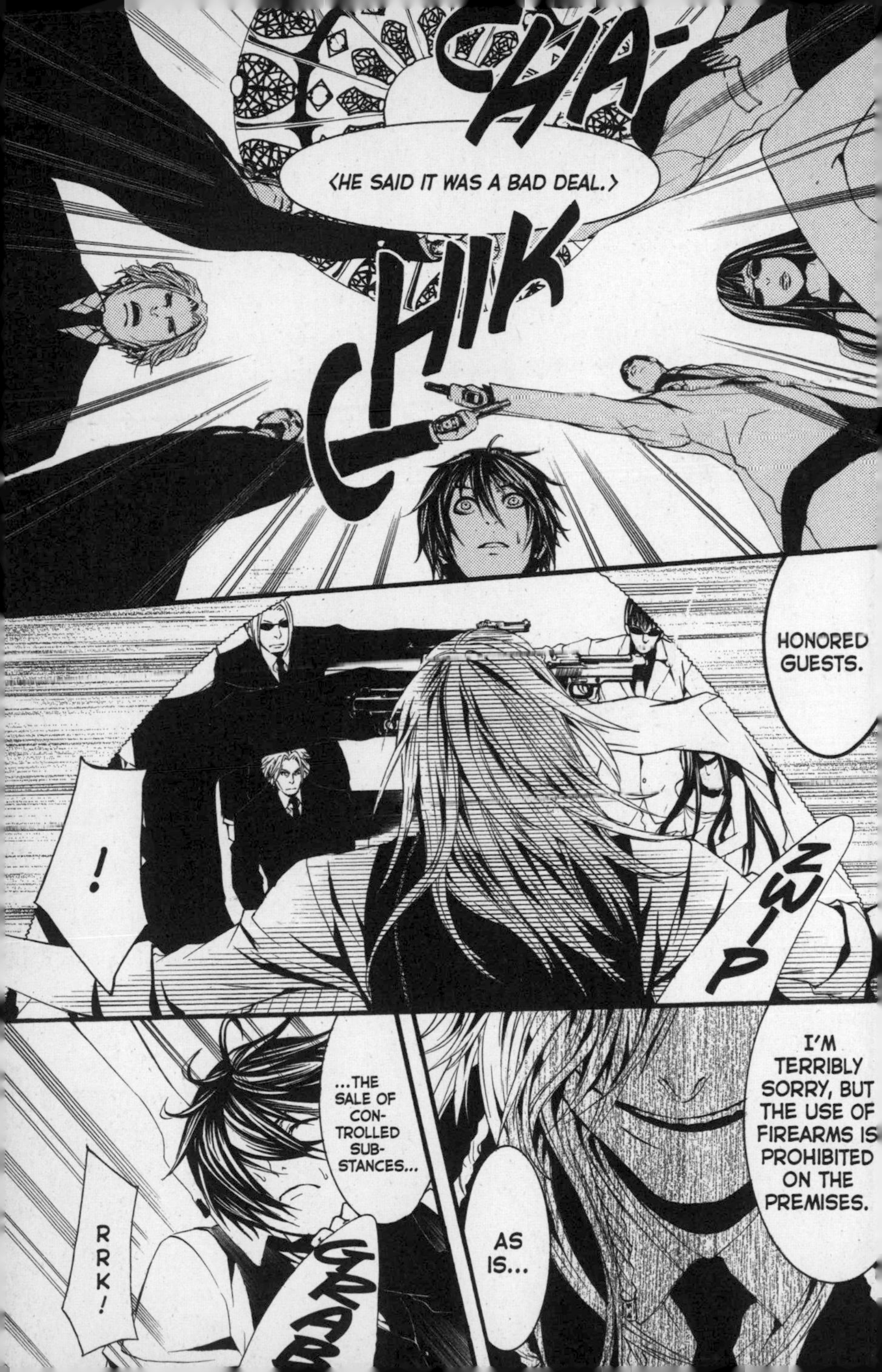
CHA-
<HE SAID IT WAS A BAD DEAL.>
CHIK
HONORED GUESTS.
ZWIP
!
I'M TERRIBLY SORRY, BUT THE USE OF FIREARMS IS PROHIBITED ON THE PREMISES.
AS IS...
...THE SALE OF CON-TROLLED SUB-STANCES...
GRAB
RRK!

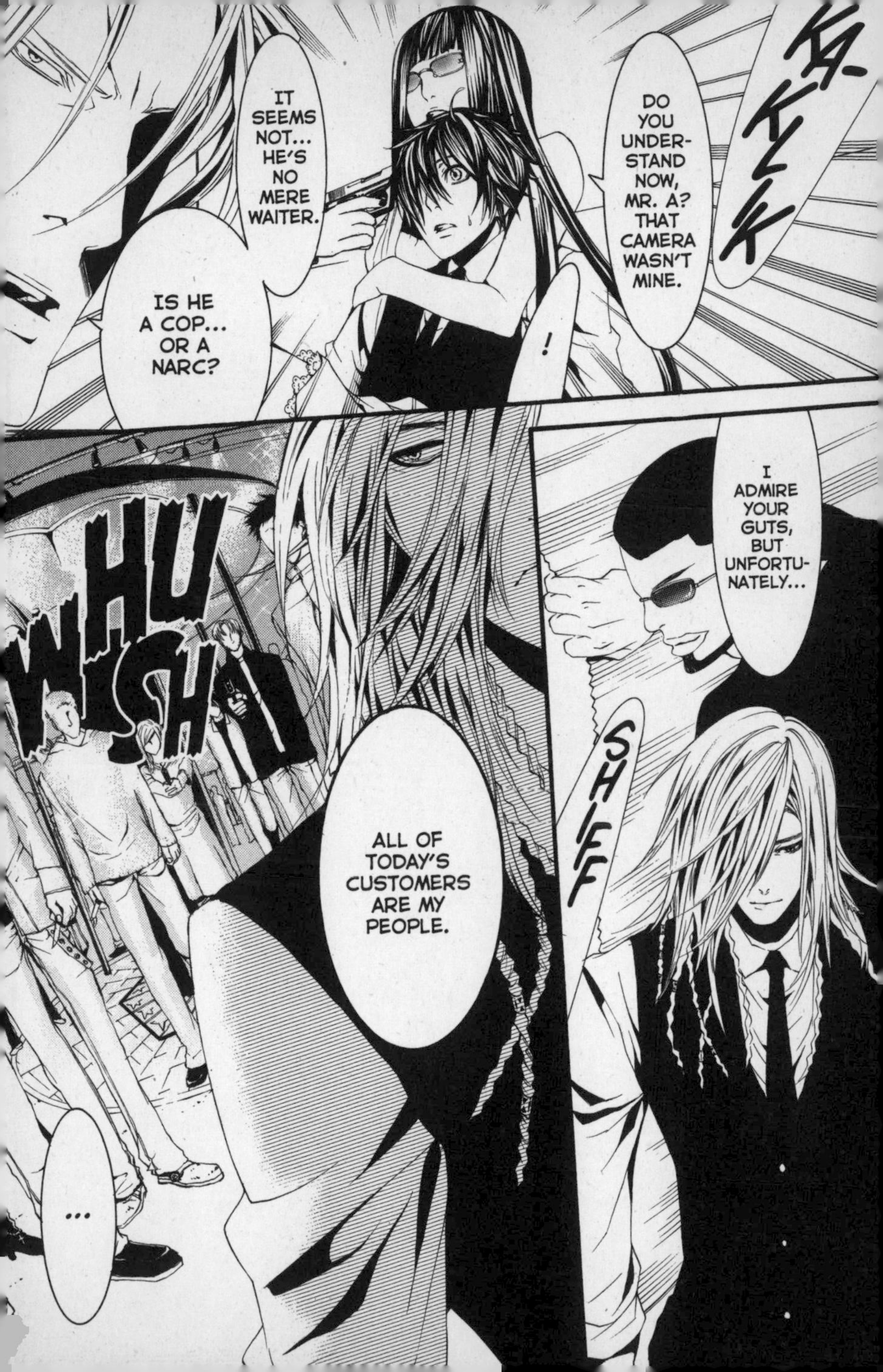
KA-KLIK
DO YOU UNDER-STAND NOW, MR. A? THAT CAMERA WASN'T MINE.
!
IT SEEMS NOT... HE'S NO MERE WAITER.
IS HE A COP... OR A NARC?
I ADMIRE YOUR GUTS, BUT UNFORTU-NATELY...
SHIFF
ALL OF TODAY'S CUSTOMERS ARE MY PEOPLE.
WHUSH
...

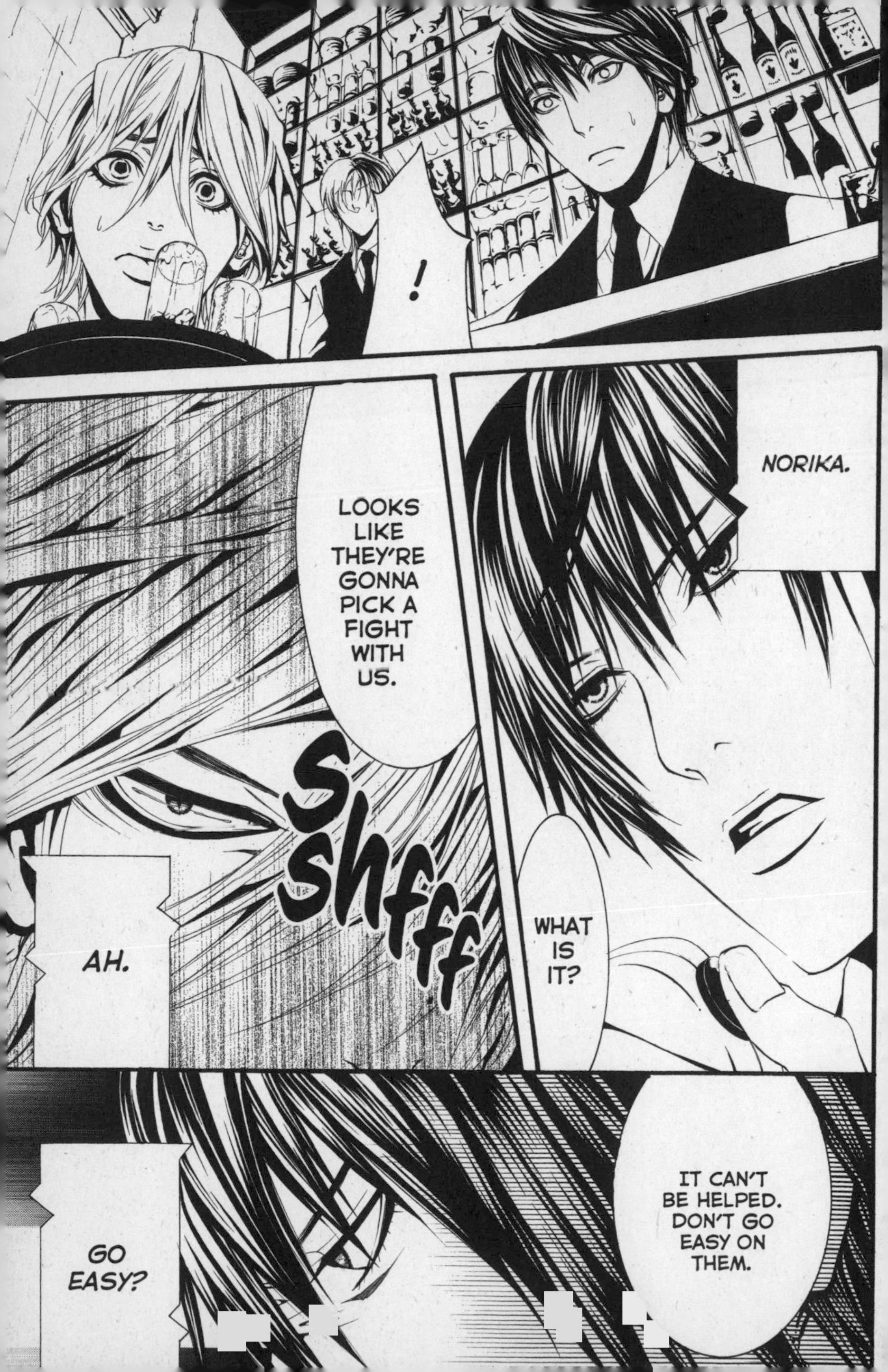
!
NORIKA.
WHAT IS IT?
LOOKS LIKE THEY'RE GONNA PICK A FIGHT WITH US.
SHFFF
AH.
IT CAN'T BE HELPED. DON'T GO EASY ON THEM.
GO EASY?

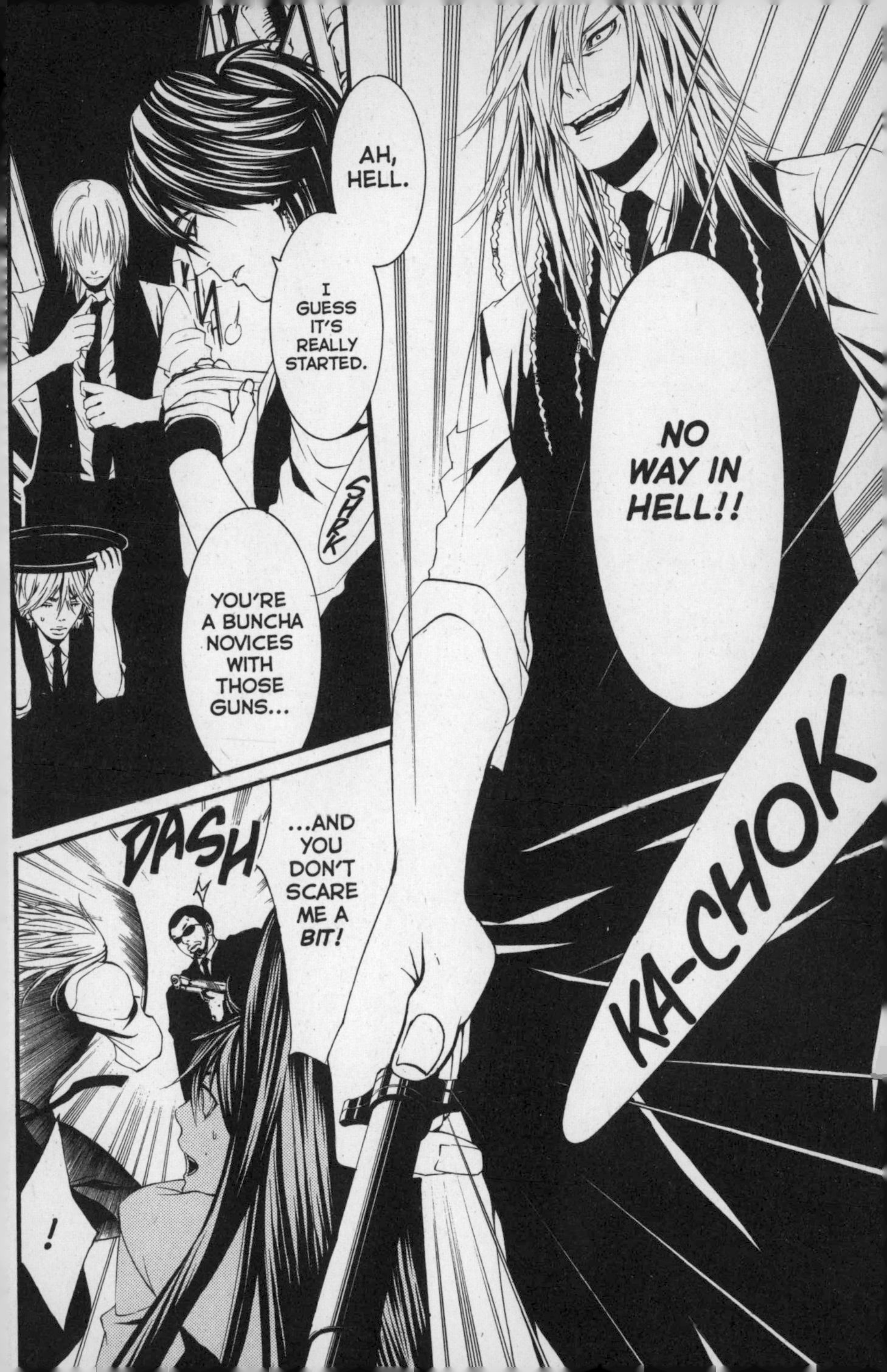
NO WAY IN HELL!!
KA-CHOK
AH, HELL.
I GUESS IT'S REALLY STARTED.
SHRK
YOU'RE A BUNCHA NOVICES WITH THOSE GUNS...
DASH
...AND YOU DON'T SCARE ME A BIT!
!

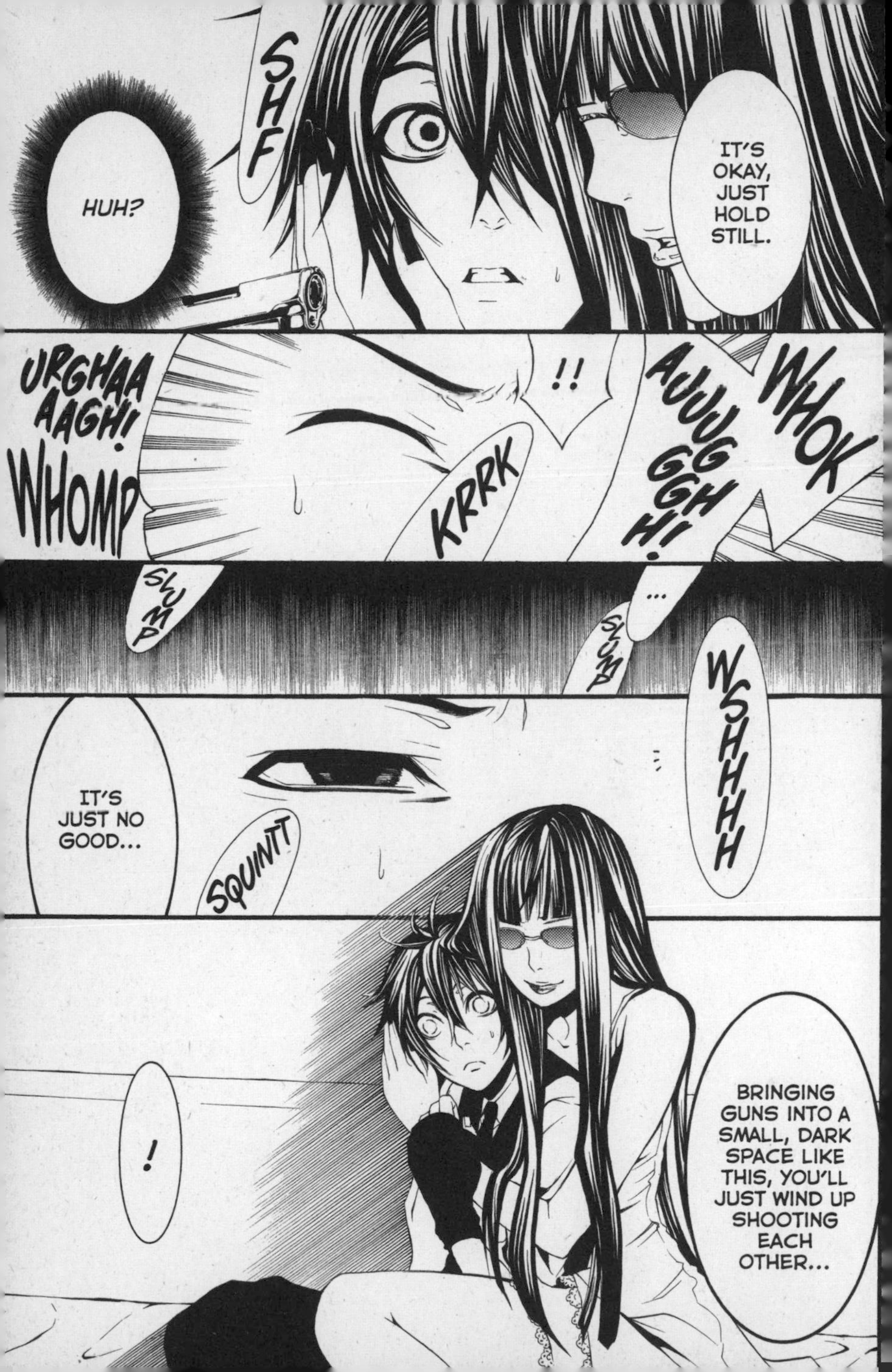
IT'S OKAY, JUST HOLD STILL.
SHF
HUH?
WHOK
AUUUGGGH!
!!
KRRK
URGHAAAAGH!
WHOMP
...
SLUMP
SLUMP
WSHHHHH
SQUINTT
IT'S JUST NO GOOD...
BRINGING GUNS INTO A SMALL, DARK SPACE LIKE THIS, YOU'LL JUST WIND UP SHOOTING EACH OTHER...
!

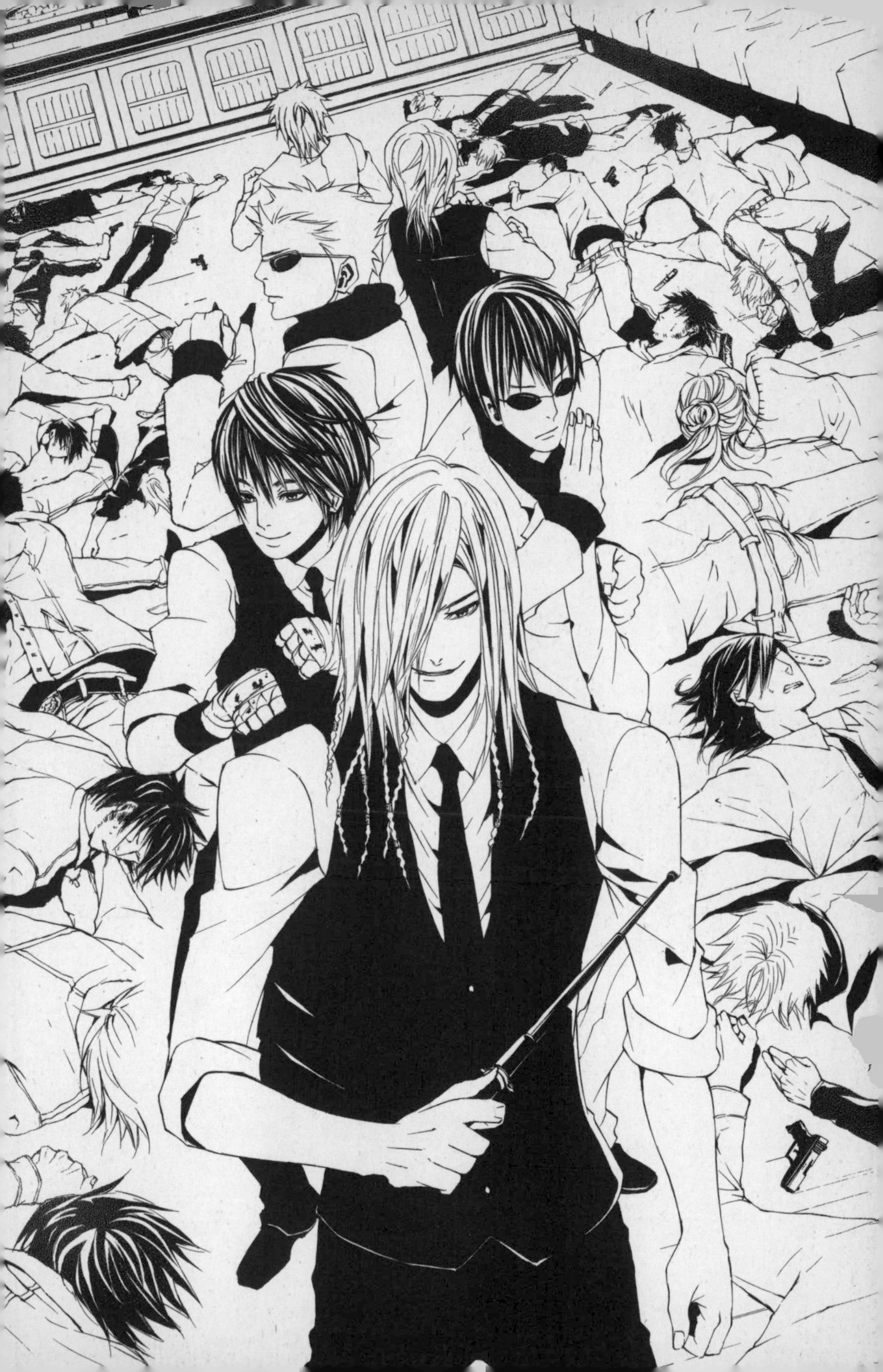

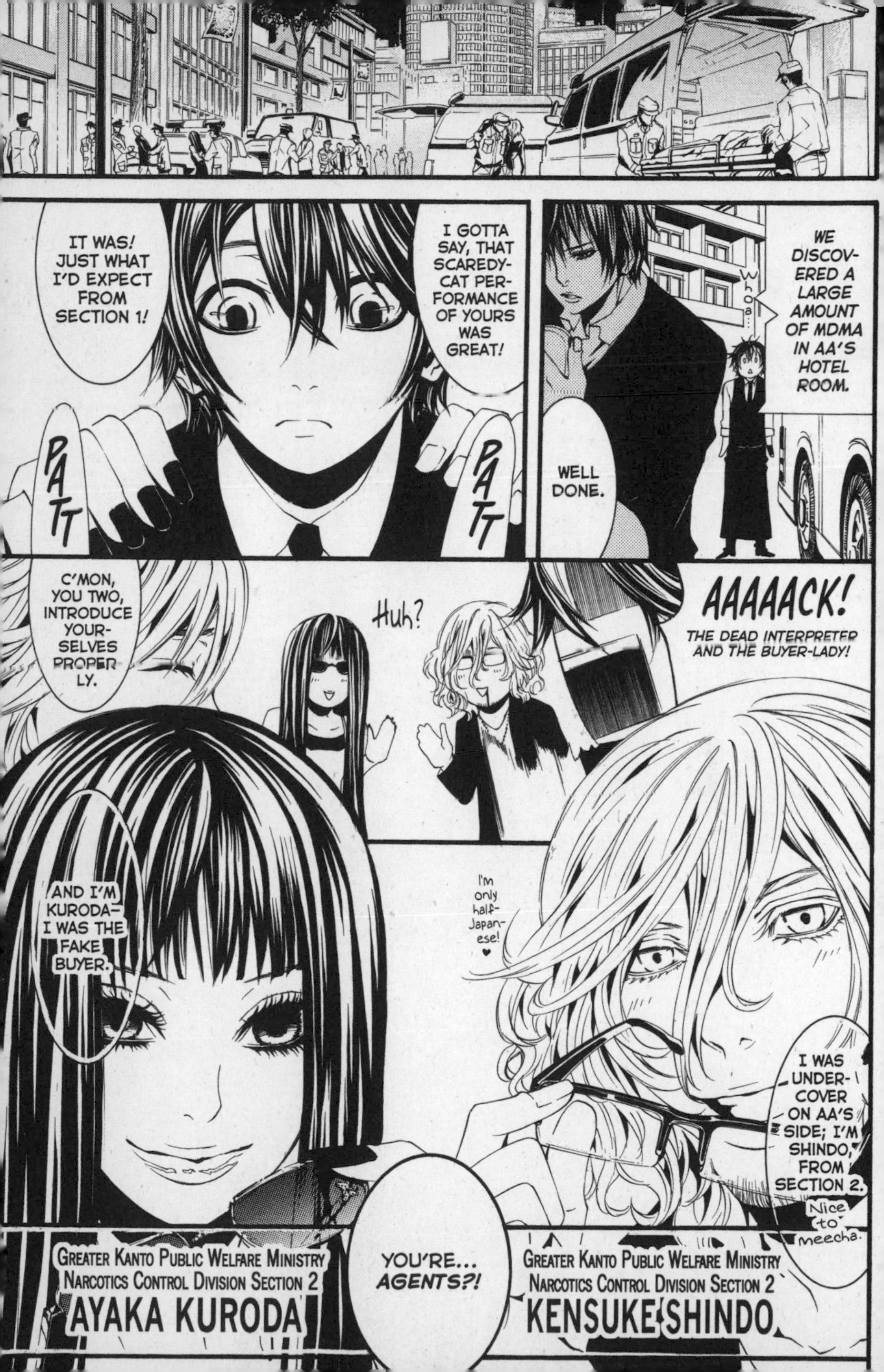

I GOTTA SAY, THAT SCAREDY-CAT PERFORMANCE OF YOURS WAS GREAT!
PATT
IT WAS! JUST WHAT I'D EXPECT FROM SECTION 1!
PATT
WE DISCOVERED A LARGE AMOUNT OF MDMA IN AA'S HOTEL ROOM.
Whoa...
WELL DONE.
AAAAACK!
THE DEAD INTERPRETER AND THE BUYER-LADY!
Huh?
C'MON, YOU TWO, INTRODUCE YOURSELVES PROPERLY.
I WAS UNDERCOVER ON AA'S SIDE; I'M SHINDO, FROM SECTION 2.
Nice to meecha.
I'm only half-Japanese! ♥
AND I'M KURODA-I WAS THE FAKE BUYER.
GREATER KANTO PUBLIC WELFARE MINISTRY NARCOTICS CONTROL DIVISION SECTION 2
KENSUKE SHINDO
YOU'RE... AGENTS?!
GREATER KANTO PUBLIC WELFARE MINISTRY NARCOTICS CONTROL DIVISION SECTION 2
AYAKA KURODA

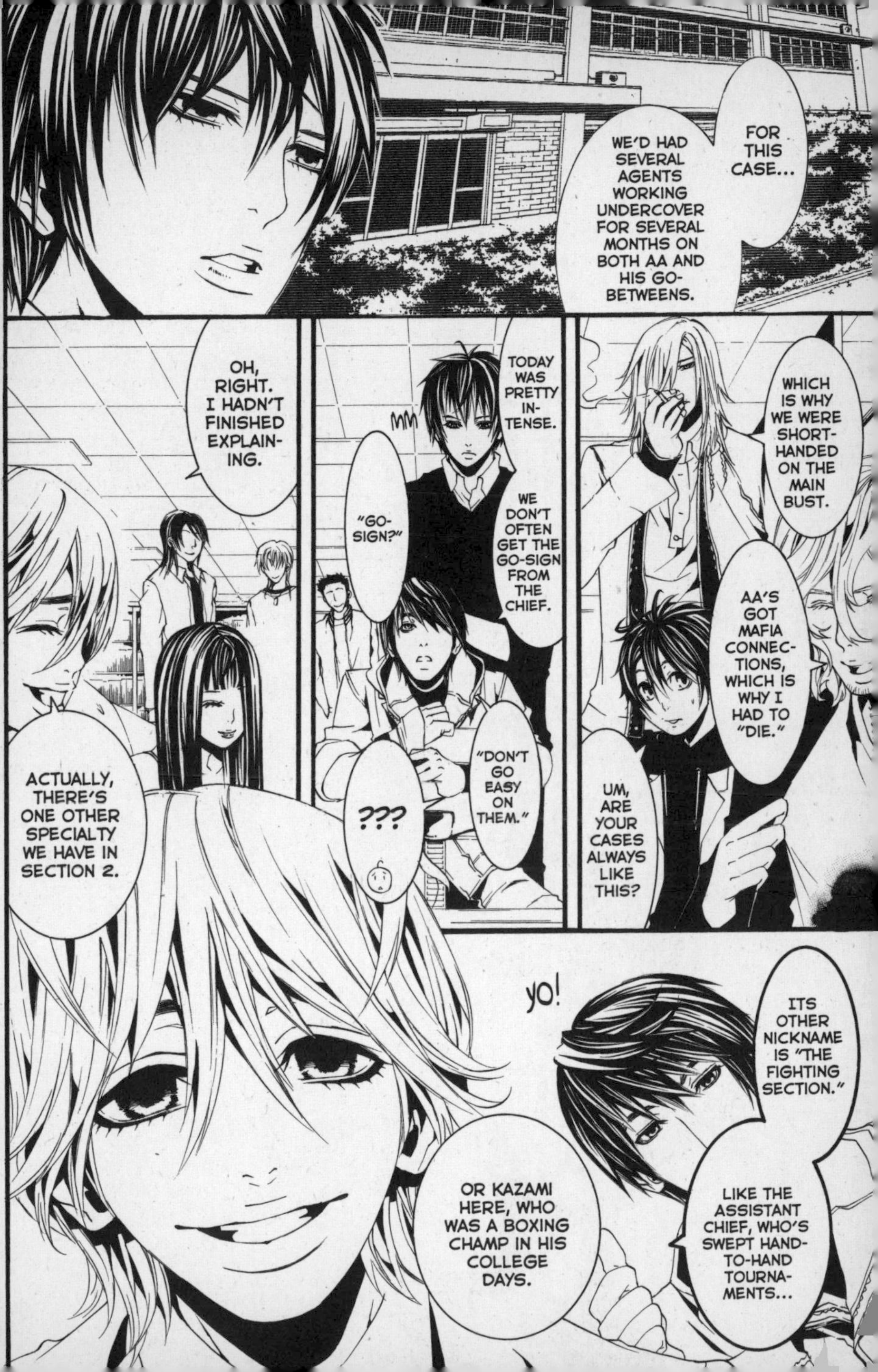
FOR THIS CASE...
WE'D HAD SEVERAL AGENTS WORKING UNDERCOVER FOR SEVERAL MONTHS ON BOTH AA AND HIS GO-BETWEENS.
WHICH IS WHY WE WERE SHORT-HANDED ON THE MAIN BUST.
AA'S GOT MAFIA CONNECTIONS, WHICH IS WHY I HAD TO "DIE."
UM, ARE YOUR CASES ALWAYS LIKE THIS?
TODAY WAS PRETTY IN-TENSE.
MM
WE DON'T OFTEN GET THE GO-SIGN FROM THE CHIEF.
"GO-SIGN?"
"DON'T GO EASY ON THEM."
???
OH, RIGHT. I HADN'T FINISHED EXPLAIN-ING.
ACTUALLY, THERE'S ONE OTHER SPECIALTY WE HAVE IN SECTION 2.
ITS OTHER NICKNAME IS "THE FIGHTING SECTION."
YO!
LIKE THE ASSISTANT CHIEF, WHO'S SWEPT HAND-TO-HAND TOURNA-MENTS...
OR KAZAMI HERE, WHO WAS A BOXING CHAMP IN HIS COLLEGE DAYS.

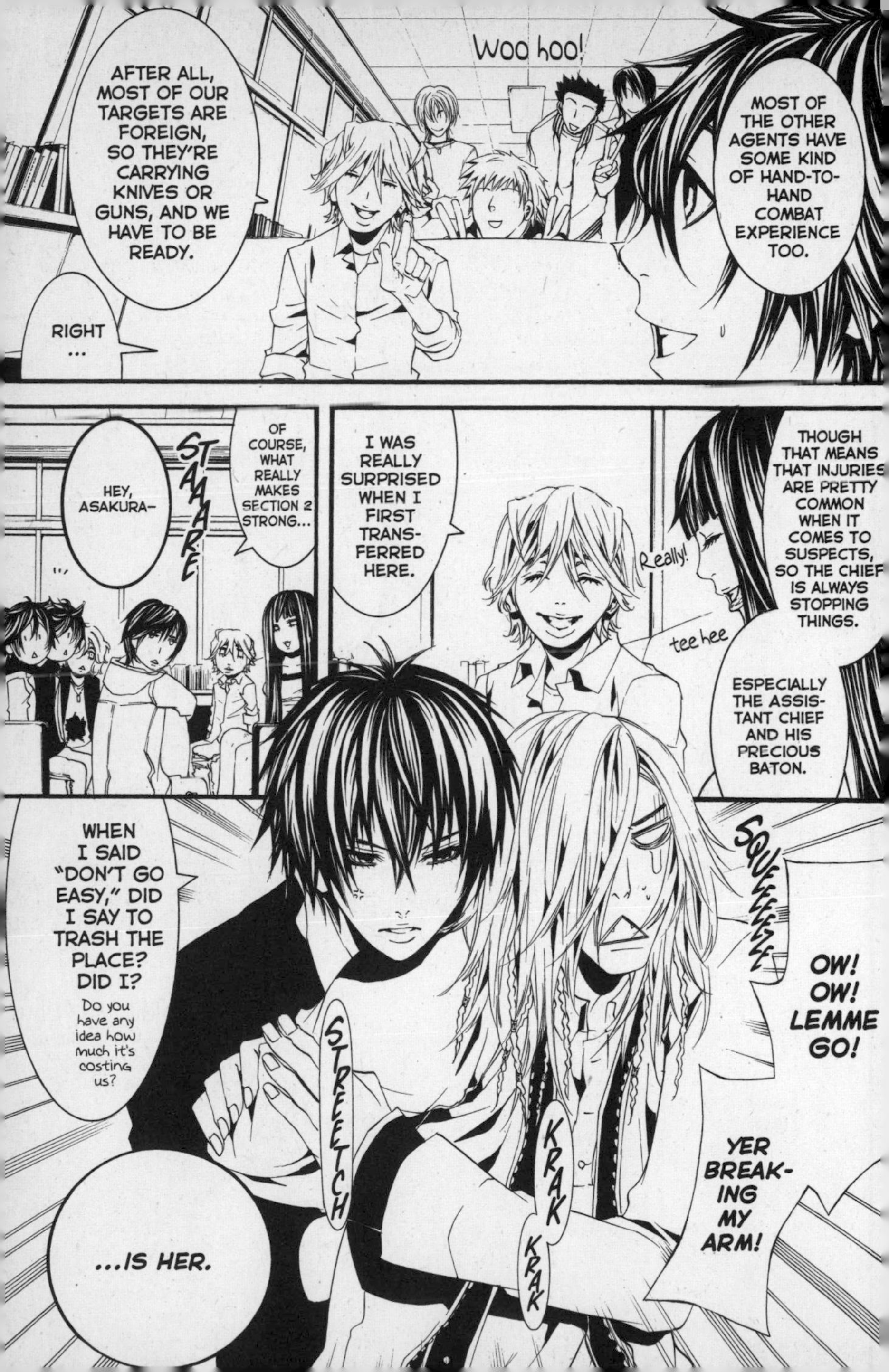
MOST OF THE OTHER AGENTS HAVE SOME KIND OF HAND-TO-HAND COMBAT EXPERIENCE TOO.
Woo hoo!
AFTER ALL, MOST OF OUR TARGETS ARE FOREIGN, SO THEY'RE CARRYING KNIVES OR GUNS, AND WE HAVE TO BE READY.
RIGHT ...
THOUGH THAT MEANS THAT INJURIES ARE PRETTY COMMON WHEN IT COMES TO SUSPECTS, SO THE CHIEF IS ALWAYS STOPPING THINGS.
Really!
tee hee
ESPECIALLY THE ASSISTANT CHIEF AND HIS PRECIOUS BATON.
I WAS REALLY SURPRISED WHEN I FIRST TRANSFERRED HERE.
OF COURSE, WHAT REALLY MAKES SECTION 2 STRONG...
STAAAARE
HEY, ASAKURA-
SQUEEEEEZE
OW! OW! LEMME GO!
YER BREAKING MY ARM!
WHEN I SAID "DON'T GO EASY," DID I SAY TO TRASH THE PLACE? DID I?
Do you have any idea how much it's costing us?
STREEETCH
KRAK KRAK KRAK
...IS HER.

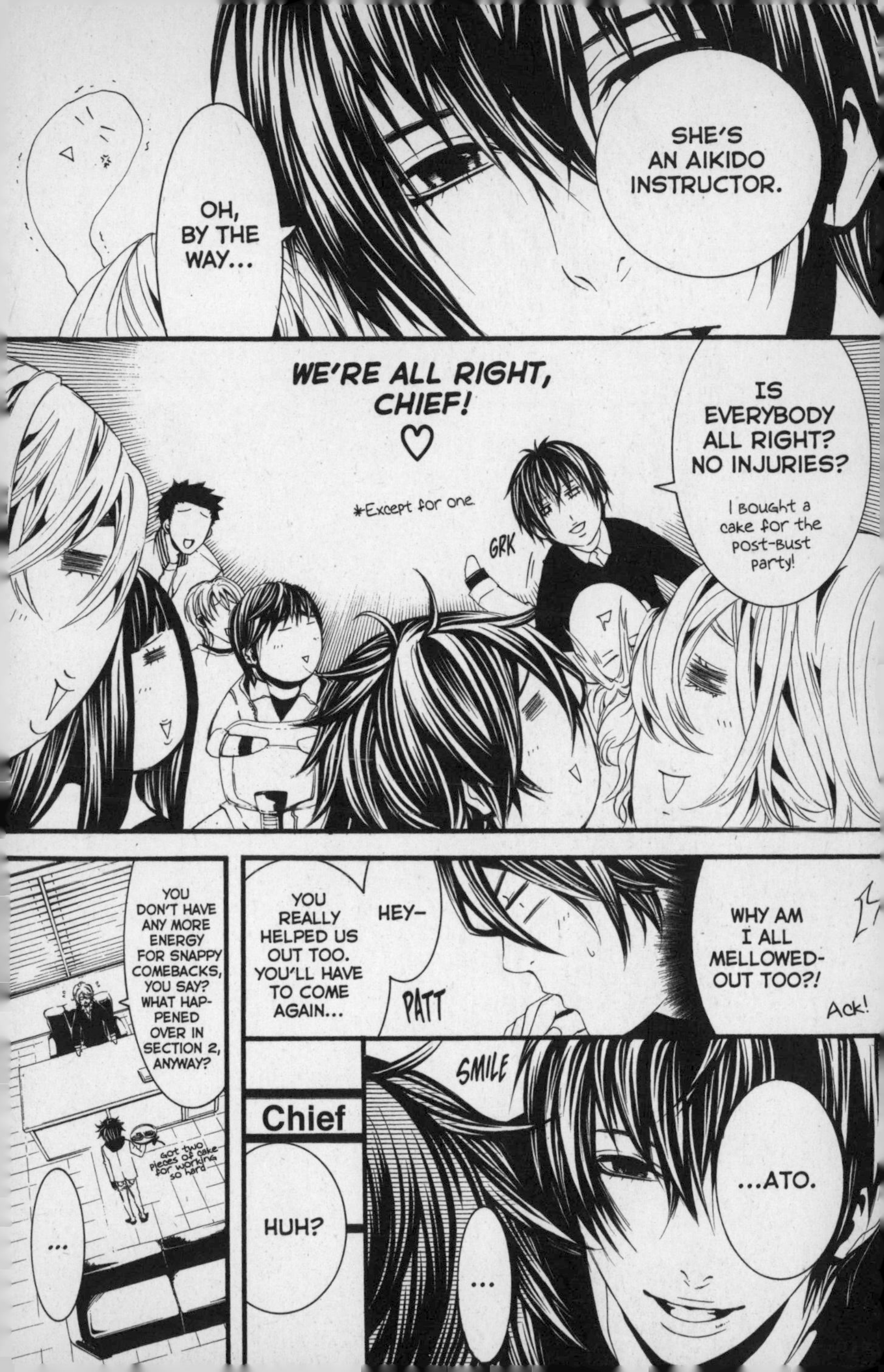
SHE'S AN AIKIDO INSTRUCTOR.
OH, BY THE WAY...
IS EVERYBODY ALL RIGHT? NO INJURIES?
I bought a cake for the post-bust party!
GRK
WE'RE ALL RIGHT, CHIEF! ♡
*Except for one.
WHY AM I ALL MELLOWED-OUT TOO?!
Ack!
HEY—
PATT
YOU REALLY HELPED US OUT TOO. YOU'LL HAVE TO COME AGAIN...
SMILE
...ATO.
...
Chief
HUH?
YOU DON'T HAVE ANY MORE ENERGY FOR SNAPPY COMEBACKS, YOU SAY? WHAT HAPPENED OVER IN SECTION 2, ANYWAY?
Got two pieces of cake for working so hard
...

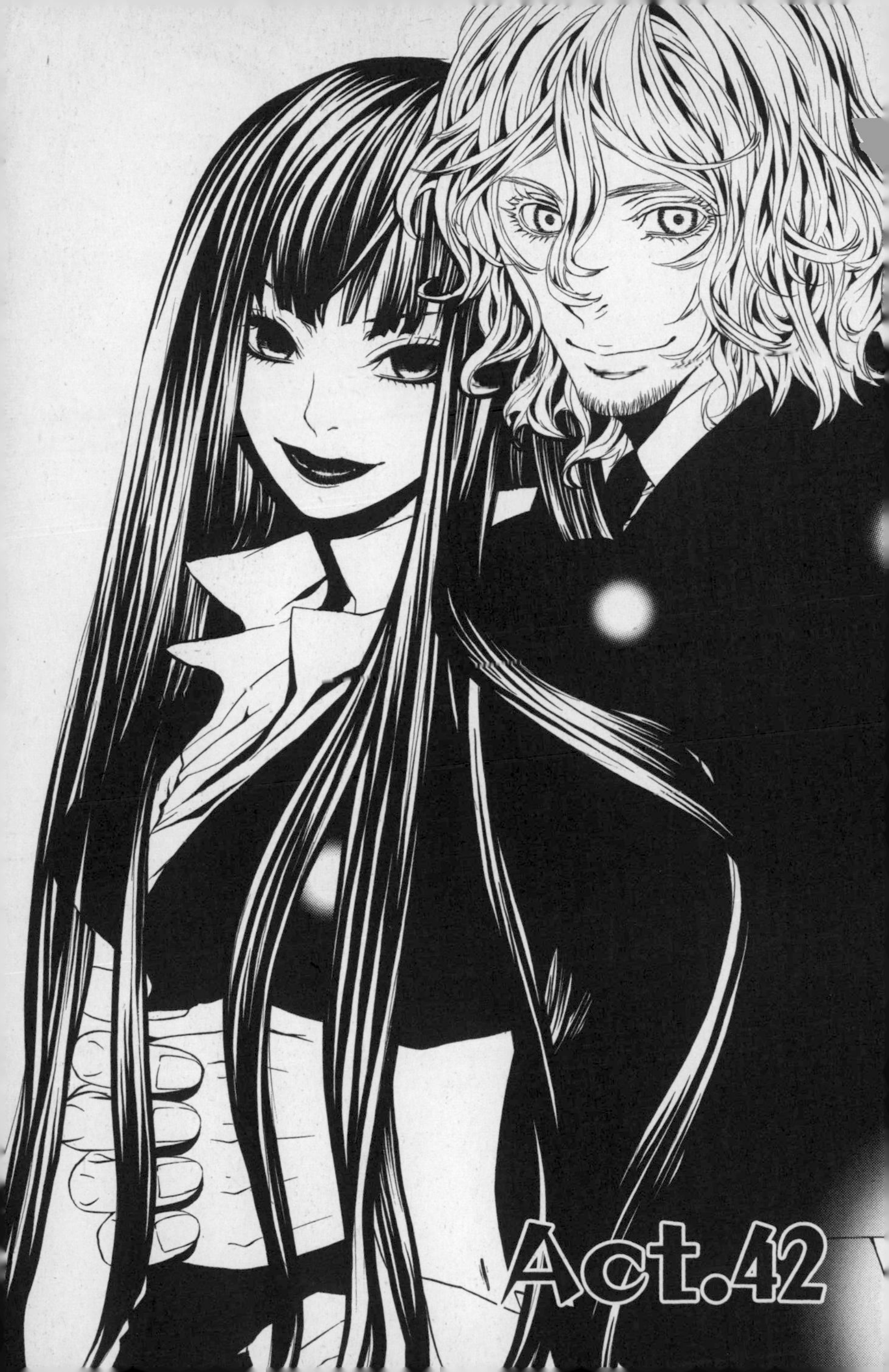
Act.42

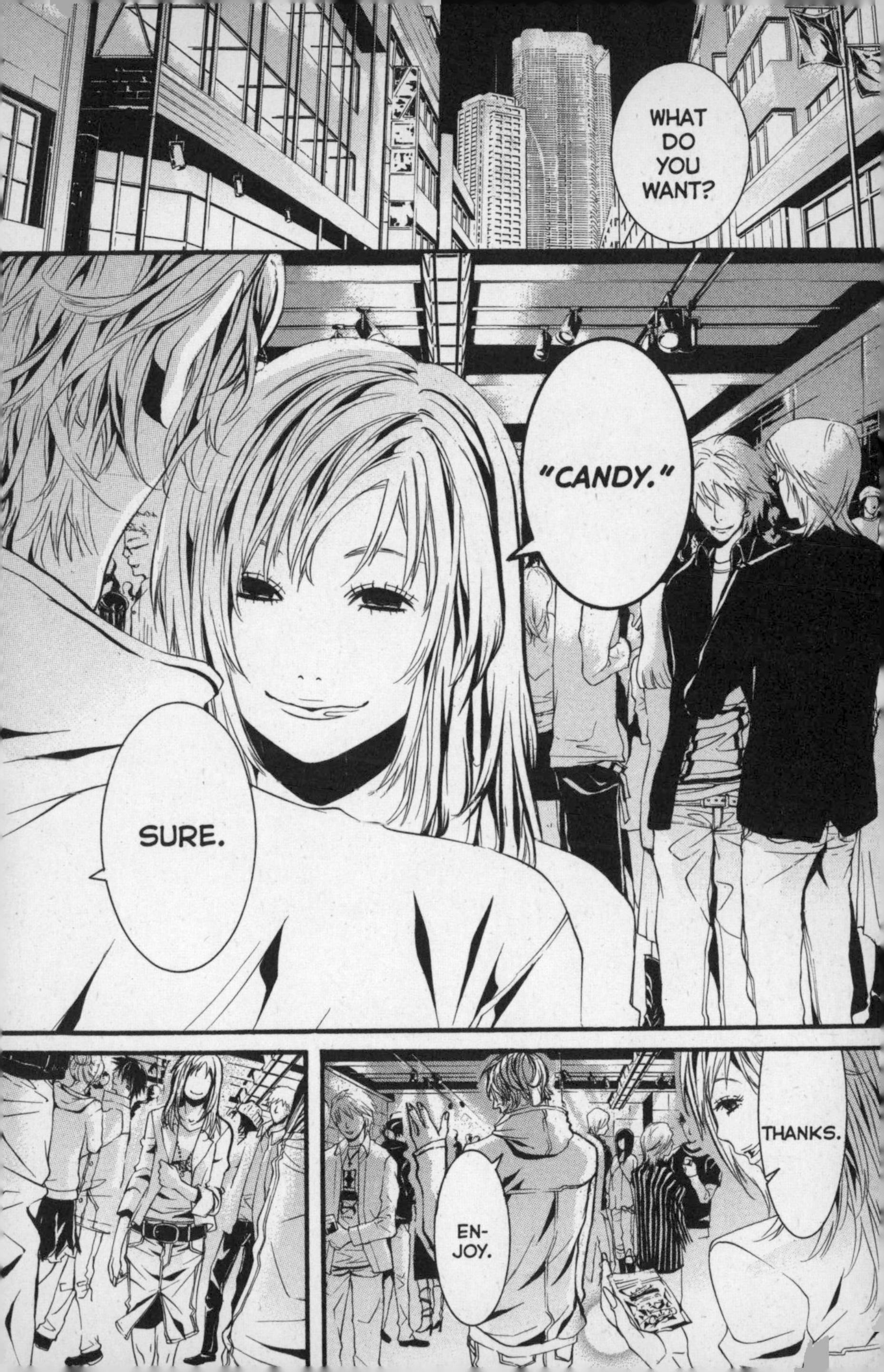
WHAT DO YOU WANT?
"CANDY."
SURE.
THANKS.
EN-JOY.

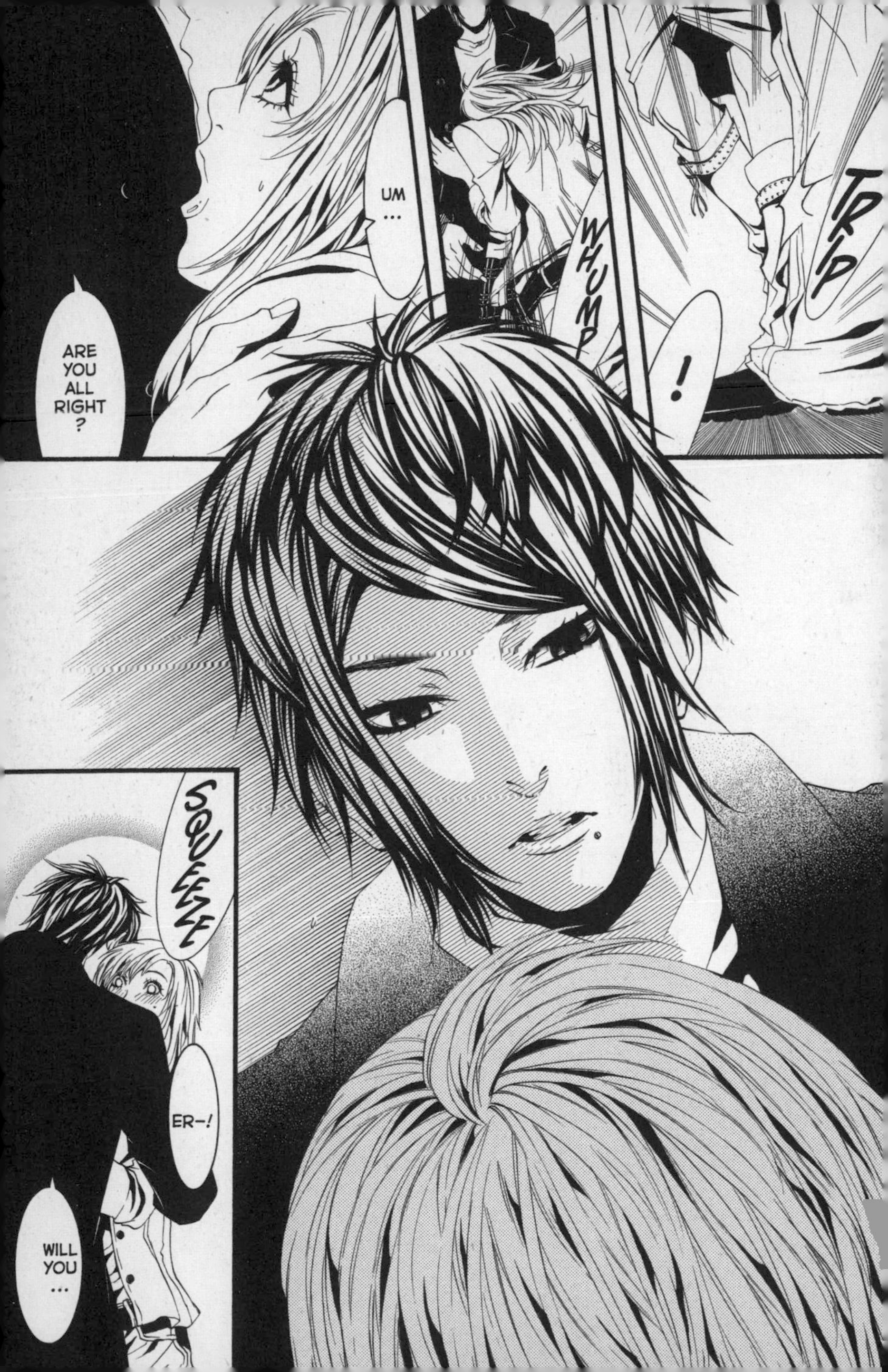
TRIP
!
WHUMP
UM ...
ARE YOU ALL RIGHT?
SQUEEZE
ER-!
WILL YOU ...

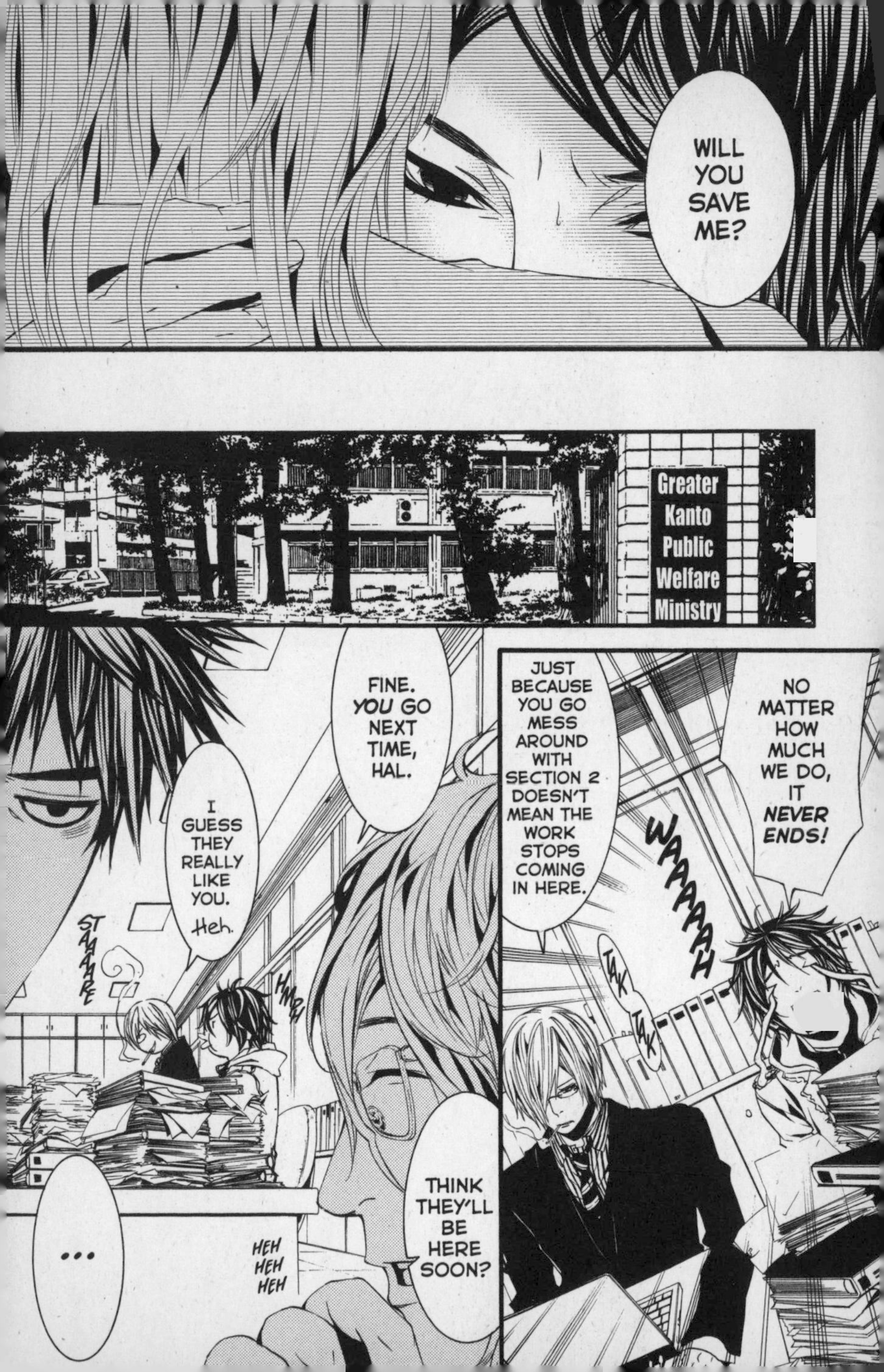
WILL YOU SAVE ME?
Greater Kanto Public Welfare Ministry
NO MATTER HOW MUCH WE DO, IT *NEVER ENDS!*
JUST BECAUSE YOU GO MESS AROUND WITH SECTION 2 DOESN'T MEAN THE WORK STOPS COMING IN HERE.
WAAAAAAH
TAK TAK
FINE. *YOU* GO NEXT TIME, HAL.
I GUESS THEY REALLY LIKE YOU.
Heh.
STAAARE
HMPH
THINK THEY'LL BE HERE SOON?
HEH HEH HEH
...

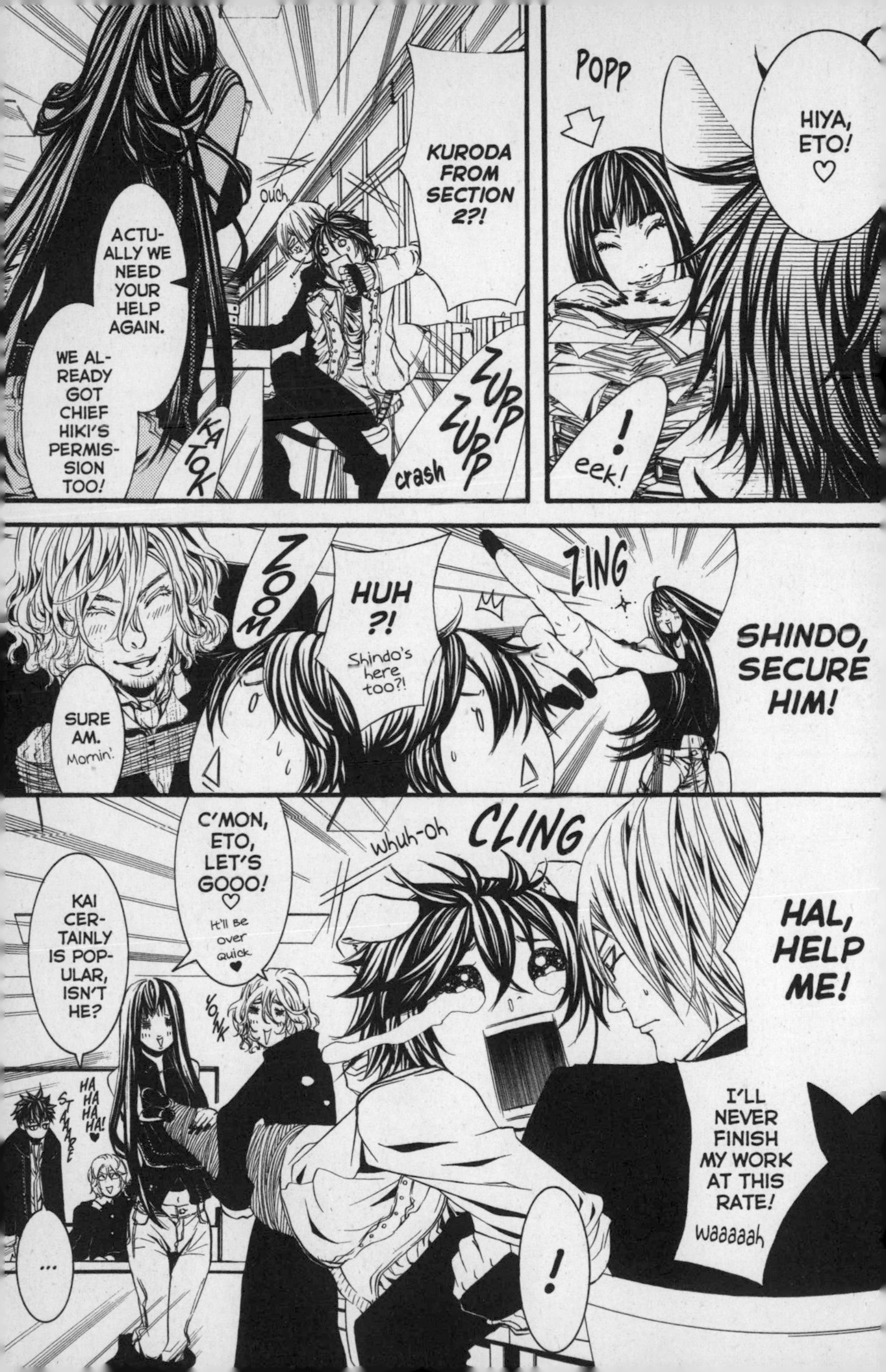

POPP
HIYA, ETO! ♡
eek!
!
KURODA FROM SECTION 2?!
ouch
ACTUALLY WE NEED YOUR HELP AGAIN.
WE ALREADY GOT CHIEF HIKI'S PERMISSION TOO!
ZUPP ZUPP
crash
KATOK
SHINDO, SECURE HIM!
ZING
HUH?!
Shindo's here too?!
ZOOM
SURE AM.
Mornin'.
HAL, HELP ME!
CLING
I'LL NEVER FINISH MY WORK AT THIS RATE!
waaaaah
!
whuh-oh
C'MON, ETO, LET'S GOOO! ♡
It'll be over quick ♥
YONK
KAI CERTAINLY IS POPULAR, ISN'T HE?
HA HA HA HA! ♥
STAAARE
...

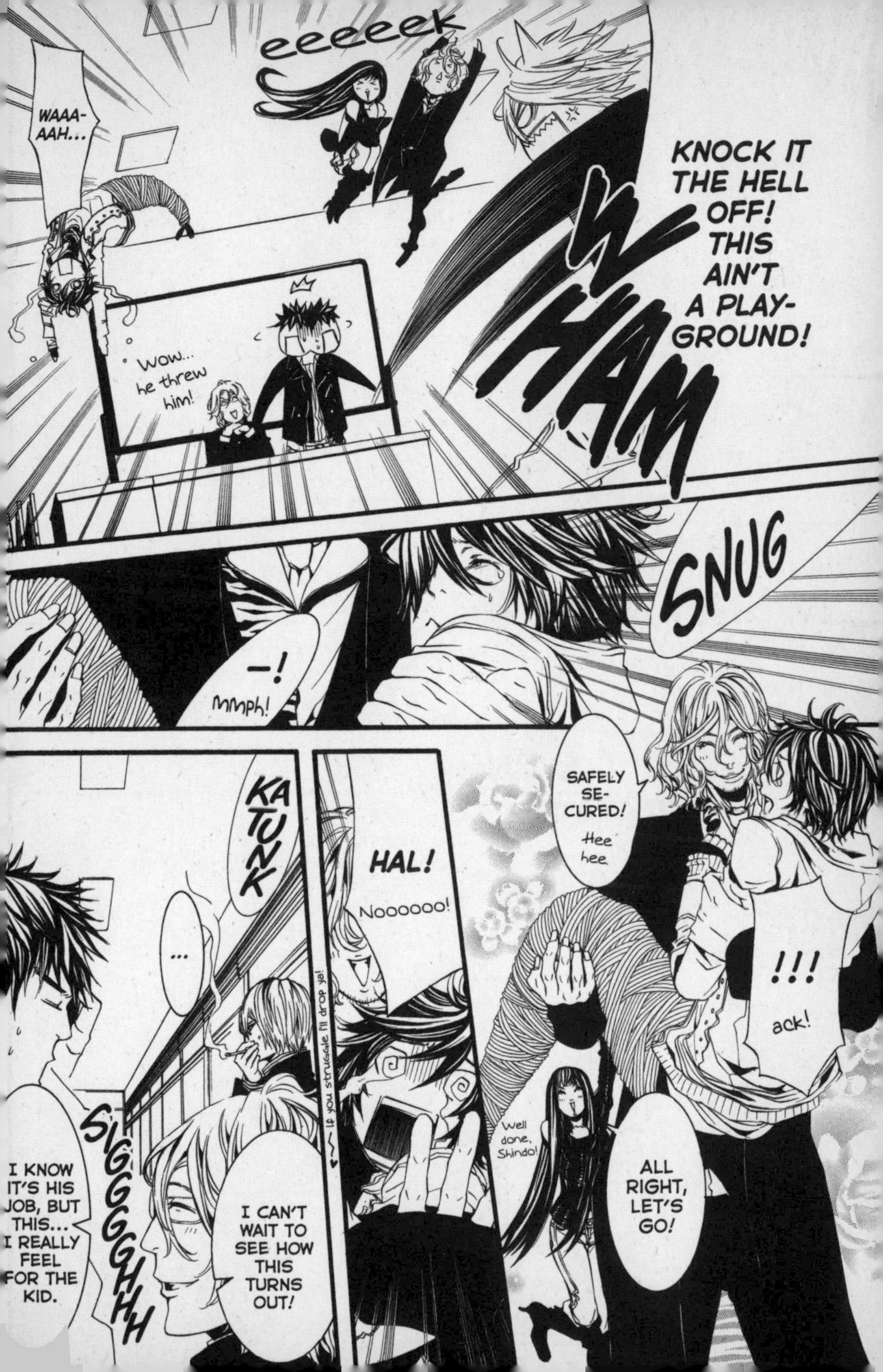
eeeeek
KNOCK IT THE HELL OFF! THIS AIN'T A PLAY-GROUND!
WHAM
WAAA-AAH...
Wow... he threw him!
SNUG
—!
Mmph!
SAFELY SE-CURED!
Hee hee.
!!!
ack!
ALL RIGHT, LET'S GO!
Well done, Shindo!
HAL!
Noooooo!
If you struggle I'll drop ya!
I CAN'T WAIT TO SEE HOW THIS TURNS OUT!
KA TUNK
...
SIGGGGHHH
I KNOW IT'S HIS JOB, BUT THIS... I REALLY FEEL FOR THE KID.

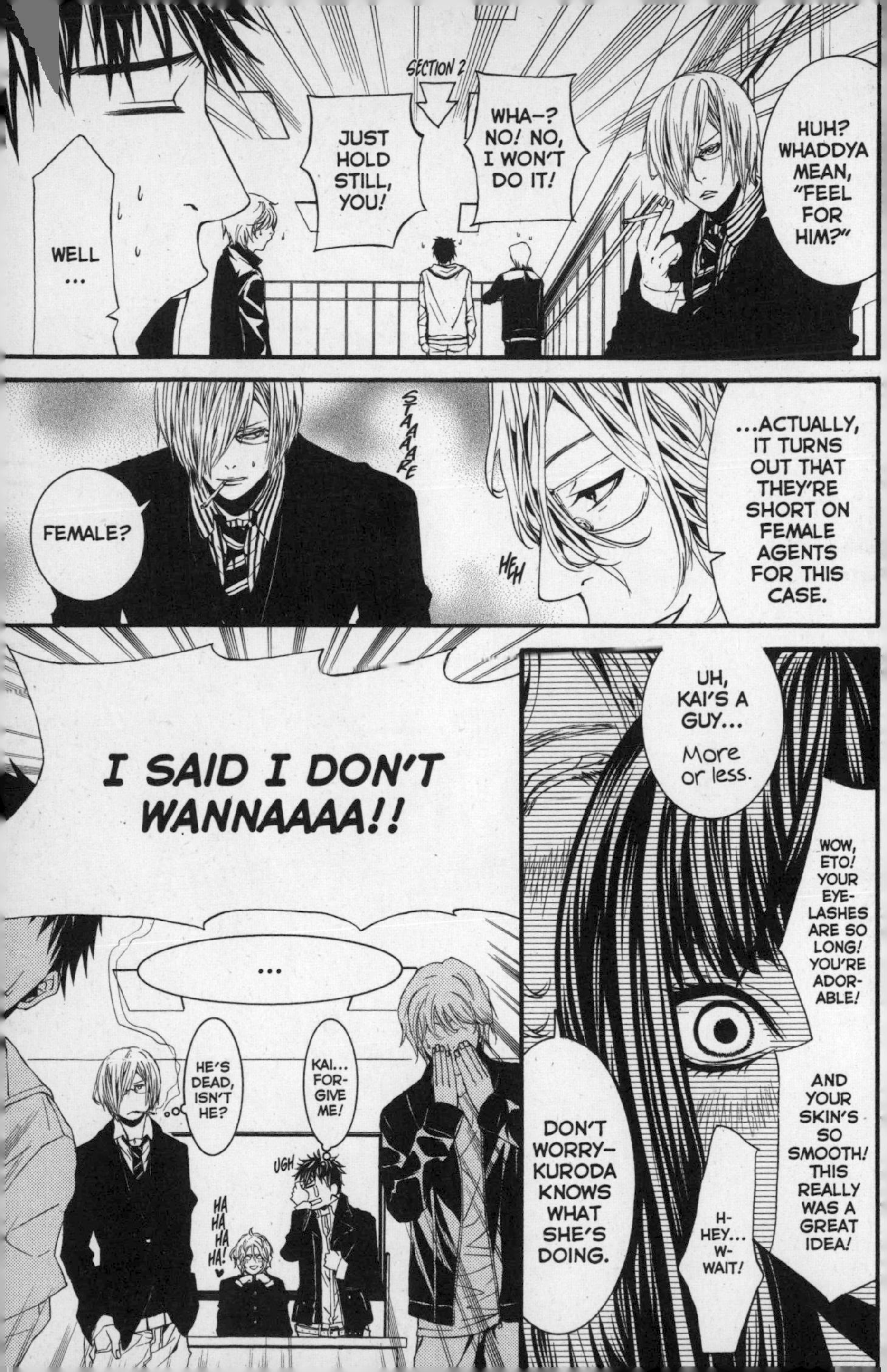
HUH? WHADDYA MEAN, "FEEL FOR HIM?"
SECTION 2
WHA-? NO! NO, I WON'T DO IT!
JUST HOLD STILL, YOU!
WELL...
...ACTUALLY, IT TURNS OUT THAT THEY'RE SHORT ON FEMALE AGENTS FOR THIS CASE.
HEH
STAAAARE
FEMALE?
UH, KAI'S A GUY...
More or less.
WOW, ETO! YOUR EYE-LASHES ARE SO LONG! YOU'RE ADOR-ABLE!
AND YOUR SKIN'S SO SMOOTH! THIS REALLY WAS A GREAT IDEA!
H-HEY... W-WAIT!
DON'T WORRY-KURODA KNOWS WHAT SHE'S DOING.
I SAID I DON'T WANNAAAA!!
...
KAI... FOR-GIVE ME!
HE'S DEAD, ISN'T HE?
UGH
HA HA HA HA!

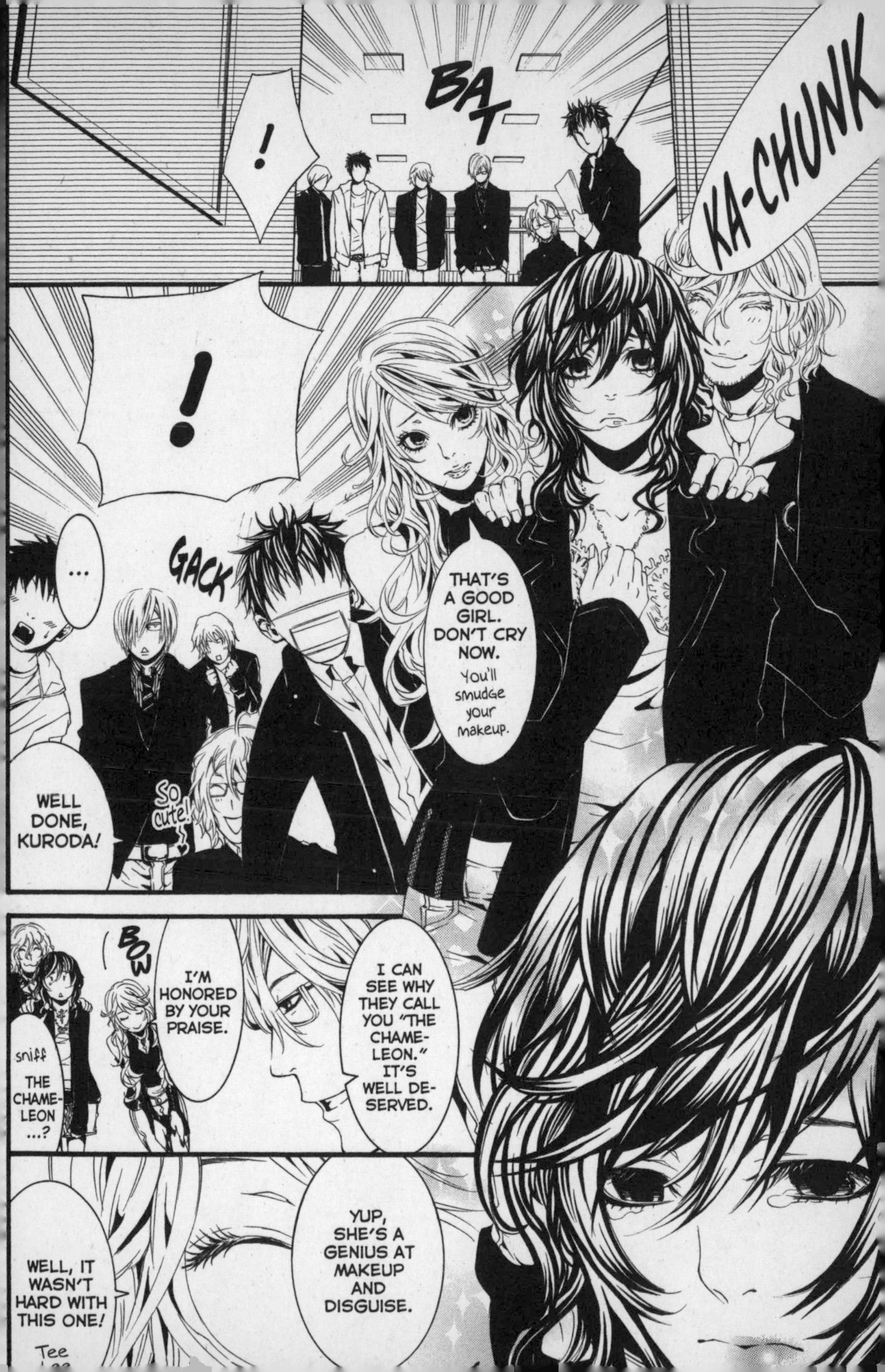
KA-CHUNK
BAT
!
!
THAT'S A GOOD GIRL. DON'T CRY NOW.
You'll smudge your makeup.
GACK
...
So cute!
WELL DONE, KURODA!
I CAN SEE WHY THEY CALL YOU "THE CHAME-LEON." IT'S WELL DE-SERVED.
I'M HONORED BY YOUR PRAISE.
BOW
sniff
THE CHAME-LEON ...?
YUP, SHE'S A GENIUS AT MAKEUP AND DISGUISE.
WELL, IT WASN'T HARD WITH THIS ONE!
Tee

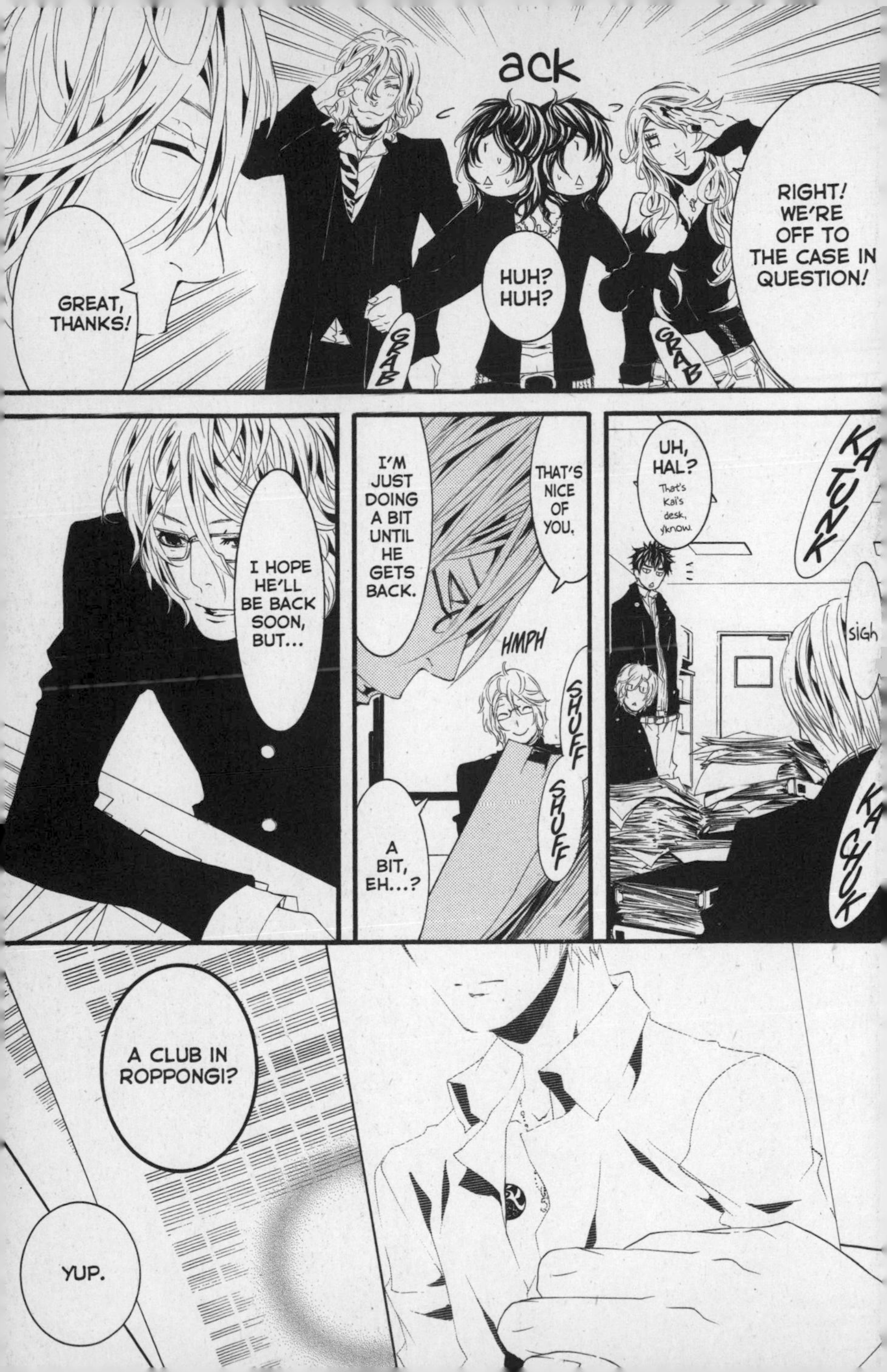
RIGHT! WE'RE OFF TO THE CASE IN QUESTION!
GRAB
ack
HUH? HUH?
GRAB
GREAT, THANKS!
KATUNK
UH, HAL?
That's Kai's desk, y'know.
sigh
KACHUK
THAT'S NICE OF YOU.
I'M JUST DOING A BIT UNTIL HE GETS BACK.
HMPH
SHUFF SHUFF
A BIT, EH...?
I HOPE HE'LL BE BACK SOON, BUT...
A CLUB IN ROPPONGI?
YUP.

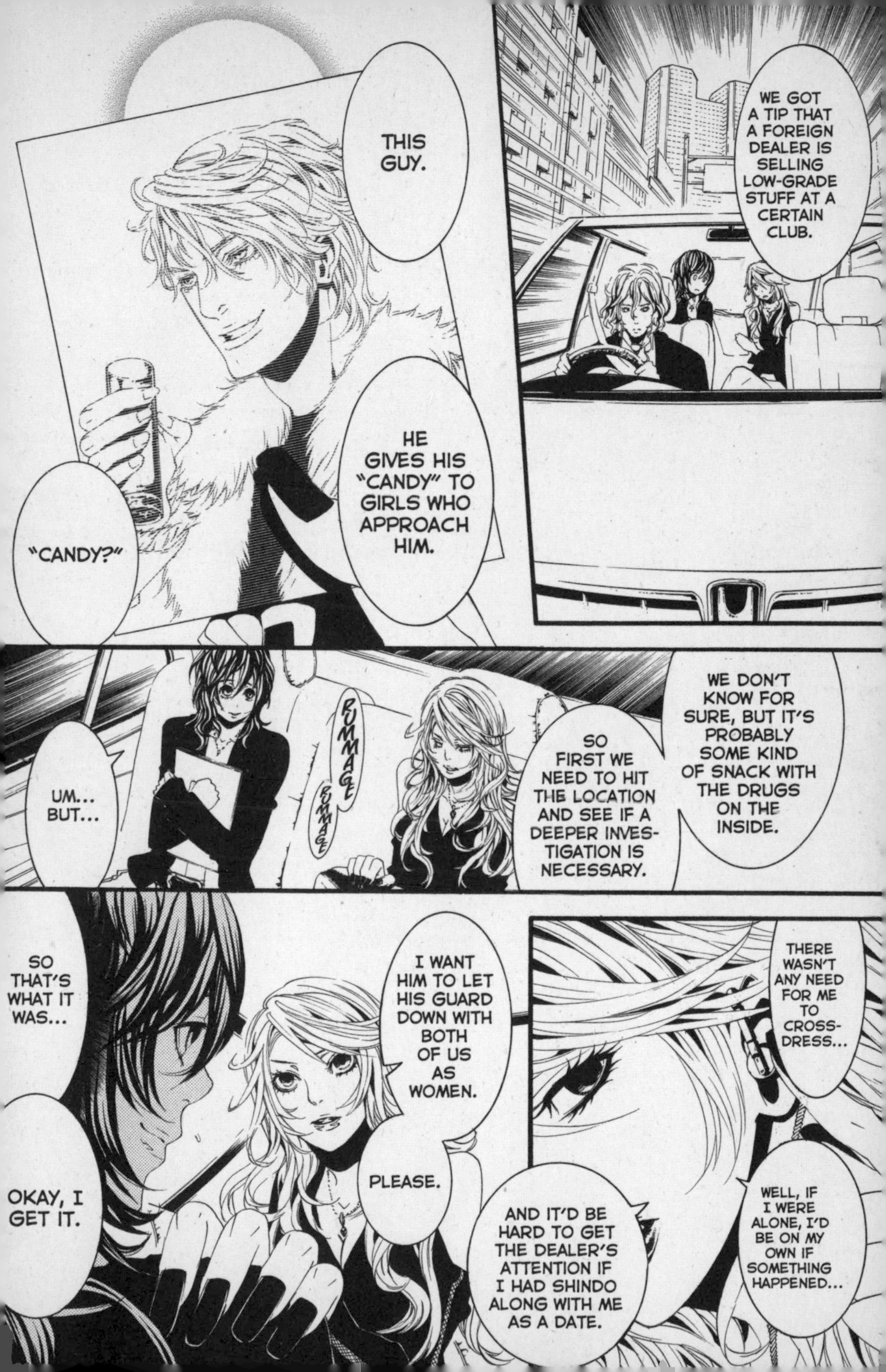
WE GOT A TIP THAT A FOREIGN DEALER IS SELLING LOW-GRADE STUFF AT A CERTAIN CLUB.
THIS GUY.
HE GIVES HIS "CANDY" TO GIRLS WHO APPROACH HIM.
"CANDY?"
WE DON'T KNOW FOR SURE, BUT IT'S PROBABLY SOME KIND OF SNACK WITH THE DRUGS ON THE INSIDE.
SO FIRST WE NEED TO HIT THE LOCATION AND SEE IF A DEEPER INVESTIGATION IS NECESSARY.
RUMMAGE
RUMMAGE
UM... BUT...
THERE WASN'T ANY NEED FOR ME TO CROSS-DRESS...
WELL, IF I WERE ALONE, I'D BE ON MY OWN IF SOMETHING HAPPENED...
AND IT'D BE HARD TO GET THE DEALER'S ATTENTION IF I HAD SHINDO ALONG WITH ME AS A DATE.
I WANT HIM TO LET HIS GUARD DOWN WITH BOTH OF US AS WOMEN.
PLEASE.
SO THAT'S WHAT IT WAS...
OKAY, I GET IT.

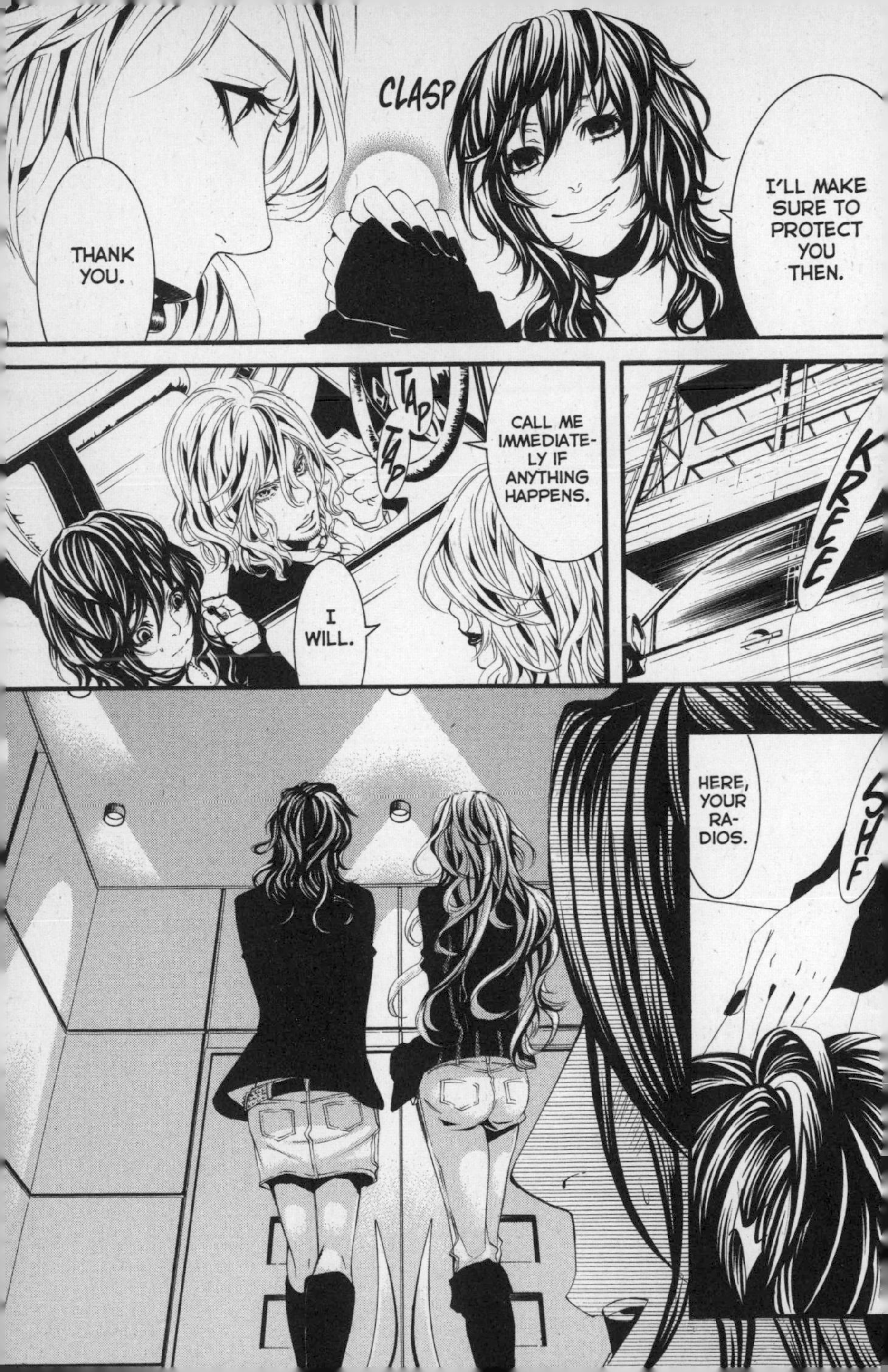
I'LL MAKE SURE TO PROTECT YOU THEN.
CLASP
THANK YOU.
KREE
CALL ME IMMEDIATE-LY IF ANYTHING HAPPENS.
TAP TAP TAP
I WILL.
SHF
HERE, YOUR RA-DIOS.

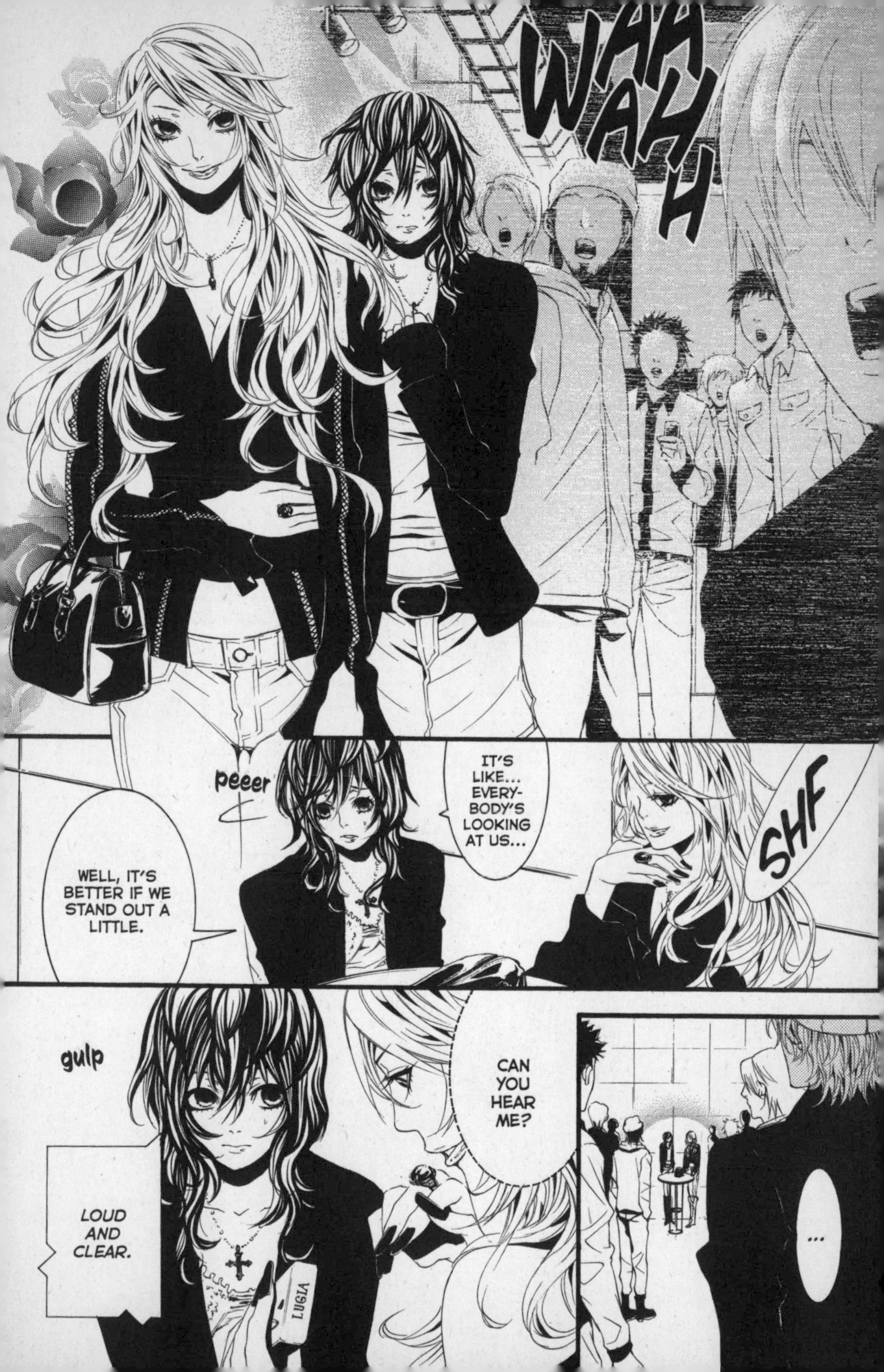
WAAAHH
SHF
IT'S LIKE... EVERYBODY'S LOOKING AT US...
peeer
WELL, IT'S BETTER IF WE STAND OUT A LITTLE.
...
CAN YOU HEAR ME?
gulp
LOUD AND CLEAR.
LUGIA

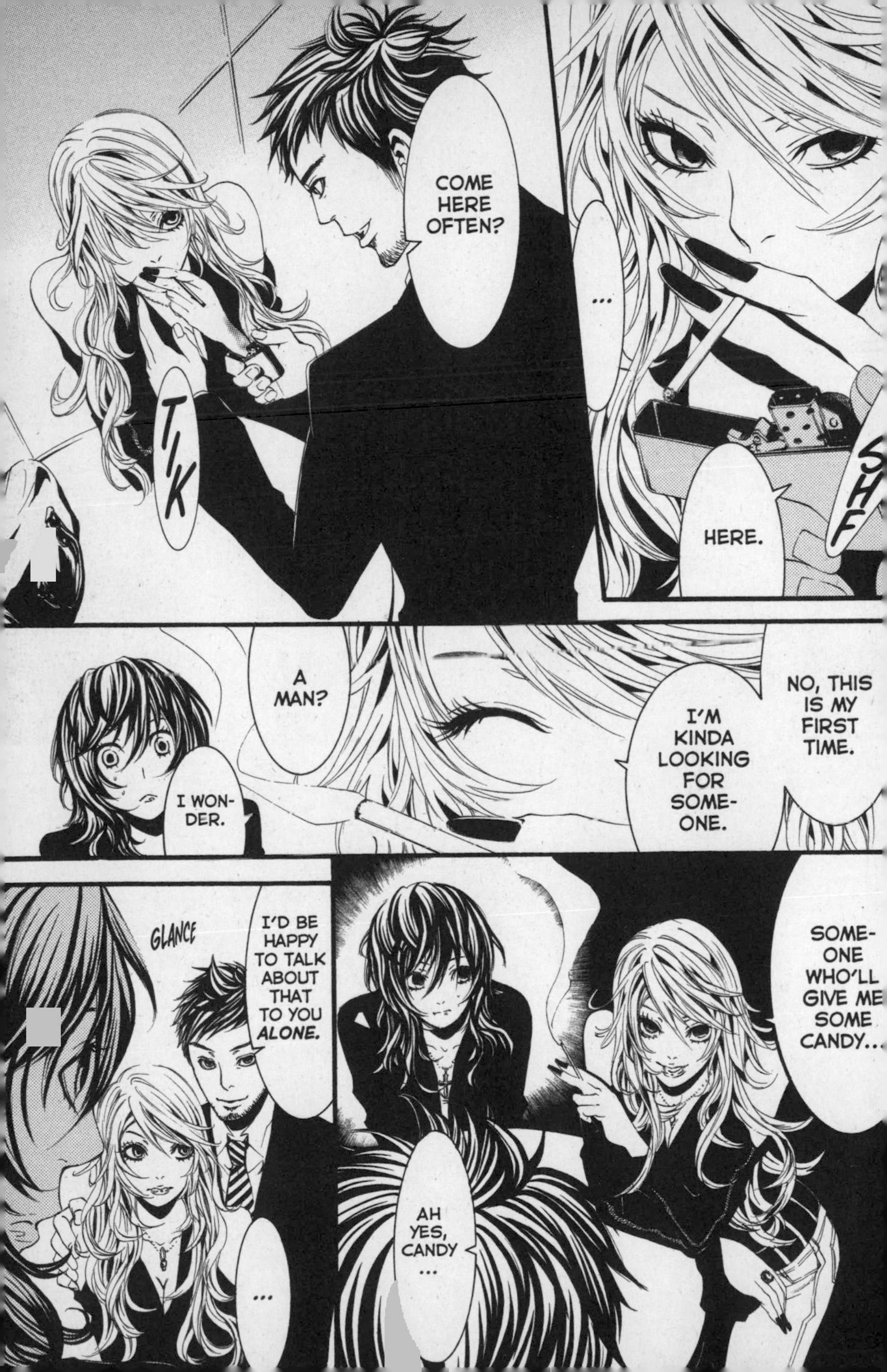
...
SHF
HERE.
COME HERE OFTEN?
TIK
NO, THIS IS MY FIRST TIME.
I'M KINDA LOOKING FOR SOME-ONE.
A MAN?
I WON-DER.
SOME-ONE WHO'LL GIVE ME SOME CANDY...
AH YES, CANDY...
I'D BE HAPPY TO TALK ABOUT THAT TO YOU ALONE.
GLANCE
...

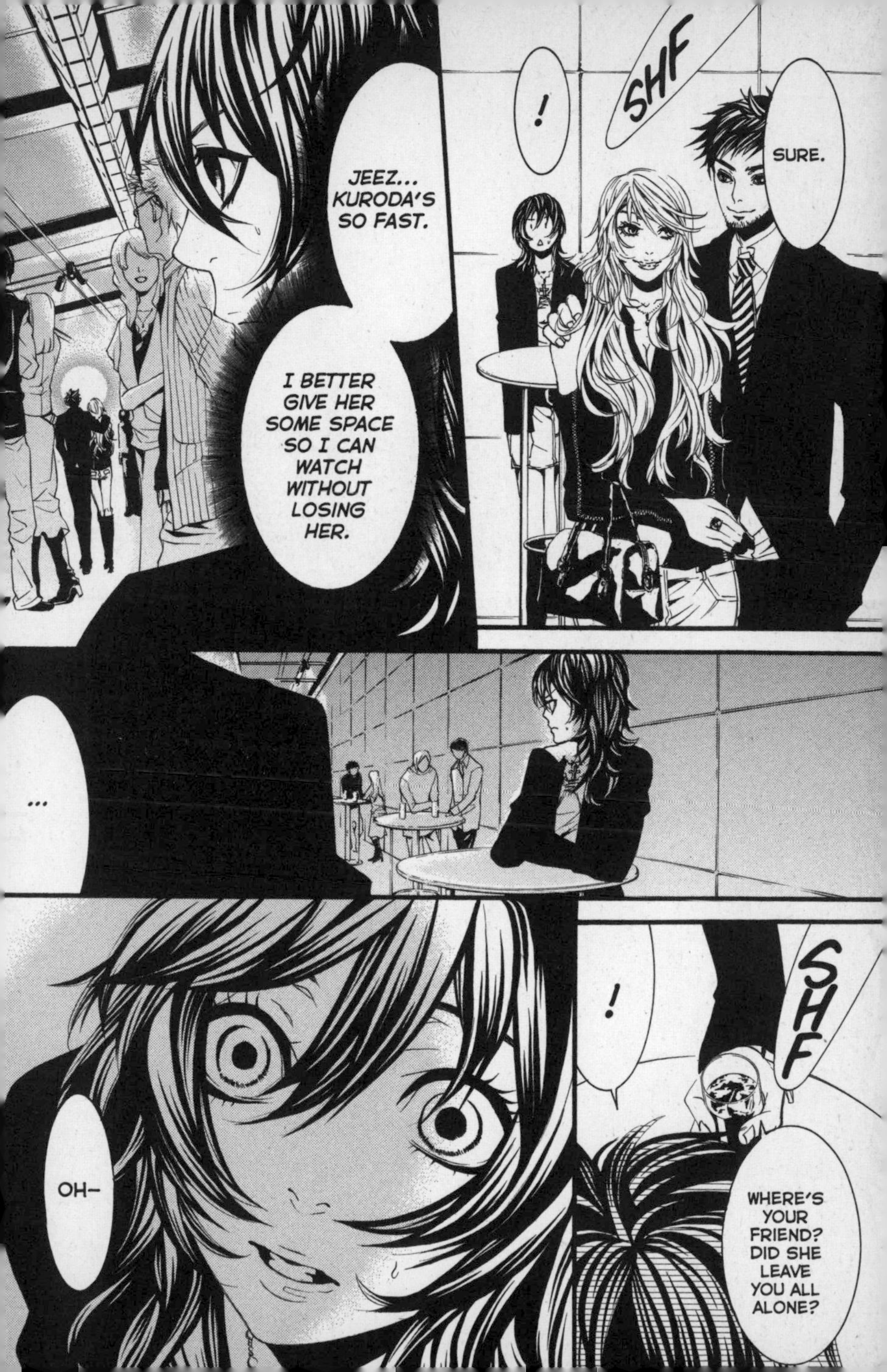
SURE.
SHF
!
JEEZ... KURODA'S SO FAST.
I BETTER GIVE HER SOME SPACE SO I CAN WATCH WITHOUT LOSING HER.
...
SHF
!
WHERE'S YOUR FRIEND? DID SHE LEAVE YOU ALL ALONE?
OH–

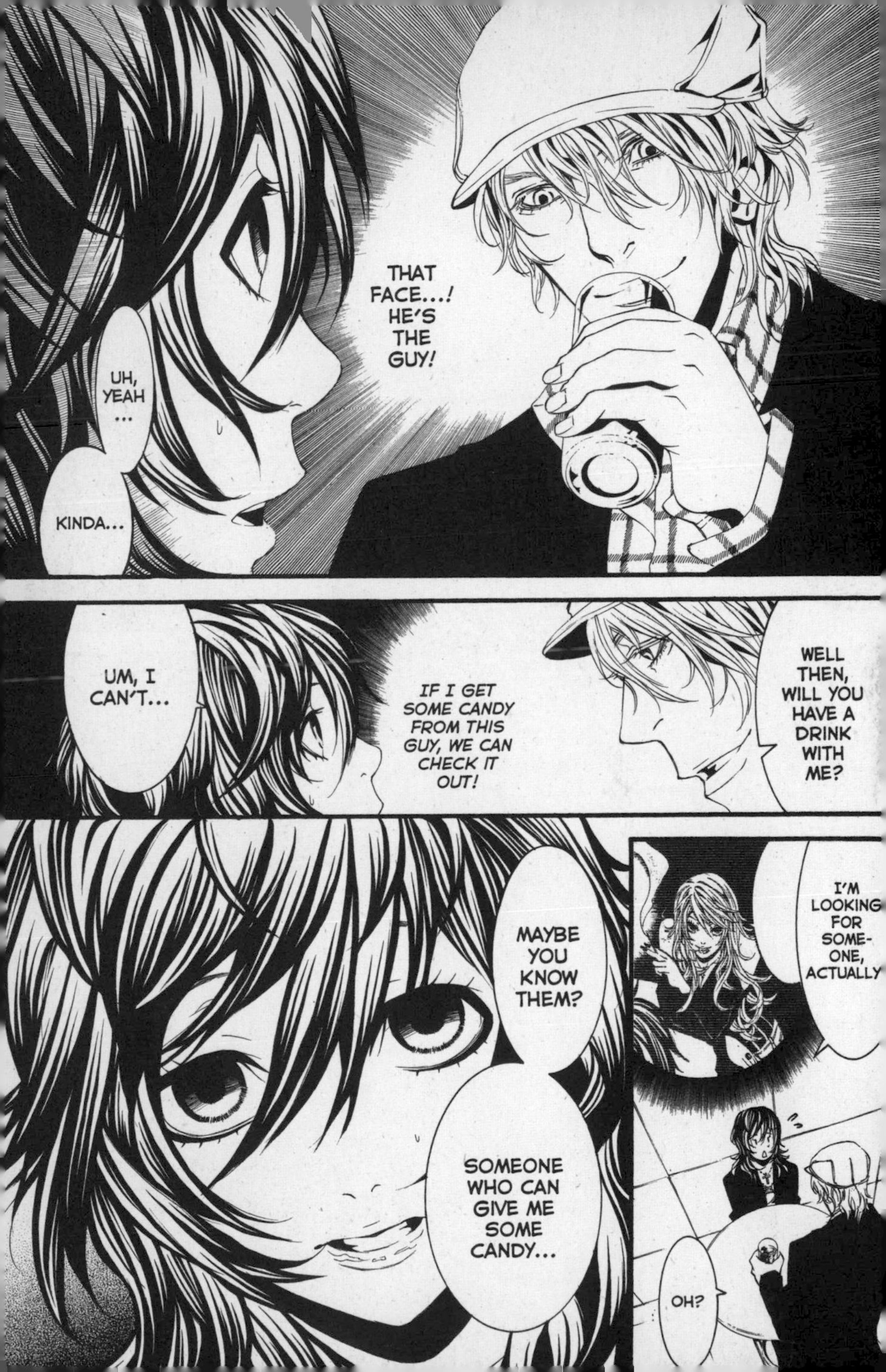
THAT FACE...! HE'S THE GUY!
UH, YEAH ...
KINDA...
WELL THEN, WILL YOU HAVE A DRINK WITH ME?
IF I GET SOME CANDY FROM THIS GUY, WE CAN CHECK IT OUT!
UM, I CAN'T...
I'M LOOKING FOR SOME-ONE, ACTUALLY
OH?
MAYBE YOU KNOW THEM?
SOMEONE WHO CAN GIVE ME SOME CANDY...

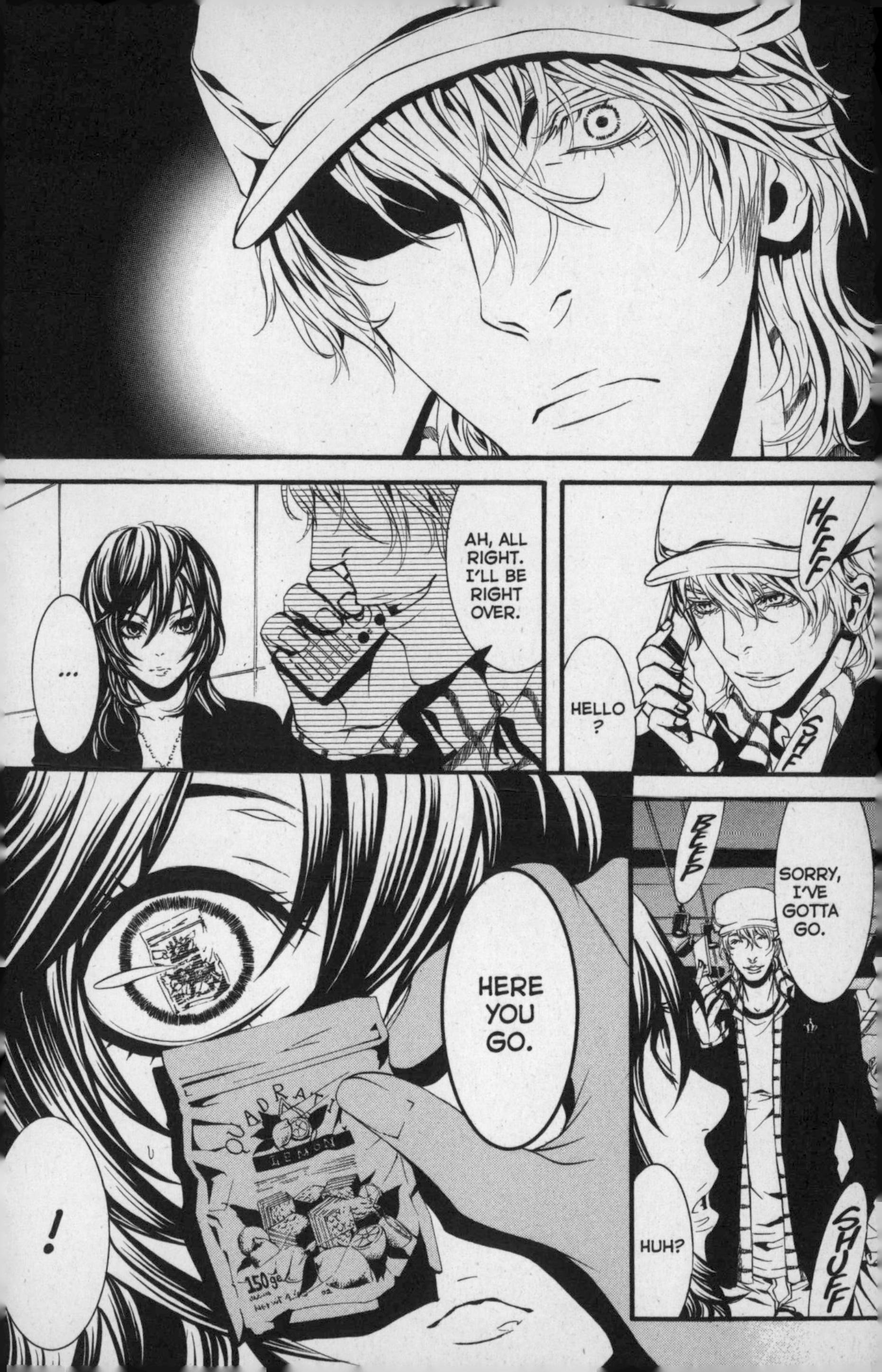
HEFF
HELLO?
SHUFF
AH, ALL RIGHT. I'LL BE RIGHT OVER.
...
SORRY, I'VE GOTTA GO.
BEEP
HUH?
SHUFF
HERE YOU GO.
LEMON
!

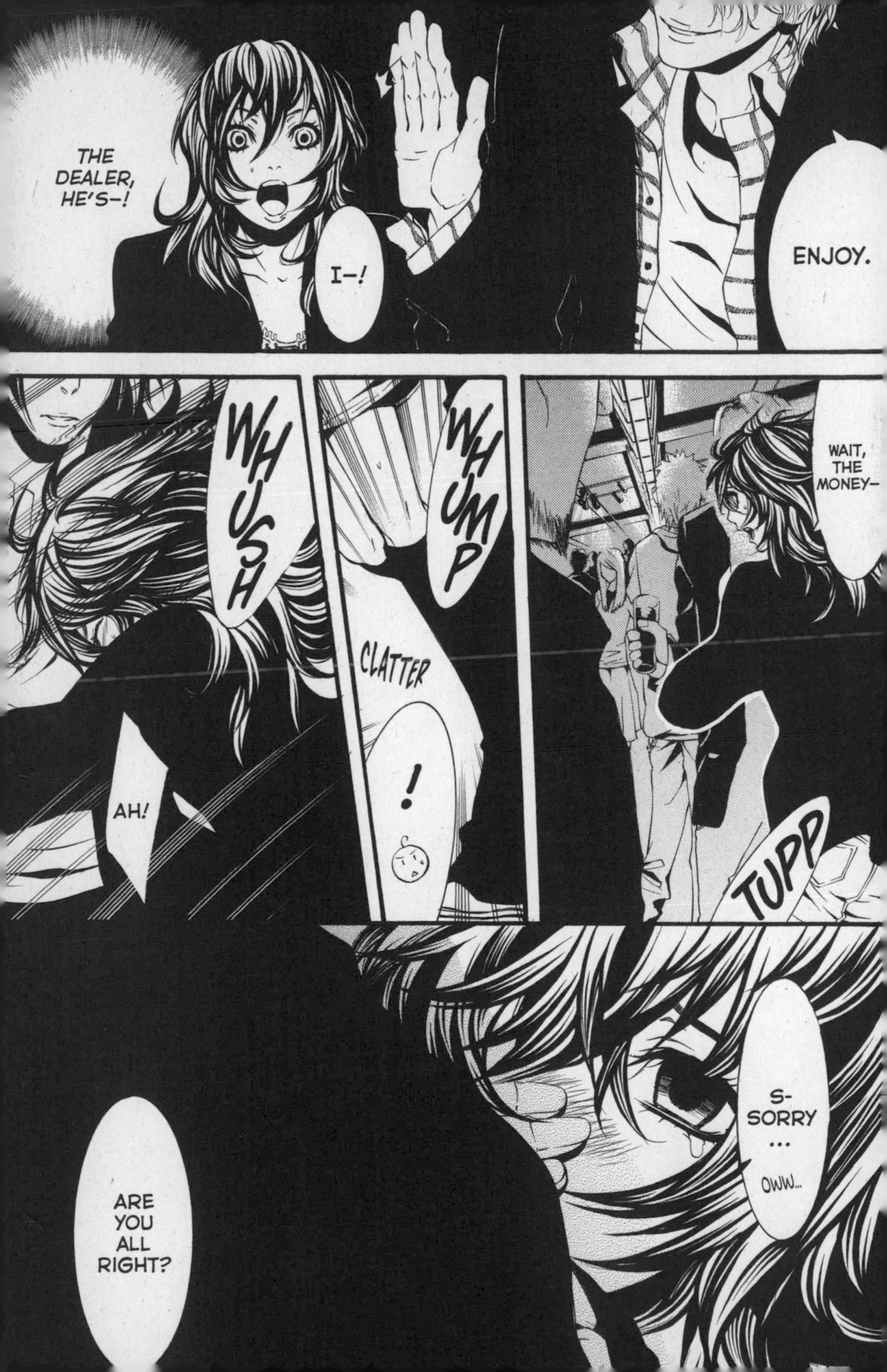
ENJOY.
I—!
THE DEALER, HE'S—!
WAIT, THE MONEY—
TUPP
WHUMP
CLATTER
!
WHUSH
AH!
S-SORRY...
OWW...
ARE YOU ALL RIGHT?

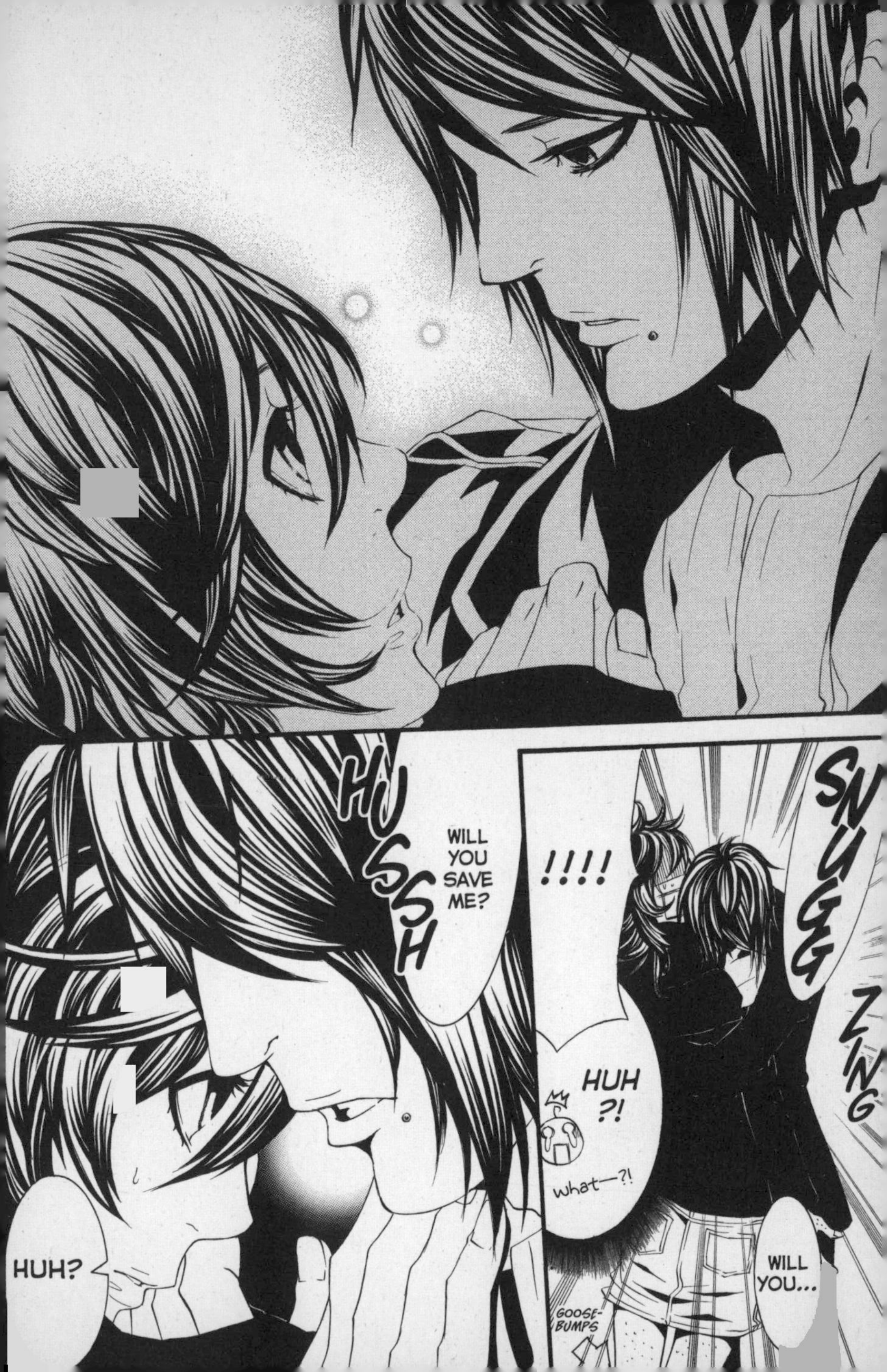
SNUGG
ZING
!!!!
HUH ?!
what—?!
WILL YOU...
GOOSE-BUMPS
HUSSH
WILL YOU SAVE ME?
HUH?

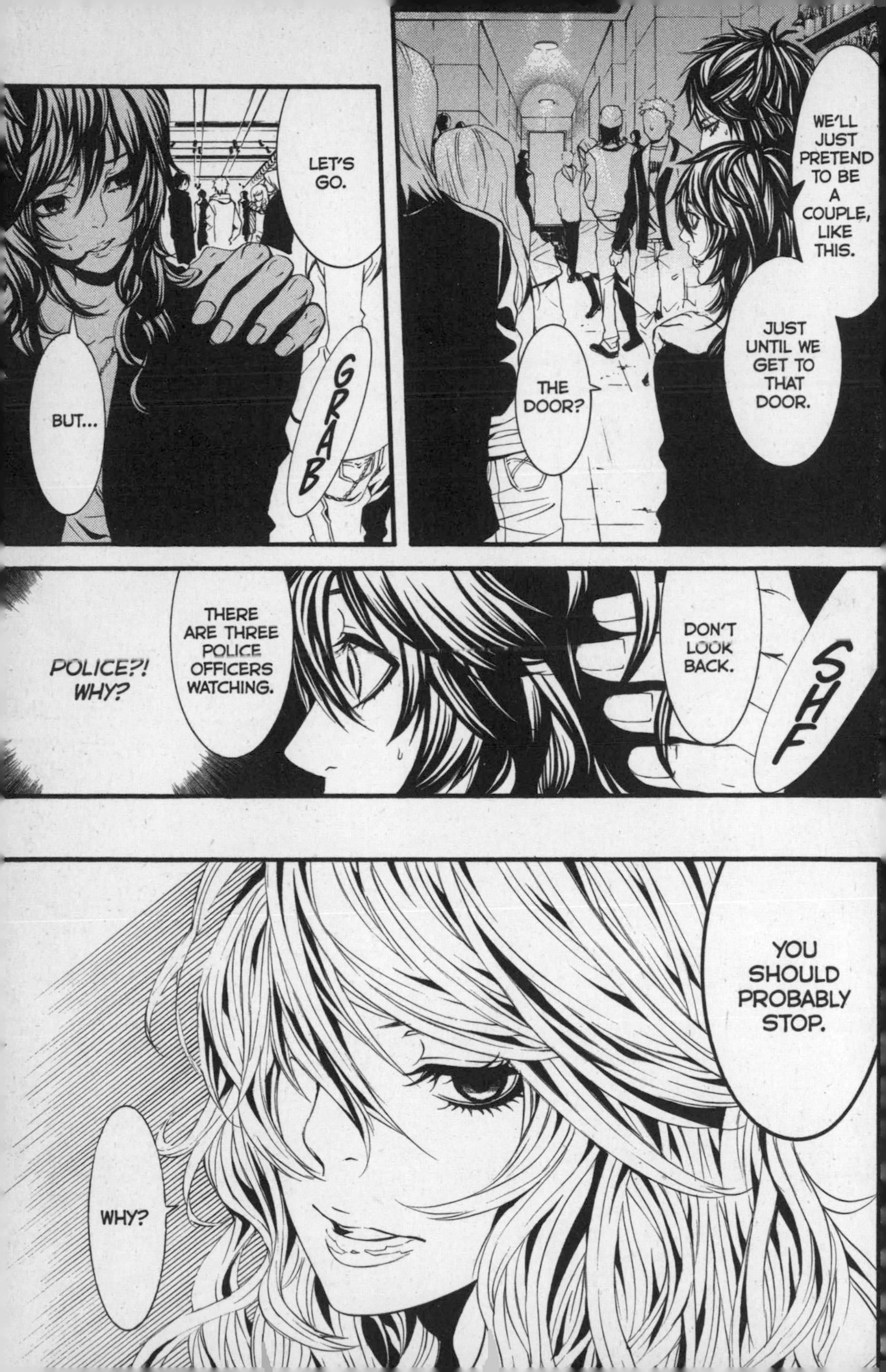
WE'LL JUST PRETEND TO BE A COUPLE, LIKE THIS.
JUST UNTIL WE GET TO THAT DOOR.
THE DOOR?
LET'S GO.
GRAB
BUT...
SHF
DON'T LOOK BACK.
THERE ARE THREE POLICE OFFICERS WATCHING.
POLICE?! WHY?
YOU SHOULD PROBABLY STOP.
WHY?

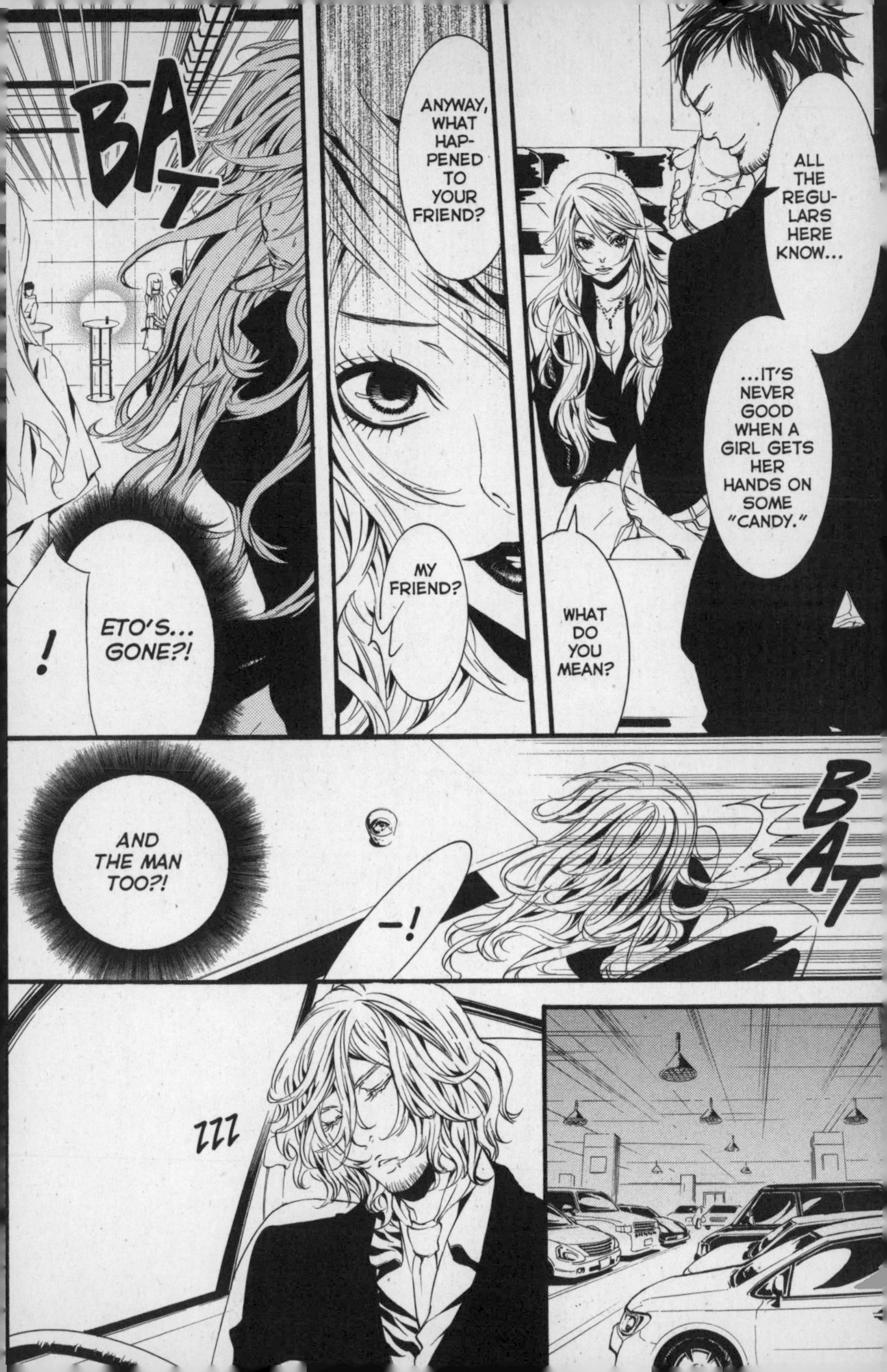
ALL THE REGULARS HERE KNOW...
...IT'S NEVER GOOD WHEN A GIRL GETS HER HANDS ON SOME "CANDY."
WHAT DO YOU MEAN?
ANYWAY, WHAT HAPPENED TO YOUR FRIEND?
MY FRIEND?
BAT
ETO'S... GONE?!
!
BAT
—!
AND THE MAN TOO?!
ZZZ

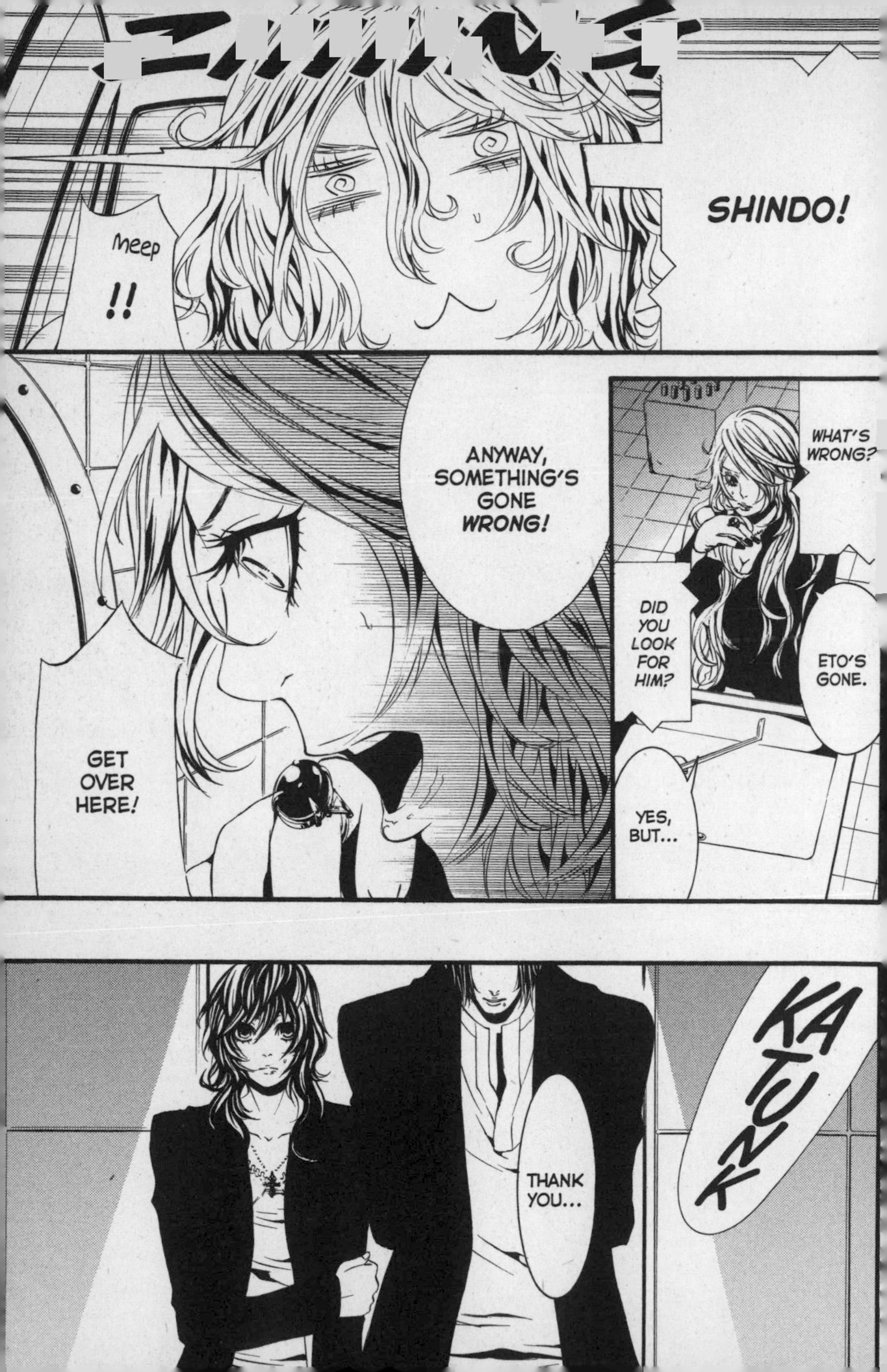
SHINDO!
Meep
!!
WHAT'S WRONG?
ETO'S GONE.
DID YOU LOOK FOR HIM?
YES, BUT...
ANYWAY, SOMETHING'S GONE WRONG!
GET OVER HERE!
KATUNK
THANK YOU...

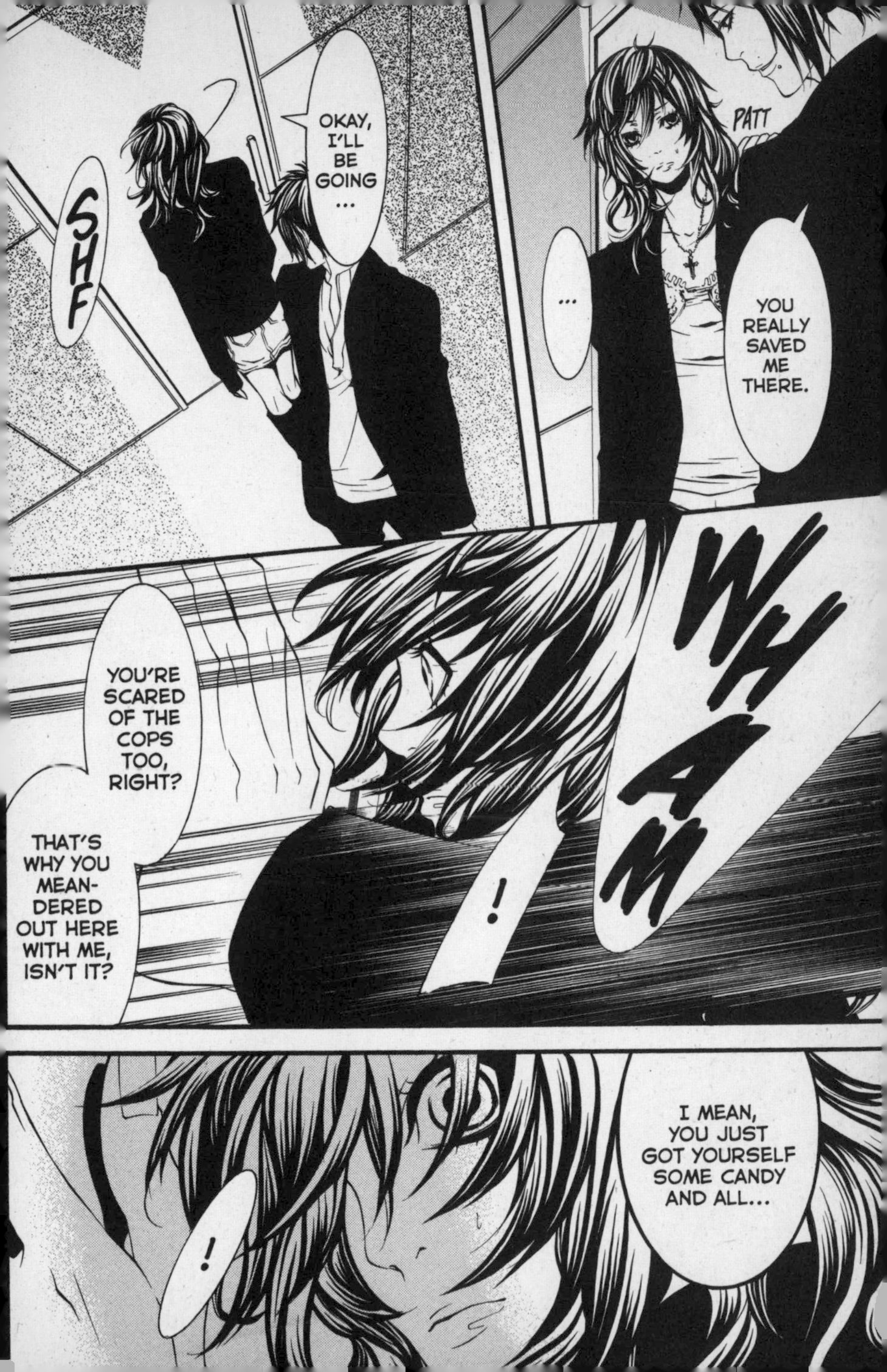
PATT
YOU REALLY SAVED ME THERE.
...
OKAY, I'LL BE GOING ...
SHF
WHAM
!
YOU'RE SCARED OF THE COPS TOO, RIGHT?
THAT'S WHY YOU MEAN-DERED OUT HERE WITH ME, ISN'T IT?
I MEAN, YOU JUST GOT YOURSELF SOME CANDY AND ALL...
!

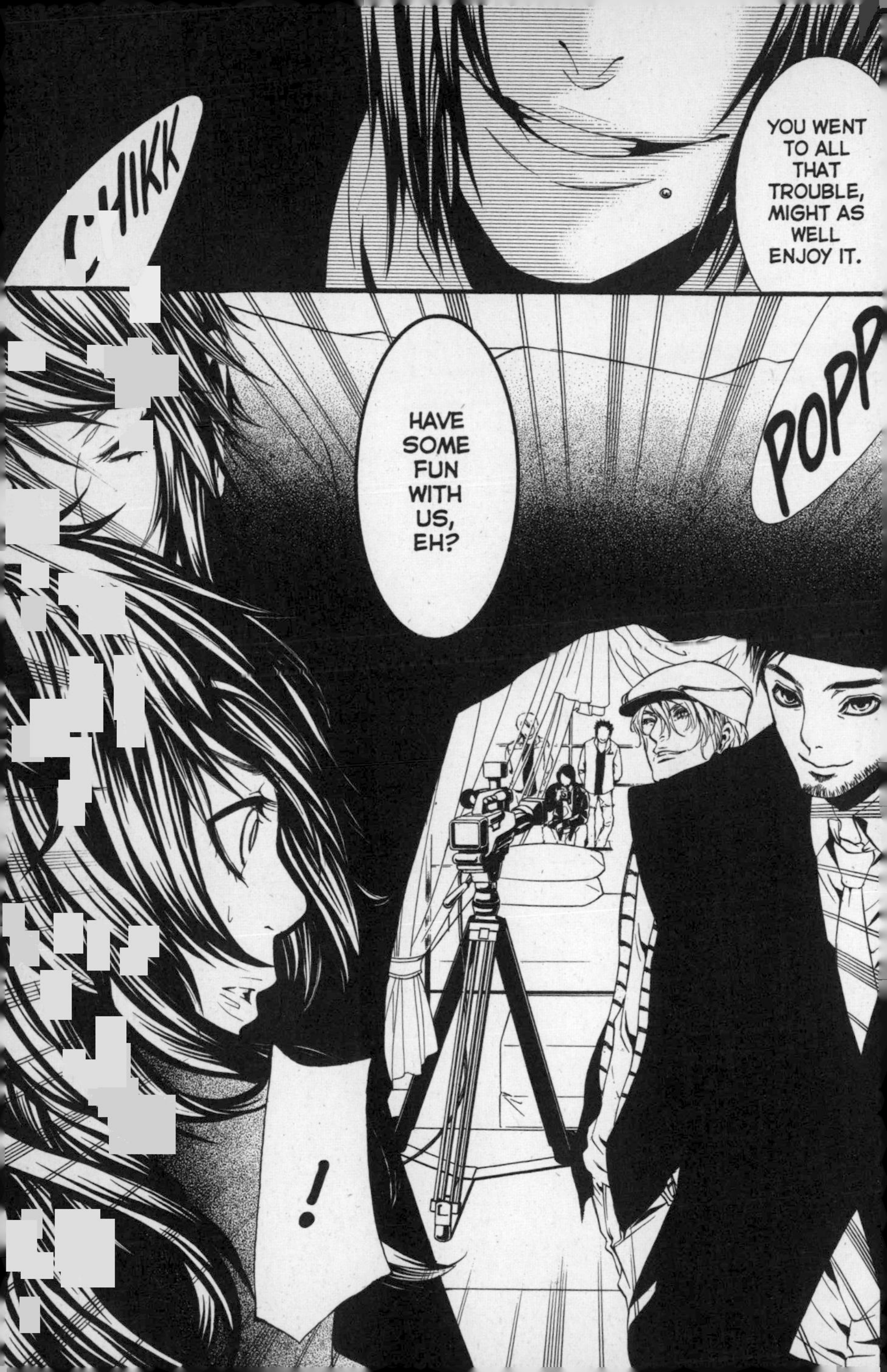
YOU WENT TO ALL THAT TROUBLE, MIGHT AS WELL ENJOY IT.
CHIKK
POPP
HAVE SOME FUN WITH US, EH?
!

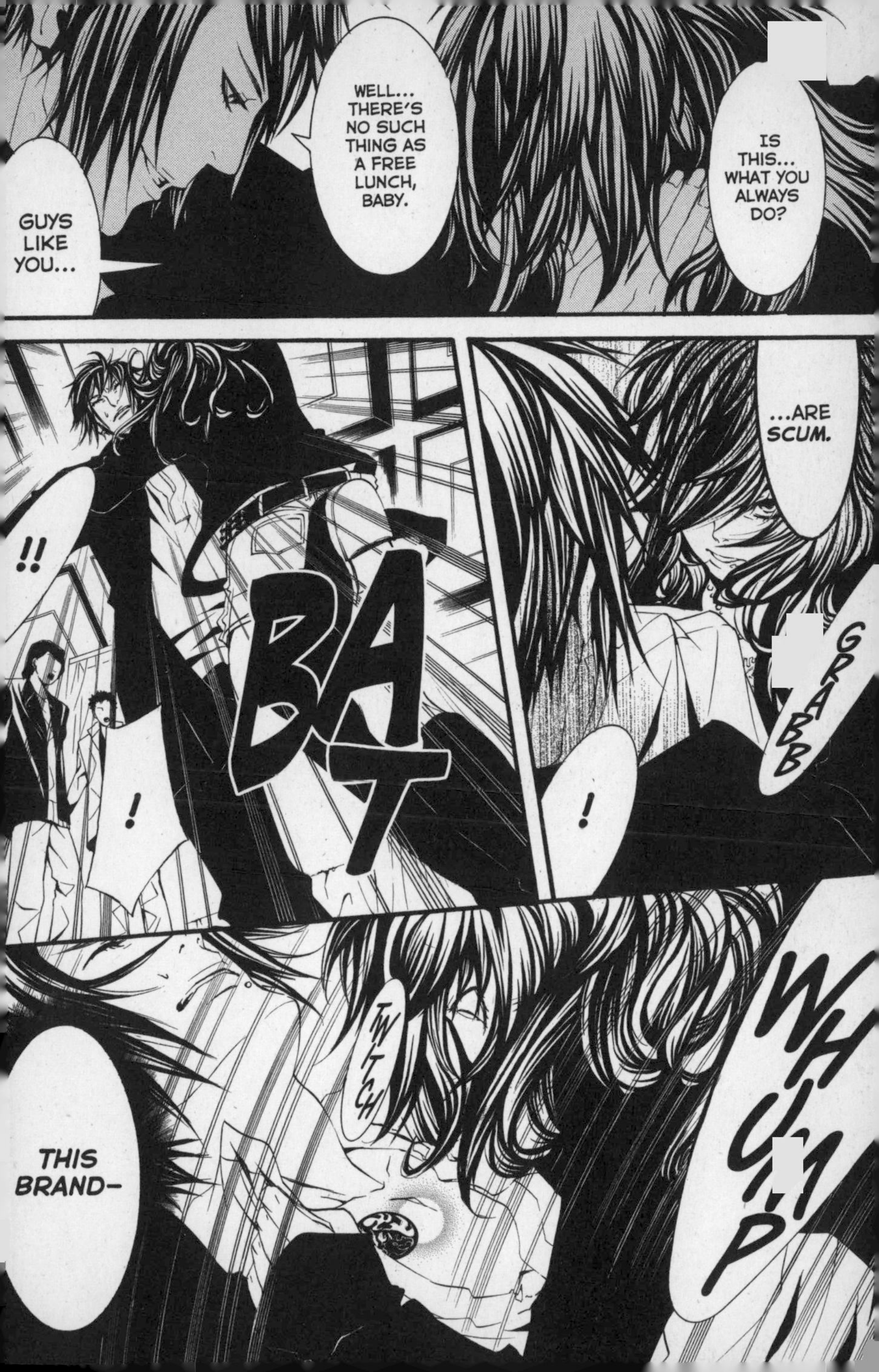
IS THIS... WHAT YOU ALWAYS DO?
WELL... THERE'S NO SUCH THING AS A FREE LUNCH, BABY.
GUYS LIKE YOU...
...ARE SCUM.
GRABB
!
BAT
!!
!
WHUMP
TWITCH
THIS BRAND–

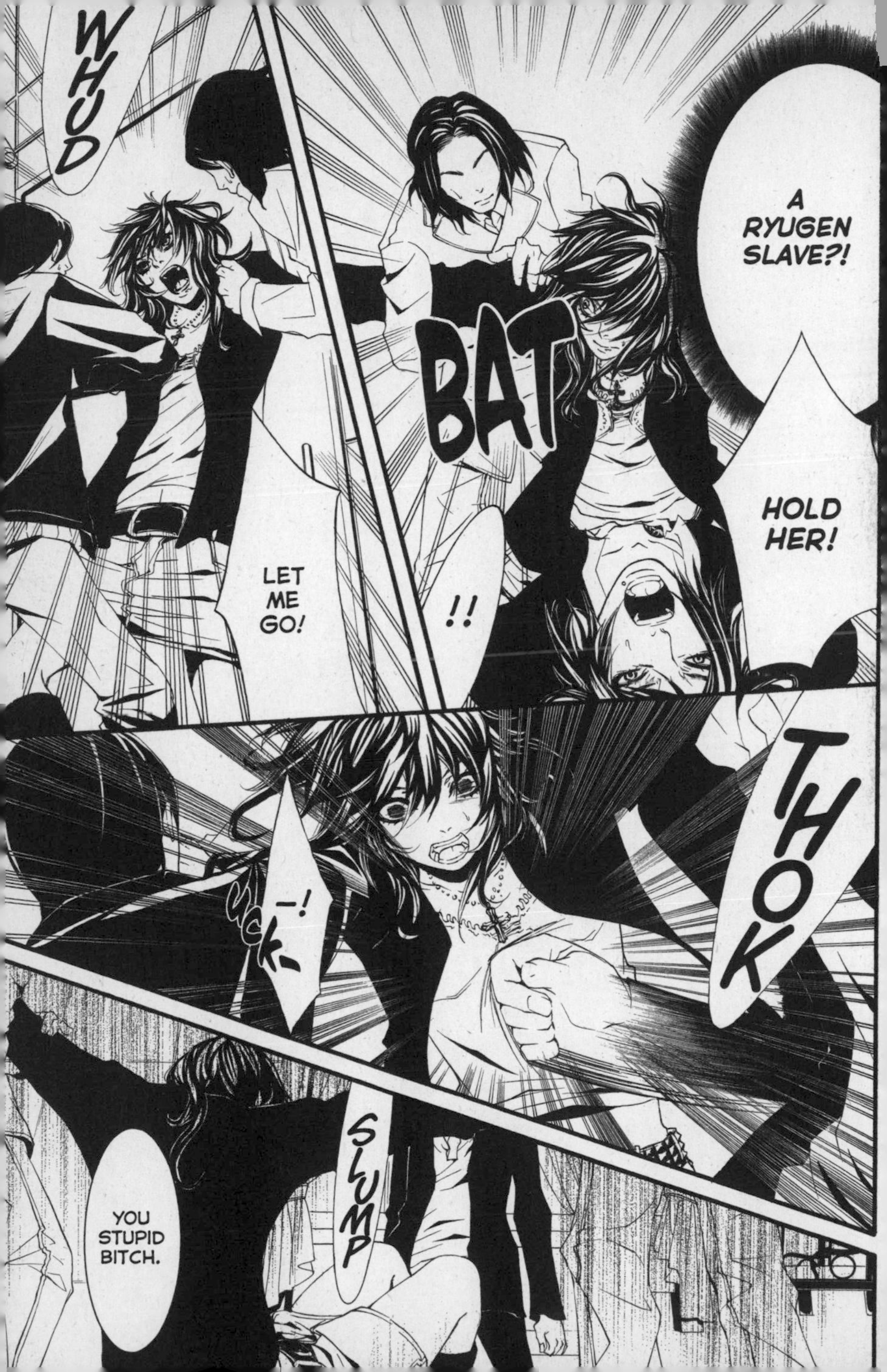
A RYUGEN SLAVE?!
HOLD HER!
BAT
!!
WHUD
LET ME GO!
THOK
—!
uck
SLUMP
YOU STUPID BITCH.

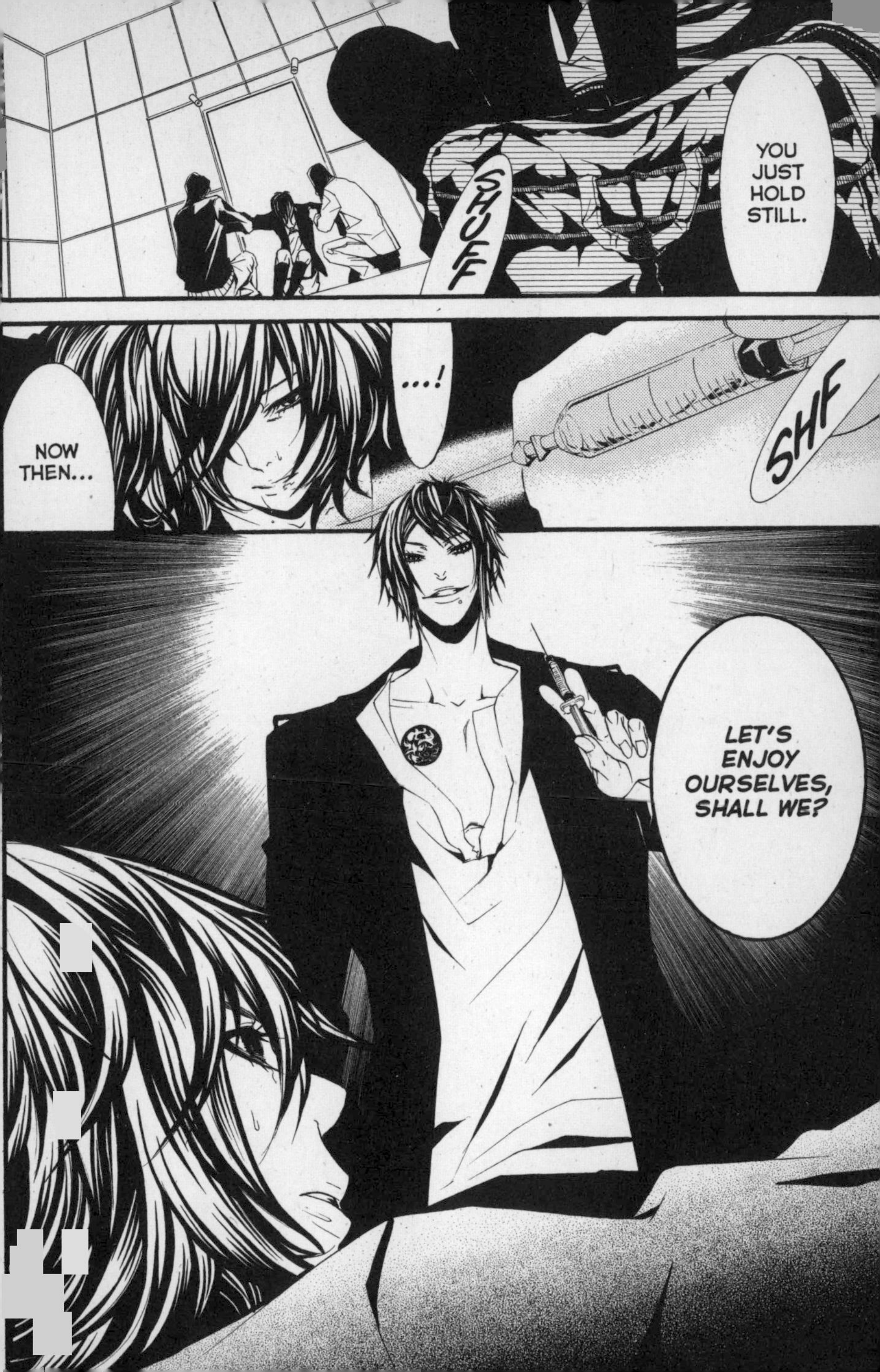
YOU JUST HOLD STILL.
SHUFF
SHF
...!
NOW THEN...
LET'S ENJOY OURSELVES, SHALL WE?

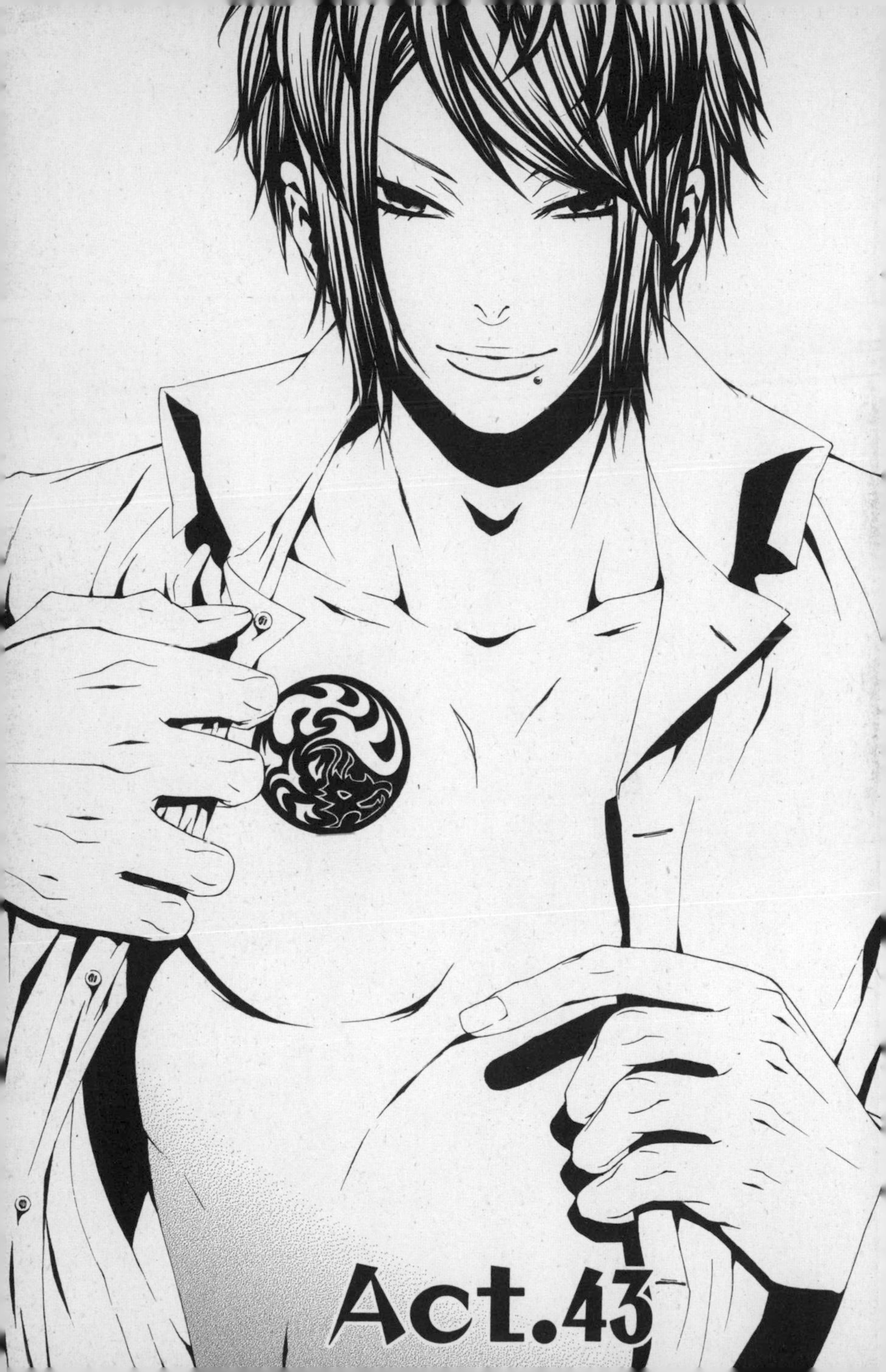
Act.43

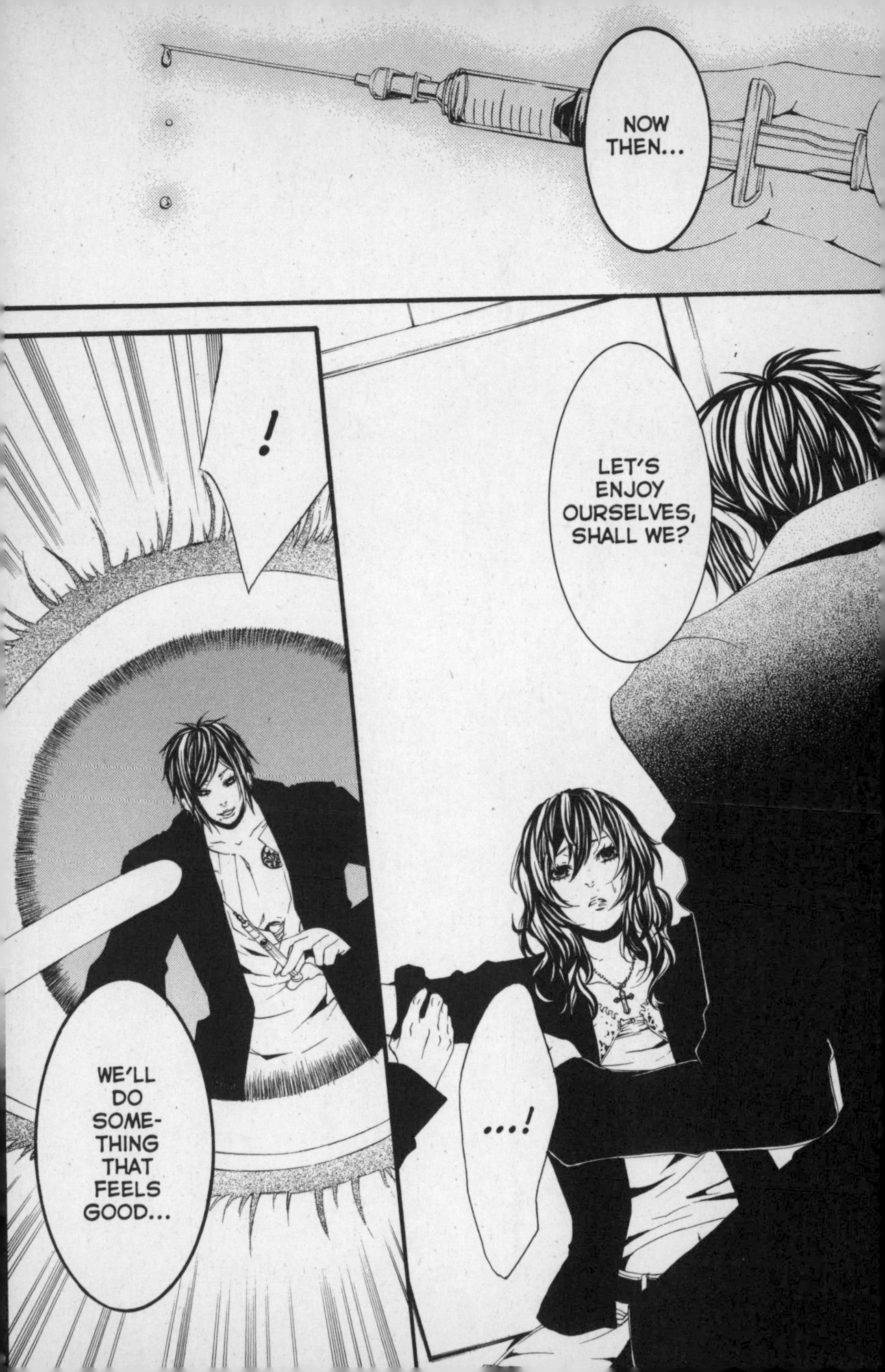
NOW THEN...
LET'S ENJOY OURSELVES, SHALL WE?
...!
!
WE'LL DO SOME-THING THAT FEELS GOOD...

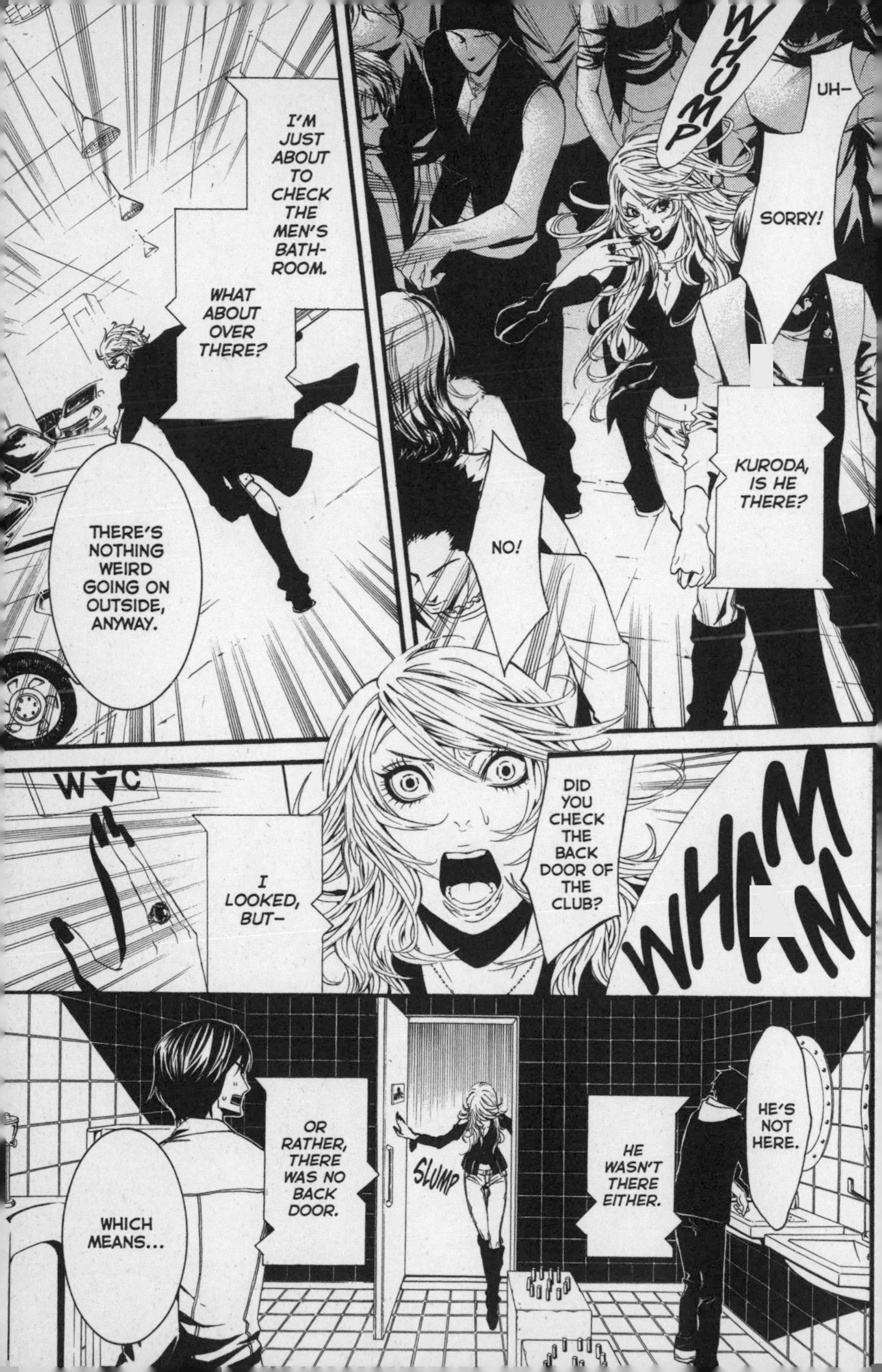
WHUMP
UH–
SORRY!
KURODA, IS HE THERE?
NO!
I'M JUST ABOUT TO CHECK THE MEN'S BATHROOM.
WHAT ABOUT OVER THERE?
THERE'S NOTHING WEIRD GOING ON OUTSIDE, ANYWAY.
WHAM
DID YOU CHECK THE BACK DOOR OF THE CLUB?
I LOOKED, BUT–
W C
HE'S NOT HERE.
HE WASN'T THERE EITHER.
OR RATHER, THERE WAS NO BACK DOOR.
SLUMP
WHICH MEANS...

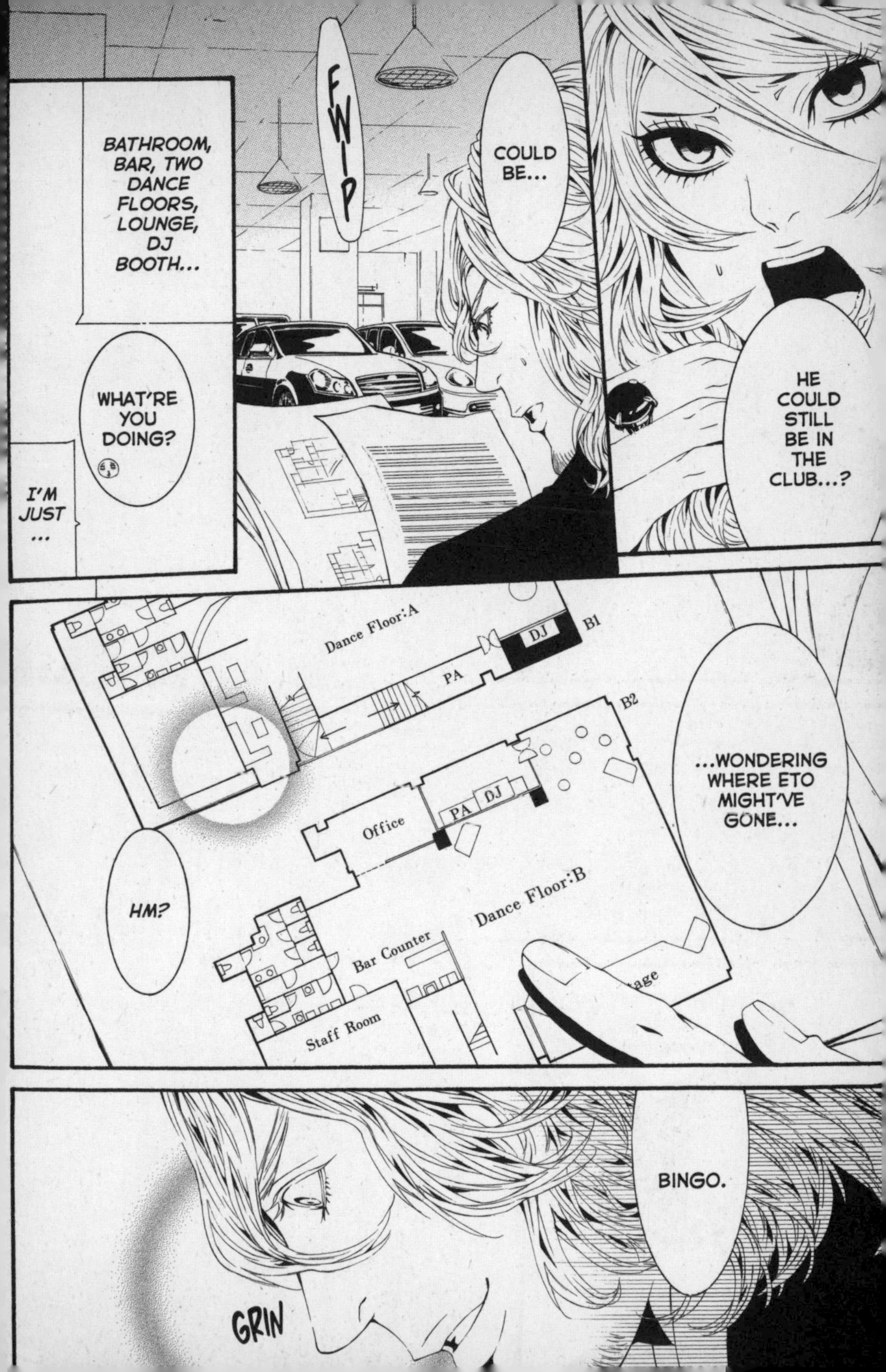
HE COULD STILL BE IN THE CLUB...?
COULD BE...
FWIP
BATHROOM, BAR, TWO DANCE FLOORS, LOUNGE, DJ BOOTH...
WHAT'RE YOU DOING?
I'M JUST ...
...WONDERING WHERE ETO MIGHT'VE GONE...
HM?
Dance Floor:A
DJ
B1
PA
B2
PA
DJ
Office
Dance Floor:B
Bar Counter
Staff Room
BINGO.
GRIN

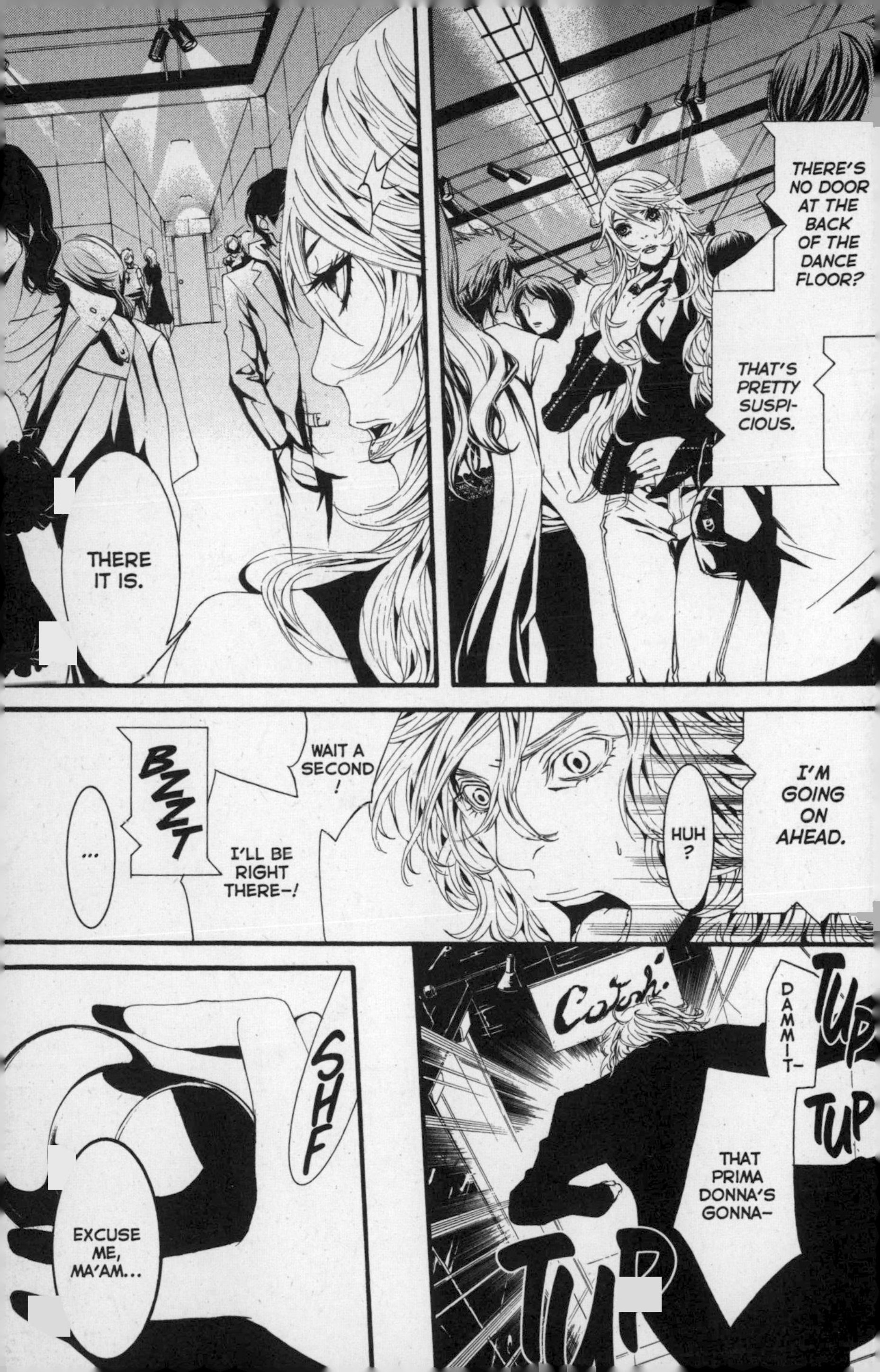
THERE'S NO DOOR AT THE BACK OF THE DANCE FLOOR?
THAT'S PRETTY SUSPICIOUS.
THERE IT IS.
I'M GOING ON AHEAD.
HUH?
WAIT A SECOND!
I'LL BE RIGHT THERE—!
BZZT
...
TUP
DAMMIT—
TUP
THAT PRIMA DONNA'S GONNA—
TUP
SHF
EXCUSE ME, MA'AM...

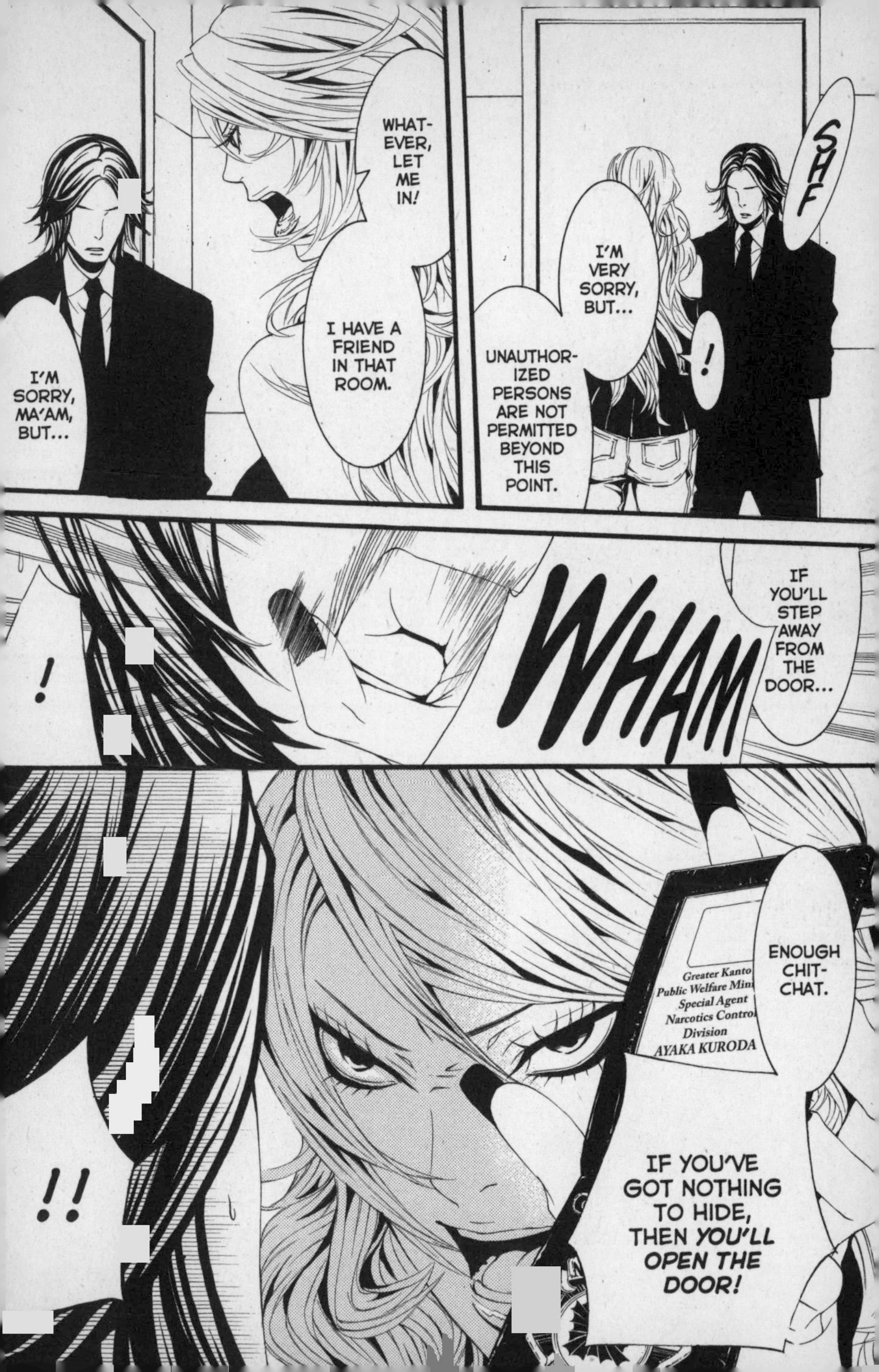
SHF
I'M VERY SORRY, BUT...
!
UNAUTHORIZED PERSONS ARE NOT PERMITTED BEYOND THIS POINT.
WHAT-EVER, LET ME IN!
I HAVE A FRIEND IN THAT ROOM.
I'M SORRY, MA'AM, BUT...
IF YOU'LL STEP AWAY FROM THE DOOR...
WHAM
!
ENOUGH CHIT-CHAT.
Greater Kanto
Public Welfare Mini
Special Agent
Narcotics Contro
Division
AYAKA KURODA
IF YOU'VE GOT NOTHING TO HIDE, THEN *YOU'LL OPEN THE DOOR!*
!!

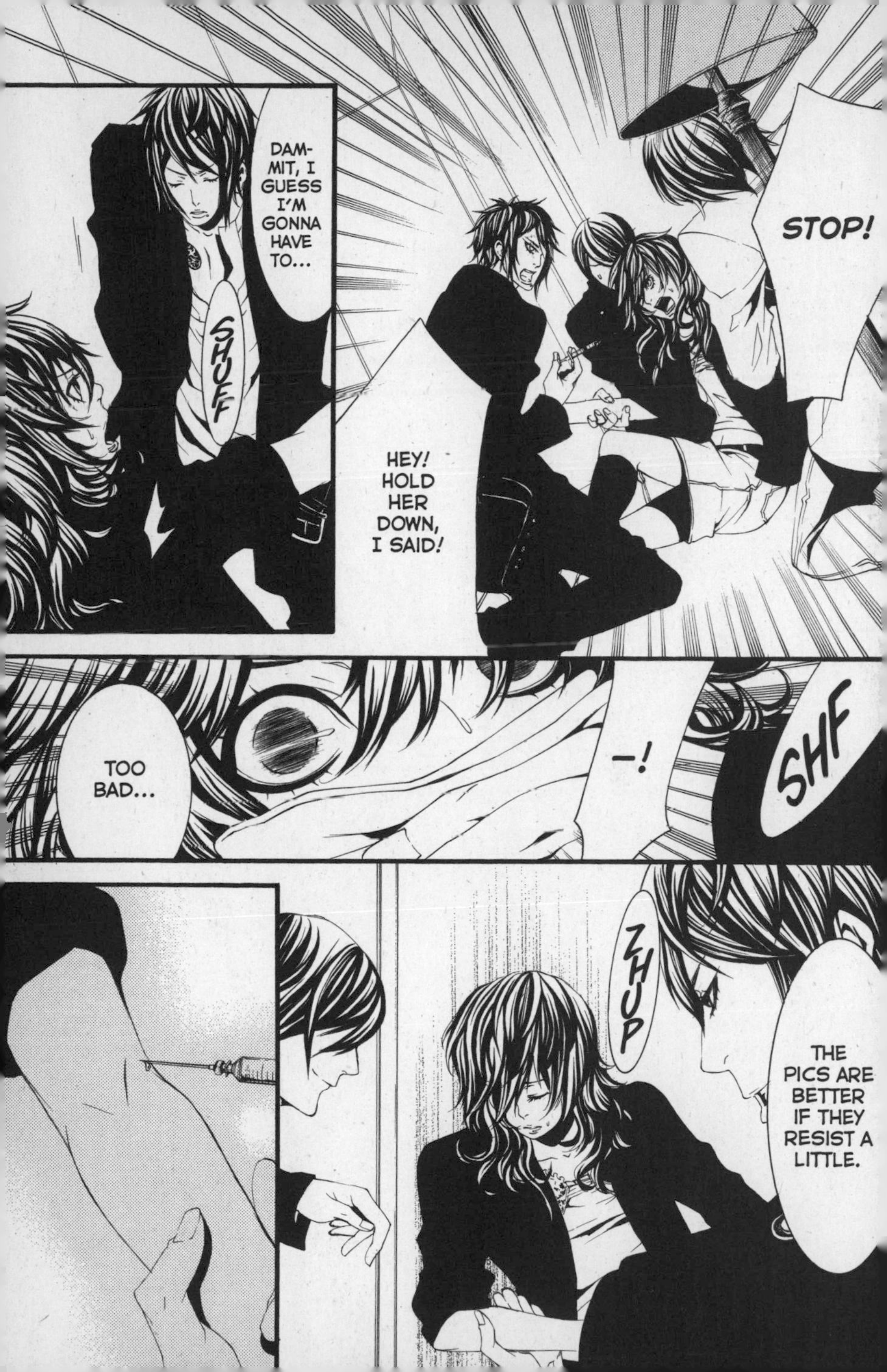
STOP!
HEY! HOLD HER DOWN, I SAID!
DAM-MIT, I GUESS I'M GONNA HAVE TO...
SHUFF
SHF
—!
TOO BAD...
ZHUP
THE PICS ARE BETTER IF THEY RESIST A LITTLE.

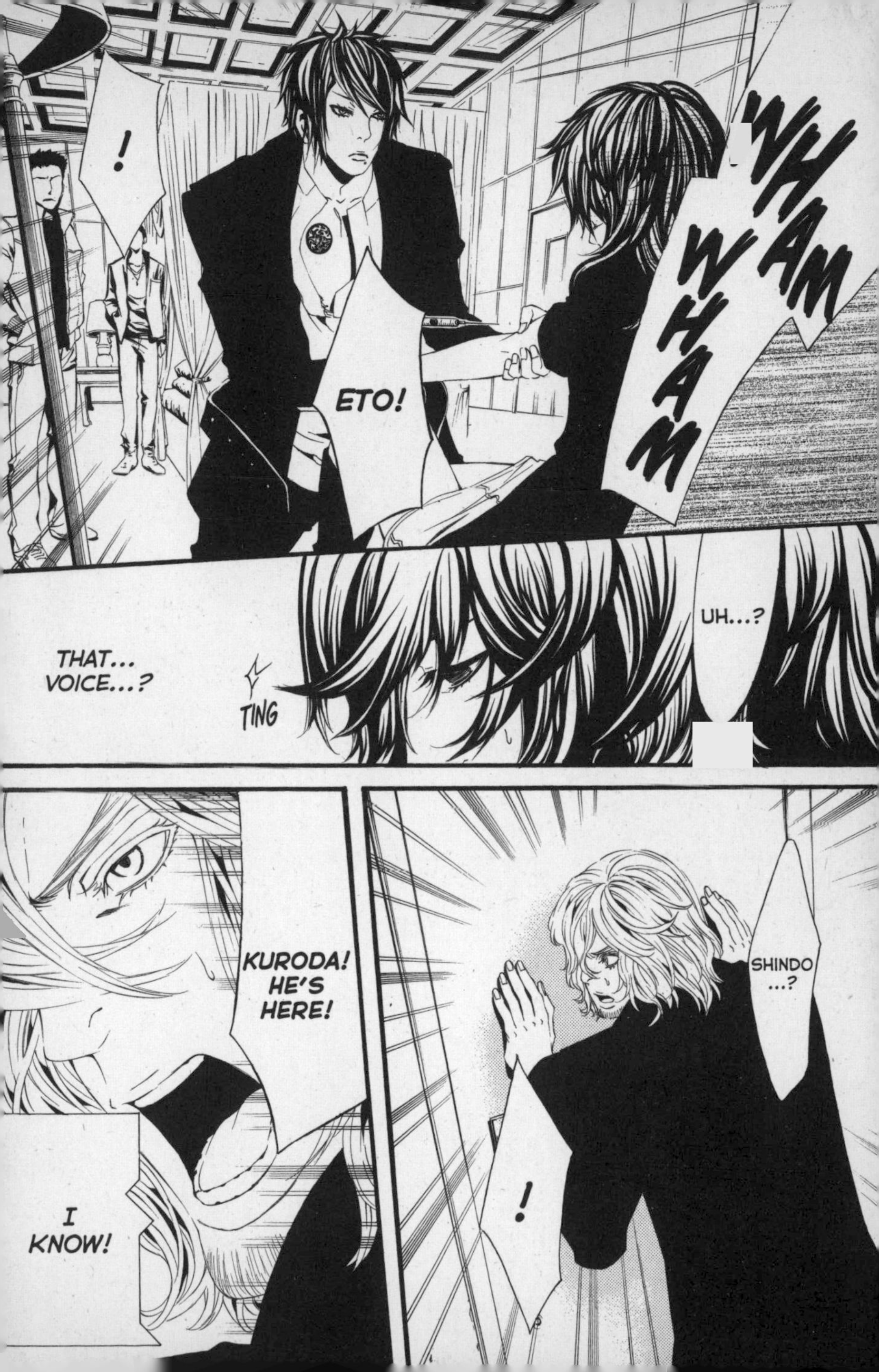
WHAM WHAM
!
ETO!
UH...?
TING
THAT... VOICE...?
SHINDO ...?
!
KURODA! HE'S HERE!
I KNOW!

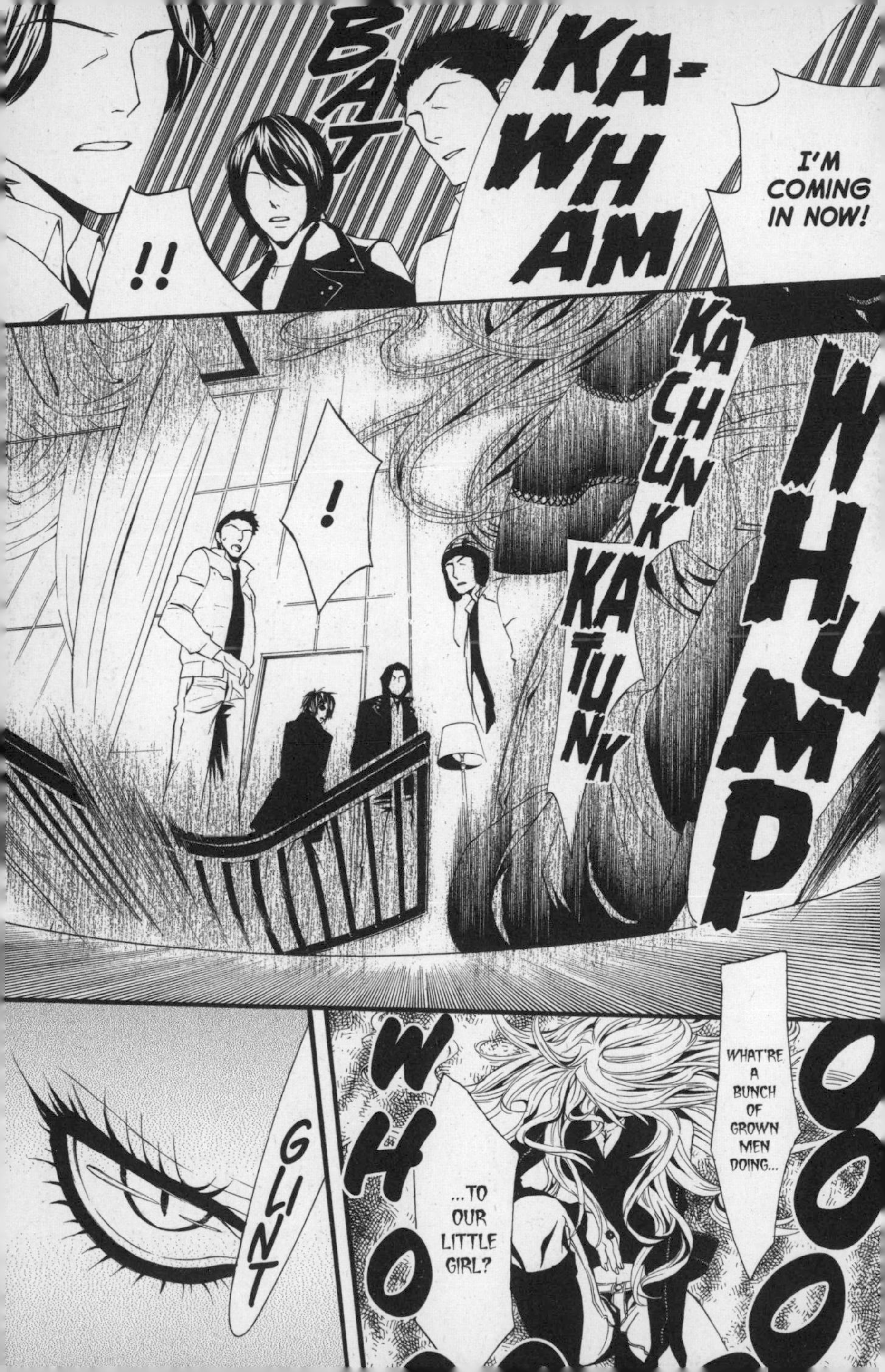
I'M COMING IN NOW!
KA-WHAM
BAM
!!
WHUMP
KACHUNK
KATUNK
!
OOOOO
WHAT'RE A BUNCH OF GROWN MEN DOING...
...TO OUR LITTLE GIRL?
WHOO
GLINT

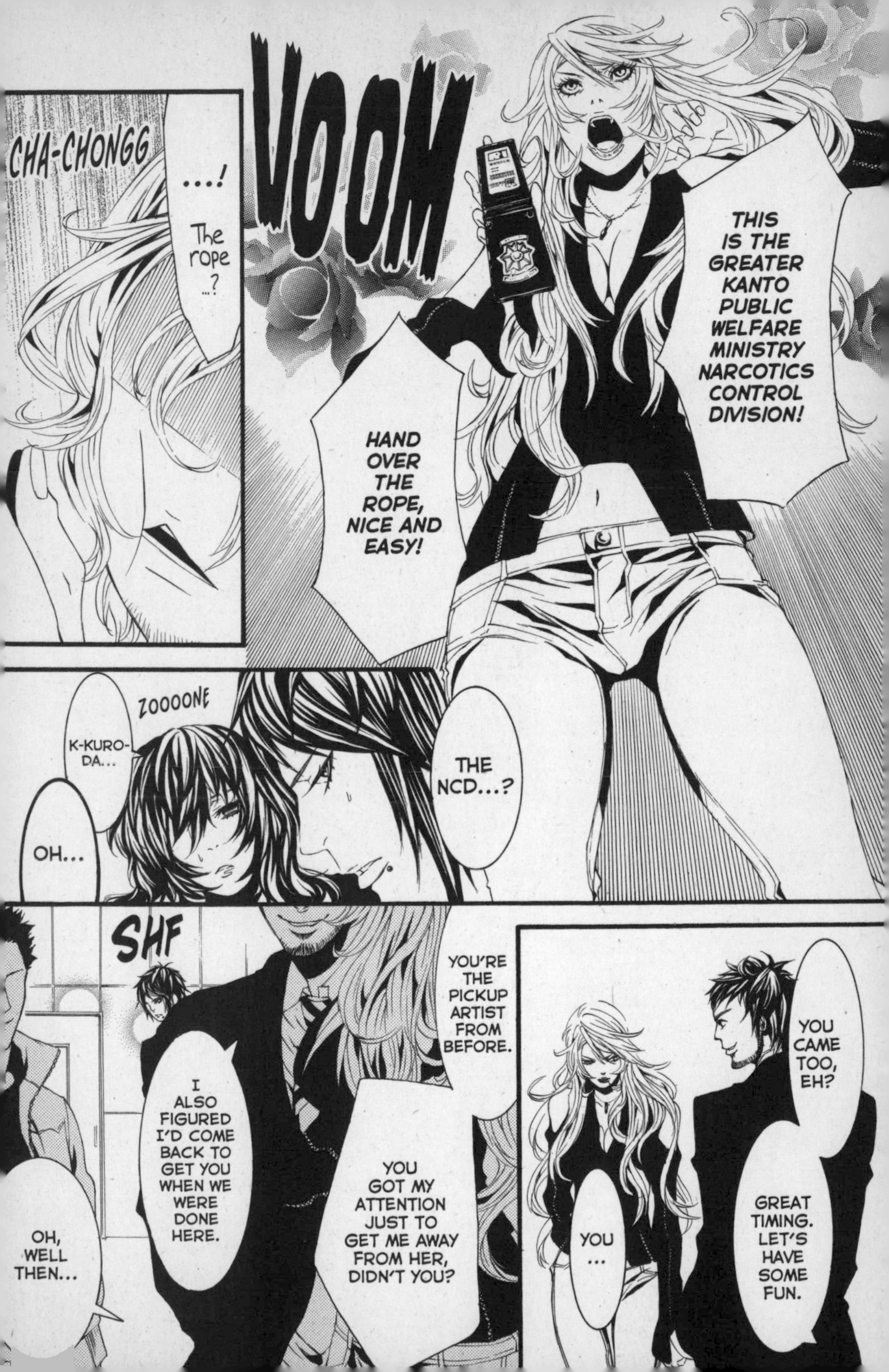
VOOM
THIS IS THE GREATER KANTO PUBLIC WELFARE MINISTRY NARCOTICS CONTROL DIVISION!
HAND OVER THE ROPE, NICE AND EASY!
CHA-CHONGG
...!
The rope ...?
THE NCD...?
ZOOOONE
K-KURODA...
OH...
YOU CAME TOO, EH?
GREAT TIMING. LET'S HAVE SOME FUN.
YOU ...
SHF
YOU'RE THE PICKUP ARTIST FROM BEFORE.
YOU GOT MY ATTENTION JUST TO GET ME AWAY FROM HER, DIDN'T YOU?
I ALSO FIGURED I'D COME BACK TO GET YOU WHEN WE WERE DONE HERE.
OH, WELL THEN...

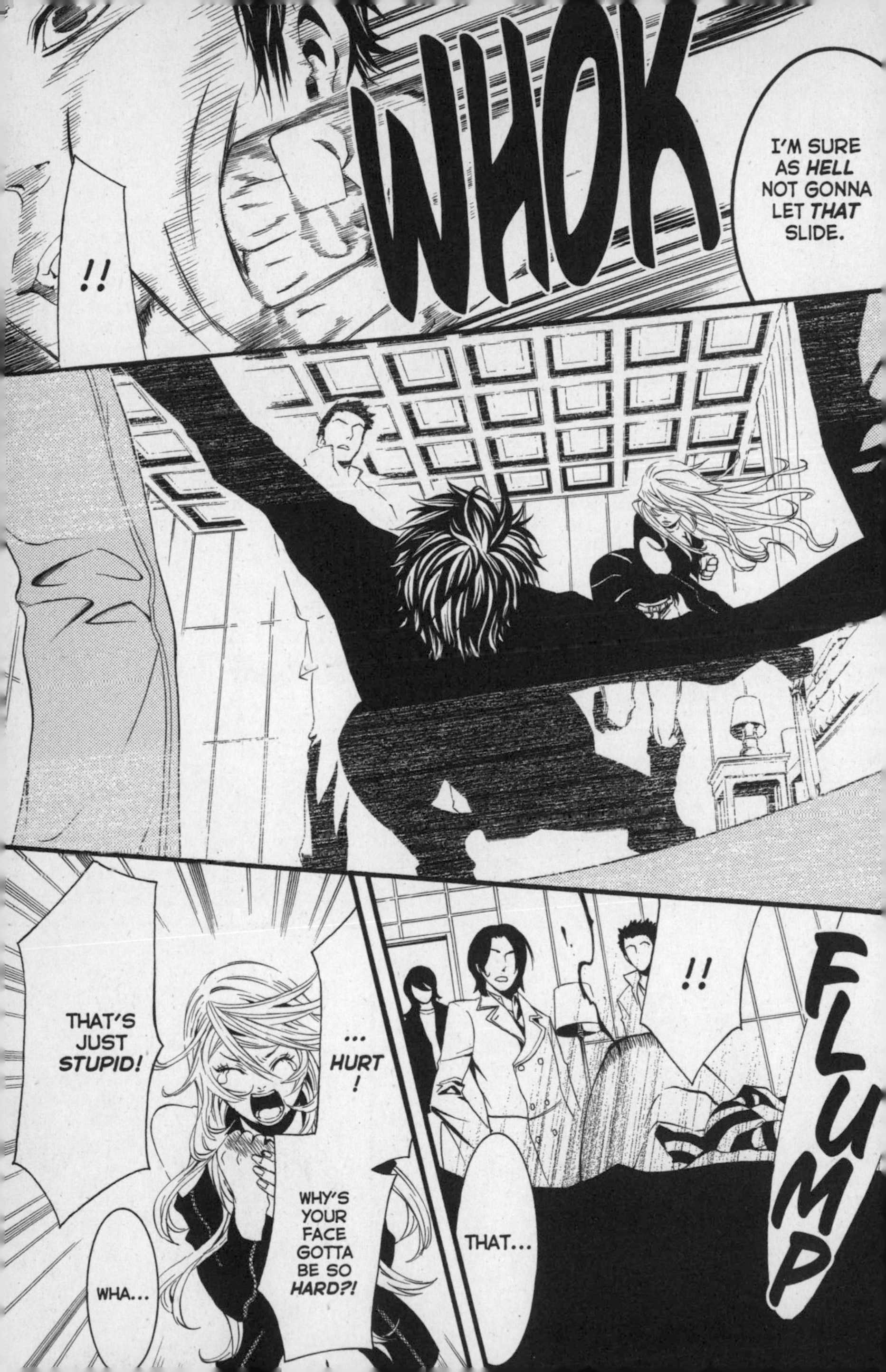
I'M SURE AS *HELL* NOT GONNA LET *THAT* SLIDE.
WHOK
!!
FLUMP
!!
THAT...
... *HURT*!
THAT'S JUST *STUPID*!
WHY'S YOUR FACE GOTTA BE SO *HARD?!*
WHA...

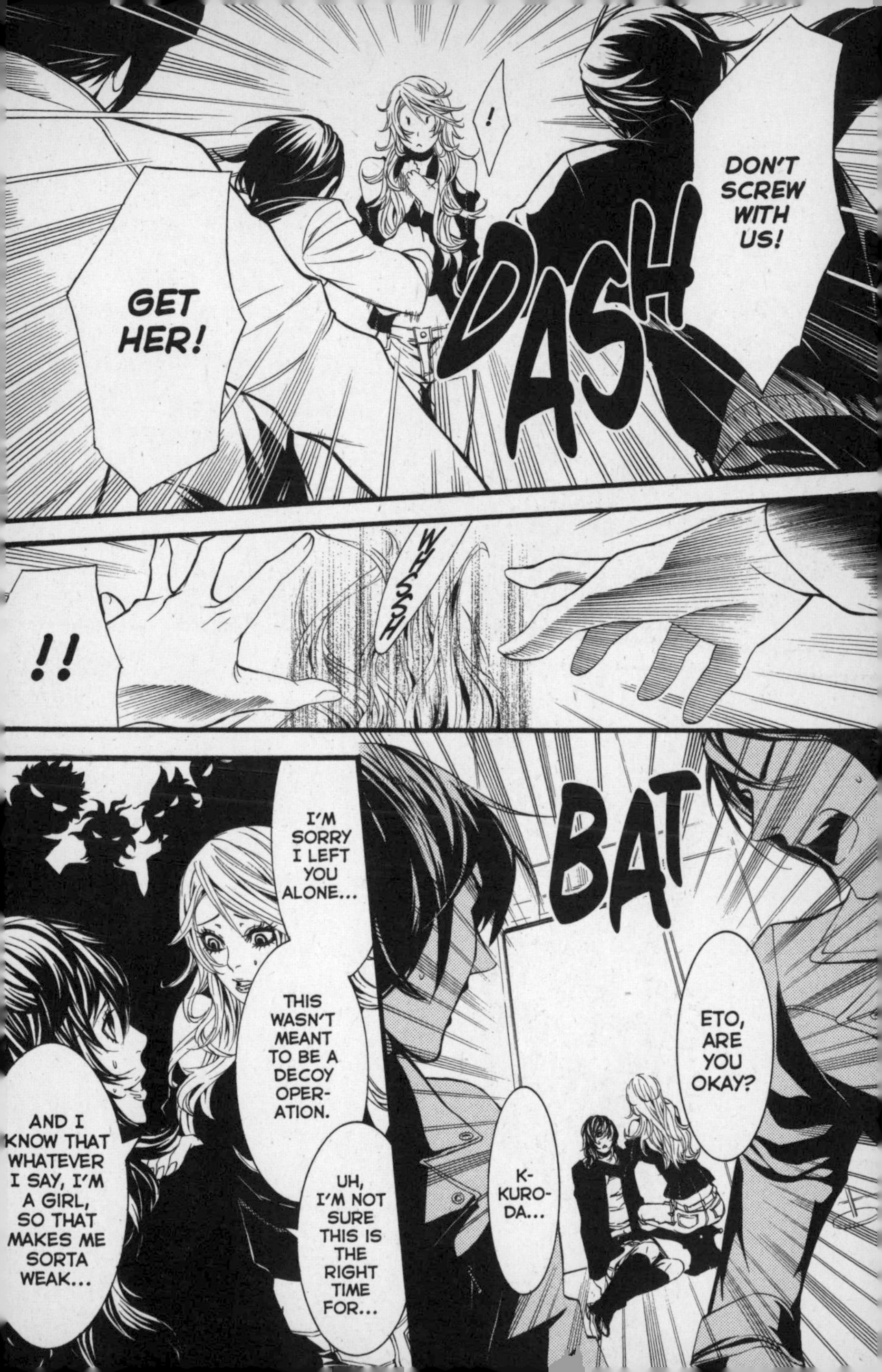

DON'T SCREW WITH US!
DASH
!
GET HER!
WHSSSH
!!
BAT
ETO, ARE YOU OKAY?
K-KURO-DA...
I'M SORRY I LEFT YOU ALONE...
THIS WASN'T MEANT TO BE A DECOY OPER-ATION.
UH, I'M NOT SURE THIS IS THE RIGHT TIME FOR...
AND I KNOW THAT WHATEVER I SAY, I'M A GIRL, SO THAT MAKES ME SORTA WEAK...

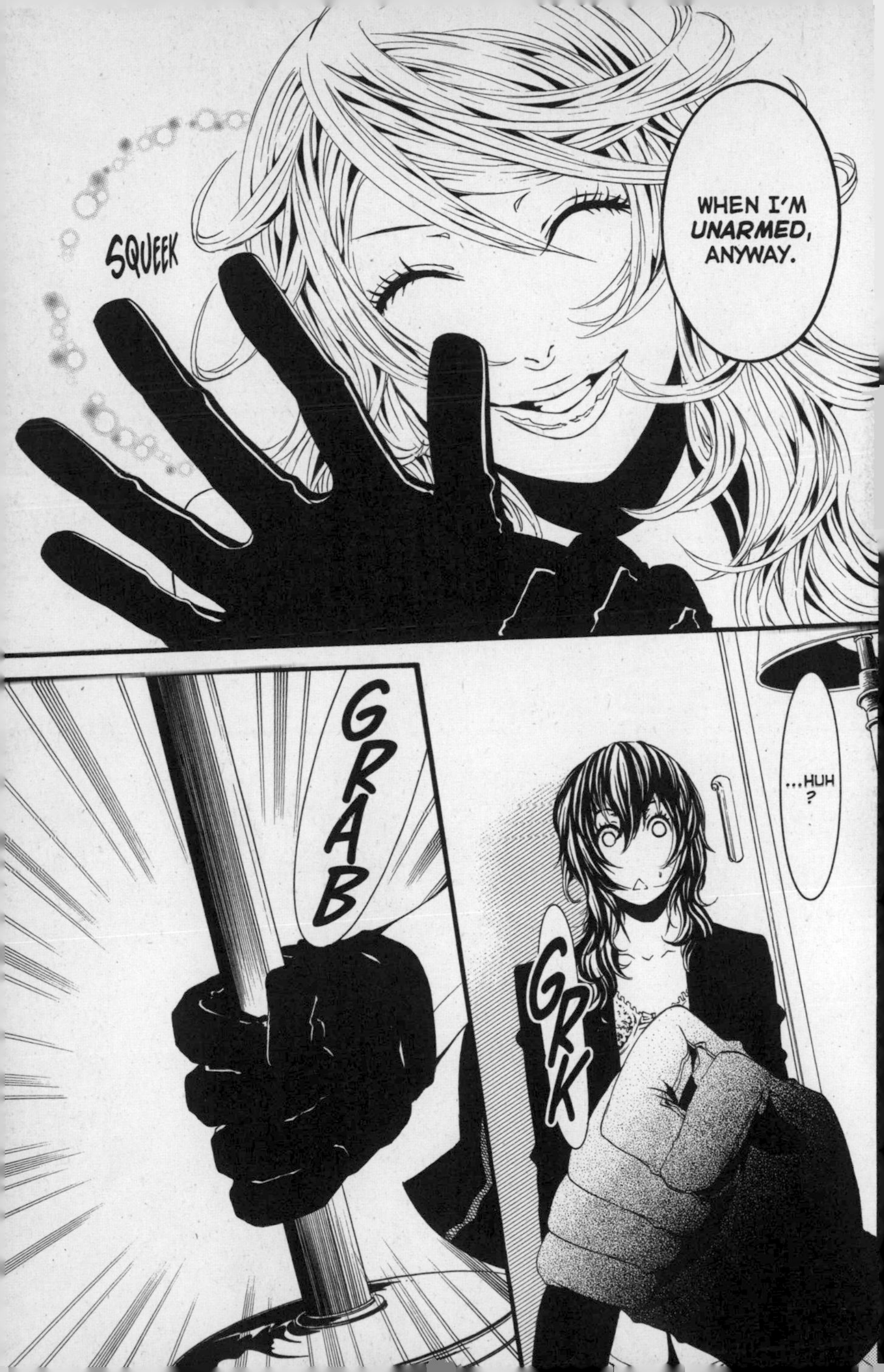
WHEN I'M UNARMED, ANYWAY.
SQUEEK
...HUH?
GRK
GRAB

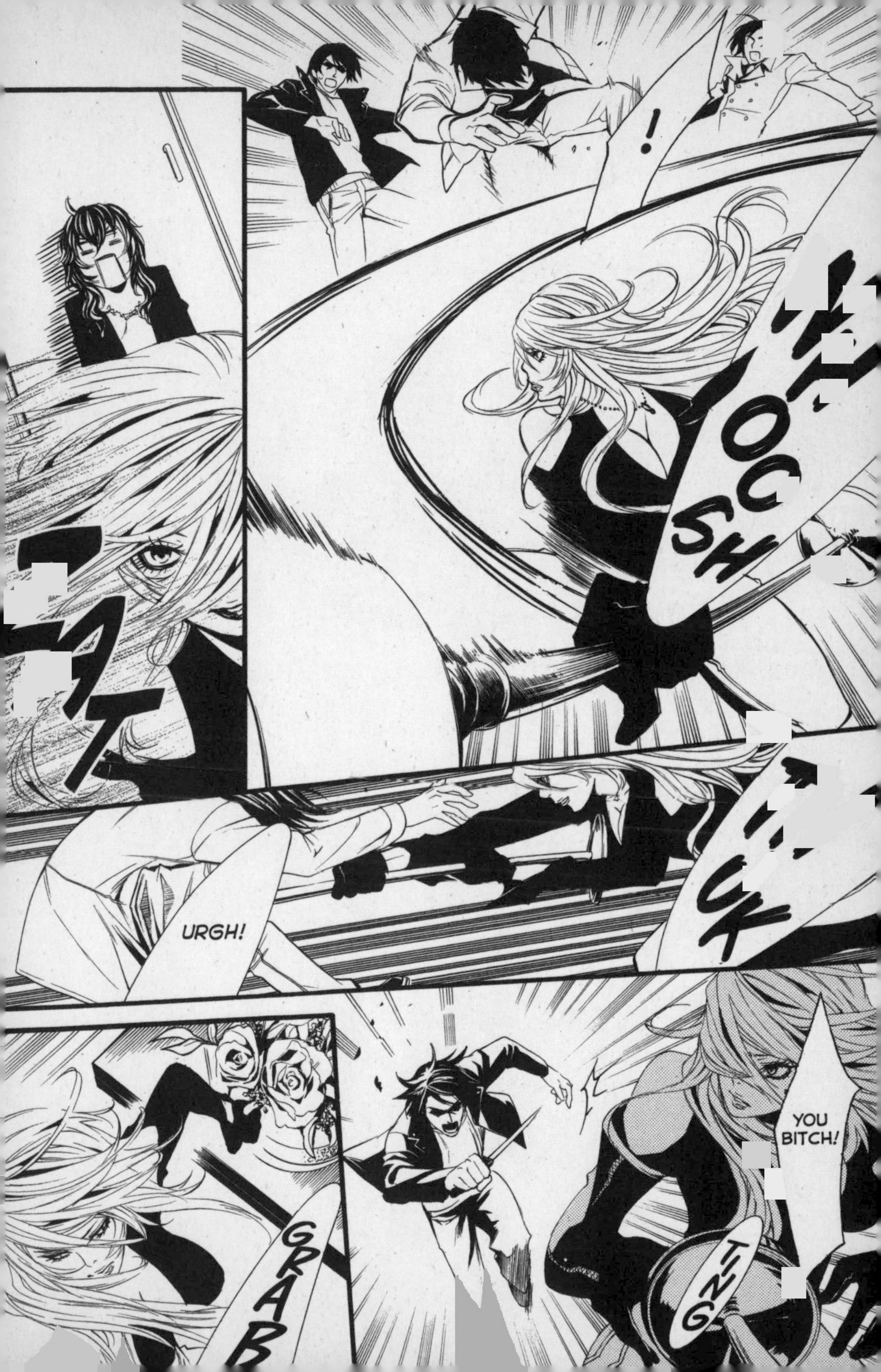
!
URGH!
YOU BITCH!
TING
GRAB

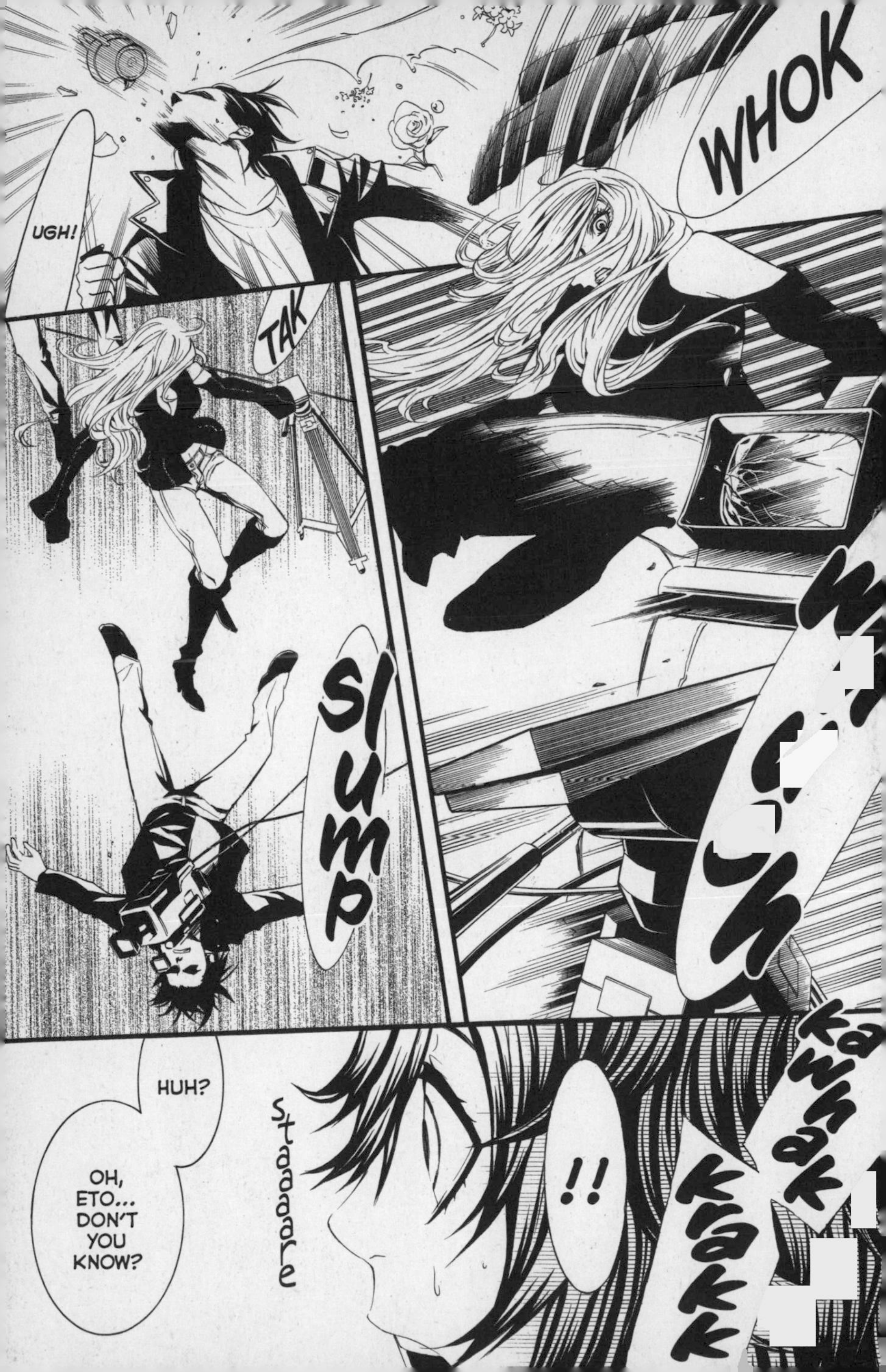
WHOK
UGH!
TAK
slump
krakk
!!
staaaare
HUH?
OH, ETO... DON'T YOU KNOW?

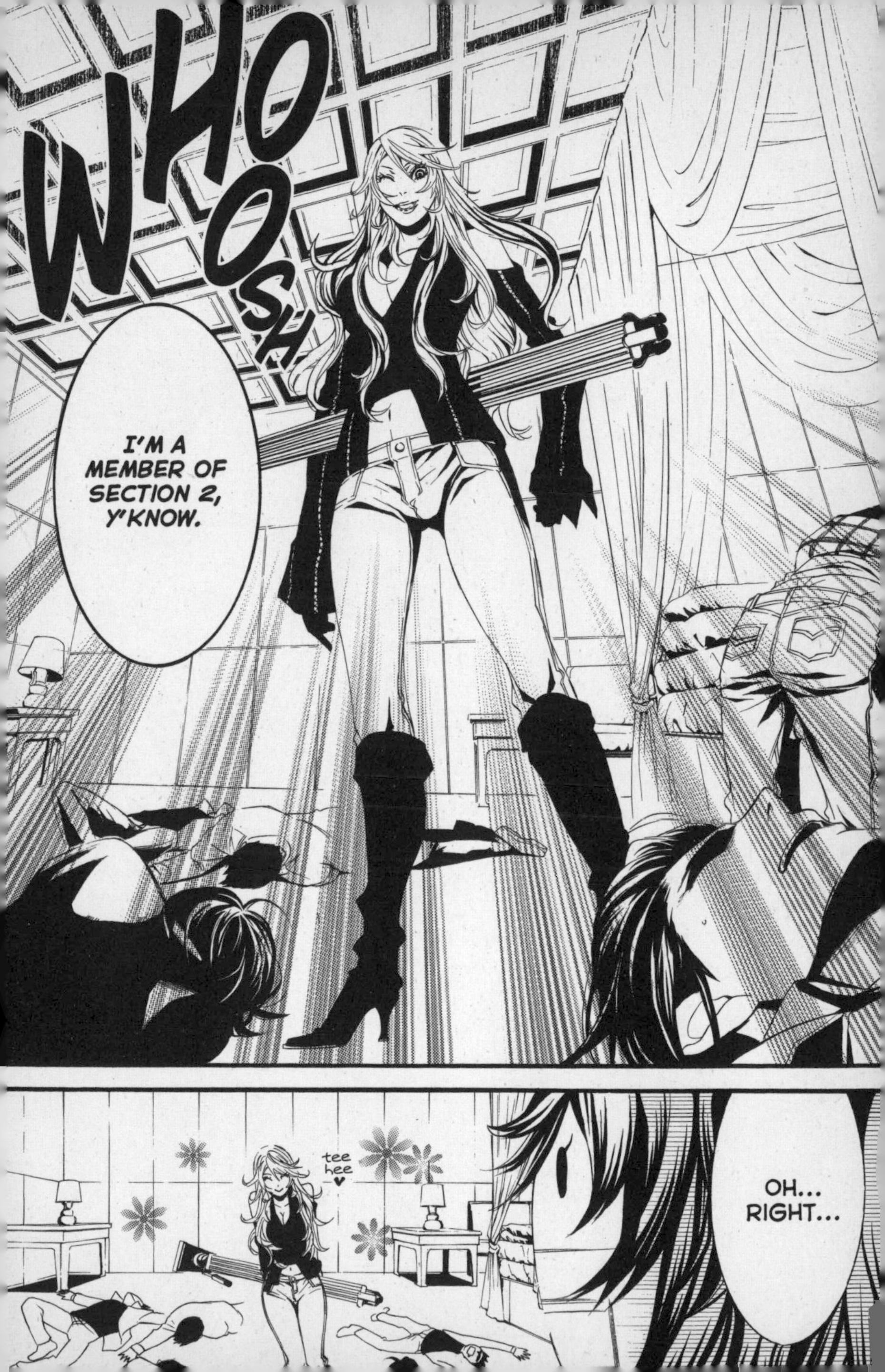
WHOOSH
I'M A MEMBER OF SECTION 2, Y'KNOW.
OH... RIGHT...
tee hee ♥

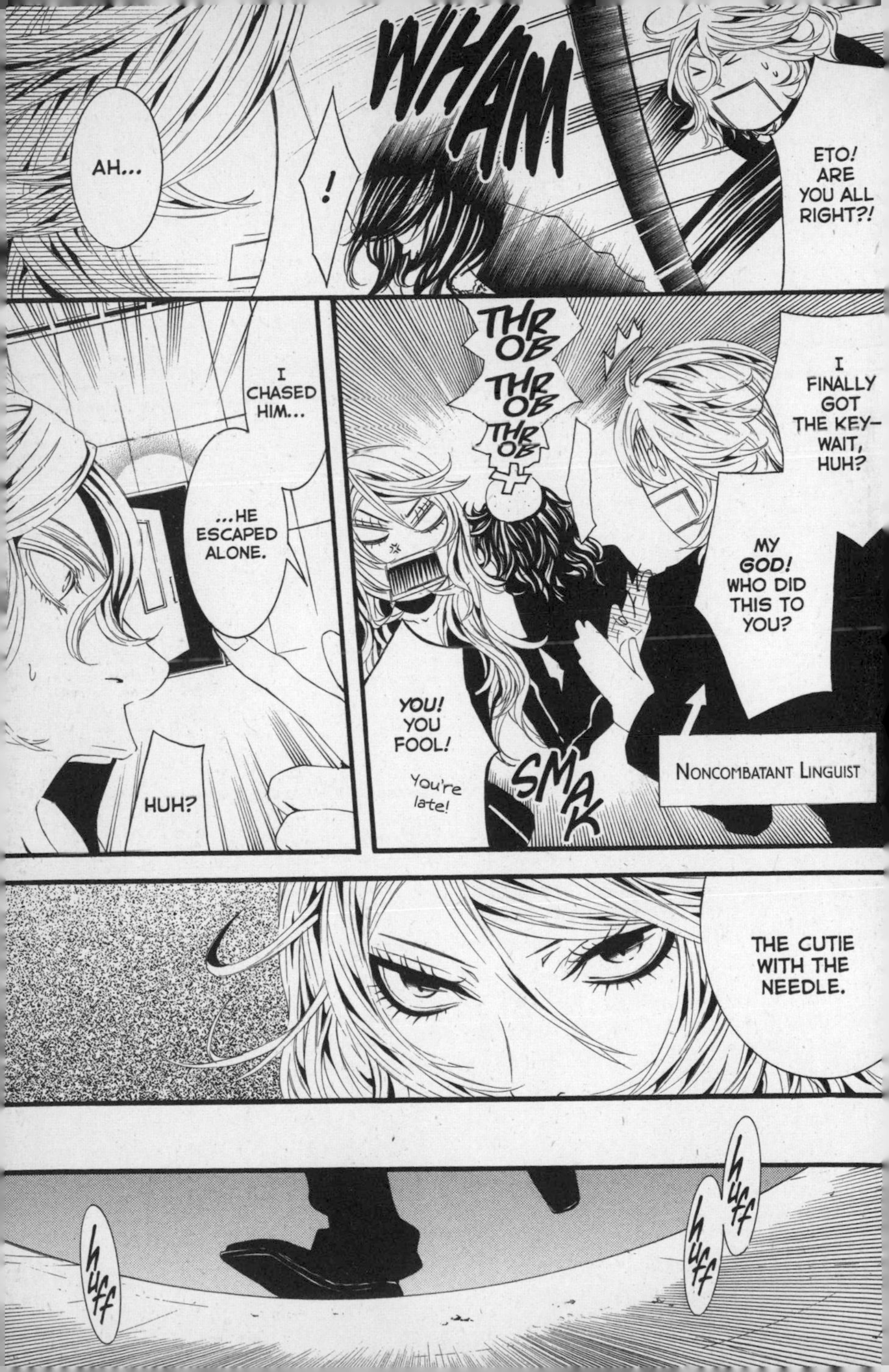
ETO! ARE YOU ALL RIGHT?!
WHAM
!
AH...
I FINALLY GOT THE KEY— WAIT, HUH?
MY GOD! WHO DID THIS TO YOU?
THROB THROB THROB
YOU! YOU FOOL!
You're late!
SMAK
Noncombatant Linguist
I CHASED HIM...
...HE ESCAPED ALONE.
HUH?
THE CUTIE WITH THE NEEDLE.
huff
huff
huff

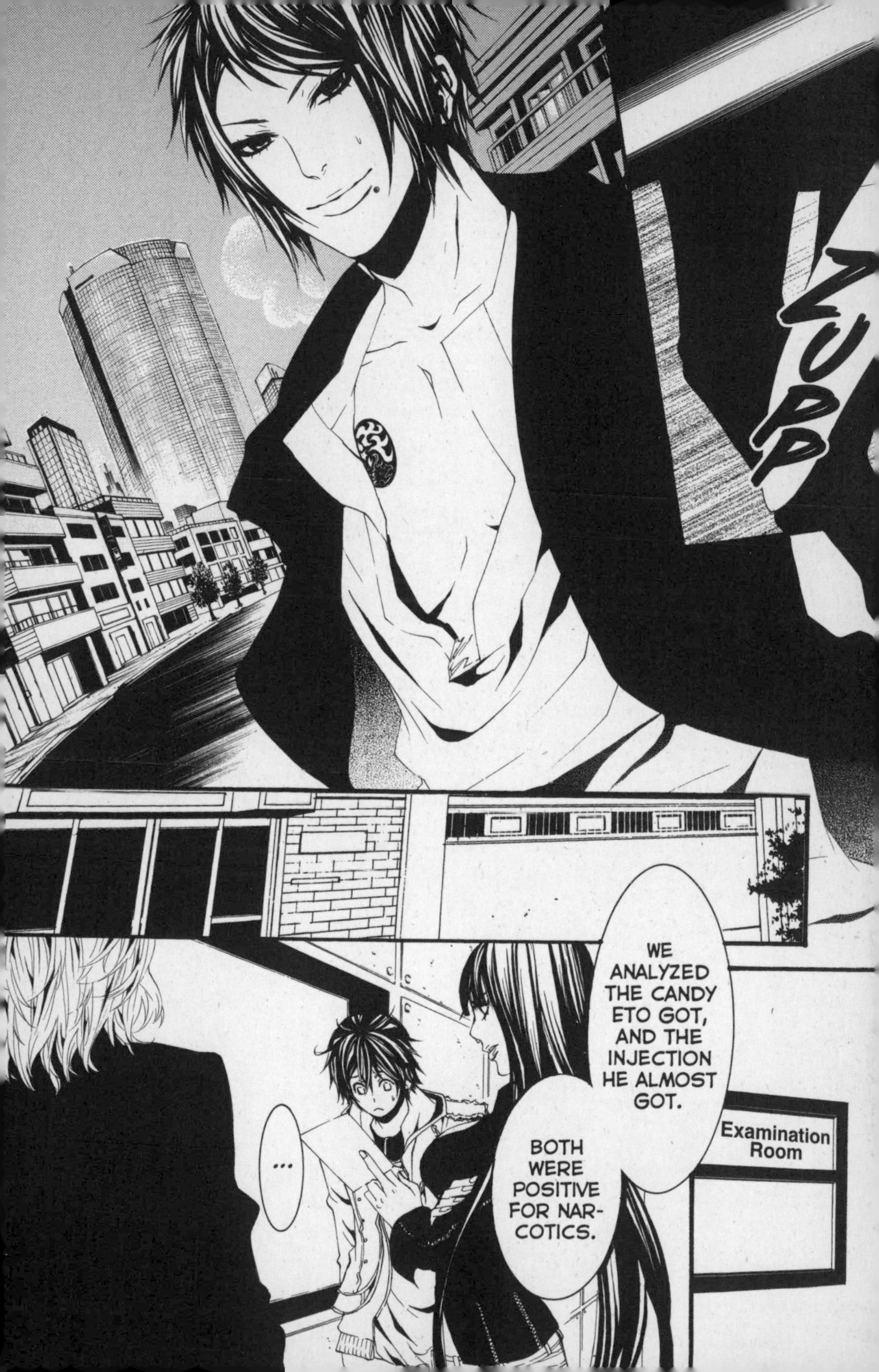
ZUPP
WE ANALYZED THE CANDY ETO GOT, AND THE INJECTION HE ALMOST GOT.
BOTH WERE POSITIVE FOR NAR-COTICS.
Examination Room
...

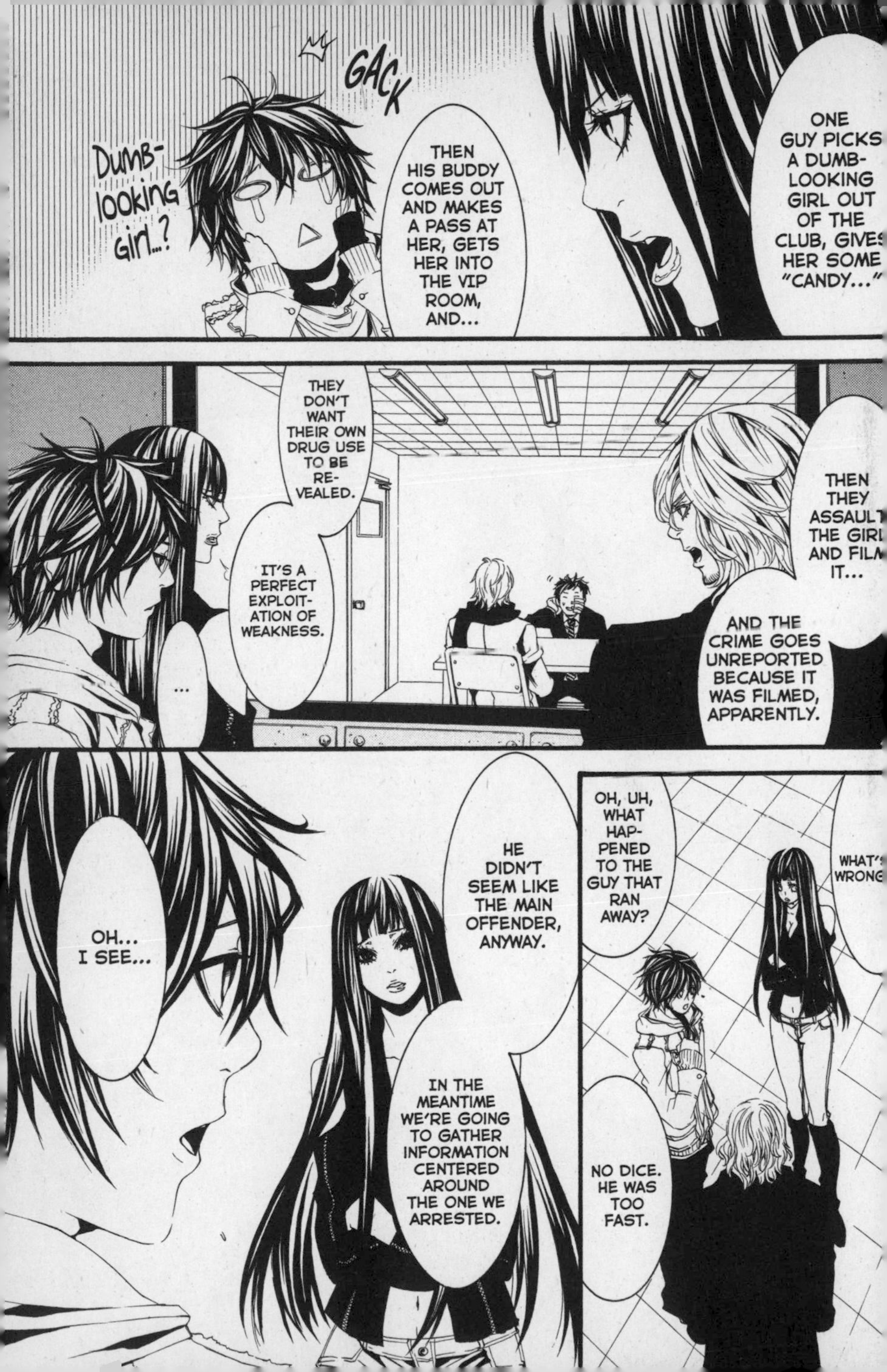

ONE GUY PICKS A DUMB-LOOKING GIRL OUT OF THE CLUB, GIVES HER SOME "CANDY..."
GACK
THEN HIS BUDDY COMES OUT AND MAKES A PASS AT HER, GETS HER INTO THE VIP ROOM, AND...
Dumb-looking Girl...?
THEN THEY ASSAULT THE GIRL AND FILM IT...
AND THE CRIME GOES UNREPORTED BECAUSE IT WAS FILMED, APPARENTLY.
THEY DON'T WANT THEIR OWN DRUG USE TO BE RE-VEALED.
IT'S A PERFECT EXPLOIT-ATION OF WEAKNESS.
...
WHAT'S WRONG
OH, UH, WHAT HAP-PENED TO THE GUY THAT RAN AWAY?
NO DICE. HE WAS TOO FAST.
HE DIDN'T SEEM LIKE THE MAIN OFFENDER, ANYWAY.
IN THE MEANTIME WE'RE GOING TO GATHER INFORMATION CENTERED AROUND THE ONE WE ARRESTED.
OH... I SEE...

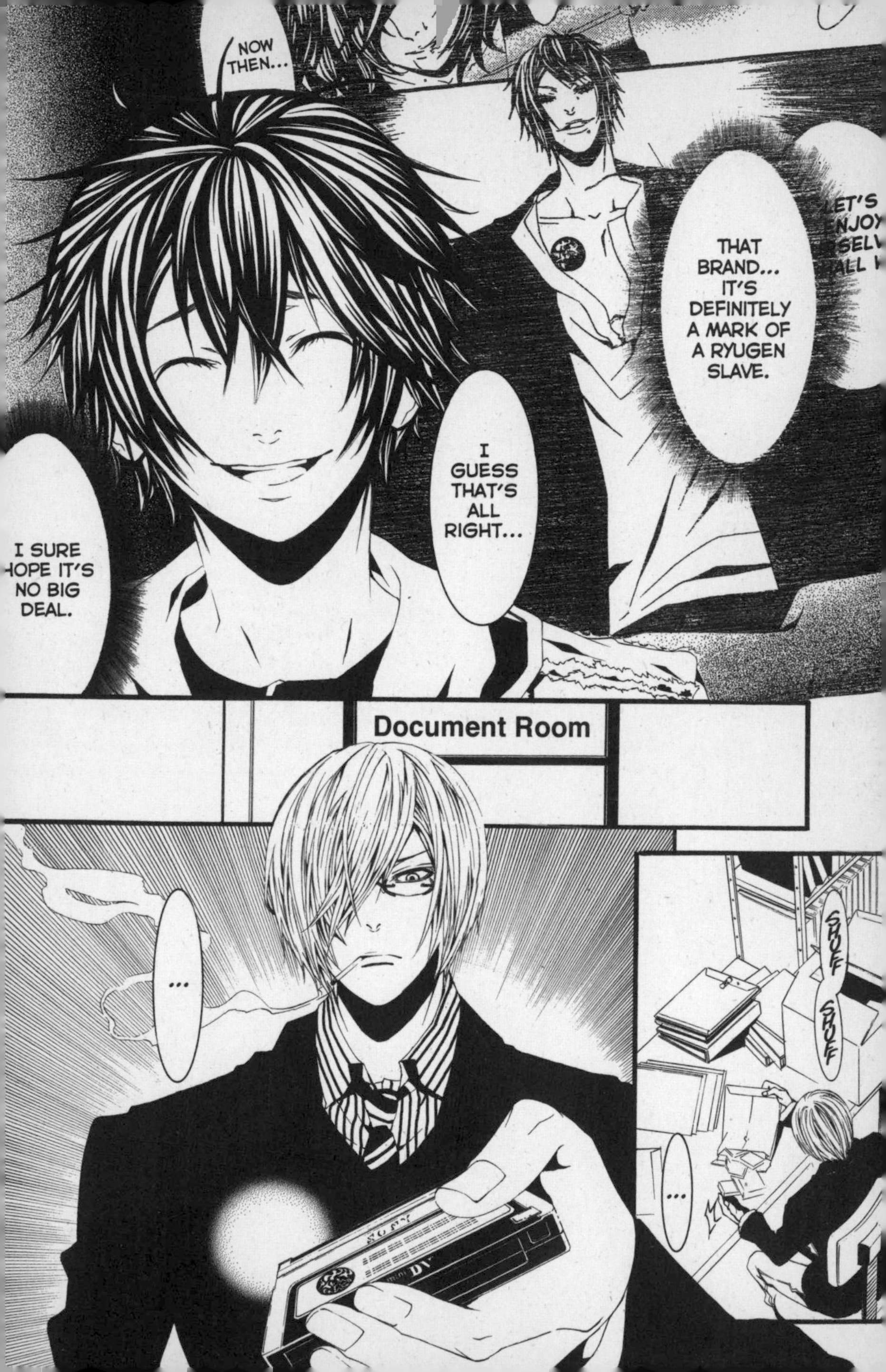
NOW THEN...
THAT BRAND... IT'S DEFINITELY A MARK OF A RYUGEN SLAVE.
I GUESS THAT'S ALL RIGHT...
I SURE HOPE IT'S NO BIG DEAL.
Document Room
SHUFF
SHUFF
...
...

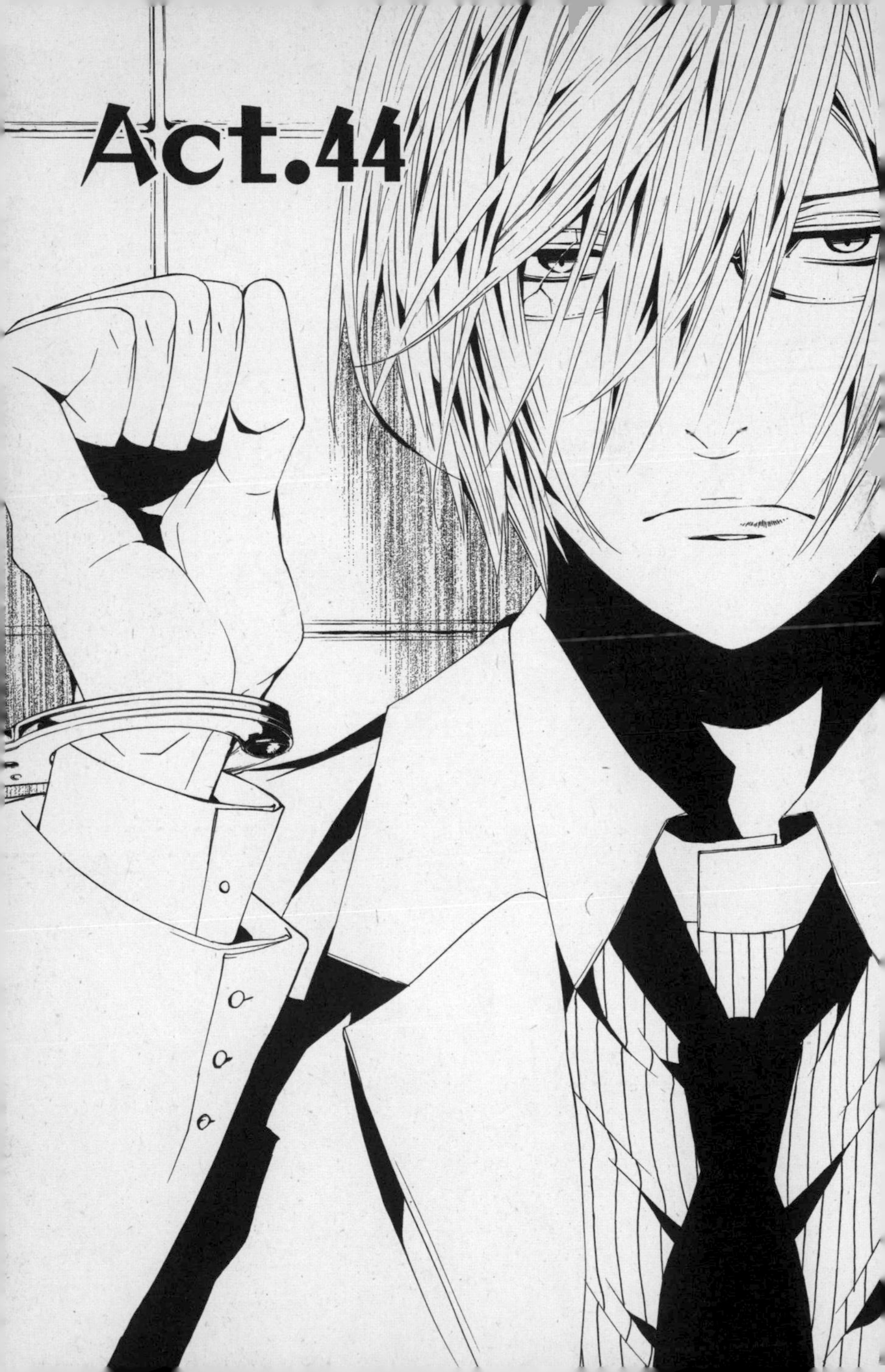
Act.44

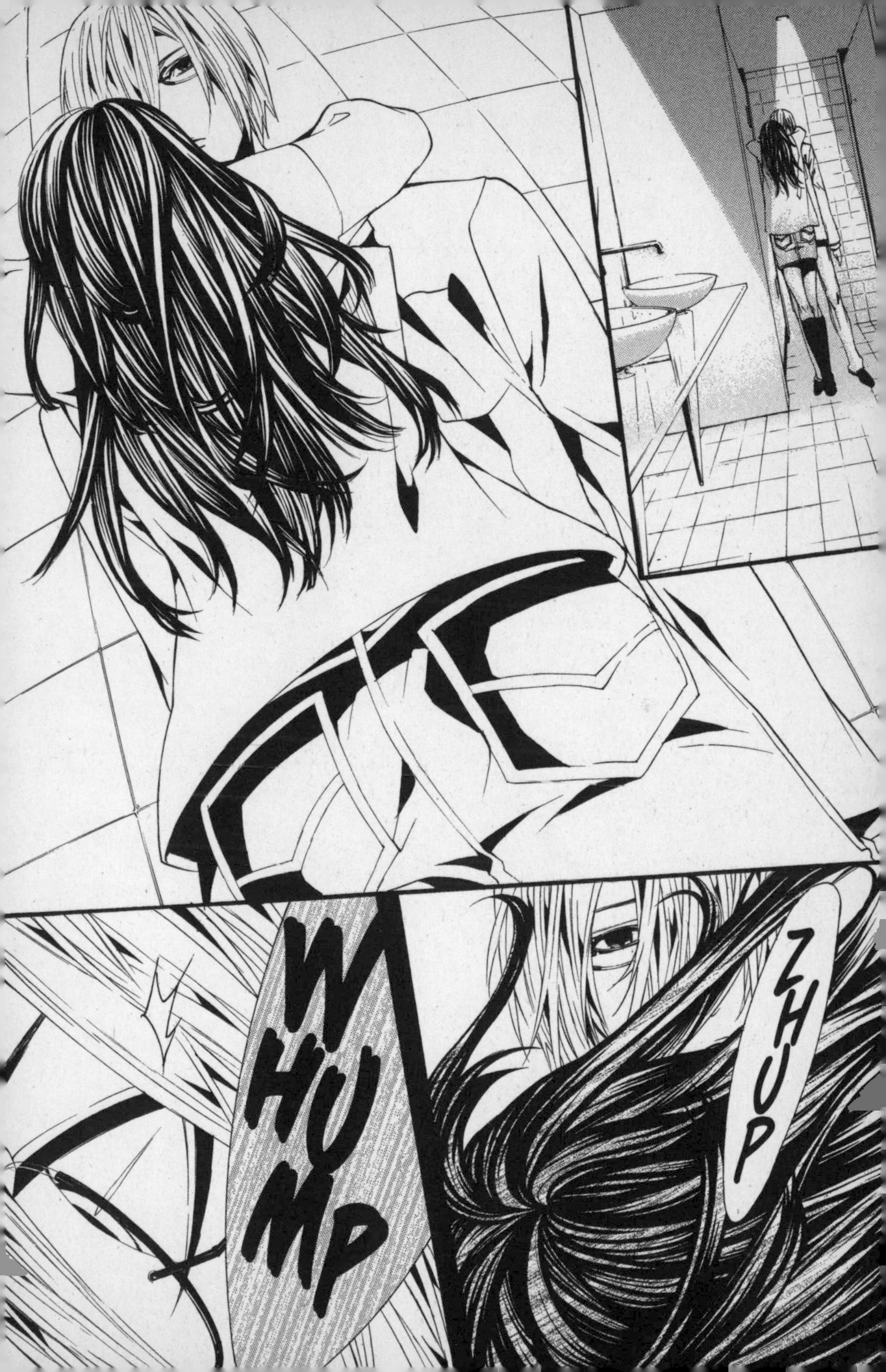
ZHUP
WHUMP

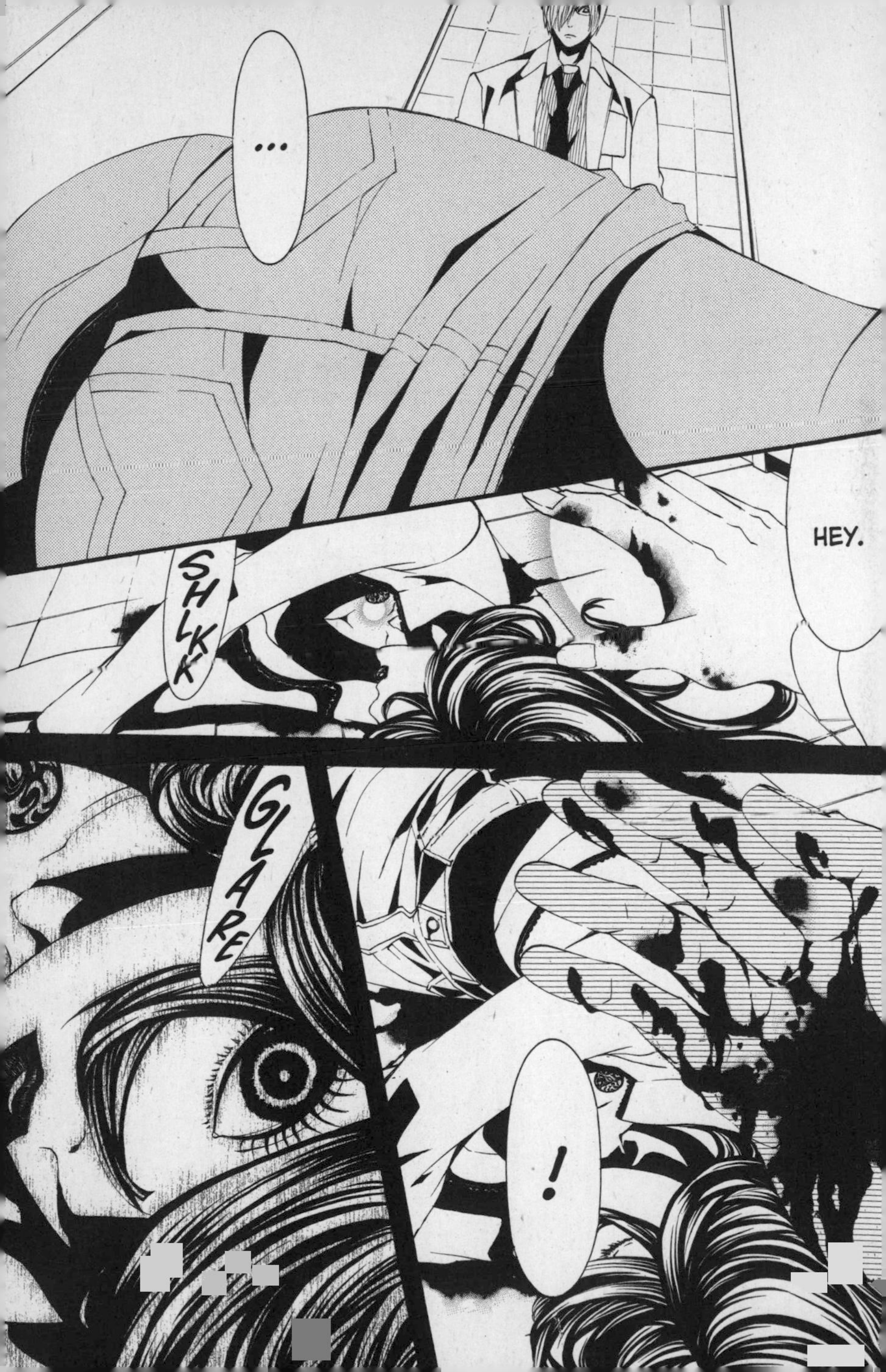
...
HEY.
SHLKK
!
GLARE

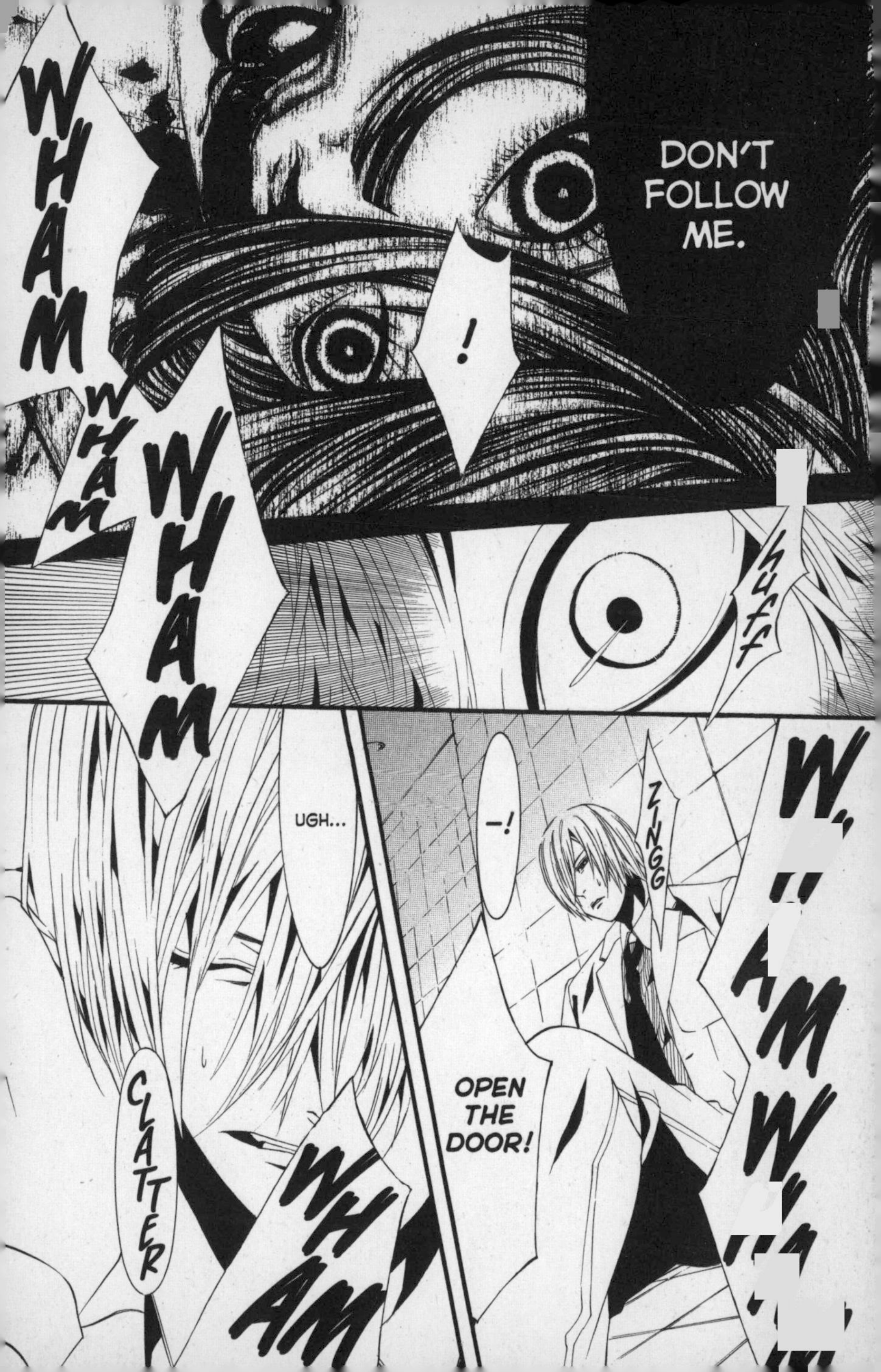

DON'T FOLLOW ME.
!
WHAM
WHAM
WHAM
huff
ZINGG
—!
OPEN THE DOOR!
UGH...
CLATTER
WHAM

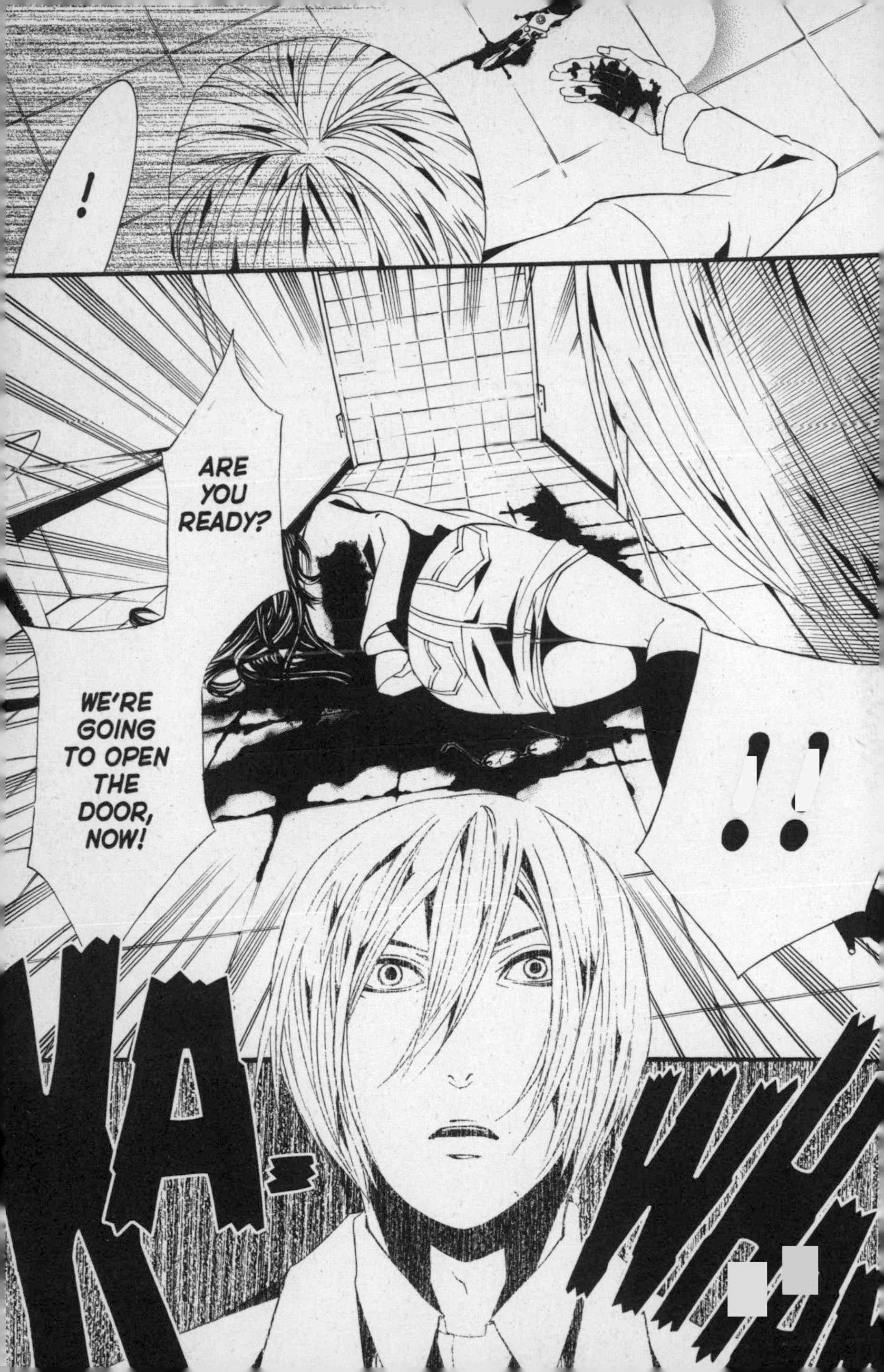
!
ARE YOU READY?
WE'RE GOING TO OPEN THE DOOR, NOW!
!!
HA-HAHA

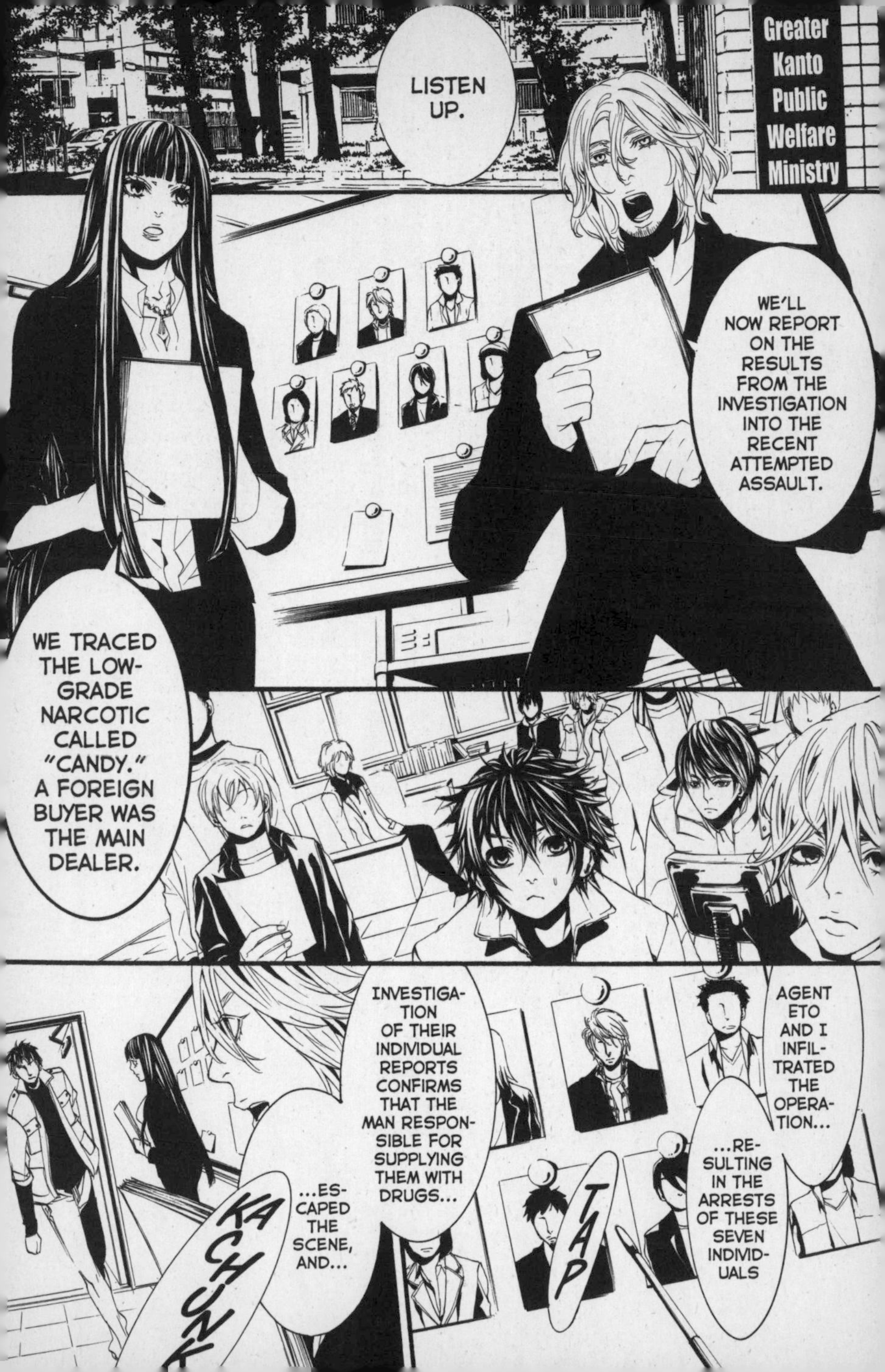
Greater Kanto Public Welfare Ministry
LISTEN UP.
WE'LL NOW REPORT ON THE RESULTS FROM THE INVESTIGATION INTO THE RECENT ATTEMPTED ASSAULT.
WE TRACED THE LOW-GRADE NARCOTIC CALLED "CANDY." A FOREIGN BUYER WAS THE MAIN DEALER.
AGENT ETO AND I INFILTRATED THE OPERATION...
...RESULTING IN THE ARRESTS OF THESE SEVEN INDIVIDUALS
TAP
INVESTIGATION OF THEIR INDIVIDUAL REPORTS CONFIRMS THAT THE MAN RESPONSIBLE FOR SUPPLYING THEM WITH DRUGS...
...ESCAPED THE SCENE, AND...
KACHUNK

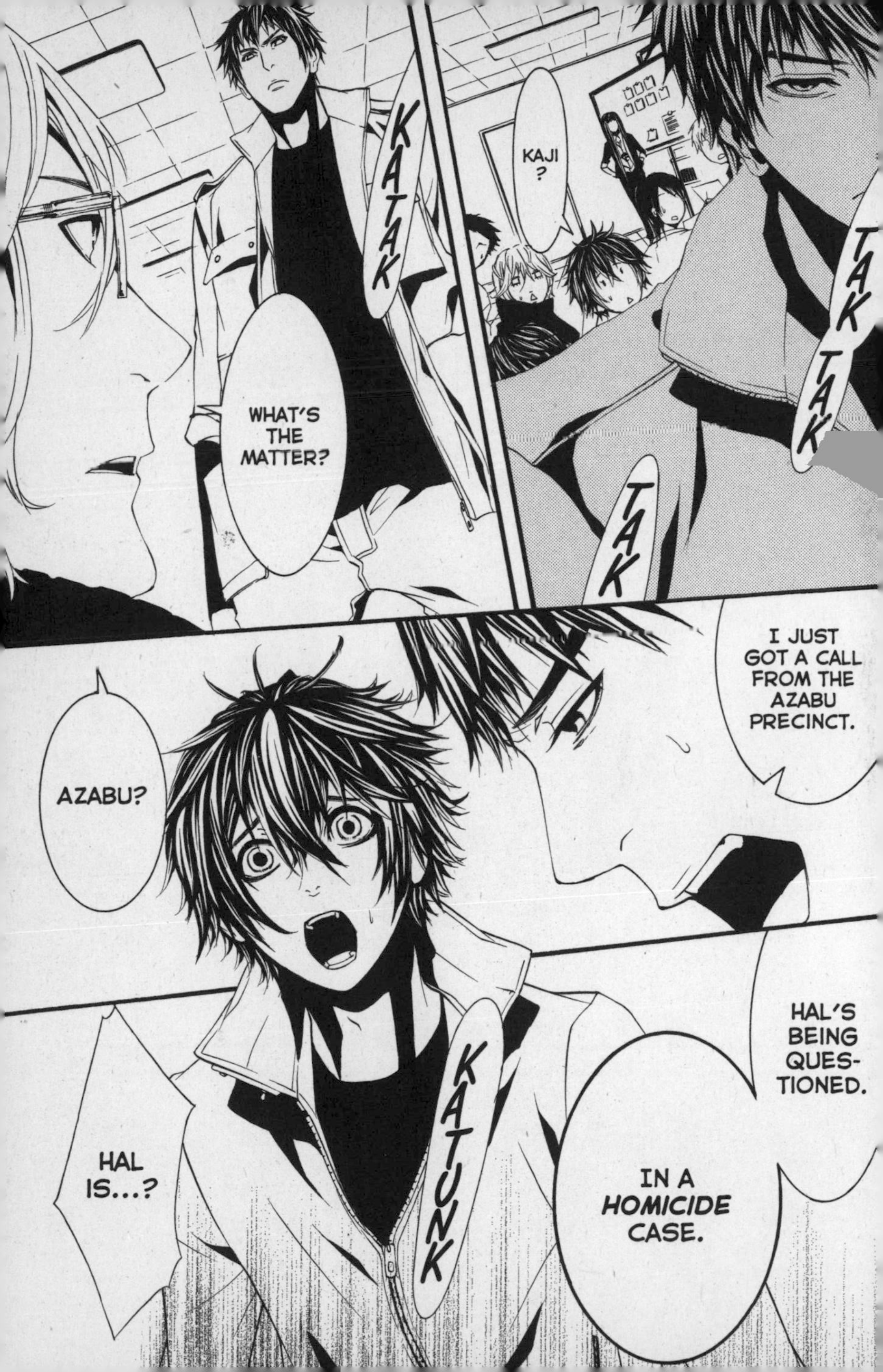

TAK TAK
KAJI?
TAK
KATAK
WHAT'S THE MATTER?
I JUST GOT A CALL FROM THE AZABU PRECINCT.
AZABU?
HAL'S BEING QUES-TIONED.
IN A *HOMICIDE* CASE.
KATUNK
HAL IS...?

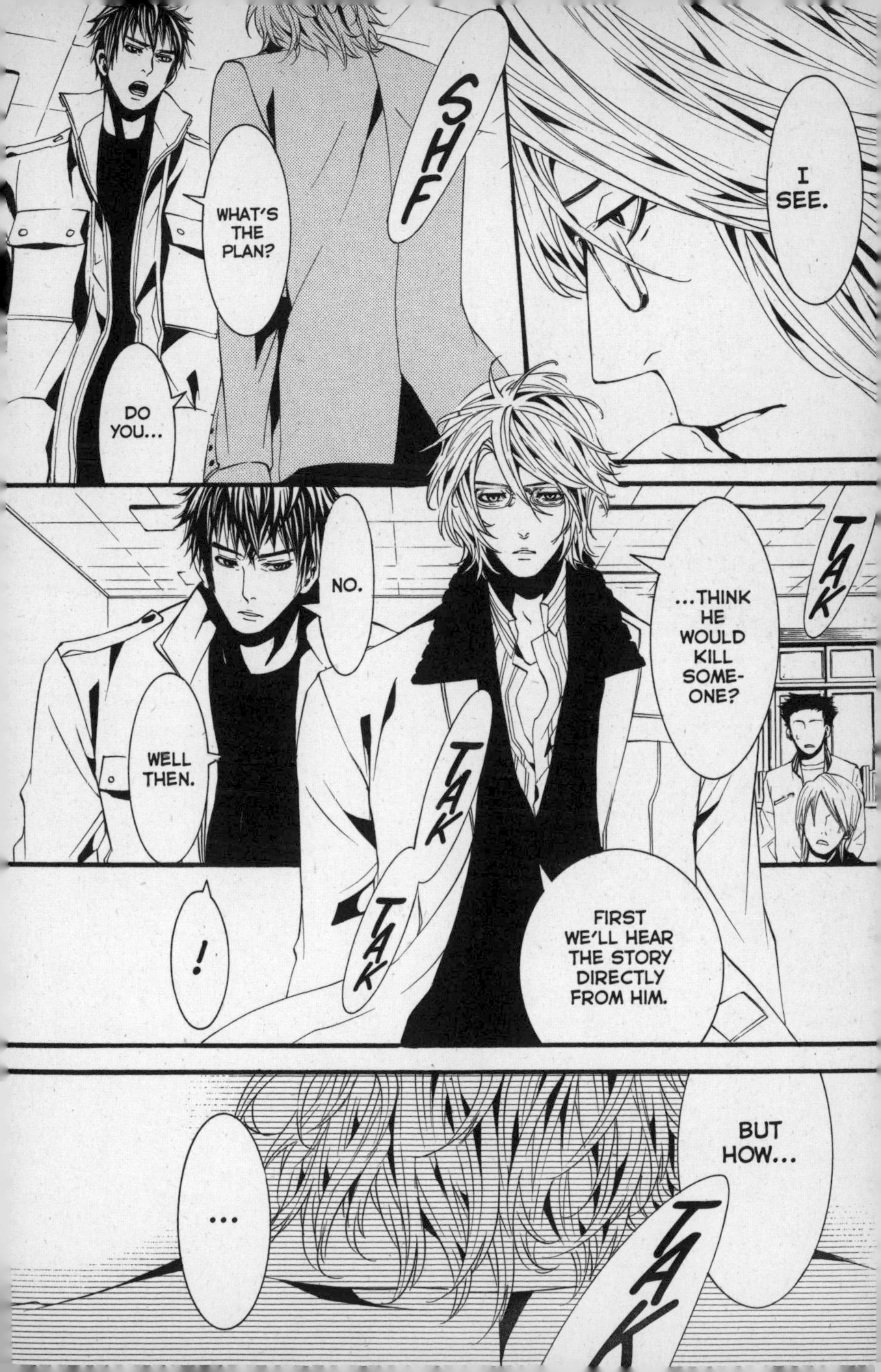
I SEE.
SHF
WHAT'S THE PLAN?
DO YOU...
TAK
...THINK HE WOULD KILL SOME-ONE?
NO.
WELL THEN.
TAK
FIRST WE'LL HEAR THE STORY DIRECTLY FROM HIM.
TAK
!
BUT HOW...
TAK
...

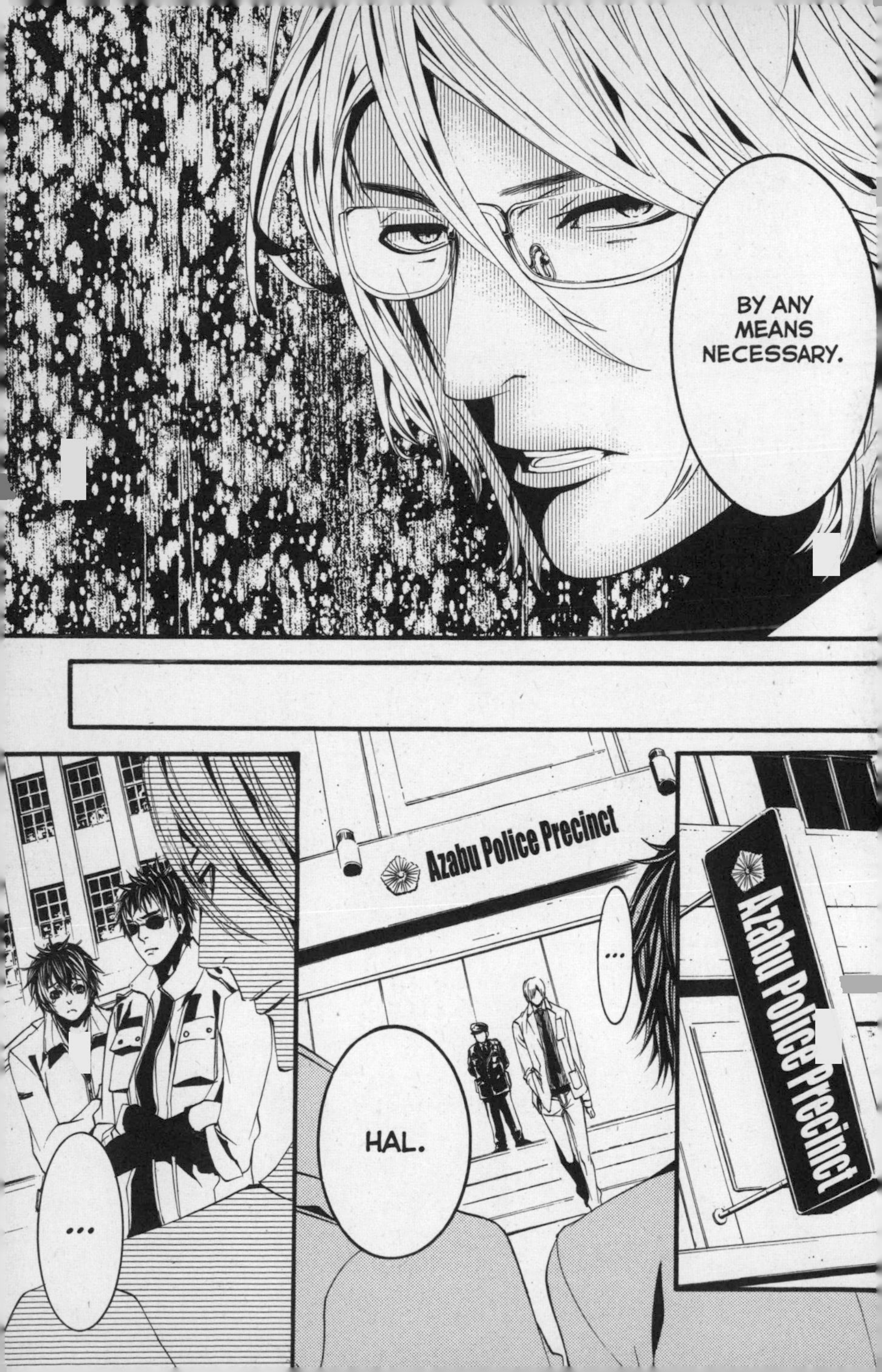
BY ANY MEANS NECESSARY.
Azabu Police Precinct
Azabu Police Precinct
...
HAL.
...

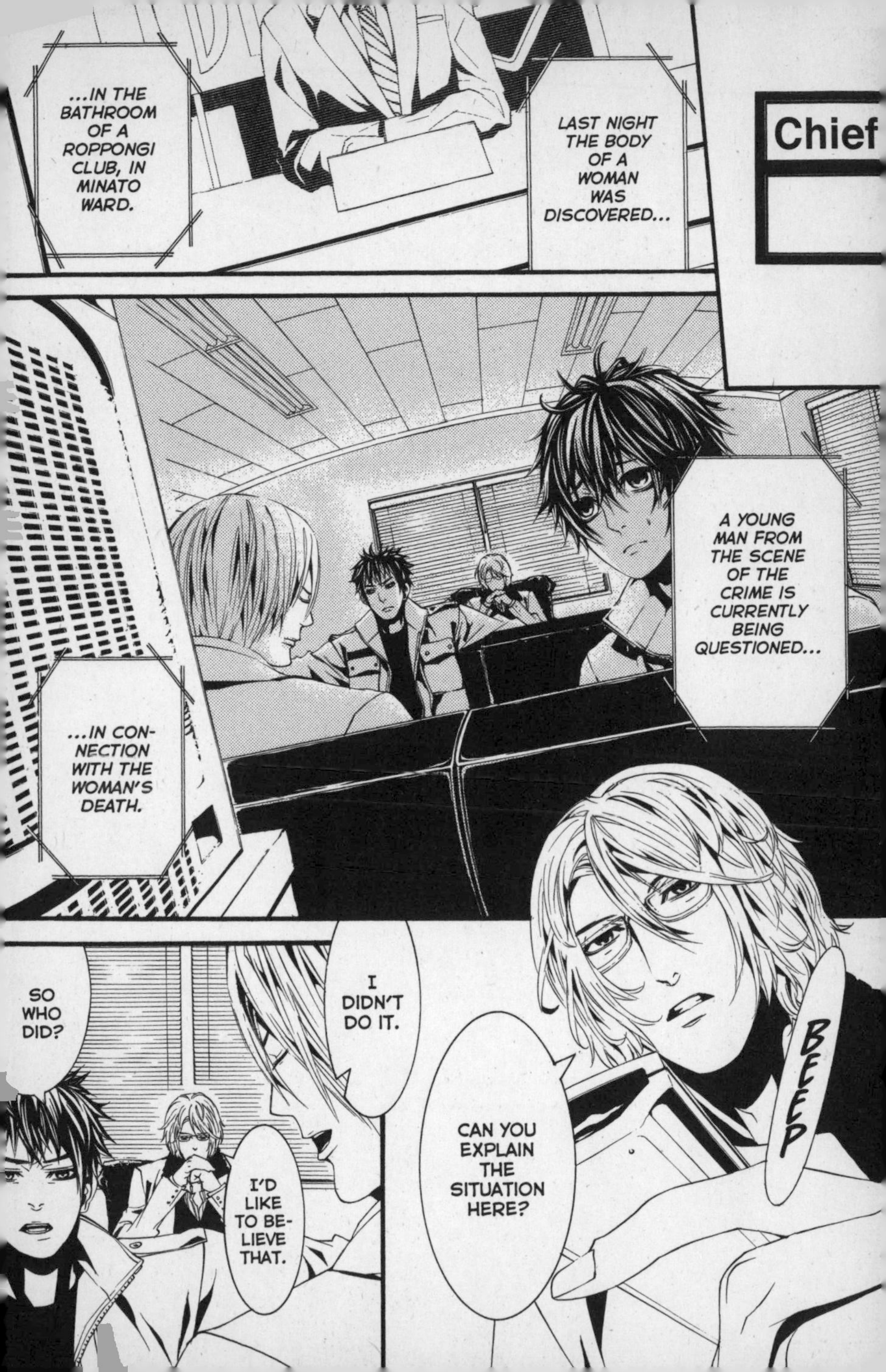
Chief
LAST NIGHT THE BODY OF A WOMAN WAS DISCOVERED...
...IN THE BATHROOM OF A ROPPONGI CLUB, IN MINATO WARD.
A YOUNG MAN FROM THE SCENE OF THE CRIME IS CURRENTLY BEING QUESTIONED...
...IN CONNECTION WITH THE WOMAN'S DEATH.
BEEP
CAN YOU EXPLAIN THE SITUATION HERE?
I DIDN'T DO IT.
SO WHO DID?
I'D LIKE TO BELIEVE THAT.

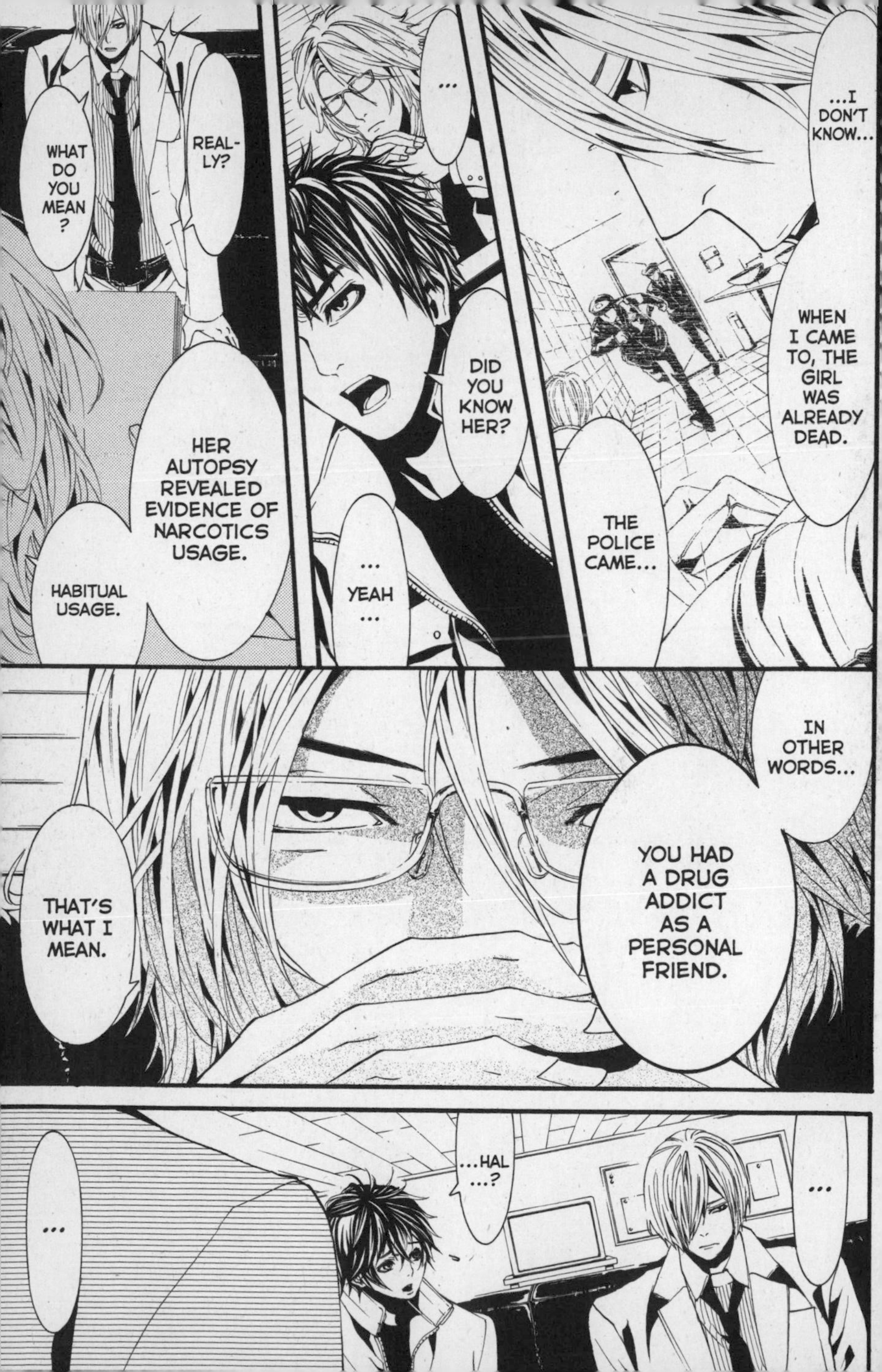
...I DON'T KNOW...
WHEN I CAME TO, THE GIRL WAS ALREADY DEAD.
THE POLICE CAME...
...
DID YOU KNOW HER?
... YEAH ...
REAL-LY?
WHAT DO YOU MEAN ?
HER AUTOPSY REVEALED EVIDENCE OF NARCOTICS USAGE.
HABITUAL USAGE.
IN OTHER WORDS...
YOU HAD A DRUG ADDICT AS A PERSONAL FRIEND.
THAT'S WHAT I MEAN.
...
...HAL ...?
...

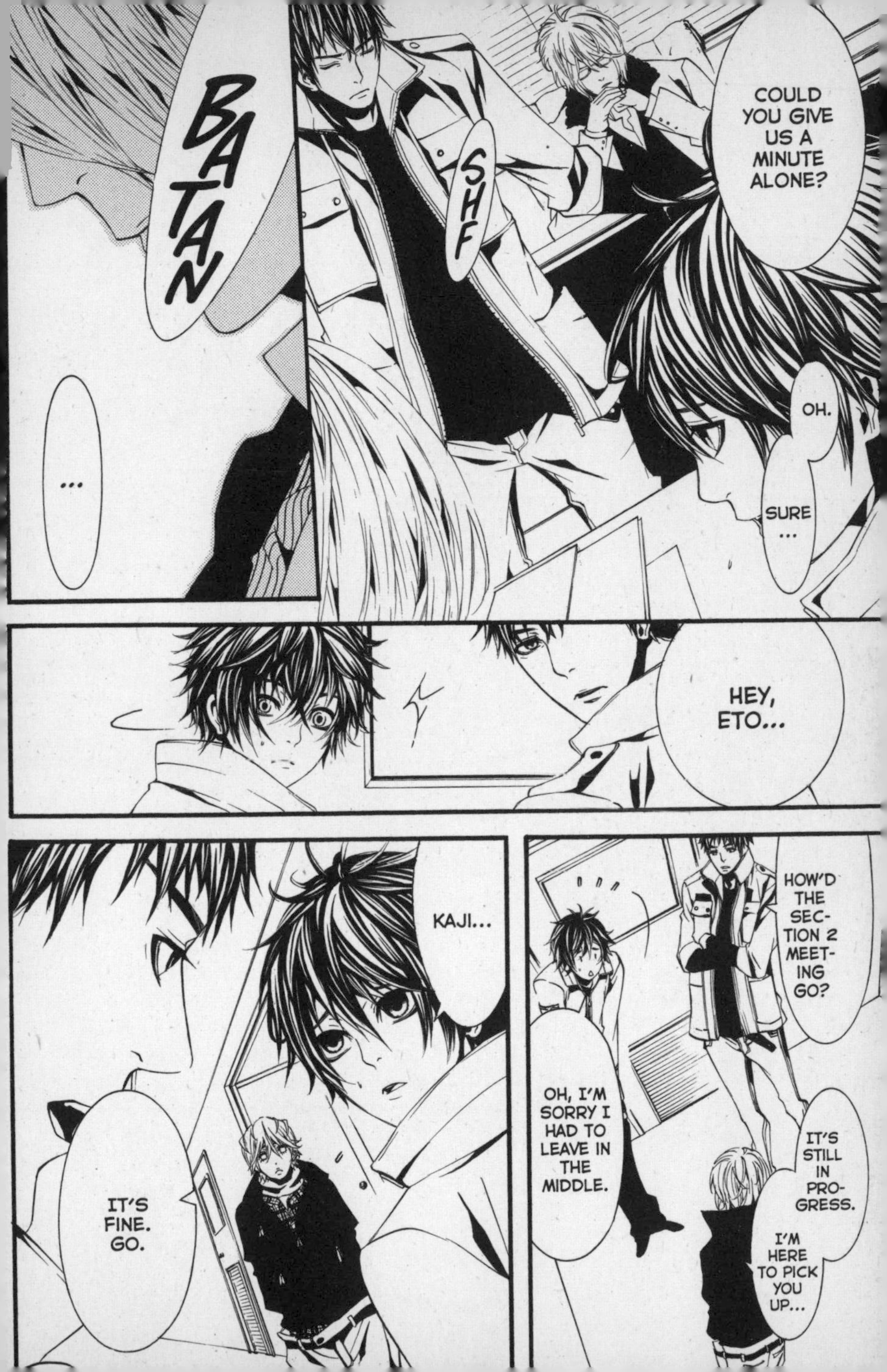

COULD YOU GIVE US A MINUTE ALONE?
OH.
SURE...
SHF
BATAN
...
HEY, ETO...
HOW'D THE SECTION 2 MEETING GO?
OH, I'M SORRY I HAD TO LEAVE IN THE MIDDLE.
IT'S STILL IN PROGRESS.
I'M HERE TO PICK YOU UP...
KAJI...
IT'S FINE. GO.

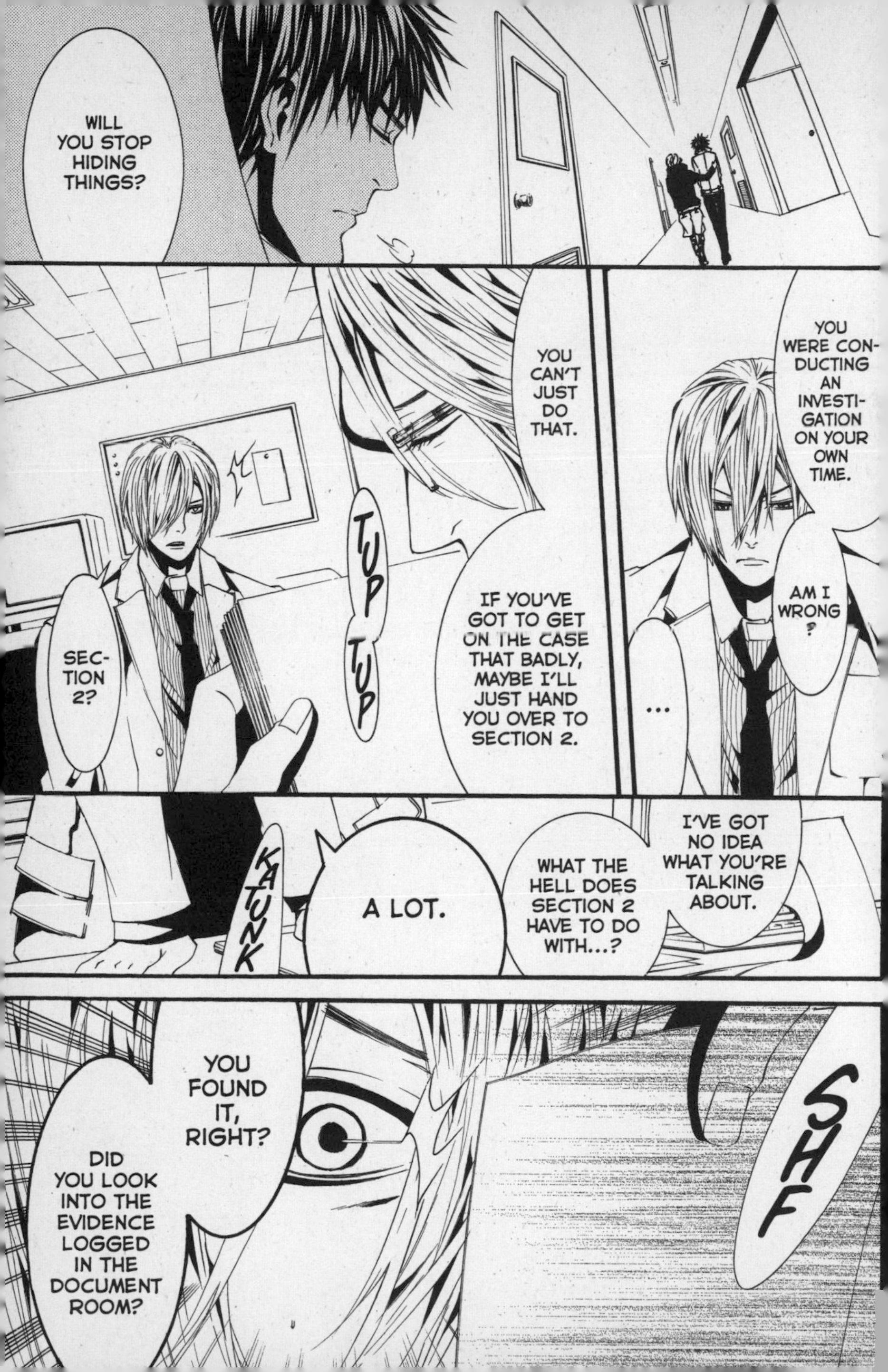
WILL YOU STOP HIDING THINGS?
YOU WERE CONDUCTING AN INVESTIGATION ON YOUR OWN TIME.
AM I WRONG?
...
YOU CAN'T JUST DO THAT.
IF YOU'VE GOT TO GET ON THE CASE THAT BADLY, MAYBE I'LL JUST HAND YOU OVER TO SECTION 2.
TUP TUP
SECTION 2?
I'VE GOT NO IDEA WHAT YOU'RE TALKING ABOUT.
WHAT THE HELL DOES SECTION 2 HAVE TO DO WITH...?
A LOT.
KATUNK
SHF
YOU FOUND IT, RIGHT?
DID YOU LOOK INTO THE EVIDENCE LOGGED IN THE DOCUMENT ROOM?

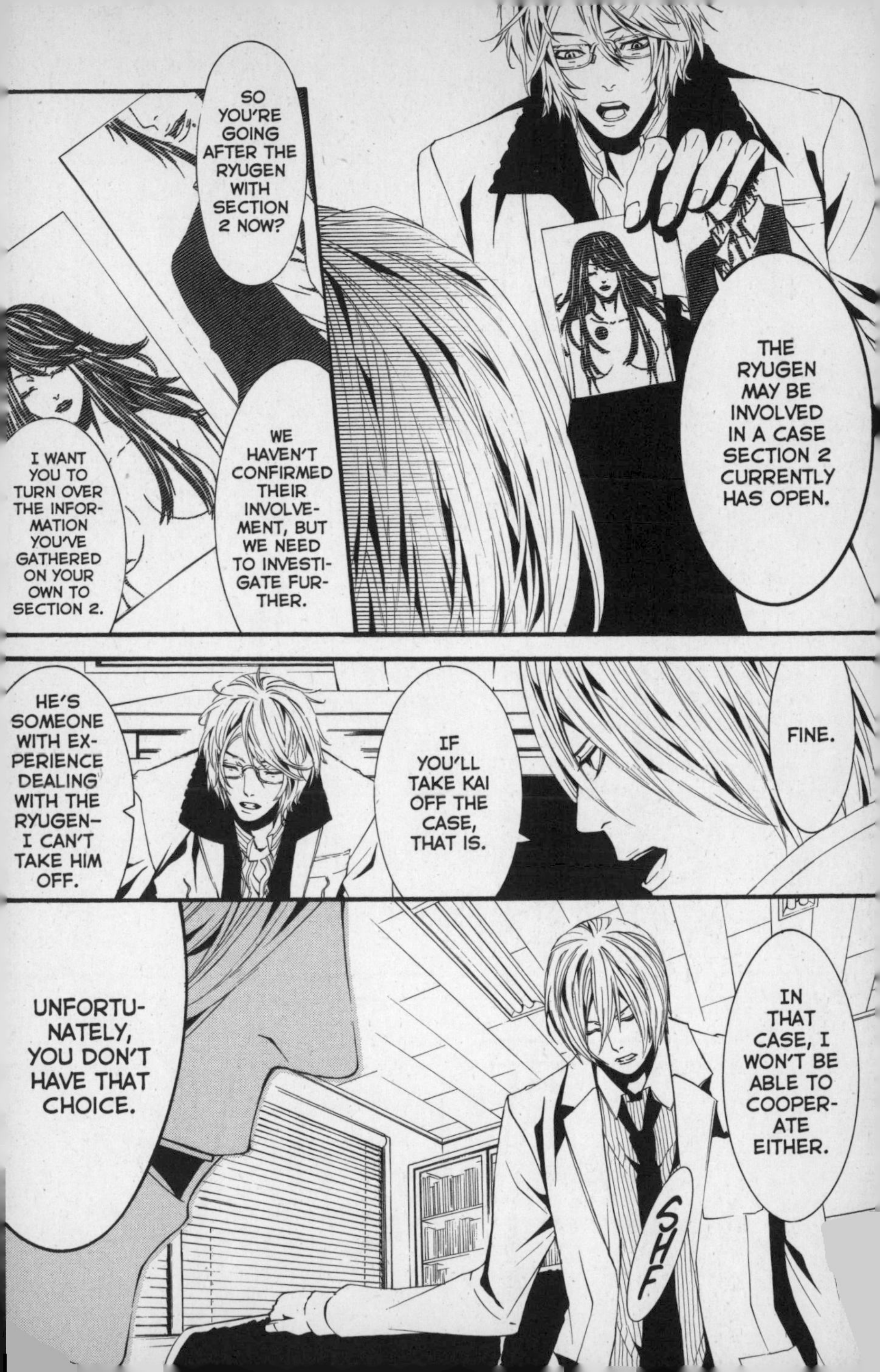
THE RYUGEN MAY BE INVOLVED IN A CASE SECTION 2 CURRENTLY HAS OPEN.
SO YOU'RE GOING AFTER THE RYUGEN WITH SECTION 2 NOW?
WE HAVEN'T CONFIRMED THEIR INVOLVEMENT, BUT WE NEED TO INVESTIGATE FURTHER.
I WANT YOU TO TURN OVER THE INFORMATION YOU'VE GATHERED ON YOUR OWN TO SECTION 2.
FINE.
IF YOU'LL TAKE KAI OFF THE CASE, THAT IS.
HE'S SOMEONE WITH EXPERIENCE DEALING WITH THE RYUGEN— I CAN'T TAKE HIM OFF.
IN THAT CASE, I WON'T BE ABLE TO COOPERATE EITHER.
SHF
UNFORTUNATELY, YOU DON'T HAVE THAT CHOICE.

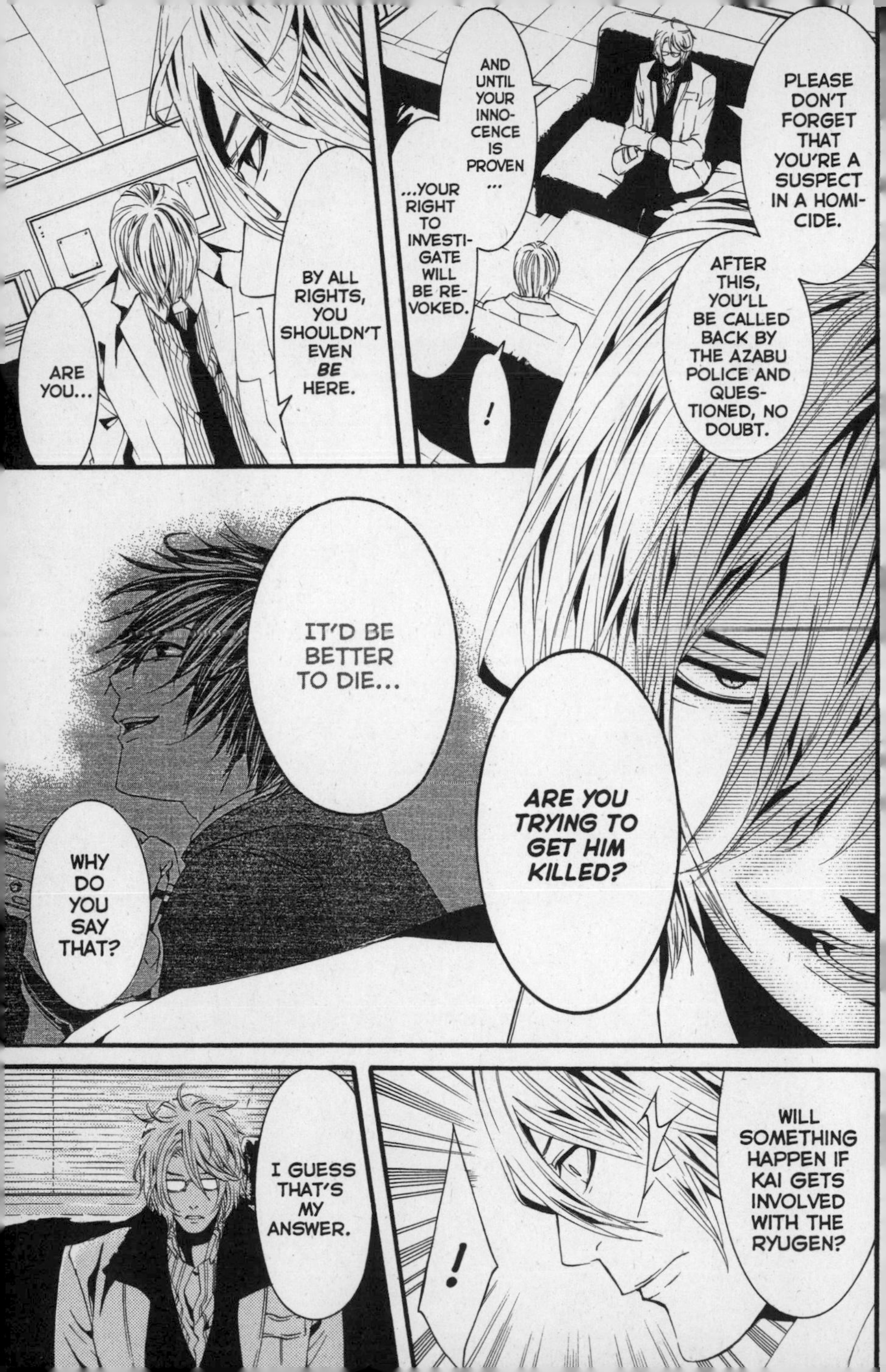
PLEASE DON'T FORGET THAT YOU'RE A SUSPECT IN A HOMICIDE.
AFTER THIS, YOU'LL BE CALLED BACK BY THE AZABU POLICE AND QUESTIONED, NO DOUBT.
AND UNTIL YOUR INNOCENCE IS PROVEN...
...YOUR RIGHT TO INVESTIGATE WILL BE REVOKED.
!
BY ALL RIGHTS, YOU SHOULDN'T EVEN *BE* HERE.
ARE YOU...
ARE YOU TRYING TO GET HIM KILLED?
WHY DO YOU SAY THAT?
IT'D BE BETTER TO DIE...
WILL SOMETHING HAPPEN IF KAI GETS INVOLVED WITH THE RYUGEN?
!
I GUESS THAT'S MY ANSWER.

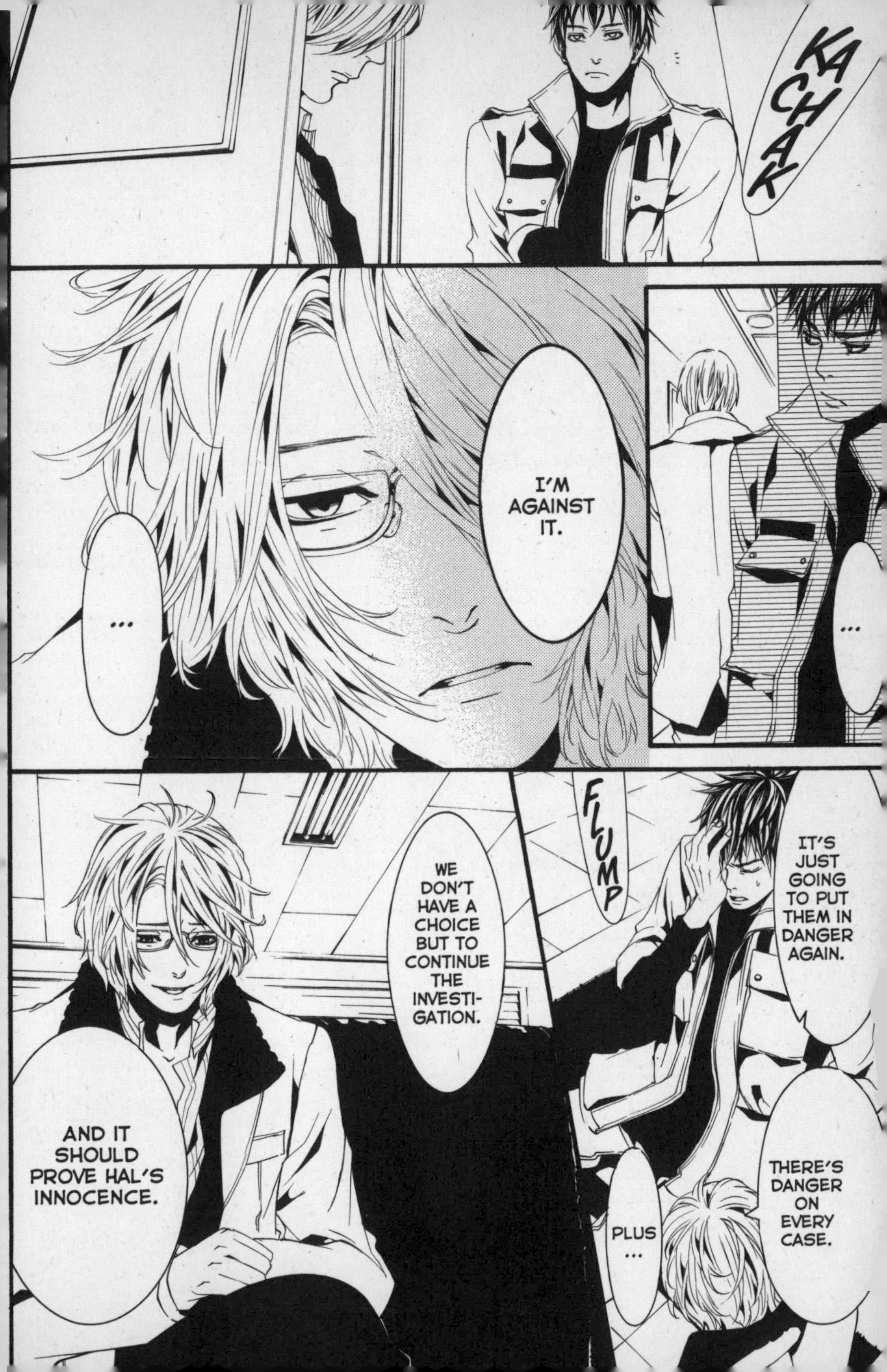
KACHAK
...
I'M AGAINST IT.
...
IT'S JUST GOING TO PUT THEM IN DANGER AGAIN.
FLUMP
THERE'S DANGER ON EVERY CASE.
PLUS ...
WE DON'T HAVE A CHOICE BUT TO CONTINUE THE INVESTIGATION.
AND IT SHOULD PROVE HAL'S INNOCENCE.

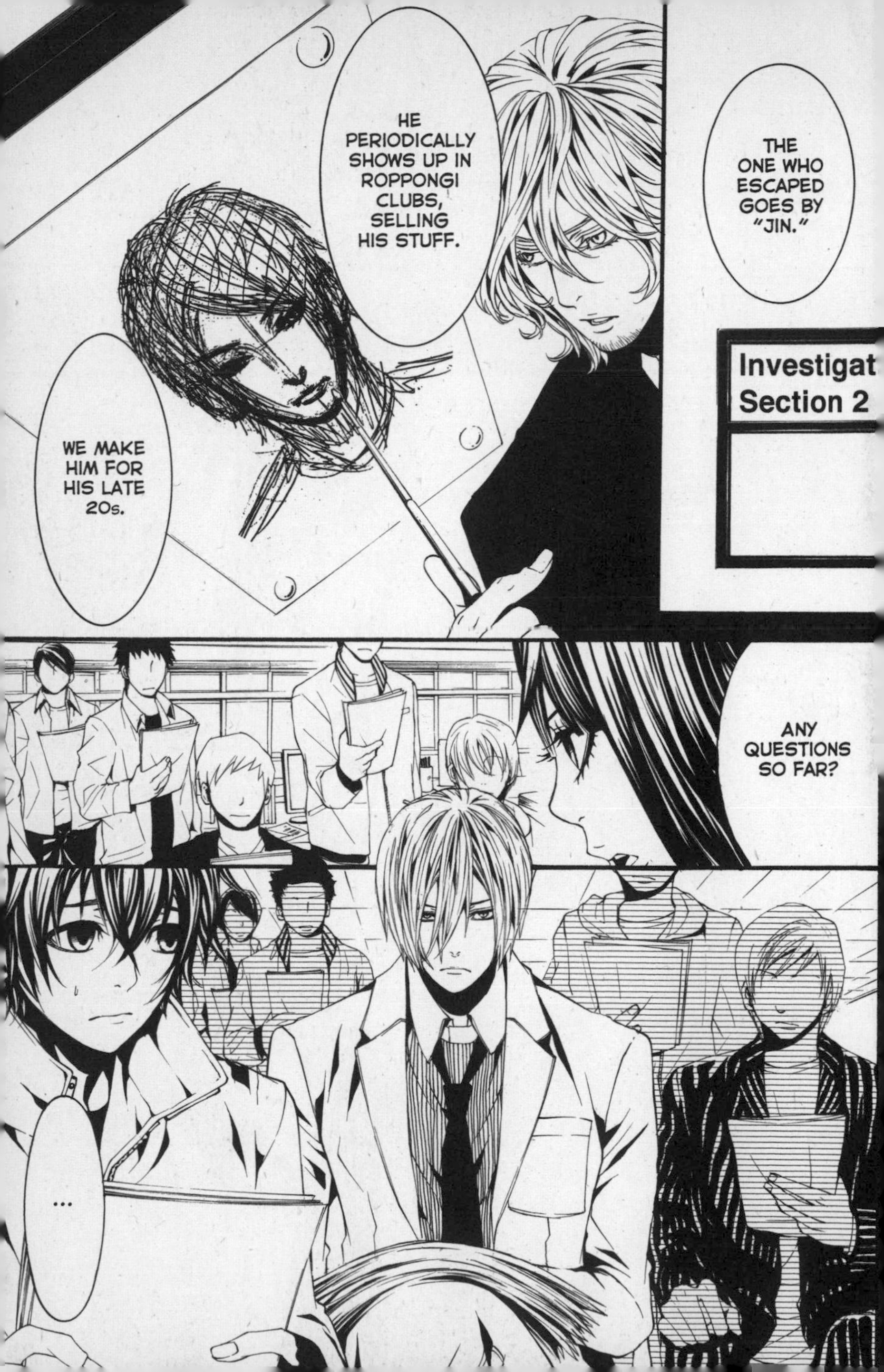
THE ONE WHO ESCAPED GOES BY "JIN."
Investigat
Section 2
HE PERIODICALLY SHOWS UP IN ROPPONGI CLUBS, SELLING HIS STUFF.
WE MAKE HIM FOR HIS LATE 20s.
ANY QUESTIONS SO FAR?
...

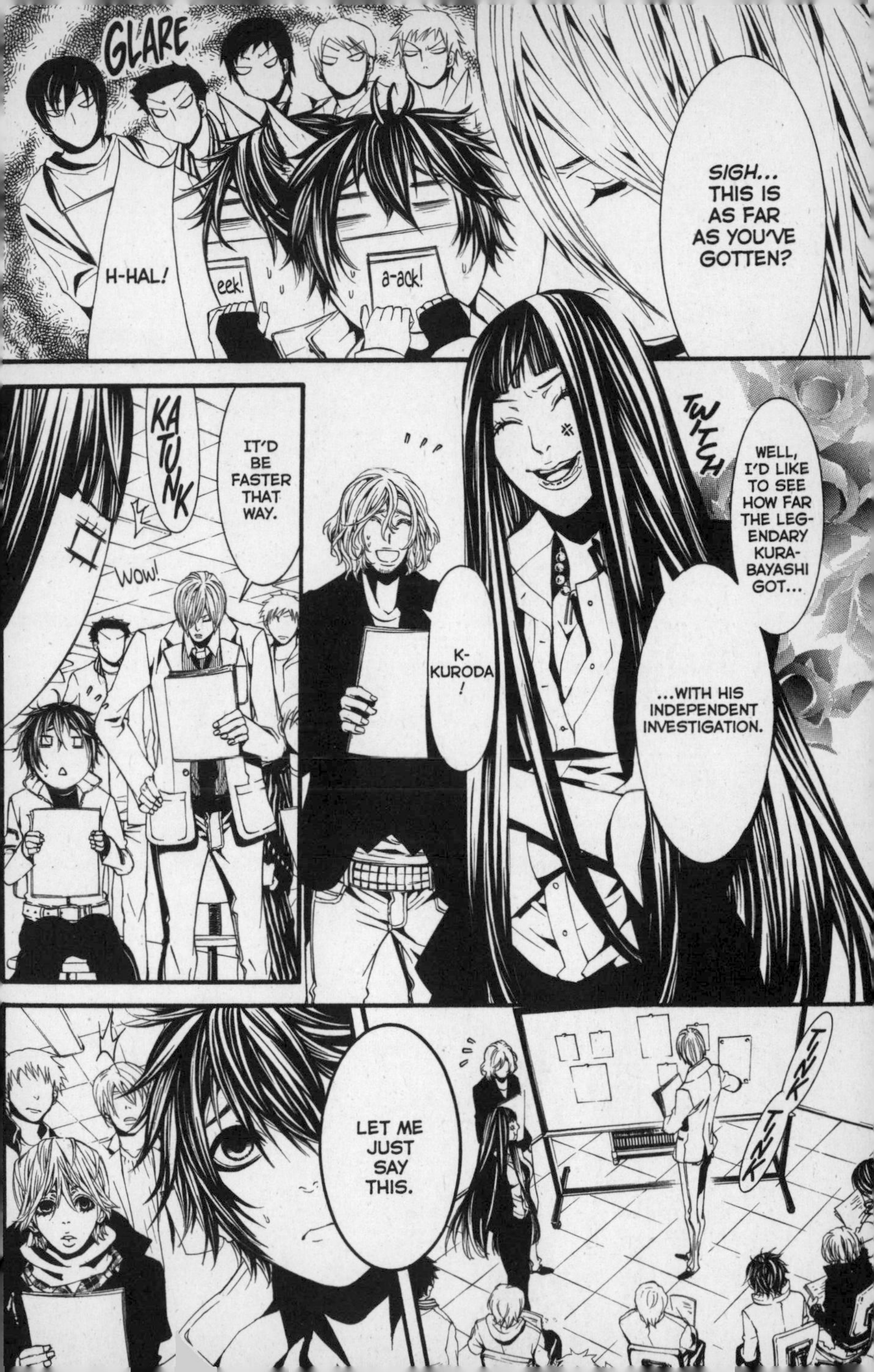
SIGH... THIS IS AS FAR AS YOU'VE GOTTEN?
GLARE
a-ack!
eek!
H-HAL!
TWITCH
WELL, I'D LIKE TO SEE HOW FAR THE LEG-ENDARY KURA-BAYASHI GOT...
...WITH HIS INDEPENDENT INVESTIGATION.
K-KURODA!
IT'D BE FASTER THAT WAY.
KATUNK
WOW!
TINK TINK
LET ME JUST SAY THIS.

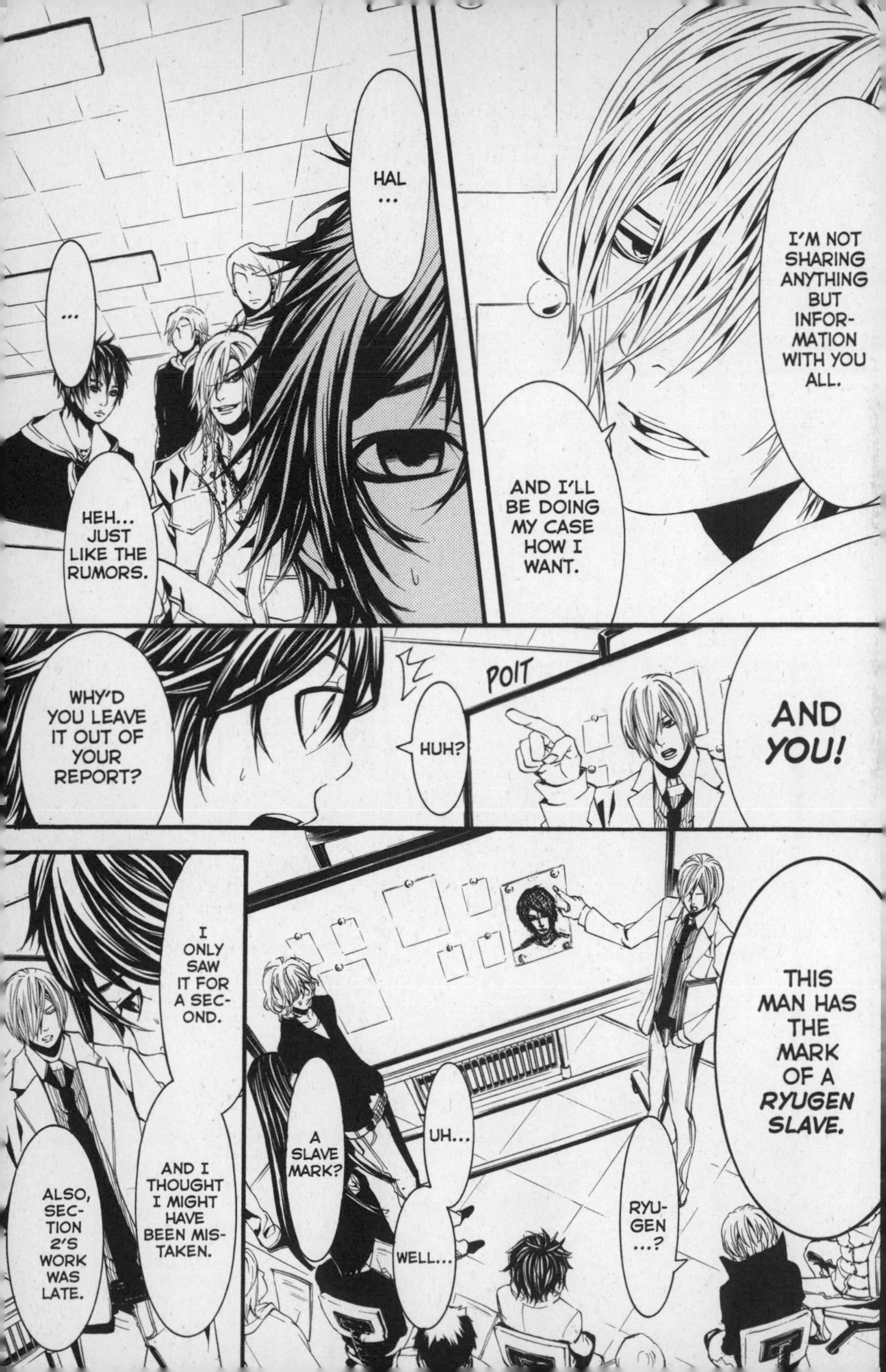
I'M NOT SHARING ANYTHING BUT INFORMATION WITH YOU ALL.
AND I'LL BE DOING MY CASE HOW I WANT.
HAL...
...
HEH... JUST LIKE THE RUMORS.
AND *YOU!*
POIT
HUH?
WHY'D YOU LEAVE IT OUT OF YOUR REPORT?
THIS MAN HAS THE MARK OF A *RYUGEN SLAVE.*
RYUGEN...?
UH...
A SLAVE MARK?
WELL...
I ONLY SAW IT FOR A SECOND.
AND I THOUGHT I MIGHT HAVE BEEN MISTAKEN.
ALSO, SECTION 2'S WORK WAS LATE.

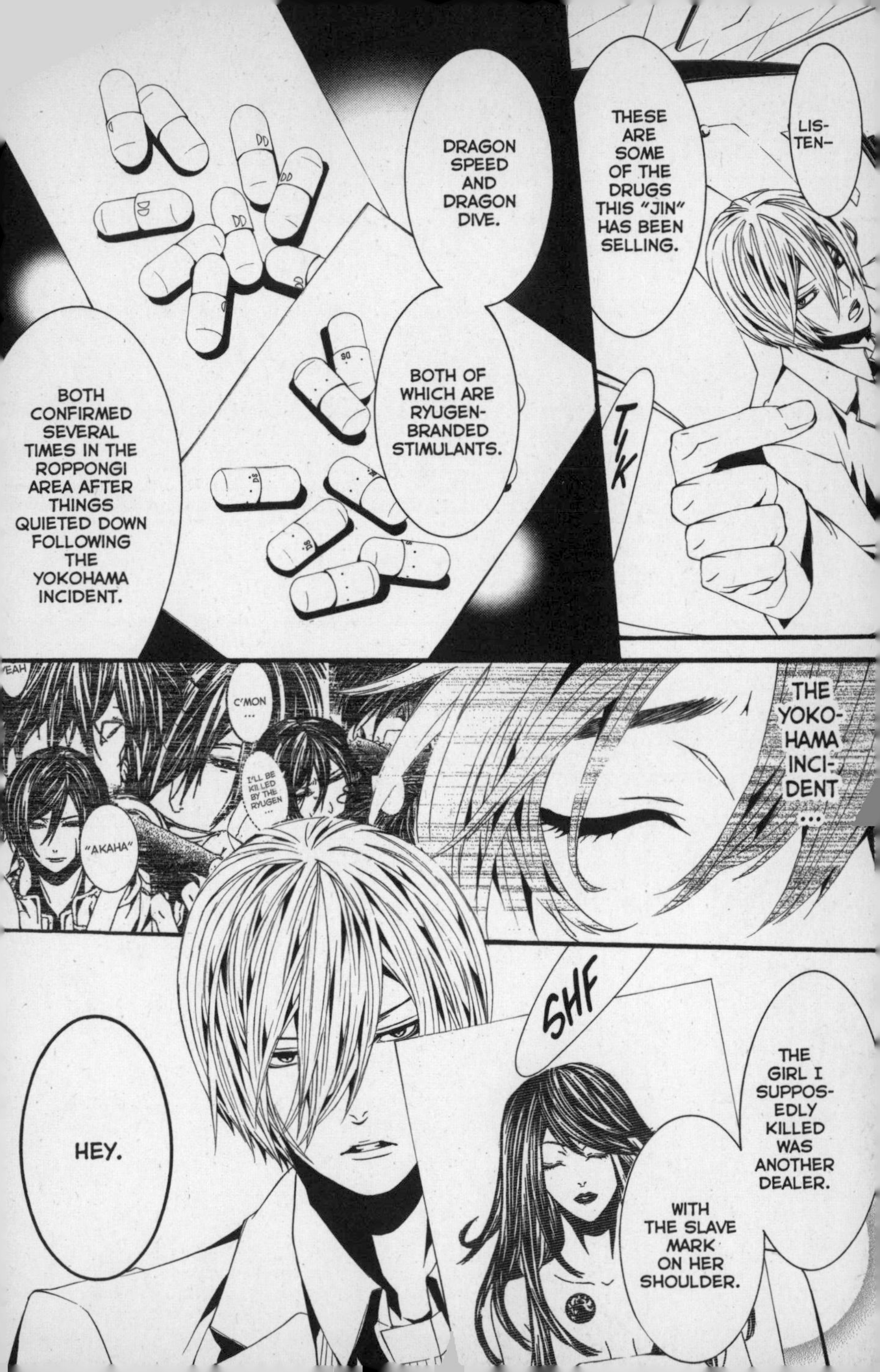
LIS-TEN-
THESE ARE SOME OF THE DRUGS THIS "JIN" HAS BEEN SELLING.
TIK
DRAGON SPEED AND DRAGON DIVE.
BOTH OF WHICH ARE RYUGEN-BRANDED STIMULANTS.
BOTH CONFIRMED SEVERAL TIMES IN THE ROPPONGI AREA AFTER THINGS QUIETED DOWN FOLLOWING THE YOKOHAMA INCIDENT.
THE YOKO-HAMA INCI-DENT...
C'MON...
I'LL BE KILLED BY THE RYUGEN...
"AKAHA"
SHF
THE GIRL I SUPPOS-EDLY KILLED WAS ANOTHER DEALER.
WITH THE SLAVE MARK ON HER SHOULDER.
HEY.

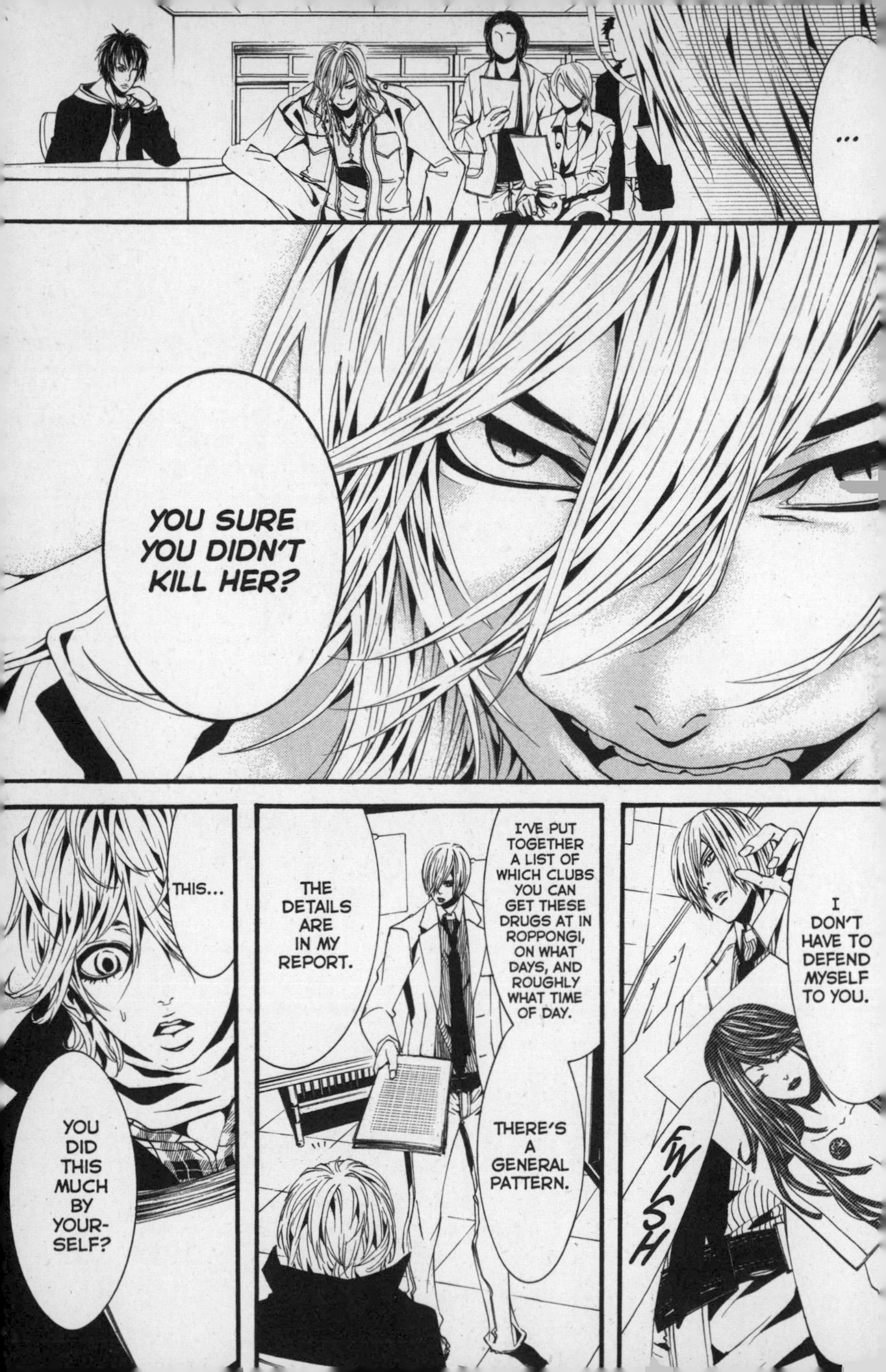
...
YOU SURE YOU DIDN'T KILL HER?
I DON'T HAVE TO DEFEND MYSELF TO YOU.
FWISH
I'VE PUT TOGETHER A LIST OF WHICH CLUBS YOU CAN GET THESE DRUGS AT IN ROPPONGI, ON WHAT DAYS, AND ROUGHLY WHAT TIME OF DAY.
THE DETAILS ARE IN MY REPORT.
THERE'S A GENERAL PATTERN.
THIS...
YOU DID THIS MUCH BY YOUR-SELF?

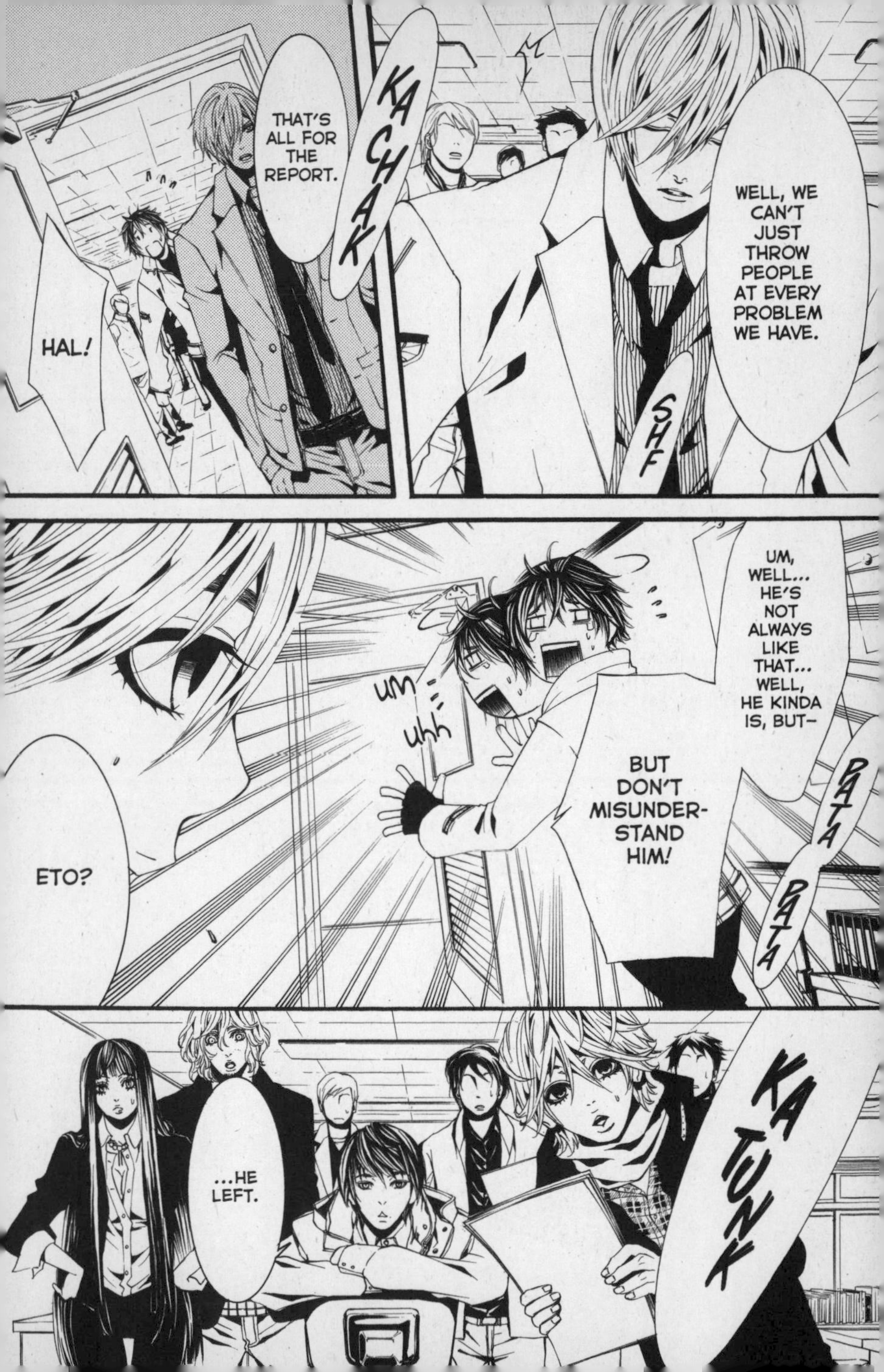
WELL, WE CAN'T JUST THROW PEOPLE AT EVERY PROBLEM WE HAVE.
SHF
KACHAK
THAT'S ALL FOR THE REPORT.
HAL!
UM, WELL... HE'S NOT ALWAYS LIKE THAT... WELL, HE KINDA IS, BUT—
PATA PATA PATA
BUT DON'T MISUNDER-STAND HIM!
um
uhh
ETO?
KATUNK
...HE LEFT.

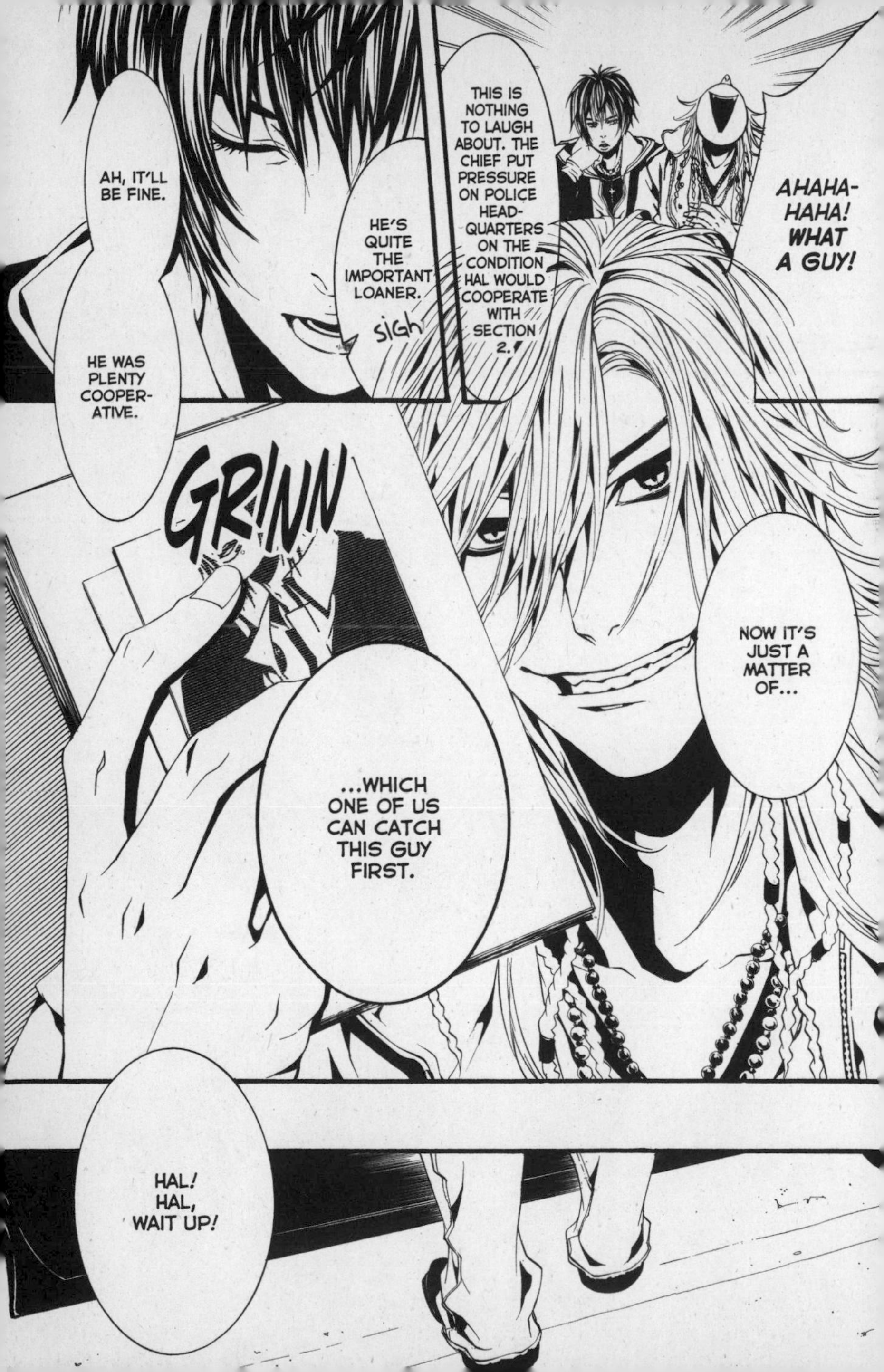
AHAHA-HAHA! WHAT A GUY!
THIS IS NOTHING TO LAUGH ABOUT. THE CHIEF PUT PRESSURE ON POLICE HEAD-QUARTERS ON THE CONDITION HAL WOULD COOPERATE WITH SECTION 2.
HE'S QUITE THE IMPORTANT LOANER.
SIGH
AH, IT'LL BE FINE.
HE WAS PLENTY COOPER-ATIVE.
NOW IT'S JUST A MATTER OF...
GRINN
...WHICH ONE OF US CAN CATCH THIS GUY FIRST.
HAL! HAL, WAIT UP!

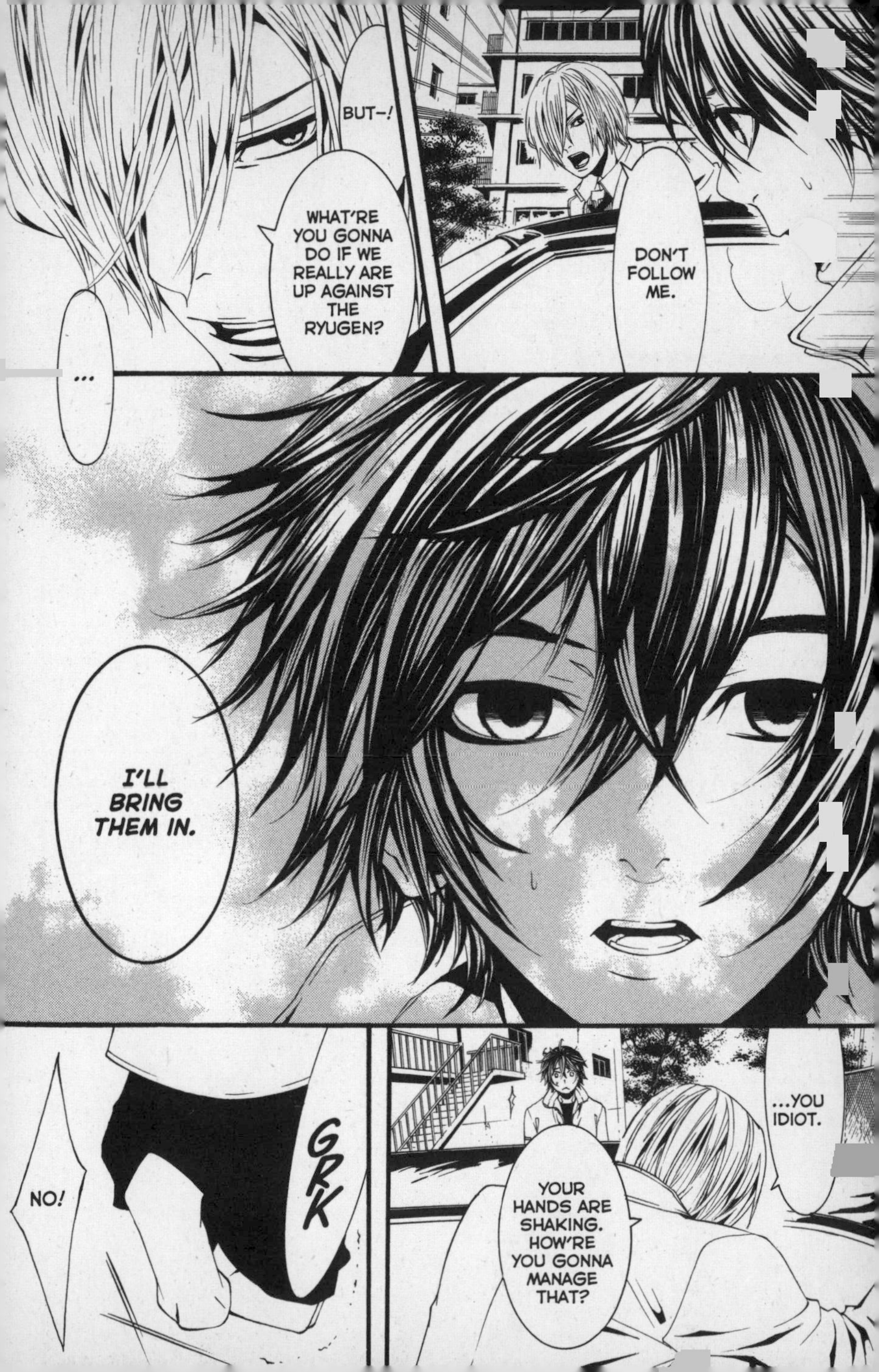
DON'T FOLLOW ME.
BUT–!
WHAT'RE YOU GONNA DO IF WE REALLY ARE UP AGAINST THE RYUGEN?
...
I'LL BRING THEM IN.
...YOU IDIOT.
YOUR HANDS ARE SHAKING. HOW'RE YOU GONNA MANAGE THAT?
GRK
NO!

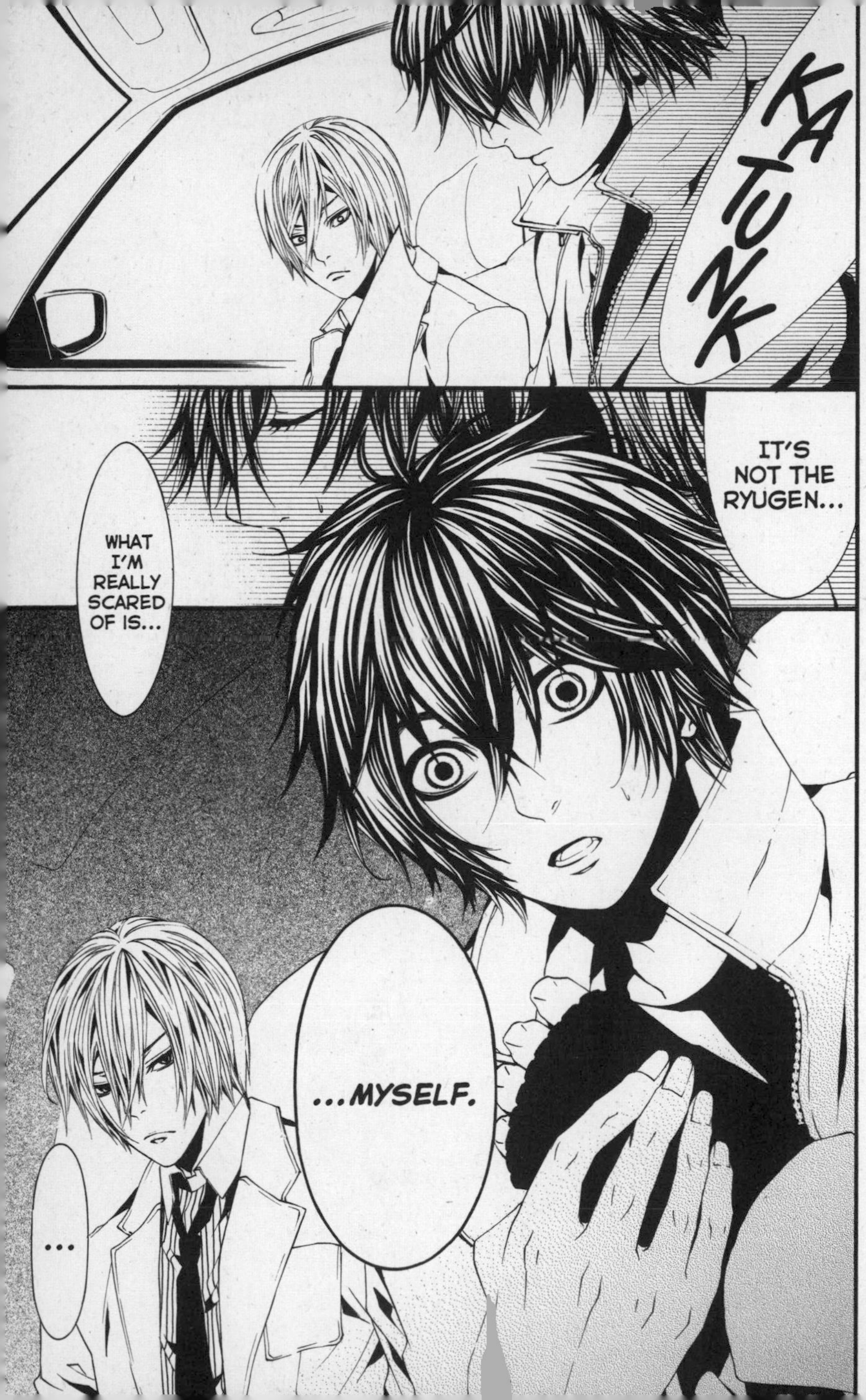
KA TUNK
IT'S NOT THE RYUGEN...
WHAT I'M REALLY SCARED OF IS...
...MYSELF.
...

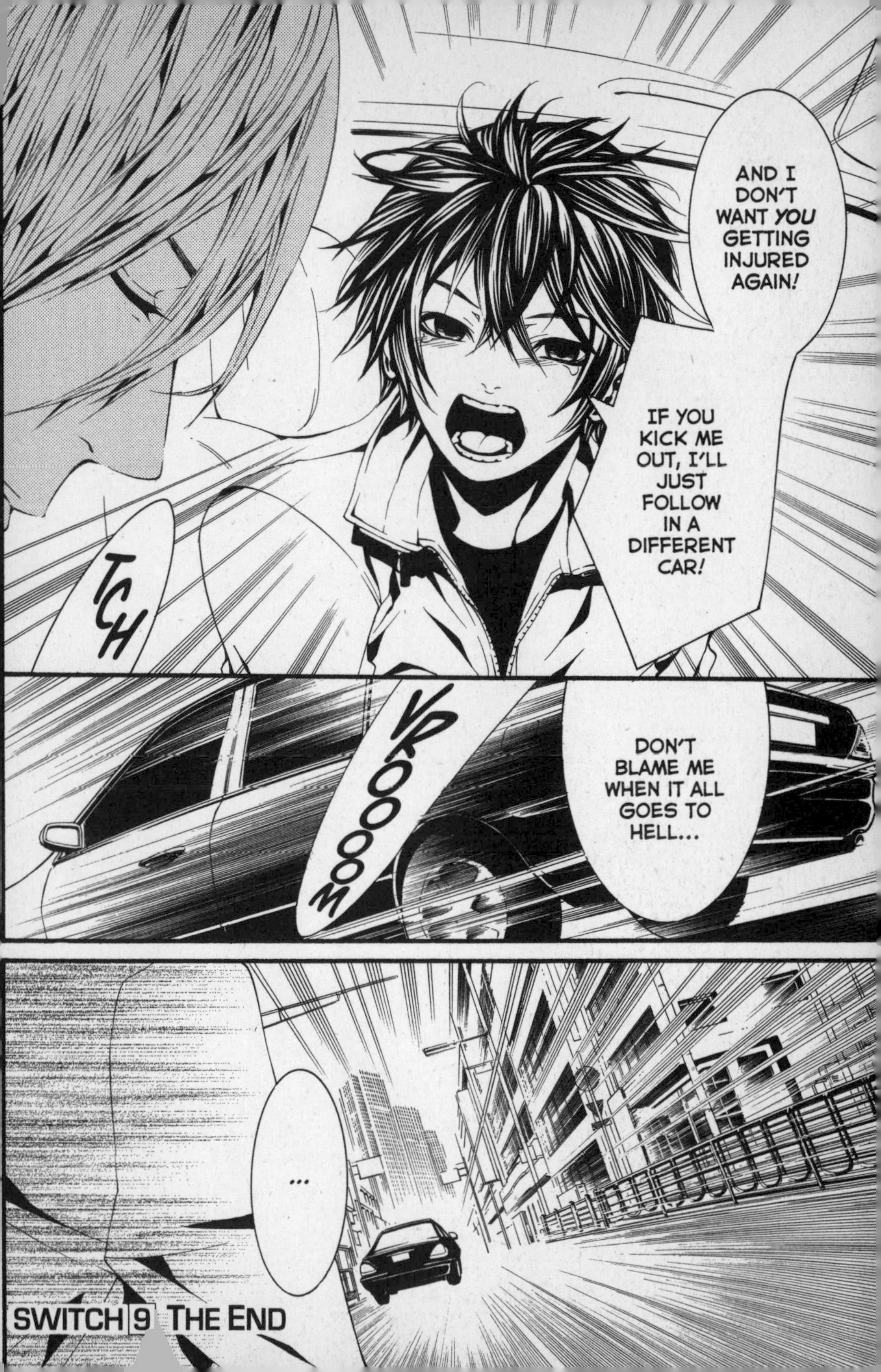
AND I DON'T WANT *YOU* GETTING INJURED AGAIN!
IF YOU KICK ME OUT, I'LL JUST FOLLOW IN A DIFFERENT CAR!
TCH
DON'T BLAME ME WHEN IT ALL GOES TO HELL...
VROOOOM
...
SWITCH 9 THE END

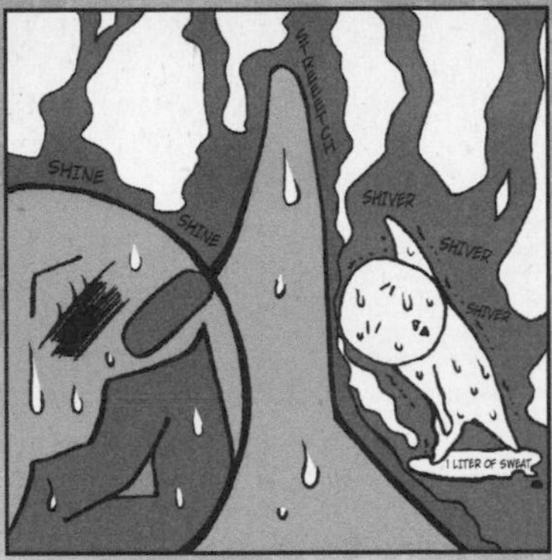
SHIVER
SHIVER
SHIVER
1 LITER OF SWEAT
SHINE
SHINE

Hot Yoga is the big thing among the normally unhealthy staff of naked ape. If you want to know what the big deal with doing yoga poses in 100-degree heat with 60% humidity is, it's that you can sweat more than a liter in an hour! When it's done, the oxygen running through you makes you feel totally refreshed. Dang, I could get addicted to this "health" thing...

naked ape is the collaboration of Tomomi Nakamura and Otoh Saki, who were born just three months apart. Nakamura, the artist, takes things at her own pace and feels no guilt for missing deadlines. Saki, the writer, also does cover design and inking and is called President by the assistants. naked ape's other works include *Black tar* and the ongoing futuristic crime thriller *DOLLS*.

SWITCH
V

Story and Art by naked ape

Translation & English Adaptation/Paul Tuttle
Translation by Design
Touch-up Art & Lettering/Susan Daigle-Leach
Design/Sean Lee
Editor/Jonathan Tarbox

VP, Production/Alvin Lu
VP, Publishing Licensing/Rika Inouye
VP, Sales & Product Marketing/Gonzalo Ferreyra
VP, Creative/Linda Espinosa
Publisher/Hyoe Narita

switch vol. 9 © 2006 naked ape/SQUARE ENIX. All
rights reserved. First published in Japan in 2006
by SQUARE ENIX CO., LTD. English translation
rights arranged with SQUARE ENIX CO., LTD.
and VIZ Media, LLC. The stories, characters and
incidents mentioned in this publication are
entirely fictional.

No portion of this book may be reproduced or
transmitted in any form or by any means without
written permission from the copyright holders.

The rights of the author(s) of the work(s) in this
publication to be so identified have been asserted
in accordance with the Copyright, Designs and
Patents Act 1988. A CIP catalogue record for this
book is available from the British Library.

Printed in the U.S.A.

Published by VIZ, LLC
P.O. Box 77010
San Francisco, CA 94107

VIZ Media Edition
10 9 8 7 6 5 4 3 2 1
First printing, July 2009

www.viz.com store.viz.com

ESSEX CG LIBRARIES

30130 5066 3102 6

ded for
drug